## Advance Praise for R
### *Eternal Questions*

"ETERNAL QUESTIONS is, truly, the Torah of wholeness. It is a guide to bringing Torah into our lives, into our bodies, into our breath, into our relationships—into realizing the expansive, transformative potential of Jewish sacred text and practice. This is the wisdom that we always need—but maybe particularly now, more than ever, during these turbulent times."
—**Rabbi Danya Ruttenberg**, author, *On Repentance and Repair*

"Why is this book of Torah commentary different from other ones? Because it is less a display of the writer's rabbinic sagacity (though he has plenty) than a practical, actionable invitation to deep, personal reflection. As its title implies, it is, first and foremost, about asking questions, grounded in a combination of traits that my friend Rabbi Josh Feigelson uniquely embodies: a sophisticated yet reverent fluency with Jewish text, a commitment to contemplative practice, and above all, what some would call menschlichkeit: decency."
—**Rabbi Dr. Jay Michaelson**, author, *The Heresy of Jacob Frank* and *The Gate of Tears: Sadness and the Spiritual Path*

"Welcome to a seat beside the warm and highly learned Rabbi Feigelson. Your heart will open and your mind lock into clarity. ETERNAL QUESTIONS is a work of wisdom and love. It welcomes all seekers to share in a deeply personal inquiry that brings Torah immediately into a reflection of the spirit."
—**Dr. Lisa Miller**, author, *The Spiritual Child* and *The Awakened Brain*

"Rabbi Josh Feigelson has penned one of the most unique works on the parsha, beautifully synthesizing worldly knowledge with classic Torah and Chassidic teaching. Interweaving genius of mind with depth of soul he creatively shows how spirituality can give wings to foundational Jewish thought and profoundly impact our lives. Rabbi Feigelson's commentary speaks directly to the heart, no doubt inspiring readers to find greater inner peace, greater meaning in life-reaching higher and higher still- to make a difference."
—**Rabbi Avi Weiss**, author, *Spiritual Activism: A Jewish Guide to Leadership* and *Repairing the World*

# Eternal Questions

*Reflections, Conversations, and*
*Jewish Mindfulness Practices*
*for the*
*Weekly Torah Portion*

Rabbi Josh Feigelson

**Ben Yehuda Press**
**Teaneck, New Jersey**

Published by Ben Yehuda Press
122 Ayers Court #1B
Teaneck, NJ 07666

http://www.BenYehudaPress.com

To subscribe to our monthly book club and support independent Jewish publishing, visit https://www.patreon.com/BenYehudaPress

Ben Yehuda Press books may be purchased at a discount by synagogues, book clubs, and other institutions buying in bulk. For information, please email
markets@BenYehudaPress.com

ISBN13 978-1-953829-38-2

22 23 24 / 10 9 8 7 6 5 4 3 2 1          20220929

# Contents

*To my parents*

*Happy and Lou (z"l) Feigelson*


*Who set me on the path of asking eternal questions*

*Eternal Questions*

# Note on Translations
# and References to Hasidic Texts

Unless otherwise noted, all translations from Hebrew texts are mine. For some classical sources, including biblical citations and major commentaries, I have consulted with available translations including those of the Jewish Publication Society and others available online at Sefaria.org.

Additionally, please be aware of a common convention in writing about Hasidic texts (and much of the classical Jewish textual literature), which is to refer to the author of a work by the name of the work. Hence, Rabbi Yehuda Leib Alter of Ger, the author of the *Sefat Emet*, is referred to frequently as "the Sefat Emet." So I might write, "The Sefat Emet says," rather than "In the *Sefat Emet*, R' Alter writes…" This reference convention may be a little disorienting for the reader who has not previously encountered it. If you experience that, you might try giving yourself a moment to wrap your head around it, perhaps saying the words out loud. To my mind, this is a wonderful tradition that conveys the sense that these texts and their authors continue to live with and speak to us.

בס"ד

# Acknowledgements

The number of people who have contributed to the creation of this book are too many to name. They include teachers, study partners, and classmates spanning four decades. In the spirit of Ben Zoma's teaching that the wise person is one who learns from everyone, I begin by acknowledging that I seek to learn from every encounter, and therefore everyone I interact with is, in some measure, my teacher, and thus a contributor to this book.

But there are some people who merit special gratitude. First among these are my colleagues at the Institute for Jewish Spirituality, many of whom are named in the Introduction and whose practices appear in these pages. Chief among these is Rabbi Jonathan Slater, who both created and shepherded IJS's Text Study program for a decade and a half and, in this instance, served as my editor. Jonathan's generous and incisive comments, his rigor and demand for clarity, and his exceptional scholarship have strengthened these essays immeasurably. Any errors or shortcomings are entirely my own.

Larry Yudelson of Ben Yehuda Press has made the hard work of publishing this book a much lighter burden. I appreciate his willingness to engage in this project and help these essays reach many more readers. Laura Logan provided excellent copy edits. Joanne Fink's cover design is a beautiful crown on this work of Torah.

I was privileged to teach these essays to several study groups as I was writing them. Each of the groups helped deepen my own understanding and contributed to my thinking and practice. One group deserves special mention, as it met for nearly the entire year of this series. My enduring thanks, therefore, to Marvin Israelow, Carol Joseph, Keith Krakaur, Donald Meltzer, Howard Sharfstein, and Jack and Judy Stern for their sustained learning and practice with me as these essays came into being.

While I have dedicated this volume to my parents, an equal measure of love and gratitude goes to my children, Jonah, Micah, and Toby, who have been my teachers and partners in the study and mindful practice of Torah.

Finally, my deepest gratitude goes to my wife, Natalie Blitt, whose love, support, and partnership makes all things possible.

# How to use this book
# or,
# What makes this book different
# from most others?

"My child, you have asked a great question."
—Hillel the Elder (Shabbat 31a)

"Truth is an eternal conversation about things that matter, conducted with passion and discipline."[1]
—Parker J. Palmer

The Talmud tells a series of stories about Hillel the Elder, one of the fathers of Rabbinic Judaism. In one story, two friends made a bet: Hillel was known for his equanimity. If one of them could get Hillel to lose his cool, the other would pay him 400 *zuz*, a hefty sum.

One of the friends mustered up his courage and went to Hillel's house late on Friday afternoon, just as the great sage was preparing for Shabbat. He pestered Hillel with a series of inane, even offensive, questions. Like a young child, each time the man would say, "I have a question to ask!" And each time, the sagely Hillel would respond, "Ask, my son, ask." The man would ask his inane question and, in every case, Hillel replied, "My child, you have asked a great question," and then would supply the answer.

At the end of the story, the man gives up: "Are you the Hillel whom they call the Prince of Israel? If so, may there not be many like you!" Why? asked Hillel. "Because I lost 400 *zuz* because of you!" True to form, Hillel responds, "Be mindful of your spirit. It is better that you should lose 400 *zuz*, and even another 400, than that Hillel should lose his temper."

The Talmud goes on from here to tell a story about three aspiring converts to Judaism who first approach Hillel's rival, Shammai, who shoos them away because of their pesky questions. They come to Hillel, who embraces them and their queries and teaches them Torah. "Eventually," the Talmud records, "the three converts came together and said, 'Shammai's ill temper would have driven us from the world; Hillel's patience brought us under the wings of the Divine Presence.'"

---

[1] Parker J. Palmer, *The Courage to Teach: Exploring the Inner Landscape of a Teacher's Life*. San Francisco: Jossey-Bass, 1998, 130.

This series of stories about Hillel is one of Jewish tradition's jewels. The stories of Hillel teach us about openness and acceptance, about what great teaching and leadership look like. When we examine them carefully, I think we find a few important qualities of Hillel—qualities that frame the book before you. And because I have hearkened to the Four Questions of the Passover Seder in the title of this introduction, I will share here four of those qualities.

## Big Questions

The first is Hillel's embrace of questions. "Ask, my child, ask," Hillel encourages the man at his doorstep. After the man asks his question, again and again he responds, "You have asked a great question, my child." Yes, he's probably being a little tongue-in-cheek. As the conclusion of the story demonstrates, he knows full well what is going on. And yet: he encourages the question-asking nonetheless. In fact, that's what Hillel does in all of these stories: he embraces and encourages questions.

Not only that, Hillel shapes those questions into something more than mere queries for information. He makes them into the basis of a relationship. Where Shammai hears the converts' questions as either interruptions or an opening to some kind of diminishment of Torah, for Hillel every question is the opening to a conversation, a moment when the Divine Presence can be made more perceptible in the world. Put another way, where Shammai sees only the question, Hillel perceives the questioner who asks it. Shammai's view of questions keeps them at bay—and likewise keeps the converts away. Hillel's approach to questions welcomes them and lifts them up—and brings the converts, and the rest of us, closer to the Divine Presence within and between them.

That approach to questions has informed my teaching for many years and it is central not only to the title of this book—*Eternal Questions*—but to its design. Every essay on the weekly parasha is framed by what I call a Big Question: A question that matters to everyone and that everyone can answer. Thus the title of the first essay, on Parashat Bereshit, is *What do you see?* The title of the first essay on Leviticus, Parashat Vayikra, is *Whose voice do you hear?* The title of the very last essay is entitled *What have we learned?*

Framing the essays this way is no small thing. In many collections of Torah portion essays, the title is often a theme: "The Closeness of God," or "A Sense of Direction" (Rabbi Jonathan Sacks on Ki-Tissa and Bechukotai, respectively); "Gifts to the Poor" (Nehama Leibowitz on Emor); "Leaving Slavery Behind: On Taking the First Step" (Shai Held on Beshallach); "The

Quest for Wholeness" (Avivah Gottlieb Zornberg on Vayishlach)[2]. I hasten to add: There is nothing wrong whatsoever with themes—as the quality of all of these, and many other, esteemed Torah commentaries should make clear. I in no way mean to denigrate these teachers of mine; God forbid.

But I do mean to do something different in titling the essays this way: to create a zone in which we—you and I and the rest of the reading public who shares these essays with us—can grow together. Twentieth century German philosopher Hans-Georg Gadamer puts it well: "Questioning opens up possibilities of meaning, and thus what is meaningful passes into one's own thinking on the subject... To understand a question means to ask it. To understand meaning is to understand it as the answer to a question."[3] By framing the essays with Big Questions, I hope to help you, and all of us, to engage with these thoughts not only as "interesting" or "thought-provoking," but as genuine invitations to reflection, conversation, and change—in your behavior, in your inner life, in your relationships with yourself, other people, and the Divine, just as I believe Hillel sought to do. They are gateways to the eternal conversation that Parker Palmer identifies as truth.

## Questions for Reflection and Conversation

That brings me to the second aspect of this book that draws its inspiration from Hillel. Big Questions are wonderful framing devices, but they are often *too big* for us to handle. *What have you lost?* (Ki Tetzei) is a beautiful question, but unless we get more specific about it, it may not actually be so useful. Thus every essay in this volume includes questions for reflection and conversation which are meant, again, to help us go beyond the reaction, "That was interesting," and instead to have some meaningful conversation with ourselves and others.

The reflection and conversation questions are generally of two types: Invitations to reflect on how the teaching intersects with your own lived experience, or an interpretive question about what the text might mean. Again, these questions are meant to be ones that are meaningful to everyone and

---

[2] Jonathan Sacks, *Studies in Spirituality: A Weekly Reading of the Jewish Bible*. Maggid Books, 2021; Nehama Leibowitz, *New Studies in Vayikra/Leviticus*. The World Zionist Organization, n.d.; Shai Held, *The Heart of Torah*. Jewish Publication Society, 2017; Avivah Gottlieb Zornberg, *The Beginning of Desire: Reflections on Genesis*. Doubleday, 1995.

[3] H.G. Gadamer, *Truth and Method (2nd Revised Edition)*. Ed. trans. J. Weinsheimer and D. Marshall. New York: Continuum Publishing, 1995/1960, 368.

that everyone can answer. They aim to require no specialized knowledge. In that way, they are also intended to help you have a conversation with another committed learner/reader regardless of their background or identity. These are meant to be questions we all share by virtue of being human. Again, in this way, my aim is to emulate Hillel, to open Torah to all of us who have bodies and have spent more than a few minutes on the planet—which is to say, everyone.

## A Diverse Array with a Hasidic Center

Every essay in this volume is centered on an original translation of a commentary by a master of the Hasidic tradition. In the same breath, I have endeavored to put these Hasidic masters in dialogue with a wide range of other writers, poets, musicians, and thinkers. In these pages you will hear the voices of the 18th-century Rabbi Menachem Nachum of Chernobyl and the twenty-first-century African American writer-poet Claudia Rankine. You will read a commentary by Rabbi Mordechai Yosef Leiner of Izhbitz (19th c.) and, a few lines later, encounter a work by Native American poet Louise Erdrich and then, in the next essay, a quote from a lecture on meaning by NYU psychologist Jerome Bruner.

My effort to include this diverse array is quite intentional, and again is in the spirit of Hillel. Like the ancient sage, we live in a time and place of remarkable cosmopolitanism. It is a moment when we are able to encounter diversity more than ever before—through our screens and phones, yes, but also in our reading, in the films we see, in the people with whom we interact. At the same time, it is also, like two thousand years ago, a moment when that very diversity can lead us to a dangerous parochialism, seducing us to label that which is different as a threatening other.

As the story of the converts demonstrates, Hillel was a boundary-crosser—and, in fact, he himself traversed boundaries as an immigrant from Babylonia to Jerusalem. He maintained the integrity of Torah while also being open to dialogue with those who were not born into Jewish life. Like the biblical paragon of wisdom, King Solomon, Hillel is depicted as one who learns from and is open to dialogue with a wide and diverse array of people. Thus my inclusion of many different voices in these essays is in service of helping us develop those same capacities for integrity and openness in order that we might grow in wisdom.

Of course, Hillel predated the Baal Shem Tov, the founder of Hasidism, by a good 17 centuries, so I cannot claim that anchoring these essays in the Hasidic tradition is inspired by him—at least, not directly. Yet some of the reasons so many have returned to studying the Hasidic masters in recent decades include their openness and embrace of all, simply by dint of their being human, and therefore being images of and vessels for the Divine. That is a fundamental orientation they share with Hillel.

Additionally, note Hillel's final words in the story with the *nudnik* questioner: "Be careful with your spirit." As any of us who have tried to keep our cool under pressure can attest, staying mindful and present, not giving in to our baser urges and flying off the handle, is fundamentally spiritual work. And it is here, in particular, that the Hasidic masters are our greatest teachers. From the Baal Shem Tov to the Maggid of Mezritch to Rebbe Nachman of Bratslav to Rabbi Yehuda Leib Alter of Ger and on and on, these great teachers of Torah were not only masters of the Jewish textual tradition, but, crucially, interpreted Torah as a spiritual practice grounded in mindfulness. In this, they made Torah come alive: it is more than simply a set of interesting or provocative ideas; it is an eternal conversation and set of practices through which we reveal the Divine Presence that resides within and amongst us.

## Ideas for Practice

This brings me to the fourth aspect of this book that makes it different: It isn't just about the ideas, or even the conversations. It's also about practicing with them. For that reason, each essay concludes not just with questions for reflection and conversation, but with a Jewish spiritual practice grounded in mindfulness. This is meant to be an opportunity to go beyond the intellectual enterprise and enable the Torah to take root in our bodies.

In case I haven't said it clearly already: It isn't enough for me that things are "interesting." Life is too short, and our times are too profoundly challenging, for "interesting" to cut it anymore. Ideas need to come with ways we can enact them—in our minds, our hearts, our bodies, our relationships, the ways we live.

Now, that doesn't mean you have to be a meditator or a yoga practitioner or even identify as a seeker in order to make good use of this book. If you have experience with mindfulness meditation, you will likely feel at home with many of the practices here. But no matter where you think you are on the spirituality meter right now, I want to invite you to try the practices included at the end of each essay.

Why? Because Torah is meant to be lived. It is an embodied practice. Judaism is not ultimately about a set of doctrines or beliefs; it is, at its core, about constructing the *Mishkan*, the Tabernacle of the wilderness—and doing so within our own hearts. All of our many *mitzvot*, from lighting Shabbat candles to returning a lost object to our neighbor to visiting the sick to giving *tzedakah,* are meant to be vehicles for connecting to the Divine Source from which we and all creation flow. (This is in keeping with the mystical understanding of *mitzvah* as *tzavta,* or connection, in Aramaic.) And while *Talmud Torah k'neged kulam,* Torah study is our greatest value, all of that study is not meant to simply stop at our brains. It isn't enough for it to be interesting. It ultimately has to extend out into our hearts, our souls, our behavior, so that it might transform our homes, neighborhoods, communities, and the world.

This, too, is part of Hillel's legacy. In the famous story of the convert who asks Shammai and then Hillel to summarize the Torah while he stands on one foot, what does Hillel answer? "That which is hateful unto you do not do unto your neighbor—that is the entire Torah, the rest is interpretation. Go and study." If you're sitting down as you read this, try to stand up on one foot. If you can't stand, try to imagine standing. Feel what it's like to balance on just one leg.

When I do so, at first I feel instability. It takes me a little while to find my balance (despite my years of marching band practice in high school). But then, perhaps like you, I find myself calming down, focusing on a point in front of me, feeling into a center of gravity in my pelvis. Eventually I sense a certain ease, an equanimity. As I do so, I bring Hillel's words to mind: The essence of the Torah is not to treat others badly, not to contribute to their suffering, to do no harm—to myself or to another. Limited in my mobility and slightly precarious, that seems to me a pretty fair summary of the most basic teaching.

Now, slowly lower your leg. What do you notice? For me, I find a renewed sense of balance and ease. I am aware of my left leg standing next to my right, supporting it. I am conscious of the mutuality and interdependence between them. While on one leg I could not go anywhere, now I can go and learn—with a book, a study partner, a community. As I do so, I am learning not just with my intellect, but with my whole self. Perhaps something like this is true for you. Try it out and see what happens!

## What Will Your Torah Be?

Many of the aspects I've mentioned here—grounding in Hasidic texts, orienting toward mindfulness, including various forms of Jewish spiritual practice, and relating the text to our own lived experience—have been hallmarks of the approach to Torah developed by the Institute for Jewish Spirituality since its founding in 1999, and particularly through the series of weekly Torah study essays developed under the leadership of Rabbi Jonathan Slater.

(This collection was originally developed as a part of that series in 2020-2021.)

While I am privileged to lead IJS now, and while this approach to studying and living Torah is deeply aligned with my own, it is very important for me to acknowledge that the book before you stands on the shoulders of a generation of teachers and practitioners who blazed a trail. Some of them, including Rabbis Nancy Flam, Sheila Peltz Weinberg, and Jonathan Slater, as well as my current colleagues Rabbis Sam Feinsmith, Myriam Klotz, and Marc Margolius, are named as teachers of particular practices or approaches. Others, such as Rabbi Rachel Cowan z"l and my colleague Michal Fox Smart, have influenced my relationship with Torah in ways that are no less important but are further below the surface.

One of the things that unites all of these teachers and the approach I have taken here is a shared belief that the most valuable and useful Torah is the Torah that responds to human questions. Like other great spiritual traditions, Torah is animated by spiritual questions we share by virtue of being human: When are we safe? When are we free? For whom are we responsible? To study Torah, to live Torah, is to enter into an eternal conversation with people past, present, and future who share these questions, to enrich and be enriched by it. That conversation is waiting for us; it is waiting for you.

In our day and age, which is marked both by so much possibility for engagement and action and, simultaneously, so much possibility for watching but not actively engaging in the world, we cannot afford for our study and living of Torah to be another form of entertainment. We must expect Torah to change us, and we must allow it to do so.

To me, that means truly opening up our life experience to a conversation through Torah. It means regularly asking, What does this story or teaching or symbol mean—in its own context and in the context of my life? How, if at all, does it resonate with my own experience? What from my own life can I bring to a disciplined discussion of Torah? And it means asking these questions not only on an intellectual level, but with all parts of our lived experience—mind, body, heart, soul, spirit.

Many have found transformative power in studying and reflecting on these essays with a *havruta,* a study partner with whom you can be truly open and honest. If you can, I would encourage you to do so. Whether or not you choose to study with a partner, I want to encourage you to engage these teachings with fullness of heart and spirit and a willingness to be honest with yourself.

Ultimately it was the openness in his students that he helped to effect, and not his techniques, that made Hillel such a successful teacher. I bless you with that same openness to spiritual transformation through Torah. Go and study.

# Bereshit: What Do You See?

## What Do We Expect To See?

A *New Yorker* cartoon caught my eye a few years ago. A little girl has drawn on the wall—a picture of a cat, a house, a sun, some hearts, herself—when her father, wearing a tie and looking angry, says, "Janey! What did I say about drawing on the walls? Perspective! Balance! Basic compositional principles!"

The joke, of course, pivots on the question: What do you see? At first glance, the reader sees a child who did something wrong. But it turns out the father sees a child who attempted to do something right, but simply didn't do it well enough.

What we see—whether with our eyes or through our broader senses of perception—is not a simple question. There is the matter of what our bodies pick up through sensation, and then there's the process of discerning which parts to pay attention to and which to ignore, which parts to recognize, how to react to the unrecognizable, and a host of other questions, most of which happen without any conscious effort on our part.

Much of the time all this conditioning is healthy, evolved over millennia to help us be safe. But a good deal of the time it's unhealthy, too. Our conditioned sensory perceptions—sight, hearing, taste, touch, smell—lead us not to notice things we should notice, to marginalize them, to call them other, to call them dangerous. These conditioned perceptions enable us to avoid looking at the things within ourselves that are hard or unpleasant, or to not hear the still small voice within us.

## Seeing and Naming in Parashat Bereshit

This activity of looking and labeling is central to the narrative of Bereshit, and especially the work of Creation. Read through Chapter 1 of Genesis and count how many times the Creator is described as seeing, organizing, and naming. Over the first six days described in Genesis chapter 1, the Torah tells us five times *vayar elohim ki tov*, that the Divine "saw that it was good": in verses 4, 10, 12, 18, 25. At the end of the sixth day (verse 31), the Torah states that God looked over all that God had created and found it not just good, but *very* good.

Further, all this seeing leads to separating, naming, and categorizing:

> God saw that the light was good, and God separated the light
> from the darkness.
> God called the light Day, and the darkness God called
> Night. And there was evening and there was morning, a first
> day. (Gen. 1:4-5)

Like the day and the night, the Holy One goes on to separate water from
land, to name the earth and the sky, to create plants and animals "of their
kind"—that is, of individualized and variegated species—and, of course,
human beings. In a final act of this categorizing and differentiating, the
Creator separates the seventh day from the others by making it holy: Shabbat.

> And God blessed the seventh day and declared it holy, because
> on it God ceased from all the work of creation that God had
> done. (Gen. 2:3)

All of this action of seeing, separating, categorizing, grouping, labeling
and naming is, of course, fundamental to us as humans. As we know from
the science of human development, we are creatures of language and we
construct our worlds precisely in this way. Likewise, we find this process
embedded in the Creation story as that which characterizes the human being.
The story of Bereshit specifically draws attention to this in chapter 2, verse 19:

> And the Ineffable formed out of the earth all the wild beasts
> and all the birds of the sky, and brought them to the human to
> see what he would call them; and whatever the human called
> each living creature, that would be its name.

Adam, the human created in the Divine image, reciprocates the Creator's
action by assigning names to nature—seeing, labeling, categorizing, organizing a world.

## Learning, or Expanding Consciousness

Yet further on in the story of Bereshit, a rupture occurs—a moment of
awakening, again through a moment of seeing (Gen. 3:6-7):

> When the woman saw that the tree was good for eating and a
> delight to the eyes, and that the tree was desirable as a source

of wisdom, she took of its fruit and ate. She also gave some to her husband, and he ate.

Then the eyes of both of them were opened and they perceived that they were naked; and they sewed together fig leaves and made themselves loincloths.

Adam and Eve eat from the Tree of Knowledge of good and bad. They taste the fruit and suddenly their consciousness is transformed. As Rashi comments on this phrase: "Scripture speaks here with reference to intelligence [or, perhaps, "the mind's eye"]) and not with reference to actual seeing" (Rashi, Gen. 3:7). Adam and Eve open their eyes in the figurative sense—they become awake to a new reality.

Reflecting on this idea, the 19th-century Hasidic master Rebbe Nachman of Breslov writes,

> When one attains expanded consciousness, it is the aspect of "Then the eyes of both of them were opened" (Genesis 3:7)—and Rashi comments: This refers to wisdom. For [judgments] are mitigated primarily by means of wisdom, expanded consciousness. (Likkutei Moharan 74:13)

Rebbe Nachman invites us to reflect on the ways in which the figurative opening of our eyes, our expansion of wisdom, entails disrupting the process of perception and judgment. That is, the process that happens all the time in our subconscious mind which enables us to almost instantaneously perceive, name, categorize, and judge things and people in the world must be interrupted for us to gain wisdom. That process is vital to our survival, and yet our learning and growth depends on our ability to step out of it, above it—to the balcony, as it were. From that perch, we can give ourselves the opportunity to first know directly what we perceive, in its neutral, undefined, objective state, before we label it and judge it. In a word, that is how we gain wisdom.

## Seeing, Discerning, and Acting

Of course, while this disruption of the perceive-name-judge process is necessary for greater wisdom, it is insufficient for greater justice. To actually bring about transformation, we have to not only allow ourselves to see and perceive differently—we also have to allow and move ourselves to act on the basis of our awakened consciousness. Langston Hughes's poem "I Look at the World," invites us to reflect on how we might translate awakened consciousness to action in the world.

> I look at the world
> From awakening eyes in a black face—
> And this is what I see:
> This fenced-off narrow space
> Assigned to me.
> I look then at the silly walls
> Through dark eyes in a dark face—
> And this is what I know:
> That all these walls oppression builds
> Will have to go!
> I look at my own body
> With eyes no longer blind—
> And I see that my own hands can make
> The world that's in my mind.
> Then let us hurry, comrades,
> The road to find.[4]

For Hughes, the act of sight and perception at first leads to resignation and acceptance of the world as it is: a fenced-off place assigned to him. But as he continues to look, he becomes gradually more aware of himself and the way that he sees, and he realizes that the walls constraining him can be viewed differently, not only as forces of oppression, but as something silly that can and should go away. As he gazes at himself one more time with a newly-awakened consciousness—eyes no longer blind—he realizes that his hands, his legs, his entire being can become activated in service of repairing and transforming the world he sees in his mind.

Hughes provides us with a vision of how our own inner work to grow in wisdom and understanding can lead to a transformative, embodied engagement with the world beyond the mind. That, I would suggest, is our tradition's vision, too: that our learning, our perceiving, and our deeper understanding help us take wise and courageous action.

---

[4] Langston Hughes, "I Look at the World." *Poetry* (2009).

## Questions for Reflection and Conversation

- When you think of someone who models wisdom, who comes to mind? Why?

- Can you think of a moment when you've become aware of ways you were unconsciously labeling and judging someone or something? What happened?

- What is something you have woken up to about your life that you'd like to change? What obstacles might be preventing you from doing so? How might you overcome them? Who could help you?

## Ideas for Practice

- Make an intention this week to notice the way you notice. What do you pay attention to? If you have a meditation practice, try being mindful of what sounds pass through your ears, what images come to your mind. Before you label them or let them go, try simply holding them in your mind's eye, non-judgmentally. How might you label them differently? What else might you notice about them? How might that change your judgment?

- As you go outside this week, make an intention to notice something more than you normally do. If you have a regular route for walking or running, make an intention to perceive something beyond what is in your line of sight or field of hearing, smell, or touch. Try journaling about what you notice.

- Consider your answer to the last question above. What is a change you'd like to make in the way you live or inhabit the world? Can you identify someone who could help you overcome the obstacles to making that change? Try arranging a conversation with them and perhaps invite them to hold you accountable by texting you in a few days and asking, "How are you doing with the change you're trying to bring about?"

# Noach: When Do We Feel Secure?

One of the enduring questions of the story of Noah is why he seemingly
failed to save anyone other than his immediate family from the flood. In contrast to Abraham, who goes to bat for the people of Sodom and is characterized
in rabbinic literature as welcoming new converts to his flock, Noah seems to
have gone about his business building the ark and preparing for the destruction
without attempting to save or even engage his neighbors. Why?

## Pride and Humility: Two Types of Tzaddik

The 19th-century Hasidic master Rabbi Levi Yitzchak of Berditchev (1740-
1809) takes up this question in his *Kedushat Levi* and offers the following
explanation:

קדושת לוי נח:ב
יש שני מיני צדיקים שעובדים הבורא יש צדיק שעובד הבורא ואין
לו חשק רק להיות עובד הבורא ומאמין שיש לו כח בעליונים להנהיג
העולמות כרצונו כמו שאמרו חכמינו ז"ל... הקדוש ברוך הוא גוזר
וצדיק מבטל הגזירה לטובה ויש צדיק אחד שעובד הבורא ברוך הוא
והוא שפל בעיני עצמו מאוד ומאוד וחושב בלבו מי אני שאתפלל
לבטל הגזירה לכן אינו מתפלל לבטל... וזה שפירש רש"י אף נח
מקטני אמנה היה, רצה לומר נח היה קטן בעיניו באמונה שהוא
צדיק תמים שיכול לבטל הגזירה שלא היה חשוב בעיני עצמו כלום.

Kedushat Levi, Noach:2
There are two types of righteous leaders (*tzaddikim*) who serve
the Creator: There is the *tzaddik* who serves the Creator and has
no other desire than to do so. This one believes that her power
can influence the uppermost realms, as our Sages taught... "The
Holy Blessed One decrees and the *tzaddik* transmutes the decree
into goodness." But there is another type of *tzaddik* who serves
the Holy Creator. This one is exceedingly humble in his own
eyes and thinks to himself, "Who am I that I should pray to
cancel a divine decree?" And so, he doesn't ... This is as Rashi
commented, "Noah was of little faith."[5] That is to say, Noah was
little in his own eyes—he did not have faith in himself that he
was a *tzaddik* who could cancel a decree, for he did not think
anything of himself at all.

[5] Rashi Genesis 7:7:2

According to the *Kedushat Levi*, Noah's greatness—his humility—also yielded a shadow side. In contrast to his 10th-generation descendant Abraham, Noah seemingly lacked a sufficient sense of security in his own self-worth necessary either to believe that his actions could have any effect on others or, perhaps, to even imagine taking that kind of action. (The *Kedushat Levi* goes so far as to quote the great kabbalist Rabbi Isaac Luria who suggests that, in order to repair this spiritual defect, Noah was reincarnated as Moses—who, while described as the most humble person on the earth, nevertheless both rebuked his fellow Israelites and God.)

## Pride and Humility in Relation to Creation

Perhaps Noah's humility comes in reaction to what he sees around him. The Talmud describes the generation of the flood like this:

> **Sanhedrin 108a**
> The Sages taught: The generation of the flood became haughty due to the goodness that the Holy Blessed One bestowed upon them… That caused them to say to the Holy One: "Depart from us; for we desire not the knowledge of Your ways. What is the Almighty, that we should serve Him, and what profit should we have if we pray unto God?" (Job 21:14–15). The members of the generation of the flood said: Do we need the Creator for anything, even for the drop of rain that God causes to fall? We have rivers and springs from which we take our supply of water; we do not fear the Divine. The Holy Blessed One said: With the goodness that I bestowed upon them, with that they infuriate Me and with it I will sentence them, as it is stated: "And behold I will bring a flood of water." (Genesis 6:17)

As Noah looks at the people in the world around him, he seemingly perceives an entire generation of supremely self-confident people. They aren't just secure in themselves, they're something more than that—they're arrogant. They thought they had mastered the world. But, as the Talmud relates, in so doing they lost the sense of humility needed to stay in right relationship with Creation and Creator. Arrogance and inappropriate humility can both create a false sense of security—often leading to disaster.

This description is evocative not only because of the arrogance of the generation of the Flood, but because the particular shape of their arrogance is one that strikes close to home for us today. Just when they thought they were secure, the world was upended and exposed their vulnerability. Conversely Noah, who in the *Kedushat Levi* and Rashi's account is lacking in self-security, becomes one of just a handful of survivors, along with his family, of a planetary catastrophe, secure inside the Ark.

Of course, most of us live in the space between these two poles. On the one hand, there are times when we feel a sure sense of security in ourselves that can enable us to take courageous action or speak courageous words: When we stand up to a bully, when we ask someone on a date, when we call our senator's office. On the other, we can also sometimes experience a profound and even debilitating feeling of insecurity that can keeps us from speaking or acting: When we fail to say something that might make us feel emotionally vulnerable, stay silent when we see others being abused, or not show up when we know we're needed.

For our personal and collective well-being, we need to spend quite a bit of time reflecting on how we can develop a healthy sense of security—neither overconfident nor undernourished. We want to be self-secure enough to take courageous action, but not so secure that we become arrogant like the generation of the flood. We want to live in a space of what leadership theorist Ron Heifetz has termed "Productive disequilibrium"—a zone in which we are just secure enough to do things that our resistance might otherwise lead us not to do.

## Educating for Spiritual Balance

One of the greatest lessons Judaism offers in this regard comes from a combination of the Mishnah and Maimonides in his laws of Torah study. In *Pirkei Avot* (2:5), Hillel the elder teaches that "The embarrassed person cannot learn, and the overly-strict person cannot teach." A thousand years later, Maimonides expanded on this idea in describing the ideal relationship of teacher and student:

> Mishneh Torah, Laws of Torah Study 4:4
> When a master gives a lesson which the disciples did not understand, she should not get angry at them and be moody, but go over it again and repeat it even many times, until they understand the lesson in depth.
>
> Likewise, a disciple shall not say, "I understand", when he did not really understand; but he should come back and ask even many times.
>
> If the master gets angry at him and becomes frustrated, he may say to her: "Master, it is Torah, and I need to learn it, but my mind is short of understanding!"

There are so many delightful things about this passage, but for our purposes the one I most want to call attention to is the way both learner and teacher share responsibility for holding the learning environment. The teacher, of course, has the responsibility not to allow their frustration to get in the way of their patience. She cannot feel so sure of herself that she is closed off to compassion and wisdom on her feet when her lesson doesn't go according to plan.

That much we would have expected. But what makes this passage so remarkable is the responsibility Maimonides places on the student. The student cannot be so worried about the insecurity he may experience by making himself vulnerable that he fails to speak up when he doesn't actually understand. To translate to the Noah story, the student cannot be over-humble and insecure to the point that he doesn't speak up—to raise a question with his neighbors ("Why are you doing the things you're doing?") or with the Holy One (as Abraham will say ten generations later, "Will not the Judge of the World do justice?"[6]).

## Covenant: Between Self-Confidence and Self-Negation

At the same time, Maimonides's framing offers us a vantage from which to take stock of the Divine as well. God seems to fail the test of the teacher—losing patience with the students and becoming angry. The Creator acknowledges as much after the Flood in making the covenant with Noah: "YHVH said to Godself: 'Never again will I doom the earth because of humans, since the devisings of their minds are evil from their youth; nor will I ever again destroy every living being, as I have done'" (Gen. 8:21). The Torah here gives us the image of the Divine as learning teacher, registering and responding to the needs and limitations of the beings with which it seeks to live in relationship—the essence of covenant.

In a teaching he made for Yom Kippur during the first year of the Covid-19 pandemic, my teacher and colleague Rabbi Jonathan Slater expanded on this idea of covenant as he reflected on the liturgical poem *ki hinei kachomer*, "Like the Potter's Clay," traditionally recited on Yom Kippur evening. The refrain of that poem is, *labrit habet v'al tefen layetzer*: "Look to the covenant and do not turn to the *yetzer*—the accuser, the negative and judgmental impulse." In this poem, we seemingly remind God of the promises the Divine entered into long ago, the cognizance the Creator took of our potential for life between the poles.

Importantly, however, Jonathan taught that we can also read this as a prayer to ourselves—to look to the covenant and not to the *yetzer*, the self-judgmental impulse within us, which would lead us to either the pole of excessive self-

---

[6] Gen. 18:25.

assurance or self-debasement. The covenant is not just a reminder to God. It is a reminder, an invitation and calling to us, to find the balance between speech and silence, taking space and making space, a sense of security and sureness in the world and ourselves and an acknowledgement of our profound limitations.

## Questions for Reflection and Conversation

- When you think about someone who embodies a balance of self-assurance and humility, who comes to mind? Do you consider them a model of behavior for you? Why or why not?

- Can you think of a time when you were able to overcome a feeling of insecurity in order to take a risk or do something which you were afraid of? If so, what happened? Who or what helped you? If not, what do you sense prevented you?

- When have you received critical feedback or rebuke? What did it feel like? What made it memorable? What, if anything, do you wish might have been different about it?

- Do you consider finding the balance between self-assurance and humility to apply to your spiritual practice or your relationship with the Divine? When, how, why or why not?

## Ideas for Practice

- In your meditation practice, let your attention turn toward a memory of a time you spoke up or failed to speak up. How does your body feel? What emotions arise? Try to investigate them. Use the R.A.I.N. practice—Recognize the sensation, Allow it to be present, Investigate where it's coming from, and practice Non-identification: Remember that you are not only these sensations or emotions.

- As you're going about your activities this week, make an effort to bring your attention to the ways in which your body is secure and the ways in which it's vulnerable. What helps you to feel more secure? What helps you to allow yourself to be more vulnerable?

# Lekh-Lekha: Who is in Your Family?

## Abram and Lot: Who is a Brother?

In the midst of a battle between the warring kings of ancient Canaan, we learn that Lot, Abram's nephew, was taken captive. Yet when Abram is informed about it, the Torah tell us:

> "And Abram heard that his brother was captured."
> (Gen. 14:14)

Most translations render the word *akh*/אָח in Hebrew not as a literal brother but as "kinsman" or "relative." Which makes sense, of course, as Lot is the son of Abram's brother Haran. Rashi suggests as much in his comment on Genesis 13:8, where Abram first refers to Lot as his brother:

> Abram said to Lot, "Let there be no strife between you and me, between my herdsmen and yours, for we men are *akhim*/אַחִים."

Commenting on this verse, Rashi explains *akhim* means *krovim*—relatives, kinsmen, close relations.

Yet Rashi also points us to a midrash that says something slightly different:

> Were they literally brothers? No—the verse means they had similar facial features. (Bereshit Rabbah 41:6)

In this telling, kinship is not only an issue of familial relation but takes on an additional dimension of physical similarity.

What do these alternative implications of the notion of brotherhood mean? And how might we deepen our awareness and experience of kinship by unpacking and reflecting on them? These are our questions this week.

## Brotherhood, Sisterhood, and Extended Boundaries

It seems uncontroversial to say that in referring to Lot as a his *akh*, Abram signals that he feels a greater responsibility toward Lot than other people. In essence Abram says to Lot, "We are brothers—and therefore we shouldn't fight, we should be at peace, and if anything ever happens to you, I'll risk my life to rescue you." Such a definition of brotherhood accords with uses of the term familiar to us from literature, film, sports, fraternal societies. Consider Shakespeare's Henry V in his dramatic St. Crispin's Day speech (Act IV, scene iii):

> We few, we happy few, we band of brothers;
> For he to-day that sheds his blood with me
> Shall be my brother; be he ne'er so vile,
> This day shall gentle his condition

The initiation rite of fighting for a cause, sharing suffering, shedding blood—these are the things that, conventionally, establish a bond of brotherhood that, in the case of the British at the Battle of Agincourt or troops on the beaches of Normandy, could traverse boundaries of class and station. Even if you've never been a soldier or on a sports team or a member of a fraternity, this sense of brotherhood is probably a familiar one.

But the very language of "brotherhood" harbors some particular traits that invite additional attention. As historian Mary Ann Clawson observed in her study of nineteenth-century fraternal orders in America, "Fraternalism is an identifiable social and cultural form" with four particular characteristics: "a 'corporate' idiom, ritual, proprietorship, and masculinity."[7] For our purposes, the last of these is perhaps particularly salient: "Brotherhood" is a gendered term, bound up with conceptions of masculinity like those King Henry gestures at as he rallies the troops. Its inclusivity rests on an act of exclusion—those who are my brothers are those with whom I make common cause to battle the enemy, exert might, and exercise power.

This undertow in the current of brotherhood becomes all the more palpable when contrasted with the language of sisterhood. Consider this example from a 1985 address by the Black lesbian writer Audre Lorde entitled "Sisterhood and Survival." Lorde describes her travels around the globe and then observes, "All over the world I found black women coming together around their identities, questioning and re-defining what that Africanness could mean, within our particular communities, and upon the world stage." In particular, she reflects that these Black women shared a common experience of suffering and oppression at the hands of colonial powers. Lord then marshals that common identity to, among other things, summon her sisters to identify with and take courageous action on behalf of Black women and

---

[7] Mary Ann Clawson, *Constructing Brotherhood: Class, Gender, and Fratnernalism.* Princeton: Princeton University Press, 1989, 5.

men in apartheid-era South Africa. She concludes with the powerful reflection, "We are sisters, and our survivals are mutual."[8]

Like Shakespeare's brotherhood, Lord's sisterhood does not rest strictly on genetics—though appearances, particularly in skin color, explicitly or implicitly matter to both. In both cases the notion of siblinghood serves to extend our moral imagination beyond those with whom we share chromosomes. But in the case of brotherhood, the roots of that extension seem more planted in excluding a shared other; in the case of sisterhood, they stem more from identifying a common experience of suffering, regardless of who perpetrated it.

## More Than Just a Pretty Face

In his *Mei Hashiloach*, the 19th-century Hasidic master Mordechai Yosef Leiner (1801-1854) comments on the midrash's suggestion that Abraham and Lot shared facial features. He writes that, despite the fact that their outward appearances and actions were indistinguishable, nevertheless God was aware of a deep internal difference between uncle and nephew. Leiner's son, Yaakov (1828-1878), elaborates on the point in his *Beit Yaakov* (Lekh-Lekha 21:9):

בית יעקב, לך לך 21:9

לוט עשה על הגוון כמו שפעל אברהם אבינו ועשה, אברהם היה
עוסק בהכנסת אורחים ובגמילות חסדים וכן עשה גם לוט. אכן
אברהם אבינו עשה זאת מעומק לבו, ולוט אף שפעל ועשה כפעולת
אברהם אבל רק על הגוון נדמה לו, ועומק לבו היה מלא שנאה
להשי"ת.

Beit Yaakov, Lekh-Lekha 21:9
On the surface, Lot acted just as Abraham did: Abraham welcomed guests and extended loving kindness, and so too did Lot. But Abraham did these things from the depths of his heart. By contrast, Lot, even though he did exactly the same things—only on the surface did they appear the same. But in his heart of hearts, Lot was full of hatred for the Blessed Ineffable One.

Setting aside the *Beit Yaakov's* idiomatic invocation of hatred of the Divine

[8] Audre Lorde, "Sisterhood and Survival." *The Black Scholar* 17.2 (1986).

on the part of Lot, what is particularly intriguing here is the idea that, despite striking physical, genetically-derived similarities, Abraham and Lot are profoundly different. Their stories bear this out: simply contrast the welcome Abraham extends to guests and the way that Lot does in Parashat Vayera (next week). Or, looking back on our text here, simply note that Abram is the one who repeatedly invokes the language of brotherhood toward Lot, while Lot does not reciprocate the gesture. This would suggest that the midrash, as read through these Hasidic masters, in fact points up the profound limitations of the racial or genetic model of kinship, and suggests, instead, that spiritual communion involves transcending it.

## Returning to Gender: Of Brothers, Sisters, and Communion

By way of concluding, let's consider one more midrash on the subject of Abraham and brotherhood. In this case the midrash is based on a verse in Song of Songs (8:8):

> We have a little sister, whose breasts are not yet formed. What shall we do for our sister when she is spoken for?

In a striking moment, Midrash Tanhuma (Lekh Lekha 2:1) identifies the little sister in the verse with none other than Abraham. In her masterful study, *Genesis: The Beginning of Desire*, Avivah Zornberg translates and comments on this passage:

> Why is Abraham called "sister?" Because he sewed the whole world together in the presence of God! [This is a pun on the words *ahot* (sister) and *la-ahot* (to sew) ...] *He was like a person who tears apart and sews together*—therefore he is called 'sister.'

"Abraham is called *ahot*," Zornberg writes, "because he represents the desire to reintegrate (*ehad* [one], *ahot* [sister], and *la-ahot* [to sew] are clearly connected) his own world with God."[9] Abraham—the one who extends notions of kinship, welcomes guests, brings converts under the wings of the Divine presence, who is identified with the *middah* or attribute of *Hesed* or loving connection—is deeply motivated by an impulse for unification. So much so that the midrash doesn't bat an eye at identifying him with the sister of the Song of Songs.

---

[9] Zornberg, *The Beginning of Desire*, 95.

Yet Zornberg also notes a paradox suggested by the midrash: Abraham's "radical activity is dual: 'tearing and sewing,' rending and rendering one. As he comes to understanding and resolution, [Abraham] uncovers further mysteries, invitations to love."[10] This, I would suggest, reflects a basic animating tension in developing and maintaining a spiritual community: How to hold the sensation of unity while allowing room for individuation and distinctiveness; of seeking mystical union while acknowledging our finiteness and separation.

Rabbi Angela Buchdahl of Central Synagogue spoke to this dynamic in a widely-viewed Yom Kippur sermon following the summer of racial justice protests in the United States and around the world in 2020. Reflecting on years of people implying or outright telling her that she doesn't "look Jewish," Buchdahl recounted her own and others' pain at being excluded from a sense of belonging in the Jewish community on the basis of their *klaster panim*, those same facial features that made Abraham and Lot look like brothers. Strikingly, however, Buchdahl lands on the metaphor of family:

> I don't deny that heredity is an important, meaningful element for our People. It is powerful to imagine an ancestral line of Jews going all the way back to Sinai. But I'm suggesting that it is time to stop thinking of Jewish Peoplehood as a race. Instead, think of Jewish Peoplehood as a family...
>
> You can be family through birth. But also, adoption. Or choice, like conversion. You can even become the closest of family through a covenant, as one does in marriage. Our covenant with God is the foundation of Jewish Peoplehood.[11]

Buchdahl's invocation of covenant provides her, and us, with a way to experience a sense of kinship that includes and yet expands beyond simple biology. Like marriage, the paradigmatic form by which people become family—even siblings-in-law!—the experience of shared access to, membership in, and identity through Abraham's covenant invites us to extend our imaginations of who is in our family.

---

[10] Ibid.

[11] Angela Warnick Buchdahl, "'We Jews are not a race': A rabbi of color speaks personally on Yom Kippur." *The Forward*, September 28, 2020.

## Questions for Reflection and Conversation

- If you have a family photo of a blood relative, take a look at it. Do you see yourself in it? Do you see others? Why or why not?

- Is there someone you treat like family even though they are not a blood relation? What is the nature of that relationship, of your sense of responsibility to them?

- Have you been a member of an organization that refers to its members as brothers or sisters? If so, what do those terms bring up for you as you reflect on them now? If not, what do you imagine it might be like to be part of such an organization?

## Ideas for Practice

- In meditation practice this week, consider bringing to mind relationships of people whom you consider at varying levels of connection: relatives, intimate friends, soulmates, acquaintances, allies, partners. What does each of these people bring up for you? What feelings arise? Try to investigate those sensations non-judgmentally and see if you can arrive at greater insight about how you categorize people.

- In his final speech to the Israelites, Moses says, "It is not only with you that I make this covenant, but with those who are standing here with us today before *YHVH* our God and those who are not with us here this day" (Deuteronomy 29:13-14). Bring to mind someone you don't know personally—from the past, the future, or today—and try writing them a letter. What do you want to ask them? What might you share about your own sense of kinship with them?

- This week make an intention to consciously interact with one person each day as if they were your sibling. What do you notice about your interaction? How is your speech, your face, your voice, your body affected? What might it be like to keep up this kind of practice?

# Vayera:
# Where Do We Draw Our Boundaries?

## Boundaries in the Torah Portion

In a poem entitled "Fooling God," Native American writer Louise Erdrich writes:

> I must be tireless as rust and bold as roots
> growing through the locks on doors
> and crumbling the cinderblocks
> of the foundations of his everlasting throne.[12]

Erdrich's poem evokes the organized, hierarchical power of religion in order to undermine it. ("I must become and file everything under my own system / so we can lose him and his proofs and adherents," she writes later.) This image from the beginning of the poem, of roots that grow through locks on doors and cinderblocks in the foundation of the edifice, is particularly striking, and it sets the stage well for our discussion this week of Parashat Vayera under the framing question: Where do we draw our boundaries?

Vayera is preoccupied with this question on a range of levels. In the opening scene we find Abraham, recovering from his circumcision at age 99, who nevertheless breaks the boundaries of his home in order to welcome and receive guests. Later in the parasha this boundary of home is thrust into high relief as the threshold of Lot's house becomes a boundary under pressure from a mob outside. Further on we find Hagar and Ishmael cast out of home entirely, into the unbounded wilderness.

In at least two instances the parasha invites us to reflect on the boundaries of private thought and shared communication: "And YHVH said: Can I keep from Abraham what I intend to do?" (18:17); and later, when Avimelech complains to Abraham that he kept from him the crucial information that Sarah was not (only) his sister, but his wife. In both these instances, the boundaries of thought, speech, and relationship are stretched and interrogated. Likewise, both these cases are woven through with another type of boundary, that of morality, which receives its most direct treatment in the stories of Lot's daughters and the *Akedah*, or Binding of Isaac.

---

[12] Louise Erdrich, "Fooling God." *Poetry* (1989): 223.

## The Capacity to Contain Multitudes

Commenting on Genesis 18:17, the early Hasidic master Rabbi Chaim of Tchernovitz (1760-1817) offers a reflection on this theme of boundaries as he considers the difference between human beings and the Divine.

**באר מים חיים 18:17:1**

אין כמדת הקב"ה מדת בשר ודם. כי הנה בשר ודם, אם יארע
לו איזה דבר שיהיה על ידי זה בשמחה וגילה ורנה, אז לא יוכל
לפעול אז שום בחינת הכעס ודין. ואומר "לא אעשה עתה זאת",
ויהיה מונח לזמן אחר. וכן כשיהיה בכעס וזעף גדול, לא יוכל
אז לעשות דבר השמחה והחסד. כי האדם הוא בעל גבול ומדה,
וכשימולא כל גופו בדבר אחד, לא יוכל אז עשות השני. כי לא
יהיה בקרבו שני הדברים, להיות ממולא בדבר אחד עד גבולו.
אבל לא כן הקב"ה, שהוא בעל בלתי גבול ותכלית. וכשהוא עושה
חסד גדול ורחמים מרובין לאחד, אף על פי כן באותו רגע הוא דן
למכעיסיו ועוברי רצונו. וכן להיפוך, כביכול: כשהוא בכעס וזעף
גדול, בזה לא ימנע מעשות החסד והשמחה לעושי רצונו.

Be'er Mayim Chayim 18:17:1
The Holy Blessed One is not like a human being. For when something happens to us that causes us to feel happiness or joy, we are unable to behave with anger or judgment. Rather, we will set it aside for a later time, saying "I can't deal with that now". Likewise, when we are angry and upset, we are unable to do something joyous and loving. For a human being is inherently limited, and when one emotion fills our body, we cannot enact its opposite. Just as two physical bodies cannot occupy the same space, so, too, two strong emotions cannot fully take up our emotional space. Not so the Holy Blessed One, however, Who is not bounded in this way. When the Creator acts toward a person with generosity and compassion, even at the very same moment the Holy One can judge those who anger It and transgress God's will. And so, too, the opposite: When the Creator is angry and in a rage, even so nothing prevents Them from showing love and happiness to those who do Their will.

Reb Chaim points us to a more internal dimension of boundedness and boundaries. Unlike God, who is *Ein Sof,* infinite, unending in time or space, human beings are finite creatures who live in physically delimited bodies that take up physical space and exist for discrete periods of time. Thus, according to his teaching, we can't really inhabit—or be inhabited by—two contradictory head- or heart-spaces at once: We can't be completely angry and loving at the same time, just as we can't be in our own home and the building across the street simultaneously. Not so the Infinite, who is able to be both angry and compassionate, destructive and constructive, at the same time and in the same place. In this case, according to the Tchernovitzer, that leads the Redeemer to rescue Lot, even as the destruction of Sodom and Gomorrah takes place. The capacity of the Divine to hold two opposites at once is highlighted in the destruction, an event which, through the birth of Moab that comes about in its wake, leads, *mutatis mutandis*, to Ruth, King David, and the Messiah. Just as God is destroying, God also brings about salvation.

While Reb Chaim seems emphatic in his belief that human beings cannot mirror the Divine capacity for simultaneous contradiction, he nevertheless opens the door to the question of paradox that is famously evoked in Walt Whitman's "Song of Myself" (Whitman was born in 1819, two years after Reb Chaim died):

> *Do I contradict myself?*
> *Very well then I contradict myself,*
> *(I am large, I contain multitudes.)*

While we can't be in the same place at the same time, we know from our own experience that through acts of imagination we can transport ourselves to times and places outside our present reality. Sometimes that can be a wonderful, creative thing—enabling us to remember loved ones or special moments or fantasize about stories past and future. And sometimes, of course, it can also be a form of distracting ourselves from a reality we don't want to focus on. In my own life, this distraction is something I try to counteract through mindfulness practice when I allow myself to bring attention to the negative thought or feeling and then, through investigation and non-identification, to come to a deeper awareness that I am not beholden to that thought or feeling, and a clearer understanding of what in my life is bringing it about.

## Boundaries and Pluralism

In our own time, the Israeli teacher Rabbi Shimon Gershon Rosenberg, known as Rav Shagar (1949-2007), has struck a chord with an increasing readership in the Modern Orthodox communities in Israel and North

America for his explorations of philosophy and Hasidism. The question of boundaries, particularly those that function to determine if something is Jewish or external to Judaism, is a recurring theme in his writing. In an essay developed in 2002, he reflects on the boundaries of faith and doubt:

> The doubting of faith's universal absoluteness—postmodernism excels at this—has a balancing, productive role: It does not stifle our capacity to experience and believe in ourselves, but it does generate boundaries. The postmodern believer's awareness of the contradictions between various faiths, and of the paradoxes inherent in his own world, can stabilize him, rendering him more sensitive, ethical, and humble.[13]

Here Rav Shagar points us to the perhaps surprising way that doubt can actually provide a sense of boundaries and humility by helping us remain attuned to the limitations of our knowledge. Whatever truth we may glimpse is but a partial truth. That lesson may seem obvious when applied to those who profess fundamentalist belief in religious truth. But Shagar's lesson applies equally for those of us who draw other kinds of dogmatic boundaries, too: Our steadfast beliefs in whatever we hold to be true are ineluctably partial by dint of the fact that we are human. And so, stepping outside of ourselves to examine the bounds of our faith, wherever they are, is essential for being mindful. In our practice, we can aim to become more aware of those boundaries on which we rely—words, concepts, people, relationships, physical objects—and to more deeply appreciate both the work they do for us and the fact that, though we may live *within* them, we are not synonymous *with* them.

At the same time, Rav Shagar goes on to argue for not only being mindful of our boundaries, but also subverting them—particularly through the awareness that, by virtue of our shared humanity, we also share a great deal of truth. Rav Shagar writes that the pluralism suggested by the paragraph above

> must be augmented by a universal dimension, meaning the knowledge that, beyond our various cultural differences, there is a universal truth shared by all humans, that "the earth is all of one piece" [Babylonian Talmud Bava Batra 67a]... The world is not merely a collection of assorted cultures whose

---

[13] Shimon Gershon Rosenberg, "Justice and Ethics in a Postmodern World," in *Faith Shattered and Restored: Judaism in the Postmodern Age*. Jerusalem: Magid Books, 2017, 117.

distinct contexts preclude intercultural communication; there is a common kernel of humanity...

By combining this universal point of view with doubt in the universality and absoluteness of any individual stance, every culture can accept other cultures as true alternatives that carry a kernel of truth. If more of us humbly acknowledge the limited capacity of the individual to utter absolute statements, perhaps we can establish justice and ethics alongside a renewed human solidarity.[14]

## Boundaries and Connections

Having explored dimensions of the boundaries of our embodied emotions and thoughts through the Tchernovitzer Rebbe, and the boundaries of larger bodies of truth and language in the work of Rav Shagar, I want to bring us back to the organic orientation with which we began through Louise Erdrich. In this case, I want to invoke a contemporary of Erdrich's, the Jewish poet Marge Piercy.

In one of her most famous poems, "Seven of Pentacles,"[15] Piercy pens a moving midrash on the scene of the Tarot card by the same name. Running through the scene she describes is a meditation on the idea of boundaries, and in particular the way in which organic life works its way above, below, around, and through boundaries in order to connect. She charts how the natural world is deeply interconnected beneath the surface of the earth: That is, the boundary of earth itself is true—it gives us ground to stand on—but it also conceals the fecund life underneath. Given our own limitations, out of sight equals out of mind—and thus we need to cultivate an active awareness of that life beyond the boundary of the surface.

With this reality in mind, Piercy exhorts us to connect, to weave together, to overcome the boundaries. That which is real, Piercy seems to say, is not only what the boundaries suggest. Indeed, reality—*real* connections, which cross boundaries; *real* houses, which are open like Abraham's—lies in the traversing of borders, the linking of things that have their own separate identities and yet are paradoxically and simultaneously part of something more.

---

[14] Ibid. 118.

[15] Marge Piercy, "The Seven of Pentacles." *Selected Poems of Marge Piercy*. Circle of Water, 1982.

## Questions for Reflection and Conversation

- Can you think of a time you erected a boundary—in the physical world, in a relationship, in another part of your life? If so, what led you to do so? How did you feel afterward? What can you say about what was lost and what was gained?

- When, if ever, have you journeyed across a boundary? What led you to do so? How did you feel afterward? What was lost and what was gained?

- This Torah portion often evokes strong responses in readers because of the ways the characters stay within or cross boundaries. You might have an innate judgment about Abraham's actions in binding Isaac, or about God's actions at Sodom. How, if at all, does bringing awareness to the question of boundaries offer you other perspectives or new ways you might understand them?

## Ideas for Practice

- In meditation this week, allow your consciousness to center on a boundary. It could be physical, emotional, conceptual. Explore what comes to mind, what sensations you experience around it.

- Bring to mind some of the characters from this very rich Torah portion and consider the boundaries they stay behind or transgress: Abraham, Sarah, Hagar, Ishmael, Lot, Lot's daughters, Avimelech, Isaac, God. Make a list of the boundaries you note. Then look a second time and see if you note other ways to imagine those boundaries, or even to redraw them. Try to notice what, if anything, arises for you as you do.

# Chayei Sarah:
# How Do We Tell Our Stories?

## The Reality of Repetition

The bulk of Parashat Chayei Sarah is taken up with the story of Abraham's servant (traditionally referred to as Eliezer, though in fact his name is unspecified in the Torah text) who is sent by his master to find a wife for Isaac from among Abraham's native kinsmen in Aram-Naharaim. Within that story, an unusual amount of space is devoted not only to narrating what happened, but also to detailing how Eliezer *tells* the story of what happened. That is, the story is first told by the omniscient narrator of the Torah, and then is repeated by Eliezer himself when he speaks to Abraham's family.

While the two accounts are certainly similar in their general details, they are not quite consistent on numerous little matters. The medieval Spanish-French commentator Rabbi David Kimchi (Radak, 1160-1235) observed the divergence within the repetitions and admitted the case seemed to be a head-scratcher: "We cannot explain the reason for all the additions and omissions in [Eliezer's] account, for they are legion," says Radak. But he explains, "[Eliezer] told them all that had gone between himself and his master, his transactions with Rebecca, and that God had providentially arranged matters just as Abraham had promised. His emphasis on this point was to impress on them that they had no alternative. They could not stop the girl from accepting the marriage offer since the matter was from God." That is, the particular way that Eliezer narrated the story was to essentially force Rebecca's family to accept that her marriage to Isaac was a *fait accompli*. Radak concludes, "The recapitulation involves merely a variation in wording, but the sense is the same. This is unavoidable in reported speech: it preserves the sense but not the exact wording."[16]

Radak's comments, along with the entire episode, invite us into deeper reflection on how we tell our stories. In one sense, Radak seems to be describing the eternality of the game of telephone: the conditions of human communication lend themselves to alteration, degradation, adaptation, magnification, elaboration, etc. It's just the way things work, and it was as true 800 years ago in medieval France as it was 3,000 years ago in ancient Mesopotamia.

---

[16] Radak on Genesis 24:39 as quoted in Nehama Leibowitz, *New Studies in Bereshit/Genesis*, World Zionist Organization, n.d., 236.

## Who's the Audience?

Yet not all changes in our stories are due simply to forgetfulness on our part. Often, we consciously or subconsciously alter our stories because of who we're talking to. When someone asks me for the story of my career, I find I tell that story in a pretty similar way—even verbatim duplication. Or when I tell the story of how my wife and I met. Or the birth of our children. Or many others. I imagine you, too, have these kinds of stories—ones that are well-rehearsed and polished from repetition. But frequently I observe that these stories are adjusted ever so slightly—a different word here, a little embellishment of a detail there, leaving out this tiny piece, and so on. I imagine we do this because of our perception of the person we're talking to and the subtle ways we intuit they might need to hear the story. Or perhaps, if we're being really honest, we change our narration based on how we want to be perceived by the listener as we tell the story.

Expounding on the commandment to tell the story of the Exodus from Egypt at the Passover Seder, Rabbi Yehuda Leib Alter of Ger (1847-1905) offers an illuminating reflection on the power and possibility of storytelling:

שפת אמת פסח תרל"ה ה

וכל המרבה לספר ביציאת מצרים הרי זה משובח. שהסיפור ביציאת מצרים מביא דעת כמ"ש ולמען תספר באזני בנך כו'. וידעתם כי אני ה'. ומאחר שיציאת מצרים נאמרה בתורה והתורה ניתנה לישראל יכולין לעורר כח הגאולה כי יציאת מצרים יוצא מכח אל הפועל ע"י הסיפור. כמו ענין תורה שבכתב ושבע"פ שבנ"י מחדשין טעמי תורה. וזה כחן בפה שע"י שמוציאין הדברים בפה מגלין הטעמים הנסתרים לבוא לידי גילוי.

Sefat Emet, Passover 1875:5

The more one tells the story, the more praiseworthy one is. For the story of the Exodus from Egypt brings conscious awareness [da'at], as it is written, "That you will tell the story in the ears of your children and your children's children—the wonders I performed in Egypt and the signs I put in their midst—and you will be consciously aware [v'yidatem] that I am YHVH" (Ex. 10:2). Since the Exodus is told of in the Torah and the Torah is given to the people Israel, we are able to arouse the power of redemption—for the exodus from constriction happens by means of telling the story... This is the power of the mouth: by means of bringing forth words out of our mouths, we uncover hidden meanings and arrive at revelation.

For the Sefat Emet, those subtle changes in how we narrate stories—whether "the story" of the Exodus (can we possibly say there is only one story?) or the stories of our own continuous liberation from various forms of constriction, our own personal *Mitzrayims*—are the very vehicle by which the liberation happens. And not only liberation, but revelation: A deeper awareness of the truth of our existence. This truth can be obscured when we focus only on the reality of our freedom, and don't then move to the simultaneous reality of our lives as vessels for the Divine in the world. The fact of our own liberation must become a revelation of Divinity in the world—for ourselves, and for others. The more we tell the story, the deeper we can go in our awareness of the fact that the story is just a story, and the more we can come to appreciate the many ways we can narrate our lives. Of course, that's only when we pay attention. If we mindlessly narrate our stories, whether at the Seder or on the phone, then that enhanced awareness remains beyond our comprehension.

It's important to point out that, for the Torah, the object of storytelling at Passover is the listener—the child. And the Haggadah itself, based on the Mishnah, instructs us to alter the story so it is learner-appropriate—hence the Four Children section of the Seder. But the Talmud also tells us that, even if we are having a Seder alone, we are required to ask ourselves a question and tell the story in response. The Sefat Emet helpfully reminds us that, even when we are telling the story to others, we are constructing and changing and adapting and telling the story to ourselves. Perhaps we are just as much the primary audience for our stories as those to whom we tell them.

## Changing Our Stories by Telling Them

Psychotherapist Estelle Frankel elaborates on this theme in an essay describing her professional practice of integrating Hasidic storytelling into her therapeutic work:

> All verbal therapies are, in effect, "narrative therapies," focused on altering the problematic stories people tell themselves. Psychotherapy offers the patient a chance to edit or rewrite his story by framing it within a larger context or by making room for alternative story lines. And by telling his story to a sympa-

thetic listener, namely, the therapist, the patient can begin to discover a new inner voice—that of a "sympathetic narrator." This simple change in voice transforms the story. Events from the past are not just *relived* but *recast* in a new light. The past is recontextualized by the compassionate awareness and insight therapist and patient bring to it in the present moment.[17]

Frankel builds on the Sefat Emet's observation that the act of telling our stories can be one of redemption. But she makes explicit what is implicit in the rebbe's writing: Our stories of personal constriction, suffering, trauma—telling these stories to a sympathetic listener can often be the very instrument of liberating ourselves from their hold on us, both because someone else is with us in our suffering and, even more so, because in telling the story we develop compassion for ourselves.

Jewish mindfulness practice can be indispensable for bringing about this kind of change, and indeed for becoming something like a compassionate listener to ourselves. When we bring a story to consciousness during practice and allow ourselves to investigate it nonjudgmentally, to recognize that it is but one way of understanding our experience, we enable ourselves to go to the balcony and look down on the story from various angles. In so doing, we engage in the work that both Frankel and the Sefat Emet describe of liberating ourselves from the negative hold our stories can have on us. We can start to see other ways of understanding the stories of our lives and those of the others with whom we share our existence, arriving at the deeper *da'at* or mindful awareness to which the Sefat Emet refers. And we move toward an experience of revelation, a moment in which we can sense the Divine moving in our lives and making possible an infinite array of stories.

### Questions for Reflection and Conversation

- Read through Genesis 24:1-26 and compare it with the recapitulation in verses 35-48. What do you notice that's the same? What do you see that's different? Why do you think Abraham's servant makes the changes to the story that he does?

---

[17] Estelle Frankel, "Sacred Narrative Therapy: Hasidism, Storytelling, and Healing." Green, Arthur and Ariel Evan Mayse. *A New Hasidism: Branches.* Jewish Publication Society, 2019, 301.

- What is one story you tell frequently? It could be about your career, a spouse or good friend, the birth or death of a loved one, or something else. Tell that story to someone and observe how you tell it. Then see if there's another way to tell it—from a different perspective, or focusing on some other detail than you usually do. What, if anything, do you notice about the story? Why might you tell it the way you usually do? Might you consider other ways of telling it?

- Ask a good friend or loved one to tell you about a story they think of you as telling frequently. Listen to how they narrate it. How does it compare with the version you have in your mind? How does it make you feel to hear them tell it?

### Ideas for Practice

- In meditation practice this week, make an intention to bring to mind a story you tell about yourself or someone close to you. Note how the story makes you feel—emotionally and in your body. Consciously, then, step out of the story, examine it, and investigate why you might tell it the way you do. See how it feels to bring greater awareness to the story.

- As you go about your week, make an intention to notice one moment each day when you have an opportunity to tell a story. It could be with a friend or loved one, at work, or with a customer service representative. Bearing in mind the character virtue of *shemirat hadibbur,* or mindful speech, try to pause before you start telling your story and consider how you want to tell it. Notice how practicing *hitlamdut,* or self-awareness, before you start speaking makes you feel—and how it might affect the course of the interaction.

# Toldot:
# How do we know?

Chapter 27 of the Book of Genesis, which forms the dramatic core of Parashat Toldot, serves as a lynchpin between the lives of Isaac and Jacob. A major theme of Isaac's life is that, to a great extent, he is acted upon by others. This intersects with a major theme of Jacob's life: deception. Just as happened during the Akedah, Isaac is the victim of the actions of others. And just as Jacob will be the victim of deception on his wedding night and later at the hand of his sons, in this parasha Jacob is the one who perpetrates deception on his father.

As the Latin phrase attributed to Sir Francis Bacon puts it, *Scientia potentia est*, Knowledge is power. This is something of an underpinning assumption for much of Western thought. Yet the story of Parashat Toldot invites us to reflect on what we mean by knowledge, and the true source of our power. How do we know what we think we know? Can we bring greater awareness to our assumptions, to the biases and limitations in our knowing minds? How might that point us to ways of knowing beyond the highly intellectualized conception we often call knowledge? And, how might that help us better know ourselves and the lives we live?

## Sensing Doubt

The contemporary mindfulness teacher Ruth King offers us a starting point. King offers this description of how perception, thought, and belief interact with one another:

> We perceive something through our senses. There is a sense organ and a sense object—eyes see, ears hear, nose smells, body feels, tongue tastes, and mind thinks. Once we perceive, the mind habitually jumps to thoughts and feelings about what is being perceived; these thoughts and feelings are rooted in past experiences, past conditioning. Thoughts and feelings then influence the mood of our mind. When perceptions, thoughts, and feelings are repeated or imprinted through experiences, they solidify into view or belief. View then reinforces perception. This cycle becomes the way in which we experience and respond to the world.[18]

King's description resonates with what we encounter in the parasha as Isaac

---

[18] Ruth King, *Mindful of Race*. Sounds True Press, 2018, 106.

and Jacob engage in a multisensory encounter involving sight, smell, taste, touch, and hearing. "Come closer that I may feel you, my son—whether you are really my son Esau or not," Isaac says in verse 21. And in the next verse, "So Jacob drew close to his father Isaac, who felt him and wondered, 'The voice is the voice of Jacob, yet the hands are the hands of Esau.'" Over and over again, the text emphasizes Isaac's uncertainty of his conscious knowing, his distrust of the conflicting inputs of his senses, and perhaps his own intuition.

We can feel Isaac's discomfort in the narrative, a discomfort that King helpfully describes:

> Essentially, we think we know something, and then we are off and running—all based on past experiences, preferences, and beliefs. And usually, but not always, it's all in our minds or, at a minimum, worthy of questioning. When we perceive and when thoughts and emotions are simultaneously activated, those thoughts and emotions proliferate, creating a state of fear and anxiety driven by what the mind is believing in that moment. In such moments, we are removed from presence; we vacate the premises of body and mind and are fixated on view.[19]

In Isaac's case, the rising tension of his encounter with Jacob finally spills over when he realizes he has been deceived: "Isaac was seized with very violent trembling" (v. 33). The trauma of the encounter touches Esau: "When Esau heard his father's words, he burst into wild and bitter sobbing" (v. 34). That trauma further gives way to a threat of violence that will hover over the brothers' relationship for decades to come: "Now Esau harbored a grudge against Jacob because of the blessing which his father had given him, and Esau said to himself, 'Let but the mourning period of my father come, and I will kill my brother Jacob'" (v. 41).

The spiraling collateral damage is rooted deeper in prior moments of unknowing. The whole of this drama is set in motion when Rebecca, overhearing Isaac instruct Esau to bring him a cooked dish in order to help him enter a state in which he could pronounce blessing, pushes her son Jacob to intercede in deception. But note: Isaac prefaces the entire conversation by saying, "I am old now, and I do not know how soon I may die" (v. 2). This state of uncertainty, doubt, question—this is the mood of the entire chapter.

---

[19] Ibid. 107.

## Unknowing Knowing: As If

The problematics of this passage have long been front and center for rabbinic commentators. What would it mean that the Divine blessing was given to Jacob through an act of subterfuge? Would it call into question the Jewish people's claim to our special relationship with YHVH? And what would it say about Jacob, the ancestor from whom the entire people springs, that he engaged in such deception? Would the blessing he received be truly a blessing if it came about not through the knowing bestowal by Isaac, but by an unwitting mistake? The stakes are high—for us, as recipients of this legacy, and for our self-understanding as intentional agents in the world.

For our purposes, which focus more on how we might understand this passage in terms of mindfulness practice, Rabbi Yisrael Hopstein (1737-1814), the Maggid of Kozhnitz, offers a tantalizing idea:

עבודת ישראל, תולדות
אע"פ שיצחק לא ידע על בוריו שזה הוא יעקב בנו, עכ"ז יצאו הדברים
מפיו ברוח הקודש כאילו יודע.

### Avodat Yisrael, Toldot
Even though Isaac did not know for certain that this was Jacob his son, nevertheless the words came from his mouth through the Divine spirit as if he knew.

The Maggid begins with the same assumption as much of rabbinic literature: it would indeed be a problem if Isaac offered the blessing to Jacob under something less than full awareness. And yet he gracefully elides the problem of Jacob's subterfuge through the invocation of the Hebrew word *k'ilu*, "as if." Even though Isaac had his well-founded doubts about Jacob's identity, somehow in the moment the blessing came out *as if* Isaac was fully aware that this was not in fact Esau before him, but Jacob.

The liminal space of *as if* consciousness, in which we are aware of our less-than-perfect knowledge, is what I understand Ruth King to describe in the passage above. In our practice of meditation and mindfulness, we bring our attention to the fact that our knowledge is inherently imperfect, that unintended self-deception impedes us from ascertaining hidden dimensions of truth. In this, we cultivate the potential to both interrupt the process of perceiving-judging-feeling, and begin a fraught process of living in a more indeterminate space.

## Knowing and Unknowing: A Speaking Silence

Rabbi Yaakov Leiner (1828-1878) offers us another way of understanding this question of knowing by contrasting Isaac with Moses:

**בית יעקב, תולדות 35**

ויהי כי זקן יצחק ותכהין עיניו מראות. אמר אאמו"ר זללה"ה (מי
השלוח ח"א ד"ה ויהי כי זקן ובגליון אות יא) שענין יצחק שניתן לו כל טוב ארץ
ישראל, כיון שלא הורשה לצאת ממנה, אך לראותה לא זכה בשלימות
כי כהו עיניו. ומשה רבינו לא זכה ליכנס לארץ ישראל, ולראותה זכה.
והענין בזה, יען כי יצחק היה מכוון שלא מדעתו לרצון השי"ת כמו
שברך את יעקב שלא מדעתו, ובהסכמת השי"ת, ומשה רבינו ע"ה היה
צריך לילך רק על פי חכמתו, ובאם לאו היה צריך לבירורים

**Beit Yaakov, Toldot 35**

"Isaac was old and his eyes were too dim to see." Isaac was given all the goodness of the Land of Israel, for he was not permitted to depart it; yet he did not merit to see it in its fullness, because his eyes were dim. Moses [was the opposite]—he did not merit to enter the land of Israel, yet he did merit to see it.[20] The idea here is that Isaac could intuit the Divine will without conscious awareness, as when he blessed Jacob in a state of unawareness but with God's concurrence. Yet Moses had to conduct himself according to his own assessment, and when his intellectual understanding failed him and he was uncertain, he required further clarification [from the Holy One].

The Beit Yaakov's comment invites us to question the assumption that what we think we know in the moment, self-assured knowledge of how things are, is all it's cracked up to be. Isaac here is presented as a different kind of knower—one who, perhaps, is able to access a different kind of truth by virtue of a different kind of mind. His attunement with the holy, represented in this passage by the Land of Israel from which he never departs, gives Isaac a different way of perceiving and relating to the world. He perhaps has a different way of understanding or knowing what is true, one that is less bound up with agency, mastery, language, and more animated by stillness, passivity, and quiet.

Much of the work of the great American poet Mary Oliver explores this ter-

---

[20] N.B. As in Deuteronomy 3:27, where God tells Moses to look out over the land of Israel.

ritory of a different kind of knowing. I think in particular of her poem, "What is There Beyond Knowing?"[21] the title of which—a beautiful Eternal Question in its own right—invites us to reflect on the ways of knowing that exist beyond, or perhaps before, logic. Isaac, who our tradition teaches established the late afternoon prayer as he "went out to meditate in the field toward evening" (Gen. 24:63), offers us an example of how we might enter into this kind of knowing.

This is a knowing that is less dependent on precisely articulated meanings and logical postulates, which, as King describes, can frequently be a knowledge that rests on a false consciousness. Rather, Isaac's knowing is more concerned with the knowledge that can appear when we become quiet, when we open our-selves to the deeper forms of perception available to us through our bodies, our emotions, and the rest of our lives that include but transcend our intellect. This might be, as Oliver suggests in her poem "Praying,"[22] a different kind of silence in which we can hear other voices. Isaac's different way of knowing invites that other voice, one which the Hasidic masters identify as the voice of the Divine working through him to offer blessing.

### Questions for Reflection and Conversation

- How do you understand the distinction the Beit Yaakov makes be-tween Isaac and Moses and their ways of knowing? Do you find one or the other resonates with you more? Why or why not?

- What do you think the Maggid of Kozhnitz means by saying that Isaac acted as if he knew that the son standing before him was, in fact, Jacob? Have you ever had an experience where you acted as if you knew something (even if you did not know it in formed thoughts or clear ideas)? What, if anything, did you notice about the experi-ence in the moment? What, if anything, do you notice about it now?

### Ideas for Practice

- In your meditation practice this week, try bringing your attention to a challenging event or story in your life involving another person. Allow yourself to notice what feelings or sensations are triggered as you go toward the story in your mind. Then investigate without judg-

[21] Mary Oliver, "What is there Beyond Knowing." *New and Selected Poems.* Beacon Press, 1993.

[22] Mary Oliver, "Praying." *Thirst.* Beacon Press, 2007.

ment: Are there assumptions or biases that might be affecting the way you are telling the story to yourself, and which, by consequence, are arousing these sensations? Notice how it feels to recognize your assumptions. Try out what it feels like to let go of them.

- In prayer this week, consider focusing on the fourth blessing of the weekday *Amidah:*

אַתָּה חוֹנֵן לְאָדָם דַּעַת וּמְלַמֵּד לֶאֱנוֹשׁ בִּינָה:
חָנֵּנוּ מֵאִתְּךָ דֵּעָה בִּינָה וְהַשְׂכֵּל:
בָּרוּךְ אַתָּה יְהֹוָה חוֹנֵן הַדָּעַת:

You grace humans with awareness and teach humankind understanding. Grant us knowledge, understanding and intellect from You. Blessed are You, YHVH, Grantor of perception.

Take time before reciting this blessing to quiet your mind, perhaps through meditation. As you say the words, allow yourself to focus not on their specific meaning, but rather see what comes up for you as you say them. What kind of awareness or knowledge comes to you? How might our learning this week help you expand or deepen your relationship with this prayer?

# Vayetzei:
## How Do We Experience
## The Divine in Our Lives?

One of the deep features of modern life—sometimes in tension with contemporary Jewish spirituality—is the reality of historical consciousness. For generations, American Jews have attended institutions of higher education at rates that far exceed the national average. American Jewry has thus been shaped significantly by the implicit and explicit values of the academy. Most fundamental is the belief that science, and not miracles or forces that cannot be empirically verified, explains how the world works. Historical events, even when disputed as to their origins or meaning, are assessable and accessible through the scientific method; miracles outside of nature, not so much.

Faced with the choice between faith and science, most modern Jews have chosen the latter. Many of those who have tried to maintain a life of faith have found it necessary to avow a kind of willful suspension of disbelief, or a countercultural proclamation like that written by one of the great 20th-century philosophers of Judaism, Rabbi Joseph Soloveitchik: "I am a man of faith for whom to be means to believe, and who substituted *credo* for *cogito* in the time-honored Cartesian maxim."[23] The reasoning here: God is something other than us; the modern world has rejected the Divine; we people of faith nevertheless proclaim our abiding belief. No wonder Soloveitchik was lonely.

Hasidism, and its contemporary expressions in Neo-Hasidism, offers a different way of understanding, approaching, and experiencing life in the Divine image. *M'lo khol ha-aretz k'vodo,* The whole world is filled with the Divine presence (Isaiah 6:3), or *Leit atar panui minei*—there is nothing separate from the Divine, as the Zohar puts it in Aramaic (*Tikkunei Zohar,* Tikkun 57, 91b)—is the starting point for Hasidic theology. There is no empirical question to be investigated; there is no historical event to be challenged. The question is less whether or how God is present in the world, and instead how to cultivate a consciousness that can hold a paradox: Divinity suffuses our lives and, in the same breath, we are somehow, miraculously, separate and unique creatures living in time and space—and so, in history.

The opening scene of Parashat Vayetzei—the story of Jacob's ladder—is an iconic image in neo-Hasidic Torah. In Jewish meditation, the image of the ladder rooted in the ground with its head reaching up toward heaven is a mental model for the posture we aim to embody. Beyond this, both the story and its interpreta-

---

[23] Joseph B. Soloveitchik, "The Lonely Man of Faith." *Tradition* 7.2 (1965), 7.

tion mark a particularly fertile field for exploring how our ancestors have related to the Divine in their lives and how we might approach the question today.

## God Was in This Place:
## Sensing the Divine in Time, Place, and History

A prominent theme in Rabbinic commentaries on Jacob's ladder is interpreting the dream as a metaphor for Jewish history. Bereshit Rabbah (69:7) offers this reading:

> The Holy Blessed One showed Jacob the Holy Temple built [by Solomon], destroyed [by the Babylonians], and rebuilt [by the generation of Ezra and Nehemia].

Or Midrash Tanhuma (Vayetzei 2:1):

> Rabbi Shmuel bar Nachman said, "This teaches that the Holy Blessed One showed Jacob our ancestor the angel of Babylonia ascending for 70 steps and then descending; that of Medea going up fifty-two steps and then going down; that of Greece going up for 100 and then descending; finally that of Edom [Rome] going up and no one knows for how long.

These and other Rabbinic interpretations that read this scene as historical draw their power from the notion that the place that Jacob rests—"none other than the abode of God, the gateway to heaven," in Jacob's words (Gen. 28:17)—is *Har Habayit,* the Temple Mount in Jerusalem. "This is Mount Moriah, where Abraham prayed, and it is the field in which Isaac meditated" (Rashi, v. 17). This is the holiest site in the world, and thus it both seemingly drew Jacob there and then demanded of him that he pay attention. Jacob only becomes aware of that holiness after his dream. "If I had known, I would not have slept in such a holy place" (Rashi, v. 16). The Divine presence in that place, recognized and reinforced in the lives of the Patriarchs and in Jacob's (interpreted) dream, gains greater weight for being experienced in history.

This historical understanding is likely familiar to us. Even if we don't necessarily buy the Bible's version of events as historical truth, the idea that certain places are endowed with holiness, that God is more available in those places than in others, has deep roots for many people—whether those places are the Western Wall, the grave of a loved one, or a synagogue we have attended. These places, and the holiness bound in them, are accessible and known directly, through experience, and so "scientifically" historical. On the other hand, the idea that the Divine could be available to us anywhere at any time, much less that the Divine is even *within* us, is often felt to be a foreign concept.

## We Are the Temple

Yet the seeds of other, non-historical conceptions are evinced by the very same Sages who produced these historical, event-focused interpretations. For instance, while discussing the *halakha* in the case of one who cannot physically dismount from his donkey to recite the Amidah at its prescribed time, the Mishnah (Brachot 4:5) teaches:

> If he is riding on a donkey, he gets down [and prays.] If he is unable to get down, he should turn his face [toward Jerusalem], and if he cannot turn his face, he should direct his heart to the Holy of Holies.

That is—and this should be obvious, yet it bears repeating—one need not be physically present in the Temple in Jerusalem, nor even physically able to stop and face in its direction, for one's prayers to reach the Creator. Ultimately the key to heaven's gate is not to be found on Mount Moriah, but in the human heart.

Other interpretations of the story of Jacob's ladder develop this idea even further. Here, for instance, is the classic Hasidic commentary of Rabbi Levi Yitzchak of Berditchev (1740-1809) in his *Kedushat Levi:*

### קדושת לוי, ויצא 12

ויחלום והנה סולם כו' (בראשית כח, יב). דהאדם בתחילת עבודתו מתלהב לבו בקרבו בחושבו שעל ידי מתנהגים כל העולמות העליונים ובזה לבו הולך וחזק בעבודתו, ואחר כך כשכבר חזק בעבודתו אז אין חושב כלל רק להשם יתברך ושם יתברך יתענג בו שהוא יהא מרכבה לשכינה. זהו ויחלום, לשון חוזק כמו ותחלימני ותחייני (ישעיה לח, טז) דהיינו שיתחזק עבודת ה' בלבו שהוא חזק בעבודתו, דהיינו בעת התחלתו בעבודתו שצריך חיזוק החיזוק הוא על ידי זה. והנה סולם מוצב ארצה, שהוא מוצב ארצה אדם בעולם הזה. וראשו מגיע השמימה, בעבודתו מגיע למעלה. והנה מלאכי אלהים עולים ויורדים בו, שמלאכי מעלה מתעלים על ידי זהו בו, על ידי האדם. ולהיפך חס ושלום גורם ירידה כמאמר חכמינו ז"ל משחרב בית המקדש נתמעטה פמליא של מעלה כביכול. אמנם אחר כך שכבר חזק בעבודתו אז חושב והנה ה' נצב עליו, הוא על ידי עבודתו שיהא מרכבה לשכינה והבן:

Kedushat Levi, Vayetzei 12

When a person sets out in spiritual practice, devoted to serving God, their heart is on fire with the thought that, by means of their personal action, they will affect the cosmos. Their heart grows stronger, deepening in their spiritual practice. Then, when they have become grounded in their practice, they no longer think of anything but the Holy One, and Holiness then rejoices in them, for they have become a chariot for the Divine Presence.

This is the meaning of, "And he dreamed (*vayachalom*)"—it is the language of strengthening, as in the verse, "You have restored me to health (*v'tachalimeini*) and strengthened me" (Isaiah 38:16). That is, the person's spiritual practice has been strengthened in their heart, such that they now have a strong spiritual foundation. Thus, when one is just beginning, when they need encouragement, that encouragement comes by this means. "Behold, there was a ladder planted in the ground"— the person is planted in the real life of this world; "and its top reached the heavens"—through their spiritual practice they arrive at transcendence. "And angels of God ascended and descended on it (*bo*)"—the heavenly angels ascend through the very means of the individual's spiritual practice [i.e., "through him (*bo*)"] ...

Indeed, after a person becomes grounded in their spiritual practice, they become able to sense that "Hashem stands atop" not "*it*" but "*them*—the *individual*"—by means of their spiritual practice and their having become a chariot for the divine presence.

In the Kedushat Levi's telling, Jacob's experience is not about foreshadowing historical events. Rather, it is the narrative of a person developing their spiritual practice. Like the ladder, we acknowledge and embrace that, yes, we are products of this physical world—with bodies, sensations, emotions, thoughts. And in the same breath, the head of our ladder reaches to the heavens and we are able to transcend physical, temporal, linguistic dimensions and limitations.

That much is very good and helpful. But what is most radical and beautiful in the Kedushat Levi's reading is the invitation to imagine that, through our spiritual practice, through our simultaneous and paradoxical embrace of both the world as we find it and the deeper reality concealed within it, we become vessels for the *Shekhina*—we become the means by which the Divine is manifest in the world. Through our spiritual practice we "ascend" beyond the limitations of the physical world to touch the Divine (like the angels ascending); we then "descend," bringing awareness of the Holy One back with us, to fill the world (again, like the angels). When we recognize this, we can embrace the reality that God is working through us, that every moment is filled with divinity, that every place is a gateway to heaven—that in fact *we* are that gateway.

## The Courage to Be Open to the Divine

If you're reading this book, perhaps this kind of orientation is not as radical as I'm making it out to be. Yet I think it's important to emphasize how striking this approach is, particularly for a population that has uncritically digested Western assumptions about empiricism and historicism. Here, perhaps, a story from another tradition may prove useful.

In 1774, after the end of the French and Indian War (when R. Levi Yitzhak was 34 years old), the Virginia colonists wanted to thank the Native Americans who had fought with them against the French. As a gesture of gratitude, they offered to send a number of Native American men to the College of William and Mary. The tribal elders gathered and sent back this letter:

> We know that you highly esteem the kind of learning taught in those Colleges, and that the Maintenance of our young Men, while with you, would be very expensive to you. We are convinced that you mean to do us Good by your Proposal; and we thank you heartily. But you, who are wise must know that different nations have different conceptions of things and you will therefore not take it amiss, if our ideas of this kind of Education happen not to be the same as yours. We have had some Experience of it. Several of our young People were formerly brought up at the Colleges of the Northern Provinces: they were instructed in all your Sciences; but, when they came back to us, they were bad Runners, ignorant of every means of living in the woods...neither fit for Hunters, Warriors, nor Counsellors, they were totally good for nothing. We are, however, not the less oblig'd by your kind offer, tho' we decline accepting it; and, to show our grateful Sense of it, if the Gentlemen of Virginia will send us a Dozen of their Sons, we will take Care of their Education, instruct them in all we know, and make Men of them.[24]

---

[24] "Letter from the elders of the Six Nations to representatives of Maryland and Virginia, 1774." Palmer, Parker J. and Arthur Zajonc. *The Heart of Higher Education*. San

Perhaps there is something here for us to consider, too. Perhaps the ways many of us have been brought up to see precisely the *absence* of the Divine in the world need to be unlearned a bit (or more). Perhaps we need to cultivate ways of seeing the *presence* of the Creator so that we may live in right relationship with creation and its source. It is in our cultural DNA, in our ancestor Jacob, a young person setting out and spending his first night away from home, alone, and discovering that, indeed, any time and any place can be a moment of experiencing the Divine in our lives—if we can open our hearts to the possibility. We, too, can become chariots for the *Shekhina*, and, in turn, the universe.

## Questions for Reflection and Conversation

- Are there places you consider particularly holy? If so, why? When and how did they become so? If not, is there a reason?

- How do you understand the kind of grounding in spiritual practice the Kedushat Levi describes? What are some ways you try to cultivate it, if at all?

- In your own words, how do you understand the story of Jacob's ladder? What is happening to Jacob? Is it an experience you wish to cultivate or deepen in your life? Why or why not?

## Ideas for Practice

- In meditation practice this week, bring to mind the image of yourself as a *Merkavah leShekhina*, a chariot for the Divine presence. Notice what arises for you as you center your attention on it. How does it feel? Are you drawn to it, repelled by it, or something else? Investigate what might be leading you to the sensations you're experiencing.

- Try to find some regular times this week when you can physically embody Jacob's ladder—maybe when you're sitting at your desk or having your morning coffee or tea. Take a moment to feel your body firmly planted in the ground, your feet and sit bones supported by the floor or chair. Feel your back becoming the ladder with your head reaching up to heaven. Note the sensation. How does it feel to sit this way? What do you feel opening or closing in your body, in your heart?

Francisco: Jossey-Bass, 2010, 19.

# Vayishlach:
# How Do We Forgive Ourselves?

There are moments in my own life, from years or even decades ago, that I'm not especially proud of. They come up in my consciousness from time to time—while I'm washing the dishes or walking the dog. They're not grievous sins in the grand scheme of things. One of them is a time from over a dozen years ago. I had a conversation with a board member of an organization I worked for and realized later that I had completely misidentified them and spoke as though they were someone else. Another is from decades ago when I said something small but hurtful to someone I cared about.

When these moments come up in my consciousness, I find that I let out a sigh, breathing out my regret and knowing that, while at this point probably no one else remembers these little things, they remain a burden—even if a very minor one—for me.

I share this reflection by way of introducing our Big Question for this week: How do we forgive ourselves?

Imagine you are Jacob coming home after 20 years. You haven't spoken to your parents since you deceived your blind father into granting you the blessing he was intending to give your twin brother. And now, with a large family and entourage in tow, you learn that that same brother, who had sworn he would kill you, is coming toward you with 400 men. We can imagine that, in addition to fear and trepidation, you might also experience feelings of self-judgment: How could I have done this to my father? my brother? myself? my wives and children?

Or, even if you tell yourself you did what you had to do, and even if you've gained a measure of peace about it, more likely than not there are still some nagging doubts. It's hard to forgive yourself when you haven't had an honest conversation with the people you wronged two decades ago.

## Who Does Jacob Wrestle With?

Against this backdrop we come to the climactic story of Jacob's spiritual life. Like most of Jacob's stories it takes place at night, a time when things aren't as clear. After he has taken the necessary precautions, the text offers us an appropriately ambiguous narrative (Gen. 32:25-26):

> Jacob was left alone. And a man wrestled [*vaya'avek*] with him until the break of dawn.

When he saw that he had not prevailed against him, he wrenched Jacob's hip at its socket, so that the socket of his hip was strained as he wrestled with him.

Translating this passage is notoriously difficult, particularly the word *vaya'avek*. While usually rendered as "wrestled," it is also, in noun form, a word for dust. Rashi, for instance, offers three different possibilities:

> Menachem (ben Seruk) explains: "a man covered himself with dust," taking the verb as connected in essence with *avak* "dust." It would mean that they were raising the dust with their feet through their movements. I, however, am of the opinion that it means "he fastened himself on", and that it is an Aramaic word… It denotes "intertwining", for such is the manner of two people who vigorously strive with one another—one clasps the other and twines himself round him with his arms. Our Rabbis of blessed memory explained that he was Esau's guardian angel. (Genesis Rabbah 77:3)

An additional midrash suggests that the angel was not that of Esau but was in fact named Israel—the very name that the angel gives Jacob after their encounter. Taken as a whole, the lack of clarity around not only the identity of the man but what precisely he and Jacob were doing contributes to the sense that there is something powerful yet subtle going on. In the darkness, alone, Jacob struggles with a force that is potent, almost overwhelming, seemingly both inside and out. It would thus appear to be not a battle fought in the open, but something internal, psychological, spiritual. It is a struggle within Jacob's soul. And I would suggest, supported by the texts we will study below, that Jacob's struggle is ultimately over doing *teshuva* for his past sins, and that it is grounded in the challenge of showing compassion to himself.

## Regret and Forgiving Ourselves

Rabbi Elimelech Weisblum of Lizhensk (1717-1787) offers a powerful reading of Jacob's encounter in his *Noam Elimelech*. His interpretation refracts the biblical story through the lens of *teshuva*, the conscious return of our mindful awareness to our best intentions. It builds on a passage from the Talmud:

Rav Amram taught in the name of Rav: "There are three sins from which no person is spared each day. They are: Having sinful thoughts, failing to be fully attentive during prayer, and *lashon hara*, malicious speech." But do you really think that a person cannot go through the day without uttering *lashon hara*? Rather, Rav was referring to uttering *avak lashon hara*—the "dust of", i.e., words with a bare trace of, malicious speech. Rav Yehuda taught that Rav said: "The majority of people sin to some extent regarding theft, a minority of people regarding sexual matters, and everyone regarding *lashon hara*." But do you really think that all people sin with regard to malicious speech? Rather, Rav was referring to *avak lashon hara*, "raising the dust" of malicious speech. (Bava Batra 164b)

These two statements of Rav focus on the fine gradation between *lashon hara*, malicious speech, and *avak lashon hara*, a hint of malicious speech. The former is generally understood to involve a direct statement about another person, while the latter involves a statement that could be interpreted negatively about another. It is not a direct comment, but an indirect statement that nonetheless could lead to reputational harm.

For the purposes of the Noam Elimelech, the idea of *avak lashon hara* provides an opening to explore Jacob's encounter, which, as we discussed above, hinges on the very same word, *avak*. In this interpretation, the emphasis on *avak* opens up a reading of the story in which Jacob's lonely wrestling was in fact an act of *hitbodedut*, deep personal spiritual reflection, on very fine aspects of his past, relationships, and character.

**נועם אלימלך, וישלח**

או יאמר "ויותר יעקב לבדו ויאבק כו'", דהנה הצדיק השלם העובד ה' באמת הוא מסתכל תמיד ברוממות אל וגדולתו יתברך, ומתבודד עצמו במחשבתו לעלות במחשבתו ממדריגה למדריגה עד רום המעלות, וגם רואה תמיד בשפלות עצמו, וזוכר חטאת נעוריו כמו שכתוב וחטאתי נגדי תמיד, ואפילו החטאים שאינם חטאים גמורים רק כמו אבק, כמו שאמרו חז"ל שלשה דברים אין אדם ניצול בכל יום אבק לשון הרע כו', הם לזכרון לפניו תמיד והם בעיניו כחמורות שבחמורות, ומתחרט עליהם ושב בתשובה שלימה מאהבתו ית', ותשובתו עולה עד הכסא הכבוד ונעשה הכל זכיות, כמו שאמרו חז"ל שזדונות נעשים לו כזכיות בעושה תשובה מאהבה.

וזהו "ויותר יעקב לבדו", ר"ל בעת שהיה יעקב אבינו ע"ה

בהתבודדות מחשבתו בבדידות גמור, אז "ויאבק איש עמו" ודרשו
חז"ל שהיו מעלים אבק עד כסא הכבוד, פירוש, "ויאבק איש" היינו
אבק החטאים שהם עם כל איש, כל זה היה "עמו" לנגד עיניו כנ"ל,
והיה מעלה האבק עד כסא הכבוד ע"ד שאמרו חז"ל גדולה תשובה
שמגעת עד כסא הכבוד, "עד עלות השחר" פירוש עד שהעלה הכל
לפני השכינה, כנסת ישראל הנקראת אילת השחר.

**Noam Elimelech, Vayishlach**

The completely righteous person who truly serves the Source
of Being always sets their sights upward, on the greatness of
the Holy One. They sequester themselves in their thoughts in
order to ascend from level to level unto the very heights, all the
while being mindful of their own individual lowliness. They
remember the sins of their youth, as it is written, "My sin is
always before me" (Psalms 51:5). This applies even to those sins
which are not truly sins but are rather like *avak,* fine dust. As
our Sages taught, "There are three sins from which no person
is spared each day [including]... *avak lashon hara,* words with a
bare trace of malicious speech." The righteous person constantly
remembers these seemingly minor transgressions, and they are
in her eyes like the most severe of sins. She regrets them and returns from them completely out of love, and her returning rises
up to the Divine throne and transmutes all her transgressions
into merits, as our Sages taught, "When one does *teshuva* from
love, their willful sins are as though transformed into merits."

This is the meaning of "And Jacob was alone." It means to
say that at that moment Jacob practiced the most profound type
of *hitbodedut,* deep self-reflection. And then, "a man wrestled
with him—*vaye'avek ish imo,*" as our Sages interpreted, "they
[wrestled] raising dust/*avak* upwards to the Divine throne."
That is, the dust of sin that every person has—all of this was
"*imo*/with him", with Jacob, and he raised it up to the Divine
throne, illustrating the teaching of the Sages, "So great is *teshuva* that it reaches the Divine throne." "Until the dawn began
to come up"—meaning, until Jacob had raised up everything
before the Divine Presence (*Shekhina*), the Congregation of
Israel, which is called *Ayelet Hashachar,* the doe of the morning.

Lofty language notwithstanding, the Noam Elimelech transforms Jacob's
encounter with the angel into a struggle all of us engage in all the time simply

by virtue of being human. We regret things and they haunt us: Words we spoke or failed to speak, gestures we made or failed to make, actions we took or failed to take. It isn't only the actions we think of as obvious mistakes, but the smaller, micro actions that we may only regret on further inspection—even ones that, when we did them years ago we thought were the right thing to do but now, with hindsight, we can see we inflicted pain. This, it would seem, was what was keeping Jacob up that night.

Like Jacob, we don't always have the chance to seek forgiveness from the people we may have wronged. Just as often, even that forgiveness isn't really enough for us to liberate ourselves from our anxiety. That brings us to the crux of the issue, namely that genuine *teshuva* rests on our ability to show compassion and forgiveness to ourselves. While the person we wronged may grant us forgiveness, ultimately that forgiveness doesn't really relieve us until we accept it—until we have self-compassion. That is what enables us not to be trapped by our past actions, to continue to move through life, gain wisdom, and realize that we are, in fact, a *biryah hadasha,* a new being—not precisely the same person we were when we did wrong in the past.

*Hitbodedut,* self-reflection and introspection, is one important spiritual path toward this kind of personal healing. It involves dedicating serious time to being alone, preferably in nature, but in any case, in a manner where we feel no one will hear or interrupt us. We allow our attention to focus on whatever that moment from the past is that is bothering us. We allow ourselves to stand on the balcony and look at our past action, to feel the hurt we may have caused, the shame we might experience, and the many other feelings present in the moment. The distance of the "balcony" provides a sense of safety, where it is possible to allow otherwise difficult feelings to be present without overwhelming us, and without running away. In this space we are free to say, "I regret that past action. I am grateful for the forgiveness I've received, and I am committed to seeking it if I have not yet. I am able now to forgive myself for it. I am a new being, a wiser person, and I will take what I have learned from my experience with me into the rest of my life, now hopefully better able not to make the same mistake again." In addition to honest conversation with the person we have wronged, this conversation with ourselves is indispensable for genuine *teshuva.*

## Wrestling and Letting Go

In her poem "Wrestling," a commentary on Jacob's encounter with the angel, contemporary poet Joy Ladin sees Jacob engaged in a struggle rooted years earlier, when he took advantage of his blind father.

The angel gropes,
searching out the sinew of light,
the blessing you stole in disguise
from a father who could only love
what he couldn't recognize.

Like classical commentators, Ladin suggests multiple possibilities about the identity of Jacob's mysterious opponent. The angel, she writes,

claims to be your father's God;
your father himself, abashed and blind;
the fear that took his eyes.
You wish you could let him go. Lose
to keep him alive. Dissolving
in the breaking light,
he begs you to let him fly[25]

In Ladin's poem, Jacob struggles to let go—of his father, of the abuse Jacob inflicted on him, and presumably of all the other pain and anxiety that came in its wake: through words spoken and unspoken, false presences and long absences. Like the Noam Elimelech, she invites us to see ourselves in our ancestor Jacob, no more and no less than a person with a body, a soul, a conscience, and many stories, struggling to be whole. For both Ladin and the Noam Elimelech, this is a story of Jacob's *hitbodedut*, his deep soul-work, to forgive himself for his past deeds as he returns, literally and figuratively, to his family and his home.

### Questions for Reflection and Conversation

- Can you bring to mind a small moment in your life—not one of the "big" stories, but a seemingly "little" regret—that comes up for you every now and then? Why do you think this episode recurs for you? Is there something unresolved, something that prevents you from showing yourself compassion over it? Why might that be? What do you imagine, now, you might bring to that story, perhaps to change it, or change you?

---

[25] Joy Ladin, "Wrestling." *The Future is Trying to Tell Us Something: New & Selected Poems.* The Sheep Meadow Press, 2017.

- What do you think the Noam Elimelech means when he writes that every person has *avak,* the dust of sin? What, if anything, do you consider *avak* in your own life right now, and how, if at all, are you trying to be mindful of it?

- What do you think Ladin means when she writes that the angel "claims to be your father's God/your father himself, abashed and blind?" How might the meaning of the poem change, depending on who the angel is?

## Ideas for Practice

- Try journaling this week. Reflect on a moment about which you have had a difficult time showing yourself compassion. If it's helpful, perhaps write your reflection as a letter to someone, but don't share it with them—this will allow you to be as open and honest as you can be. Try to really address the question of why you've had difficulty showing yourself compassion. After you've written your reflection, note how you feel.

- Bring to mind the moment you thought about in the first question above. Really enter into that event: feel the feelings you felt then, hear the thoughts you thought then—and don't run away. Don't let any outer movement keep you from staying connected to that moment. Allow yourself to fully experience the feelings.

- Bring your hand to your heart. Holding yourself in this manner, address yourself in the past with the loving words of the great mindfulness teacher Sylvia Boorstein: "Sweetheart, you're in pain/afraid/sad" or whatever the feeling is from the past, and how you now understand what led to that untoward interaction. With a hand on your heart, allow your new understanding of the interaction come to mind. Feel whatever you feel. Notice how your sense of the other person may change. Offer yourself some compassion: "I was doing the best I could in that moment. It was not what I wish I would have done, but that's how I behaved. I realize now it was not helpful, it was not kind. It is painful to recognize that—but I do, fully." This may free you to make amends, or to commit to acting differently now and into the future.

# Vayeshev:
# What Will Your Story Be?

My father called. "I have some news to share. I had a heart attack."

It was, thank God, a minor event and detected in time. But, he explained, he needed surgery to put a stent in his artery.

Natalie and I, and our then-infant son, lived in New York. My parents lived in Ann Arbor, Michigan. Being the Depression-era child of eastern European Jewish immigrants that he was, my Dad said, "I really don't want you to come home. It's not a big deal."

I struggled with that and wound up calling a mentor, David Lowenfeld, who gave me advice that stays with me to this day.

"There's only one question to ask: What do you want the story to be in twenty years?"

Now, I'll confess: I still didn't go home. My Dad had made his wishes clear and honoring them was important to me, and to him. And while I ultimately came to regret that decision, the lesson I learned in the story has stuck with me. I've shared the question with many students and my own children in the years since: How do you want the story to be told in the future?

Of course, we don't ultimately have control over that. But through spiritual practice, and particularly through viewing our lives as part of an eternal Torah that we bequeath to future generations, we can develop a consciousness, an orientation to living, that can inspire us, lend meaning to our actions, and nourish us with spiritual strength in difficult moments.

## Who writes our stories?

This question forms the basis of a wonderful midrash that takes as its starting point a moment in Parashat Vayeshev. You will recall that, after his brothers have determined to murder Joseph, Reuben, the eldest brother, talks them out of it. "But when Reuben heard it, he tried to save him [Joseph] from them. He said, 'Let us not take his life'" (Gen. 37:21). Instead, the Torah tells us, he convinces his brothers to throw Joseph into a pit, intending to rescue him eventually and return him to Jacob. Of course, things didn't work out that way, as Judah convinces the brothers to sell Joseph before Reuben is able to take him home.

Picking up on this this well-intentioned but poorly executed rescue by Reuben, the midrash teaches the following:

Rabbi Yitzchak the son of Maryon said: This passage comes to teach us that if a person is going to do a *mitzvah*, they should do it with their whole heart. For if Reuben had known that the Holy Blessed One would [ultimately] write about him [in the Torah], "And Reuben heard it, and delivered him out of their hand" (Gen. 37:21), he would have borne Joseph to his father on his shoulders!

The midrash goes on to cite two other instances when characters did things that were good but, seemingly, not quite as good as they might have been had they put their whole hearts into it.

If Aaron had known that the Holy Blessed One would write about him [only that, "And also, look, he is coming to meet you" (Exodus 4:14), he would have met Moses with tambourines and dances! And if Boaz had known that the Holy Blessed One would write about him [only that], "He gave her some parched corn, and Ruth ate and was satisfied, and left some over" (Ruth 2:14), he would have fed her with fattened calves!

As stated at the outset, the moral of the midrash is: If you're going to do something, do it with a full heart. Why? Because you don't want someone generations from now to read your story and say, "Wow, that was really nice—if only they had done a better job."

Yet the next voice in the midrash realizes a problem with this line of thinking: That's all well and good when God or Moses or someone with an eternal perspective is writing down your story. But who's writing down our stories nowadays?

Rabbi Kohen and Rabbi Joshua of Sikhnin in the name of Rabbi Levi: Previously [i.e., in biblical times], when a person performed a *mitzvah*, a prophet would write about it. But now, when a person performs a *mitzvah* who writes about it? Elijah writes it and the Messiah and the Holy Blessed One seal it with their hands. This is reflected in Scripture: "Then they that held the Divine in awe spoke one with another; and the Holy One hearkened, and heard, and a book of remembrance was written before God, for them that held the Divine in awe, and that thought upon God's name." (Malachi 3:16)

It's a deeply moving thought: Our stories *are* being recorded—not by anyone we can see, but by none other than the Creator of the universe.

## Living Our Life Story Knowing It Will Be Read

In his Sefat Emet, Rabbi Yehuda Leib Alter of Ger (1847-1905) elaborates on this midrash in one of his comments on the parasha from 1874:

**שפת אמת וישב ד:ו**

אילו הי' ראובן יודע כו'. פי' שהאבות כל מעשיהם הי' תורה. לאשר בכל פעולתם השתתפו כח תולדותיהם ושיזכו זרעם אחריהם. וז"ש יצוה בניו כו'. פי' שיחבר מעשיו לתולדותיו כנ"ל. לכן נקראו אבות כדאיתא אין אבות אלא שלשה. ולכן זכו שמעשיהם כתובים בתורה. ובני ישראל הוגים ומבינים ומיישרין דרכם ע"י לימוד מעשיהם בתורה כנ"ל. ואם הי' ראובן יודע שמעשיו יהיו לימוד לדורות. הי' זה סיוע לחזק עצמו. ועל כתפיו הי' מוליכו כו'. לכן צריך כל אדם ליישב עצמו איך כל מעשיו נוגעי' לזרעו אחריו לדורות:

**Sefat Emet Vayeshev 4:6**

"If Reuben had known…" I interpret this to mean that the actions of our Patriarchs and Matriarchs were Torah. That is, they were aware that the potential of their descendants was in all their actions, that their descendants would gain merit through their own actions taken in light of the lives of their ancestors. This is what Scripture means when God says of Abraham "he will instruct his children and his posterity to keep the way of YHVH by doing what is just and right" (Gen. 18:19): he connected his deeds to those of his descendants. That is why the Patriarchs are called the "Avot," as it is taught (Brachot 16b), "One may only call three [i.e., Abraham, Isaac, and Jacob] 'Avot' [but not their descendants; i.e., their deeds became Torah, but the potential of their deeds extends to their descendants]." Therefore, their actions merited to be written down in the Torah. The children of Israel reflect on these deeds, and understand them, and then strive to live in upstanding fashion by means of studying their ancestors' actions in the Torah. "If Reuben had known that his actions would be studied for generations"—had he had such an awareness, it would have strengthened him, and—"he would have borne Joseph to his father on his own shoulders." Therefore, each person must strive to think how all their actions extend to their descendants in all future generations.

The *Sefat Emet* introduces a powerful mystical dimension into the midrashic teaching. The issue isn't simply one of having a scribe around to record the events of our lives. There are at least two additional deeper dimensions. First is the notion that the lives of our ancestors are Torah to us: the text we study, the language we share, the way we understand ourselves in the world. Second is that, though we are not the subjects of the written Torah, nevertheless we are both implicated in that Torah and the lives that informed it *and* we are, ourselves, composing a kind of Torah for all of our future descendants.

For the *Sefat Emet*, the lesson is not only that Reuben should have been aware that the eyes of history were on him. It is also that had he lived with such a consciousness, that itself would have become a source of strength. He would have seen and heard all those future souls—us—holding him up at a moment that required courageous action. Because he didn't have such a consciousness, he wound up doing only half the job—he saved Joseph, but he didn't bring him home.

## Living Torah

This kind of consciousness can affect many parts of our spiritual practice, but I'd like in particular to focus on *Talmud Torah:* Torah study itself. Encountering both the written Torah and the universe of interpretation surrounding it is not merely an academic exercise. When done with preparation, a proper dose of humility and self-confidence, and in relationship with both a teacher and a *havruta, Talmud Torah* becomes a conversation extending across generations and continents. It is stepping into a world of language and story and ideas and deeds that touch on virtually every aspect of life and invite us to make our lives a literal embodiment of our spiritual consciousness.

The Sefat Emet teaches that, not only do we learn through that form of study; we seek to take what we learn and embody it in our lives—such that our own lives become stories, Torah, that will be told and studied and learned generations from now. We don't strive to live lives of meaning only because it's the right thing to do or because we seek to become vessels for the Divine presence in the world, though those are noble goals. Beyond them, we develop this kind of consciousness because we are aware that the stories of our lives are themselves Torah—Torah that was known at the time of Sinai, Torah that will be studied by our descendants in the future. In that knowledge we draw enormous strength, because we are not alone—we never have been, and we never will be.

## Questions for Reflection and Discussion:

- What do you think the Sefat Emet means when he says that the potential of the Patriarchs and Matriarchs was in their actions? How would you paraphrase that idea for yourself? How do you understand it particularly given that we may well not be biological descendants of these biblical figures? Once you articulate your paraphrase, reflect on how it makes you feel: Is it uplifting? Overwhelming? Something else?

- Have you ever encountered a moment when you were aware that your actions or behavior, the endeavor in which you are engaged, would be recounted in the future? If so, how did that affect you in the moment? How have you reflected on it since? If not, how do you imagine it might feel?

- Do you have a sense that your actions now are on behalf of people in the future? How, if at all, does that affect the way you live your life? How does it affect the choices you make in what you buy, how you use material things, the way you deploy your wealth? How does it make you feel to be implicated in the lives of people you do not, and will never, know?

### Ideas for Practice

- Before engaging in Torah study, pause to calm and focus your mind. Close your eyes. Meditate for several minutes. Allow yourself to be fully present to the experience. Whether you are studying alone or with a *havruta,* offer an intention for your study—perhaps that your *limmud Torah* will open you to making the Divine presence more manifest in the world, or that through your study you will live more with a whole heart, with fuller consciousness.

- Reserve time at the end of your study for several minutes of quiet meditation. Make an intention to take on one action as a result of your study. When you undertake the action, acknowledge fully that you are fulfilling your intention. Note how it feels to more fully inhabit your action and to feel it linked with your study.

# Miketz: How Do We Love?

The central drama of the Joseph saga springs from something we learn early on as readers of the story:

> Now Israel loved Joseph best of all his sons (Gen. 37:3).

In Jacob's case, his love for Joseph seems intimately linked to his love for Joseph's mother, Rachel: "And Jacob loved Rachel" (Gen. 29:17)—whereas, by contrast, he did not love Leah, Bilhah, or Zilpah as much. Jacob seemingly transfers his greater love for Rachel into greater love for Joseph—and for Benjamin, his younger brother. This relationship is later described by Judah so intimately: as "His [Jacob's] life is bound up with his [Benjamin's]" (Gen. 44:30).

One does not need a doctorate in family systems to know that such a situation is not likely to end well. Of course, the story of Joseph and his brothers, and the larger family into which they are born, is one of our most enduring studies in the meanings and complications of love—romantic, filial, fraternal, and in nascent form, civic or societal. And because of that, the Joseph story invites us to reflect on the question: How do we love?

## What Kind Of Love?

Western philosophy classically differentiates between *eros, philia,* and *agape* as three types of love. *Eros* has come to be understood as love that has a reason behind it—most often physical or sexual attraction, or perhaps more broadly the pleasure brought to us through the object of this kind of love. *Philia* refers to the love of friends, which likewise have a kind of reason supporting them, as we get something out of the relationship in exchange for investing in it. *Agape,* by contrast, came to be understood as love independent of any reason, like the love that a parent has for a child or that the Holy One has for human beings.

In our own tradition, *Pirkei Avot* (5:14) offers us a teaching that seems to follow this delineation:

> All love that depends on a thing, [when the] thing ceases, [the] love ceases; and [all love] that does not depend on a thing, will never cease.

Commenting on this passage, Maimonides writes:

> We explain this teaching thus: You know that if the physi-
> cal causes cease or are removed, then of necessity that which
> they cause will be removed with the removal of its cause. And
> because of this, when the cause of the love is a divine mat-
> ter — and this is the nature of true scientific inquiry — it is
> impossible for that love to be removed ever, as its cause exists
> eternally.[26]

Likely the Mishnah and Maimonides's commentary strike us as familiar
from our experience. We know intuitively that there are things we "love"
but only passingly, and other things and people we love in an ongoing and
sustained way. Our society largely truncates our language of love into romantic and sexual categories—the easier to commodify and sell them. We
casually talk about loving items of clothing, foods, and other material objects.
Sometimes even people "fall" into and out of our love. Once we experience
the pleasure of these objects of our affection, however, we often discard them.
"There is no aspect of sexuality that is not studied, talked about, or demon-
strated," observes the late scholar and activist bell hooks. "How-to classes
exist for every dimension of sexuality, even masturbation. Yet schools for love
do not exist."[27] How do we learn a love that is sustained, that will not cease?
As our Mishnah concludes:

> What is an example of love that depends on a something? Such
> was the love of Amnon for Tamar. And what is an example of
> love that does not depend on anything? Such was the love of
> David and Jonathan.

Amnon, who obsesses over his half-sister Tamar, confuses his sexual and
power drives for love. Yet, the moment he has had his way with her, the Book
of Samuel tells us he "felt a very great loathing for her; indeed, his loathing
for her was greater than the passion he had felt for her. And Amnon said to
her, 'Get out!'" (II Sam. 13:15). There is no more horrible example in literature
of confusing lust for love, nor a more vivid exemplar of its consequences.

---

[26] Maimonides, Commentary on the Mishnah, *Pirkei Avot* 5:16:1.
[27] bell hooks, *All About Love*. William Morrow, 2001, xxviii.

## True Love

With this example in mind, we should probably ask the question: Is a love dependent on something or someone else really love at all? In classical Buddhist teachings the answer is no. Only love that is grounded in and develops liberation is properly categorized as love. To borrow from the Dread Pirate Roberts in *The Princess Bride*, "Anyone who tells you otherwise is selling something"—perhaps literally.

The same is true in neo-Hasidic Torah. Consider the following teaching from Rabbi Dov Baer, the Maggid of Mezeritch (d. 1774) on Parashat Miketz (from *Torat HaMaggid*):

**תורת המגיד, מקץ**

"ואת הארץ תסחרו". הנה ב' אהבות יש. א' שהאב אוהב מעשה בנו החכם ומתפאר במעשה החכמה שעושה, או בדבר חכמה שמדבר. והב' שאוהב אותו בעצם וכל מה שמדבר לפניו הכל הגון לפניו בשביל אהבתו אותו.

והנה באהבת השי"ת אלינו אהבה א' הנ"ל כשהצדיק עושה מעש"ט ומצוות, הכל בחכמה נפלאה, ומעלה ניצוצות קדושות מה שבדומם צומח חי מדבר, ואז השי"ת אוהב מעשיו מאוד. ובזה מקשר חיצוניות העולמות להשי"ת. שהשי"ת שורה בכל מעשיו, וזה יתקן לגמרי אי"ה בביאת משיח ב"ב, כמ"ש "ומלאה הארץ דעה את מ' וגו'". וגם בהמות וחיות כולם יהיו יודעים מהשי"ת "לא ידעו וכו'".

ואהבת הב' ר"ל הוא כשהצדיק עצמו מקשר להשי"ת, והשי"ת אוהבו מאוד אותו בעצמו, ואין עושה מעשה בחכמה כמו הראשון. רק הולך בתמימות גדולה ומקושר להשי"ת. וכן השי"ת אוהבו, וזו עליות פנימיות העולמות שהצדיק הוא פנימיות העולמות.

וזה מ"ש "ואת הארץ", דהיינו האותיות מה שהם בארציות, דהכל נבראו באותיות, דהיינו הדיבור של הקב"ה. והם ניצוצות הקדושה "תסחרו", לשון עליה דהוא לשון סיבוב וגלגל.

### Torat HaMagid, Miketz

"You may trade in the land" (Gen. 42:34). We can talk about two types of love. The first is like that of a parent who loves the actions of their clever child and basks in the glory of the intelligent things they do or say. The second, however, is that of a parent who loves the essence of the child—and no matter what the child says before them, it is all well-received, because of their love for the child.

The same applies when we consider God's love for us. There is the first type which applies to the *tzaddik* who does good deeds and performs the commandments, doing so with marvelous insight. In this manner they raise up the holy sparks found in the material world, and for this God loves their actions greatly. Through this, the *tzaddik* connects the material world to the Divine so that Divinity dwells throughout Creation, ultimately bringing about the Messianic era, as it is written, "The earth shall be filled with awareness of God" (Is. 11:9)—even the animals and wild creatures will know of the Divine.

The second type of love is exemplified by the *tzaddik* who connects to the Holy One, who then loves the *tzaddik* greatly, in their essence. This *tzaddik* does not do the kinds of marvelous acts of the first type of *tzaddik*, but simply inhabits the world with great integrity, with connection to the Divine. For this reason, God loves them. This type of *tzaddik* raises up the inner, spiritual world [in contrast to the first type, who raises up the external, material world].

This is the meaning of ואת הארץ תסחרו—the letters through which the world was created, signified by א to ת, are embedded in the material world (ארציות). They are Divine speech [which brought about Creation], and they are the holy sparks that fill the world. Our task is תסחרו, to (re)turn them, and through doing so to raise them up.

What is particularly striking about this teaching in the context of our discussion of love is that, while the Maggid continues to distinguish two types of love, there is a fundamental difference between his approach and that of Greek philosophy or even the Mishnah: In either case, the Divine force of love in the universe which lives in and through us is taken as a given. It does not need to be generated by us, and it flows freely to us, gratis. The first type of *tzaddik* accesses and extends that love through action in the world. Recognizing that everything can be connected back to Divinity, this *tzaddik* does so through "good deeds and performing commandments." The second type of *tzaddik*, turning inward, rests in the Divine love, and allows it to flow to everything, extending it to all existence.

The existence of love and the reality of being a vessel for the loving lifeforce of existence are taken as conditions of life in the Maggid's teaching. They are there for us to partake of, live in, and amplify as we become conduits for the love the Creator has for us and all creation. Love, originating in the Ineffable, is not dependent on anything else; yet it depends on us to manifest it in the world. We may cease, or be removed from the world, but the love will continue.

This is a very different, profoundly countercultural approach to love than the one that predominates in our society. It starts not from the premise that we are monads, isolated from one another and therefore desperate to find the connection and sense of self-worth and purpose that love conveys. Nor do we have to generate love on our own. We neither possess it nor can contain it. Rather, this approach takes as foundational the proposition that we are all interconnected, all animated by Divine spirit, all vessels for holiness and the presence of God.

As bell hooks writes further on in her book, "Life-threatening nihilism abounds in contemporary culture, crossing the boundaries of race, class, gender, and nationality. At some point it affects all our lives... Knowing love or the hope of knowing love is the anchor that keeps us from falling into that sea of despair."[28] We draw strength from, and find refuge in, our awareness of being loved and being conduits for love. Sometimes that allows us to rest in an innerness, like the second type of *tzaddik* in the Maggid's teaching. Yet hooks wisely adds that while such a move may be necessary, it is not sufficient: "Spiritual seekers let their light shine so that others may see not only to give service by example but also to constantly remind themselves that spirituality is most gloriously embodied in our actions—our habits of being."[29]

May our practice help us experience the reality of our belovedness so that we may manifest it in service of others and the Divine.

## Questions for Reflection and Conversation

- Read the Maggid's description of the two *tzaddikim* again. Try to paraphrase the distinction he makes. What is different about them? How do you experience that difference in your own life?

- Has there been a moment when you have experienced the kind of Divine love that the Maggid or bell hooks describe? What did it feel like? Did this experience come about in any way as a result of your practice? When, how, why or why not?

---

[28] Ibid. 78.
[29] Ibid.

- When, if ever, have you sensed that you were a conduit for Divine love in the world? How did you realize it? Have you ever tried to be that conduit on a regular basis? Why or why not?

## Ideas for Practice

- In meditation practice, try bringing your attention to the sensation of feeling loved. As you give attention to your body through a body scan, offer love to your toes, feet, knees, etc., and allow space to sense love returning to you from your body. Then try bringing your attention to someone toward whom you may want to be more loving. Note how it feels to extend the love you sensed inwardly to another person.

- Building on your meditation practice, this week try to find one person toward whom you want to act as a vessel of Divine love. Consider sharing with a friend or loved one your sense of love for them. How might you convey it? Could it be through spoken word, through a letter, through art or through a meaningful act? In what other manner might you express this love?

# Vayigash:
# How Do We Connect?

The tension of the Joseph story reaches its climax this week as Judah makes a dramatic speech to spare his brother Benjamin. And Joseph, seeing that his brothers have learned from the sin they committed against him, finally reveals himself. Judah seems to pull off something remarkable here, connecting with this person who he does not realize is his half-brother and who appears to him in the stark figure of the viceroy of Egypt. An enormous amount rests on this speech and it is understood by classical commentators to be a model of biblical rhetoric—because without it, it seems like the story may have turned out differently, without the tearful family reunification that comes about in its wake.

Rashi's first comment on the parasha provides us with an opening to explore the larger question with which we frame this week's study: How do we connect? He explains Judah's opening words, "Please, my lord, let your servant appeal to my lord" (Gen. 44:18) by means of a more literal translation of the Hebrew:

"May my words penetrate into your ears."

While George Bernard Shaw is said to have quipped that the biggest problem in communication is the illusion that it has taken place, the physicality of Rashi's image calls our attention to the miraculous reality that communication can and does happen all the time. When we stop to think about it, we can appreciate just how remarkable it is that we can make sounds, or create visual or sensory symbols, which can be heard or read or touched by others, and by means of that interaction they can understand us. It's an amazing thing! In the same breath, Rashi's image reminds us of the truth in Shaw's aphorism as well: communication is far from a given. Achieving understanding can often feel as hard as trying to penetrate through the skull of another. Which makes achieving it all the more remarkable.

## Connecting Through the Divine

This brings us to a teaching of the *Ma'or Vashemesh* of Rabbi Kalonymus Kalman Epstein (1753-1825) of Krakow. The teaching builds on a midrash from Bereshit Rabbah which understands Psalm 48 in light of Judah's speech to Joseph. For instance, Psalms 48:5, "See the kings joined forces, they advanced together," is understood in the midrash to refer to Joseph and Judah confronting one another. The *Ma'or Vashemesh* builds on this midrash by employing creative gematria in service of a larger reflection on the nature of communication, and what happens not only between Judah, Joseph, and the rest of the brothers, but between the rest of us in our interactions as well.

**מאור ושמש, ויגש**

"ויגש אליו יהודה": במדרש רבה: "ויגש אליו יהודה'—"כי הנה המלכים נועדו עברו יחדיו כו'". יש לרמז בזה כך: דהנה כי ראה יהודה שצריך לקרב עצמו אל האיש הזה, וראה שצרתו צרה מאד. ע"כ היה מוכרח ליחד היחודים הצריך לדבר זה, לקרב הדיעות ומחשבות יחד.

וידוע שהשם "אהוה" הוא שם הדעת, שהוא גושפנקא דחתום בי' שמיא וארעא, כידוע כמה פעמים בספר "מקדש מלך". ששם הזה הוא שם הדעת. ע"כ כשהי' מכוין בזה השם, חיבר עצמו עם יוסף. וזהו הרמז בר"ת "ויגש "אליו "יהודה: הוא גימטריא י"ז, והוא מספר שם "אהוה. וגם השם הזה הוא מספר קטן של שם הוי' ב"ה.

לרמז שאי אפשר לאדם לבוא לבחי' הדעת, לקשר ולחבר איזה התחברות הקדושה, כ"א שיקטין א"ע תחילה. ע"כ כשהקטין יהודה א"ע, ע"כ קירב עצמו ליוסף. וביבוא לבחי' הדעת שנתחברו יחדיו יהודה ויוסף. וזהו פי' המדרש הנ"ל "כי הנה המלכים נועדו", ר"ל, נתחברו "יחדיו", "זהו יהודה ויוסף".

ועי"ז, כשנתחברו יחדיו יהודא ויוסף, ושאר כל אחיו היו באותו מעמד. ע"כ נתגלו כל הי"ב צירופי הוי' של כל י"ב שבטי "יה .... ונתעוררו כל הרחמים עליהם, ונמשך להם משם "חיים". וזהו אמצע אותיות של "ויגש "אליו "יהודא עולים בגימטריא "חיים". גימטריא אהי' הוי' אהי'. הם המוחין הגדולים. וע"י היחודים אלו המשיך ונתגלה להם יוסף, שהוכרח להתודע להם ע"י השמות הקדושים האלו כנ"ל.

## Ma'or Vashemesh, Vayigash

"And Judah came near to him"—In Midrash Rabbah this passage is interpreted in light of Psalms 48:5: "See, the kings joined forces. They advanced together." We can discern a deeper meaning here. Judah saw that he had to bring himself to this "man" [i.e., Joseph], and realized how great a challenge this was. He determined to perform the necessary unifications to speak directly to him, to bring their ideas and thoughts together.

It is known that the name א-ה-ו-ה is the name by which the Divine is accessible through awareness. It is the sign with which heaven and earth are sealed, as is explained several

times in the book *Mikdash Melekh*.[30] When Judah meditated
on this name, he connected himself to Joseph. This is hinted
at by the first letters of the words of the verse: *Vayigash Elav
Yehuda*, ‫ו-א-י‬, which in gematria add up to 17. This is the same
value as ‫א-ה-ו-ה‬.

This name, AHVH, is a miniature version of the fuller Divine name, YHVH. This reduction to the "miniature version"
points us to the lesson that it is only possible for us to arrive
at the quality of awareness necessary for making holy connections if we have curtailed our own sense of self first. Judah did
precisely this: He made himself smaller and was therefore able
to cultivate the consciousness necessary to connect with Joseph.
This is what the midrash means when it says, "The kings joined
forces": they connected together—"this is Judah and Joseph."

Once Judah and Joseph had connected, all the rest of the
brothers stood at the same level. Thus, in that moment, each
of the twelve permutations of the Divine name—one for each
tribe—were revealed… Through this revelation, compassion
was aroused, flowing through them directly from the Divine
Name, "Life". This is suggested by the middle letters of the
words in the verse: ‫ויגש אליו יהודה‬, which add up to 68, which
is the numerical value of ‫חיים‬, life. This is the same value as
‫אהיה, הויה, אהיה‬—"I will be," "I am," "I will be," which also
equal 68. [All of this gestures at] the expanded consciousness
that was present among the brothers in that moment, by means
of which they connected with one another and through which
Joseph revealed himself to them—as he was compelled to do.

In the *Ma'or Vashemesh's* telling, Judah didn't just make a great speech. He
did something cosmic, mystical. In communicating to Joseph such that his
words penetrated his brother's mind, he partook of and developed a divine
channel of connection—a connection that was latent, ready to be developed,
but that required a special kind of awareness to activate.

## Connection: Interpersonal, Communal, and Unmediated

Foundational to that connection was Judah's own self-limitation, which
we might describe in mindfulness practice as recognizing the truth of a

---

[30] R. Shalom ben Moshe Buzaglo, Morocco, Palestine, London (c.1700-1780).

situation, accepting it, investigating it with compassion, and nurturing that compassion for oneself and others. Also essential was empathy, a recognition of the suffering of the other actors in the story, most notably Jacob and Benjamin. "Please let your servant remain as a slave to my lord instead of the boy, and let the boy go back with his brothers," Judah pleads. "For how can I go back to my father unless the boy is with me? Let me not be witness to the woe that would overtake my father!" (Gen. 44:33-34). Judah develops and evinces an awareness not only of himself but of his father and half-brother. That demonstration of compassion is ultimately what makes it unbearable for Joseph to remain unrevealed, unconnected: "And Joseph could no longer bear it." (Gen. 45:1).

For the *Ma'or Vashemesh*, Judah's connection with Joseph in the moment also results in a collective moment of connection, which he understands as a moment of revelation. Like a pebble dropped in a pond, the humble, compassionate consciousness of Judah expands to touch and include all of the brothers—and to again enable a flow of divine love to connect them all. This, too, is a lesson to us about the transformative potential of acts of courageous communication carried out in the presence of a community. While one person may need to take a first step in opening up channels of compassion, ultimately we are hardwired—literally, as research on mirror neurons suggests—to recognize and respond to compassion. We want those channels of divine love to open within and between us. In witnessing such healing, we become affected by it. The divine within us is called to connect.

One final dimension of both Judah's speech and its interpretation by the *Ma'or Vashemesh* bears mention: As we read the story, all of this takes place face to face. It is not mediated by letters written on parchment and separated by weeks or months, much less through email or social media or Zoom or Facetime. The story, and likely the stories it evokes in our own lives, takes place in person and in real time. These stories are personal and unmediated—indeed, that is the final precondition before Joseph's revelation to his brothers, as he sends out his attendants and is thus able to have an intimate conversation as he reveals himself. This, too, reminds us of some fundamental aspects of the divinity that resides within and between us. As much as my words right now are hopefully entering your consciousness, possibly as conveyors and activators of divine sparks, this kind of connection is of a fundamentally different quality than if you and I were meeting in person, face-to-face in real time. Being mindful of these limitations within the possibilities for connection is itself an important aspect of our practice, too.

## Questions for Reflection and Conversation

- Does this study bring up a time in your life when you connected with someone in a spiritual way? If so, what happened? What did it feel like? What can you discern about yourself, the other person/people, and the environment, that contributed to the moment?

- What do you think the *Ma'or Vashemesh* means when he says that Judah made himself smaller before connecting with Joseph? What does it evoke for you? How, if at all, do you try to "make yourself smaller," or perhaps take up the right amount of space, in connecting with others?

- How do you understand the what the *Ma'or Vashemesh* is trying to convey by invoking gematria and divine names? Do you see it as a word game, or do you think he is saying something else? How would you put it in your own words?

## Ideas for Practice

In meditation practice this week, consider bringing to mind someone with whom you've had trouble connecting, or perhaps a relationship in need of repair. With the image of Judah and Joseph in mind, allow yourself to recognize and feel the emotions that arise when you consider this relationship: perhaps fear or frustration, anxiety, sadness, anger, hope. Try to investigate where the emotions are coming from. Gradually move toward simply allowing the emotions to be present, while allowing for the possibility of engaging with the other person with compassion. Does this process open up possibilities for you? Does it give you more choices for connecting—or for keeping things as they are, but reframing them for yourself?

# Vayechi:
# How Do We Bless?

Blessing is one of the most prominent themes in this final parasha of the book of Genesis. The bulk of chapter 48 is devoted to Jacob's blessing of Joseph's sons, Ephraim and Menashe, while most of chapter 49 documents his blessing to his own twelve sons. Yet both of these instances of blessing are less than straightforward. Jacob first blesses his younger grandson rather than the older one, an episode that seems to touch on deep chords of unease in Jacob's own past. And the blessings he offers his sons are not in all cases generous—or even blessings.

Something seems blocked in Jacob's ability to bless, a condition gestured at by commentaries on the very first verse of the parasha. Unique among all the Torah portions, Vayechi begins without a line break from the previous section. Rashi, quoting the midrash, suggests that this scribal convention reflects a deeper reality: "Jacob wished to reveal to his children the end of [their] days, but it was concealed from him" (Rashi on Gen. 47:28).

This emphasis on blessing, presented in its imperfect humanity in the character of Jacob, invites us into a deeper reflection on what exactly we are doing, or trying to do, when we offer blessings.

## Blessing With and Through Deeper Awareness

To begin, we will study two teachings of Rebbe Nachman of Breslov (1772-1810), great-grandson of the Baal Shem Tov and inspiration for Breslover Hasidism.

The first teaching expands on a discussion in the Talmud about why it is not common for Torah scholars to have children who are also Torah scholars. After proffering various possible answers (i.e., so that they should not become presumptuous or lord it over those they are meant to serve), the sage Ravina (from a late generation of teachers in the Talmud) offers another reason. He teaches that the children of these Torah scholars do not succeed them because they fail to recite a blessing before studying Torah. Rebbe Nachman builds on this teaching to offer the following:

**ליקוטי מוהר"ן 14:4 I**

וְזֶה שֶׁאָמְרוּ חֲכָמֵינוּ זִכְרוֹנָם לִבְרָכָה (נדרים פא.): מִפְּנֵי מָה תַּלְמִידֵי־חֲכָמִים אֵין בְּנֵיהֶם תַּלְמִידֵי־חֲכָמִים—מִפְּנֵי שֶׁלֹּא בֵרְכוּ בַּתּוֹרָה תְּחִלָּה; שֶׁצָּרִיךְ כָּל אָדָם, וּבִפְרָט תַּלְמִיד־חָכָם, לְבָרֵךְ וּלְהָאִיר בְּלִמּוּד תּוֹרָתוֹ בְּשֹׁרֶשׁ הַנְּשָׁמוֹת, הַיְנוּ בְּמַחֲשָׁבָה תְּחִלָּה, כִּי שָׁם שָׁרְשֵׁנוּ. נִמְצָא, כְּשֶׁמֵּבִיא

הָאָרֶץ וּבְרָכָה לְתוֹךְ תְּחִלַּת הַמַּחֲשָׁבָה, וְעַל־יָדוֹ מִתְנוֹצְצִין וּמִתְבָּרְכִין
הַנְּשָׁמוֹת, נִמְצָא כְּשֶׁמַּמְשִׁיךְ נְשָׁמָה לִבְנוֹ, בְּוַדַּאי הוּא מַמְשִׁיךְ נְשָׁמָה
בְּהִירָה וְזַכָּה, וְעַל־יְדֵי־זֶה גַּם בְּנוֹ יִהְיֶה תַּלְמִיד־חָכָם; אֲבָל כְּשֶׁאֵין מֵאִיר
וּמְבָרֵךְ אֶת הַתְּחִלָּה עַל־יְדֵי לִמּוּדוֹ, אָז כְּשֶׁמַּמְשִׁיךְ נְשָׁמָה לִבְנוֹ, הַנְּשָׁמָה
הִיא בְּחִינַת (שיר השירים ה׳:ב׳): "אֲנִי יְשֵׁנָה", וְאֵינָה מְאִירָה, מִפְּנֵי זֶה
לֹא יִהְיֶה בְּנוֹ תַּלְמִיד־חָכָם, וְזֶה מִפְּנֵי שֶׁלֹּא בֵרְכוּ בַּתּוֹרָה תְּחִלָּה, הַיְנוּ
שֹׁרֶשׁ הַנְּשָׁמוֹת, בְּחִינַת: יִשְׂרָאֵל עָלָה בְּמַחֲשָׁבָה תְּחִלָּה:

### Likkutei Moharan I:14:4

This is what our Sages taught (Babylonian Talmud Nedarim 81a):
"Why do Torah scholars not have children who are Torah scholars? Because they did not recite the blessing for Torah before
studying." Every person, and especially the Torah scholar, must
bless the Torah first. That is, through their Torah study, they
must bless and illuminate the root of all souls—i.e., the "first
in thought," for that is where the root of our soul is.

We find, therefore, when a person brings illumination and
blessing into the very first moments of thought, and through
this causes the souls [in the root/source] to shine and be blessed,
then when they cause a soul to be implanted in their child, they
surely extend to their child a pure and clear soul. As a result,
the child will also be a Torah scholar.

However, when the scholar does not illuminate and bless
the "first" through their study of Torah, then, when they cause
the soul to be implanted, this soul reflects [not this awakened
and activated world of soul, but rather] the quality of "I am
asleep" (Song of Songs 5:2). It does not shine. This is why the child
will not be a Torah scholar. And this is: "Because they did not
recite the blessing for Torah first"—i.e., [first in thought,] the
source of the souls, as in [the teaching of the Zohar], "Israel
arose first in thought."

Rather than focus on the mechanics of procreation Rebbe Nachman describes (which are both metaphorical, and medieval), I would draw our attention to the experience of blessing he outlines. I would suggest his point
is not that the recitation of a blessing before Torah study is some kind of
transactional guarantee for the scholar's children, but rather a caution in
believing that it could be so. For Rebbe Nachman speaks of a mystical reality
in which, through our recitation of a blessing before Torah study, we bring a
spark and blessing not only to the souls engaged in the study, but the broader

realm of all souls. Reciting a blessing is not a formulaic ritual, it is not merely saying the prescribed words. Clearly he is gesturing at something more: An experience in which our articulation of words of blessing reflects an inner conscious awareness through which we connect ourselves to a much deeper reality. To offer a genuine blessing requires a quality of wakefulness (i.e., not "I am asleep") that opens up our hearts and those around us—in this case, a scholar's children, who will be shaped by the presence of a parent who lives in and with this kind of consciousness. Rebbe Nachman invites all of us to practice this kind of consciously aware blessing-making.

## To Carry and Be Carried

In another teaching, Rebbe Nachman reflects on a second aspect of the reality and experience of blessing. This teaching builds on Ezekiel's vision of the Divine chariot (Ezekiel ch. 1). It invites us to consider the way blessings are not one-way affairs, but are rather more paradoxical: they are experiences that we hold and by which we are held. He begins by describing the custom at weddings in his community to offer some of the ceremonial wine not only to the couple under the huppah, but also the person who brings the wine.

**ליקוטי מוהר"ן 69:1:II**

מַה שֶׁנּוֹהֲגִים לִתֵּן בְּרָכָה לְהָאִישׁ הַמֵּבִיא הַמַּשְׁקֶה לָאוֹרְחִים אוֹ עַל הַחֲתֻנָּה וְכַיּוֹצֵא, (הַיְנוּ כְּשֶׁנּוֹשְׂאִין יַיִן אוֹ דְּבַשׁ לְאוֹרְחִים אוֹ עַל חֲתֻנָּה, אֲזַי נוֹהֲגִין לִתֵּן מִן הַמַּשְׁקֶה לְהַשָּׁלִיחַ הַנּוֹשֵׂא אֶת הַמַּשְׁקֶה, לַעֲשׂוֹת בְּרָכָה) הוּא עַל־פִּי מַה שֶׁכָּתוּב בַּזֹּהַר (פקודי דף רמב.), שֶׁיֵּשׁ כַּמָּה דְּבָרִים שֶׁהֵם נִשָּׂאִים וְנוֹשְׂאִים, וְחוֹשֵׁב שָׁם כַּמָּה דְּבָרִים שֶׁהֵם נִשָּׂאִים, דְּהַיְנוּ שֶׁנּוֹשְׂאִין אוֹתָם, וּבֶאֱמֶת אֵלּוּ הַדְּבָרִים הֵם נוֹשְׂאִים, כְּגוֹן הַמֶּרְכָּבָה, שֶׁהִיא נִשֵּׂאת וְנוֹשֵׂאת, וְכֵן הָאָרוֹן, שֶׁהָיוּ נוֹשְׂאִים אוֹתוֹ וְהוּא נָשָׂא אֶת נוֹשְׂאָיו וְכוּ'.

וְזֶה בְּחִינַת בְּרָכָה שֶׁנּוֹתְנִין כַּנַּ"ל, כִּי בְּרָכָה—רָאשֵׁי־תֵבוֹת: כִּי רוּחַ הַחַיָּה בָּאוֹפַנִּים (יחזקאל א':כ'), בְּחִינַת נִשֵּׂאת וְנוֹשֵׂאת. כִּי הָאוֹפַנִּים נוֹשְׂאִים הַחַיּוֹת, וְהַחַיּוֹת נוֹשְׂאִים אוֹתָם, כִּי רוּחַ הַחַיָּה בָּאוֹפַנִּים, וְכֵן הוּא כָּל הַמֶּרְכָּבָה, שֶׁהָאוֹפַנִּים נוֹשְׂאִים אֶת הַחַיּוֹת, וְהַחַיּוֹת אֶת הַמֶּרְכָּבָה, וּבֶאֱמֶת הַמֶּרְכָּבָה נוֹשֵׂאת הַכֹּל.

וְעַל־כֵּן זֶה שֶׁנּוֹשֵׂא אֶת הַמַּשְׁקֶה נוֹתְנִין לוֹ בְּרָכָה, שֶׁהוּא בְּחִינַת: כִּי רוּחַ הַחַיָּה בָּאוֹפַנִּים, בְּחִינַת נִשָּׂא וְנוֹשֵׂא, כִּי הוּא נוֹשֵׂא אֶת הַמַּשְׁקֶה, וְעַתָּה הַמַּשְׁקֶה מְנַשֵּׂא אוֹתוֹ.

Likkutei Moharan II:69:1

Regarding the custom of giving a blessing to the sommelier or to the wine waiter at a wedding and the like (that is, when they bring the wine or honey to the guests at the wedding, we have the custom of giving from the wine to the emissary who brings the wine so that they, too, may make a blessing): The basis for this is what is written in the Zohar (II 242a), that there are various things which are carried but which also carry. Listed there are things which are carried—i.e., people carry them—but, in truth, these things are the ones doing the carrying. The Chariot, for example, is carried and carries. So, too, the Ark; they would carry it, and it carried its carriers (Sotah 35a).

This is reflected in the notion of giving [drink to recite] a blessing, as mentioned above. The letters of *bracha* (ברכה) can be rearranged to form the acronym כרה״ב, *Ki Ruach Hachayah Ba'ophanim* ("for the spirit of the living creatures is in the wheels") (Ezekiel 1:20). This is the concept of something that is both carried and carries. The wheels carry the living creatures, and the living creatures carry them, "for the spirit of the living creatures is in the wheels." It is the same with regard to the entire Chariot. The wheels carry the living creatures, and the living creatures carry the Chariot. But, actually, the Chariot carries everything.

Therefore, we give wine to the one who brings the drink to make a blessing, which corresponds to "for the spirit of the living creatures is in the wheels"—for he carries and is carried. They carry the drink, and now the drink carries them.

In this teaching our attention is drawn to a beautiful paradox—of carrying and being carried at the same time. The consciousness of this kind of braided, interwoven interconnection is, I would suggest, a part of the awareness at which Rebbe Nachman gestured in the first teaching. When we offer a blessing, we are not simply saying a formula that enables a *mitzvah* to take place. Rather, if I can bring my attention fully to the moment, I can then open up to sense my interconnection with all others. That both requires and makes possible—holds and is held by—softening and opening up my heart.

Building on this individual awareness, if collectively we can experience this kind of consciousness, we can further cultivate a capacity for sensing our interconnectedness on a communal level. In turn, that can expand and deepen our individual experience. As important, it also has the potential to lead us to social and political transformation that reflects our collective awareness of interconnection. On both an individual and a communal/societal level, cultivating this kind of practice of blessing can help us become more self-aware and perhaps a little more humble. Through our acts of mindful blessing, we may realize that we are not, in fact, the *source* of blessing, but rather a *conduit* for it—we hold it and we are held by it.

We conclude the Book of Genesis much the way the Divine concluded the very first chapter: With acts of blessing. This, after all, is our mission, our charge as descendants of Abraham and Sarah: to be a blessing. May our practice help us hold and be held, bless and be blessed.

## Questions for Reflection and Conversation

- Have you ever received what you sensed was a genuine blessing from someone? What did it feel like? What, if anything, about the giver of the blessing helped bring it about? What, if anything, about you in that moment enabled the blessing to take root?

- Have you ever blessed someone else in this way? If so, what did it feel like? What, if anything, helped you to make such a blessing?

- Do you find offering this kind of meaningful blessing—where you bring light and life to the first impulse to bless, where you realize you are borne by those you wish to bear in blessing — to be hard for you? If not, what has helped make it easier? If so, what do you feel gets in the way? Does traditional liturgy, such as blessings for Shabbat or holidays, or daily blessings in prayer or for eating, help or hinder your ability to offer meaningful blessings? Why or why not?

## Ideas for Practice

Consider bringing renewed attention to blessings over food this week. You might try a silent breakfast or lunch, bringing awareness, intention, and blessing to each part of the eating process.

As you first contemplate eating, pause to notice your body: Do you feel hungry? Are you preparing a particular food you really desire right now? Are there sensations in your mouth, your belly, or other parts you notice? Whatever is involved in the process, try to take time to notice and appreciate it: The way your own body works to enable the preparation to take place; the many people who labored to plant, cultivate, harvest, and transport it; those who you help to sustain yourself in the process; the list can seem endless. Pause to offer gratitude to them.

As you prepare to eat, bring attention to the way your senses interact with the food. With all this in mind, before you eat, offer a blessing—perhaps both a spontaneous one of your own creation and a Jewish liturgical blessing. Eat slowly, mindfully, and appreciatively.

When you reach a point of satiety, bring your mind to the verse (Deuteronomy 8:10): "And you will eat and be satisfied and bless YHVH your God." Note how your body feels different now than before you ate. Take to heart Rebbe Nachman's words that blessing sparks and illuminates all souls. If you are so moved, offer a blessing of gratitude for the food you have just eaten—your own blessing and, perhaps, a blessing from the liturgy. When you finish the blessing, note again how it feels—in your body as well as in your mind and heart—not only to have eaten with intention, but to have offered a mindful blessing as well.

# Shemot:
# How Do We Cry Out?

We live in a paradoxical time when it comes to raising our voices. On the one hand, it has never been easier to make ourselves heard. Through video, audio, pictures, blogging, tweets, and all the various platforms of social media, virtually anyone can put out a message to the world and attempt to draw attention to a cause they care about. On the other hand, that very proliferation of media channels comes with two shadow sides. First, it is harder for any single person's voice to stand out from what becomes background noise. Second, it becomes so easy for us to speak out on everything, posting or tweeting about every cause and issue, that we exhaust even ourselves (not to mention those around us, who are more apt to tune us out) with our frequent cries.

This reality invites us to reflect on a Big Question of Parashat Shemot: How do we cry out?

We first encounter a cry in the dramatic words that close chapter 2 (vv. 23-25):

> A long time after that, the king of Egypt died. The Israelites were groaning under the bondage and cried out; and their cry for help from the bondage rose up to God. The Holy One heard their moaning, and the Holy One remembered His/Her/Their covenant with Abraham and Isaac and Jacob. The Divine looked upon the Israelites, and the Divine was aware of them.

The Italian commentator Obadia Sforno (1475-1550) explains that "they cried out (za'aku) from the pain in their hearts over their enslavement." He then connects their cry to another collective cry, in the verse (Isaiah 14:31): 'Howl, O gate; cry (za'aki) out, O city!'" (Sforno, Exodus 2:23). That is, under the weight of their collective suffering, the people cried as a collective body from the depths of their pain.

In our own time we witness this kind of crying out, perhaps most visibly in the social protests over racial injustice and police brutality. It is a kind of crying that is public and collective, happening not only through media channels but, even more powerfully, through embodied collective action. When that kind of cry rises up, it seemingly affects everyone and everything. Like the Divine in Exodus, our collective conscience hears and sees and remembers. Our awareness, da'at, is broadened and activated.

## What Kind of Cry?

But there is an earlier instance of crying in the parasha which is not public, but personal and intimate—and yet also a hinge moment in the Exodus story. After Pharaoh decrees that all the male children of the Israelites are to be killed, the baby Moses's mother puts him in a basket on the Nile and sends him off. The child is found by Pharaoh's daughter as she bathes in the river. The biblical text there notes that, "She spied the basket among the reeds and sent her slave girl to fetch it. When she opened it, she saw that it was a child, a boy crying. She took pity on it and said, 'This must be a Hebrew child'" (Ex. 2:5-6).

This moment is pivotal. In a gesture that is at once extraordinary and the definition of basic human decency, she has compassion for a crying child whom her father, the king, has decreed should die. Without her courageous compassion—like that of other women in these opening chapters of Shemot—the Exodus would not have taken place.

And yet if we read closely, there is something curious here: Why did she only realize the baby was crying when she opened the basket and saw him? Presumably she could have heard him. Rabbi Chaim of Tchernovitz (1760-1817) asks this question in the course of the following teaching :

**באר מים חיים, שמות 2:6:1**

ותפתח וגו' ותאמר מילדי העברים זה. פירוש אף שיש ביאור גם ילדי המצרים כאומרם ז"ל (סוטה י"ב.) בפסוק ויצו לכל עמו שאף על עמו גזר מכל מקום זה הכירה שהיא מילדי העברים, ואמנם להבין על פי פשוטו מאין הכירה שמילדי העברים זה.

נראה, כי לכאורה יש לשאול במה שאמר הכתוב ותראהו וגו' והנה נער בוכה וכי לבכיה צריך ראיה לראות שהוא בוכה הלא גם בלא ראיה יוכל להשמע קול הבכיה והוה ליה למימר ותשמע את קול הנער והנה בכה

ואכן אפשר לומר כי בכייתו היה על דרך הנאמר בחנה (שמואל-א א', י) ובכה תבכה, ושם ודאי היה הבכיה רק בדמעות בלי נשמע קולה שהרי נאמר שם וקולה לא ישמע וכן כאן לא שמעה קולו כי בכה בנחת וקולו לא ישמע כלל רק כשפתחה התבה ראתה שהוא בוכה ועל כן ותחמול עליו כי סברה שזה ודאי אחד משני דברים, או שכבר נחלש כחו כל כך שאינו יכול לבכות בקול כי אם בבכיית הלב או שזה מה' הוא שלא ישאג בקול בכיה פן ישמע קולו אחד ממצרים וידע כי נער שם וירד להמיתו או להשליכו מן התבה אל המים הרבים, ובין כך ובין כך נתמלאה חמלה וחנינה עליו.

ואמנם עוד דבר אחד הרהרה במה שאינו שואג בקול והוא כמו שאמרו המפרשים ז"ל בפירוש מאמר חז"ל שאמרו (ברכות ס') מעשה

בהלל הזקן שהיה בא בדרך ושמע קול צווחה בעיר אמר מובטח
אני שאין זה בתוך ביתי וכו' עד כאן, כי הלל הזקן לימד את בני
ביתו תמיד שלא יקראו תגר על מדותיו של הקב"ה ואיך שיהיה
עמהם אף בהגיעם לפעמים לאיזה מקרה רעה ח"ו לא ירימו קולם
לזעקה רק יבקשו רחמים בהכנעה בקול נמוך, ועל כן כששמע קול
צווחה אמר מובטח אני שאין זה בתוך ביתי וכו' עד כאן.
וכן היא סברה כי על כן אינו בוכה בקול גדול להיות שבוצין
בוצין מקטפיה ידיע (ברכות מ"ח.) ואינו רוצה לצעוק בקול, רק בלחש
למי שהוא עונה לחש, וזה אמרה מילדי העברים זה פירוש הנה
מעת ילידתו מתנהג כמנהג העברים ומדת העברים בו.

### Be'er Mayim Chayim, Shemot 2:6:1

She opened and she saw... and she said, "Behold this is a Hebrew child!" The Sages taught (Sotah 12a) that Pharaoh had decreed that even the Egyptian male babies were to be killed—yet
somehow Pharaoh's daughter recognized that this was a Hebrew
child. So, how are we to understand on a more basic level what
is signified by her saying that this was a child of the Hebrews?

It would seem we could begin by asking why the verse mentions that "she saw that it was a child, a boy crying"—does one
need to see in order to recognize crying? Even without seeing
the boy she presumably could have heard the sound of his cry!
In that case, the verse should have said, "And she heard the
voice of the child and behold he was crying."

Now it could be that the nature of his cry was like that of
Hannah: "She prayed to the Holy One, weeping all the while"
(I Sam. 1:10). In that case, Hannah was crying only from the
heart, with tears but no sound, as the story clearly states: "Only
her lips moved, but her voice could not be heard" (I Sam. 1:13).
Likewise, in the case of Moses, Pharaoh's daughter did not
hear his voice because he cried quietly, and his voice was not
audible in the slightest. Thus, it was only when she opened the
basket that she saw that he was crying. That led her to direct
compassion toward him. For she reasoned that the case could
only be one of two possibilities: 1) He was already so weak that
he was not able to cry out loud, but only to himself; or 2) The
matter was divinely ordained such that he would not cry aloud,
lest he be heard by one of the Egyptians, who might then kill
him or throw him into the deep. In either case, she was filled
with tenderness and compassion for him.

Further, she inferred something else from his lack of an audible cry, similar to that which our Sages taught (Brachot 60a): "There was an incident involving Hillel the Elder, who was coming on the road when he heard a cry in the city. He said: 'I am certain that the cry is not coming from my house'. And of him, the verse says: 'He shall not be afraid of evil tidings; his heart is steadfast, trusting in *YHVH*'" (Psalms 112:7). For Hillel the Elder taught the members of his household not to decry God out loud regarding the painful nature of reality. Rather, he instructed them to accept events as they came and, even if they were difficult, not to raise their voices and cry out, but rather humbly request mercy in a quiet voice. Thus, when Hillel heard a shout on his way into the city, he was sure it was not coming from his house.

It therefore stands to reason that Moses did not cry out in a loud voice, as the Talmud teaches, "A cucumber can be recognized from its blossoming stage" (Brachot 48a).[31] Rather, Moses whispered to the One who answers whispered prayer. This is the deeper meaning of "And she said, 'This must be a Hebrew child'": From the time he was born he had been brought up in the ways of the Hebrews, and their values were manifest in him.

It seems to me that the message at the heart of Reb Chaim's teaching focuses primarily on how we respond to the reality of our own suffering. The story of the infant Moses is surely particularly fraught. Yet, on another level, all of us suffer (like Moses) simply by virtue of being human and living in the world. We encounter physical and emotional pain. We witness or experience trauma. We are at the mercy of currents and streams into which we are born and placed by our parents; larger systems of power and law, through no choice of our own. Even as adults, we sometimes find ourselves floating, abandoned, seemingly without hope. We are often waiting for "Pharaoh's daughter" (or even we, ourselves) to save us.

Some of us may have more material resources available to help mitigate our own suffering. Once "saved," we may have the spaciousness to see others in need and bring our resources to their aid. In that respect, Pharaoh's daughter is

---

[31] This statement comes as the summation of a story about the sages Rava and Abaye as young children, who were asked, "Where is God?" and proceeded to point to the ceiling and the sky outside, respectively. These answers indicated their deep understanding even as young people and were understood by the Talmud to foreshadow their later greatness as sages.

an exemplary role model. But even in the absence of sufficient resources, all of us can identify with the situation of a baby in need of care by others—because we were that baby once ourselves cared for by others, and because we may have cared for other babies like him, too.

It is possible to read Reb Chaim's interpretation of the Hillel story as saying simply, "Don't complain. Be quiet and accept the suffering life doles out." Yet I think with the image of the crying baby Moses in mind, we can read Reb Chaim as inviting us to go deeper. First we are to see ourselves in the baby Moses. Then, we may be able to hear his lesson as a mindfulness teaching. He asks us to meet each moment in full awareness, recognizing that whatever is happening is indeed happening, and can't be otherwise right now—and then to consider how we might cry out. Do we cry from a place of perceived lack, of needing to fill a hole in our bellies or our hearts? Do we become angry and bitter at the cosmic forces of the universe that we sense are treating us unfairly? When we cry in anger and bitterness, is that a mindful response (it might be) or is it an unconsidered reaction (which it also might be)? What might happen if we allow ourselves to acknowledge the presence of the pain we're sensing, honor it, and, mindfully, choose a more considered form of response? That, I think, is what Reb Chaim is suggesting in this text.

## Our Freedom to Feel—and to Choose

In her book, *The Inner Work of Racial Justice: Healing Ourselves and Transforming Our Communities Through Mindfulness,* contemporary law professor and mindfulness teacher Rhonda Magee relates the story of Constantin, one of her students. In a course on racial bias, Constantin became so aggravated by what he was learning that he "came to a class session with a new level of outrage."

"*Fuck!*" he shouted loudly. "I just can't believe this happened. And at the same time, I can't believe I didn't know about this!"

The class was silent. Drawing on a mindfulness practice they had developed through Magee's teaching, they paused together with Constantin and invited "ourselves to ground in the body, to sense the support that we feel when we bring our attention to the ground beneath us. From there, we settled in and opened up to insight," including acknowledging the strong emotions aroused through the class's often painful learning.

"We sat together in silence," Magee relates.

Finally a student spoke. "'I really *feel* angry,'" the student said. "And also, shame. But also feel resistant to saying that. What good is it to feel anger? I guess I just want to better understand how this relates to where we are now, and what we can do to prevent such injustices in the future."

The student raised a crucial question. It is one of the most important questions any of us can ask, not only in such charged situations, but on an ongoing basis: Acknowledging that I feel angry and ashamed, but also wondering
what good those feelings can do, how can I mindfully choose a response that
brings about greater justice and peace? This, I would suggest, is a version of
the question into which Reb Chaim invites us: Acknowledging the many different emotions aroused in response to our own suffering, and witnessing the
suffering of others (another of the crucial events in the life of young Moses),
how do we cultivate the capacity to cry out with purpose and not just with
our first, unconsidered reaction? What will nurture compassion—for our own
pained hearts, but not only those—for those whose suffering causes us pain?

"Pausing long enough to allow ourselves to *not know*, or to feel all of the
often conflicting emotions and sensations in our bodies, is really important
if we are ever to truly change the patterns and habits we have created around
race and racism," Magee concludes.[32] Or, we might say, to break the shackles of
the psychological enslavement to which unmindful reaction contributes—the
*mitzrayim* [Egyptian bondage] which we have left, and which we must leave
anew every moment.

## Questions for Reflection and Conversation

- The *Be'er Mayim Chayim* tells a story about Hillel the Elder, who,
  according to the Talmud, taught that we should not argue with
  God about the suffering we endure. What does this position evoke
  in you? How does it make you feel? What might be a virtue of his
  position? What might be a critique?

- I have suggested here that we can interpret Reb Chayim to extend
  an invitation to mindful responsiveness to suffering. Does this
  reading differ from what you view as the plain meaning of the
  text? How does our interpretive reading resonate with you? Do you
  imagine that you might be able to internalize this lesson, to make
  it part of your life? When, how, why or why not?

- As you reflect on this teaching, is there someone from your own life
  or experience who comes to mind as a model of it? What happened
  to them? How did they exemplify a mindful response to suffering?

---

[32] Rhonda V. Magee, *The Inner Work of Racial Justice: Healing Ourselves and Transforming Our Communities Through Mindfulness.* TarcherPerigee, 2019, 204-207.

- In your own life, what tendencies do you notice about how you cry out in response to suffering—either that which you experience or that which you witness? Are there patterns in your behavior? What, if anything, would you want to change? What prevents you from doing so? Who or what might help you to do so?

## Ideas for Practice

The practice of *Tikkun Middot* that we have developed at the Institute for Jewish Spirituality involves a three-step foundation of: 1) *hitlamdut*, or non-judgmental curiosity; 2) recognizing the *bechira*, or choice, point when we are able to choose our response to stimuli in the world; and 3) *teshuva*, returning to our original intention and acting accordingly.

As you go about your week, try to notice when you are reacting and when you are responding mindfully. Make a commitment this week to, at least once a day, consciously and mindfully slow down the process of stimulus-response and engage in this three-step process.

1. At the moment stimulus (e.g., irritation/anger, fear/reticence, jealousy/desire) arises, practice *hitlamdut*. Notice the sensations, emotions, and thoughts which habitually arise for you in this kind of situation. These may vary, depending upon the situation. Recognize and accept these, just as they are. Then, determine for yourself—but also in relation to others around you—how these emotions prompt a reaction or response. See which is skillful or wholesome, and which does not serve greater connection or peace.

2. Look for the *bechirah* point, the moment in which you become aware of choices for responding in this situation, rather than reacting. What options are available? Which represent the path of the *middah*, the character trait, you seek to manifest? What, if anything, hinders you from following that path or obstructs you from making your desired choice)? Investigate this "inner obstruction" with curiosity, releasing judgment.

3. Practice *teshuvah*, returning to your intention to access your innate and natural capacity to respond mindfully, with wisdom and compassion.

# Vaera:
# What Do We Mean?

## Flying the Flag: Meaning in Mitzvot

I originally wrote this commentary on January 7, 2021, the morning after a mob invaded the United States Capitol and disrupted the counting of the presidential electoral votes. While the essays in this volume generally have avoided direct reference to specific historical events, the nature of this particular one was so jarring that I have found it hard to move my consciousness beyond it. I have felt, and continue to feel, a need to sit with it, and lean in for a bit, and reflect on the Torah with the day's heaviness on my mind and heart.

That morning, after reading that the counting was completed and the presidential election finally confirmed by Congress, I found myself moved to take our American flag and hang it on the front door of our house. I thought of my father as I did so. My Dad was our Scoutmaster growing up. He punctiliously hung the flag on national holidays. More than that, he instilled in my brothers and me a deep appreciation and love for America as a country that had given refuge to his parents, who came from eastern Europe with so many other millions of Jews; fought against fascism; provided public education and enabled him to go to college and graduate school; guaranteed equal rights and, despite its shortcomings and imperfections, gradually spread the protection of those rights to people who had been marginalized and oppressed.

As I hung the flag, I could feel all of these meanings and resonances, could sense my father's spirit working through me. And, overwhelmed by the emotional sensation, tears came to my eyes. I felt I was performing a *mitzvah*—not a *mitzvah* prescribed in the Torah perhaps, but a *mitzvah* of American civic religion. For my father, flying the flag was a *mitzvah*—a duty of citizenship, an act performed with his body, conveying meaning, connecting and weaving connections in the process, reflecting the Hasidic tradition's understanding of *mitzvah* as related to the Aramaic word *tzavta*—not only as commandment, but as that which connects.

With this idea of *mitzvot* in mind, we turn to our Big Question for this week: What do we mean? How do we make meaning, and how do we convey it? For so many of us, this is a crucial question. We aim to live lives of meaning and purpose. We want our activities, our words, our actions to be mindful and meaningful. But what do we really mean by meaning, and how do we ensure that we bring about what we mean?

## The Meaning of Meaning

In a series of lectures in 1990 at The Hebrew University entitled "Acts of Meaning," the psychologist Jerome Bruner reflected on the question of meaning, which of course is intimately tied up with questions of language. Bruner was an exponent of the notion that language is not some fixed, external thing that exists independent of and is inscribed onto the blank slate of a malleable human being. Rather, he argued, "language is acquired not in the role of spectator but through use. Being 'exposed' to a flow of language is not nearly so important as using it in the midst of 'doing.' Learning a language, to borrow John Austin's celebrated phrase, is learning 'how to do things with words.'"[33] We learn language, Bruner suggests, not only as a mental exercise, but as an embodied and social enterprise.

This insight led Bruner to articulate larger dimensions of what he termed contextualism, that is, an approach that takes cognizance of the context in which our words and actions take place. "Action requires for its explication that it be *situated*, that it be conceived of as continuous with a cultural world," he writes. "The realities that people construct are *social* realities, negotiated with others, distributed between them. The social world in which we live is, so to speak, neither 'in the head' nor 'out there' in some positivistic aboriginal form. And both mind and the Self are part of that social world."[34]

I would like to suggest that Bruner invites us to approach the question of meaning and *mitzvot*, which are precisely the kind of "learn by doing," situated and contextualized actions, he describes. We can create an outdoor hut that happens to conform to the definition of a sukkah. But until we acknowledge that we are sitting in a sukkah during the holiday of Sukkot, can we say we are fulfilling the *mitzvah* of the sukkah? Are we performing a truly meaningful act? Certainly, we're doing something—we're sitting in a hut—but that's different than doing the meaningful act of the *mitzvah* of sitting in the sukkah. Likewise, to use a classic Talmudic example, we might read the words of Deuteronomy 6:4 while perusing through Scripture in a Bible as literature course in college, but that's different than saying the *Shema* with the awareness and intention that we are doing something. While there may be meaning in both acts, the meaning in the second is clearly different than that in the first.

---

[33] Jerome Bruner, *Acts of Meaning*. Cambridge: Harvard University Press, 1993, 70-71.
[34] Ibid. 105.

## Mitzvot and Meaning

One of the things that distinguishes these acts of meaning is that, through them, we experience a sense of connection to a larger reality. Flying the flag, sitting in the sukkah, reciting the *Shema*: When we do these kinds of activities, we sense in our minds, hearts, and bodies a feeling of expansion and interconnection, a feeling of purpose, a feeling of meaning. That happens because these activities aren't just activities, but rather are bearers of spiritual energy that we can tap into if we are willing and able to open up to them.

Commenting on the verse "We must go a distance of three days in the wilderness [and sacrifice to YHVH our God as God may command us]" (Ex. 8:23), Rabbi Dov Ber, the Maggid of Mezritch (d. 1772), expands on this idea of *mitzvot*, meaning, and connection. He draws on the Jewish mystical framework of the Four Worlds in which Divine emanation flows from the supernal realm of *Atzilut*, to *Briah* (creation), *Yetzirah* (formation), and ultimately *Asiah* (action), the physical realm of limitation we inhabit. These latter three are also identified with three human capacities: thought, speech, and deed. According to the Maggid, when we perform a *mitzvah*, we unite the three lower realms and raise up the world of *Asiah* into the higher worlds of *Yetzirah* and *Briah*.

תורת המגיד, וארא

כי התורה והמצוות שהם מצומצמים בעולם הזה הם בעצמם מצויים
בעולמות עליונים, רק ביותר התרחבות, באשר היא קרובה לשורשה,
על כן צריך כל אחד לכוון בעת עשיית המצוה בדיבור ובמעשה
ובמחשבה, כי בזה מעלה את המצוות ומפשיט אותה מגשמיותה
ומקרב אותה אל שורשה ומייחדה בעולמות עליונים. והעיקר הוא
התענוג בעת עשייתה, והבן. נראה זה בחוש, כי התענוג הוא המחבר
ב' דברים, למשל דכר ונוקבא, המחברם הוא התענוג. על כן כל
איש שיעשה המצוה בדיבור ובמחשבה ובמעשה, ועליון על הכל
הוא התענוג המחברם. ובזה הוא מקשר כל העולמות להקב"ה, ואין
לך מצוה שאינה כלולה מכל התורה כנזכר, כי היא אחדות פשוט,
אך היא מצומצמת. אבל כשהתפשטה מגשמיותם, היא רחבה מאד
וכלולה מהכל, וגדולה יותר מעולם ומלואו. וזה שאמר הכתוב "רחבה
מצוותך מאוד", שהיה רואה אותה בעולמות העליונים.

כי המצוה צריך שיעשו אותה בדיבור ובמחשבה ובמעשה ותענוג
(דהיינו שצריך להמשיך עצמו לדביקות, עד שמגיע לתענוג). הנה
כשניתנה התורה בסיני, ניתנה בדיבור, וכמו שאנו רואים בודאי
מוכרח להיות שם מחשבה, כי הדיבור נמשך מן המחשבה. נמצא
שהתורה ניתנה בדיבור ובמחשבה, אבל המעשה הוא בידינו. וכאשר
אנחנו עושים המצוות במעשה, אז אנו מייחדים מעשה המצוה

שהוא עולם העשייה, עם הדיבור והמחשבה, שהם עולם היצירה
והבריאה.

וזהו "ביום חתונתו", "זה מתן תורה". ולכאורה איזה חתונה
היתה שם? אבל העניין הוא כמו שכתבתי שהיה יחוד אמת, כי עולם
העשייה היתה לו עליה ונתייחדו לעולם השמיעה שהיא כלי מוכן
לעולם הדיבור, דהיינו לקבל הדיבור עם המעשה.

ובזה מתייחד עולם העשייה לעולמות עליונים, וזהו שלושת
ימים נלך במדבר, דהיינו שלושת עולמות נלך בקבלת התורה
שניתנה בדיבור כנזכר, והבן.

### Torat Hamagid, Vaera

The Torah and the *mitzvot*, compacted as they are in this world,
exist as expanded versions of themselves in the upper realms,
where they are closer to their source. Therefore, every person
must cultivate intention at the moment they perform a *mitzvah*,
whether in word, thought, or deed: that through this *mitzvah*
they are elevating it, taking it from its worldly limitations and
reuniting it with its root in the upper worlds. And—and this
must be truly understood—the essence of this activity is joy at
the moment one is doing the *mitzvah*. We intuit this already:
that joy is what unites two separate things, for example, that
of loving partners in sexual union. Above everything else, this
kind of joy of connection is what we must bring to our performance of *mitzvot*. Through this, the individual connects all
worlds to the Holy Blessed One. There is no *mitzvah* which,
itself, does not also contain the whole of the Torah, for Torah
is all one unified whole. Even if, in this world, it has limitations,
it is ultimately infinitely broad and encompasses everything,
larger than the world and what fills it. This is the meaning of
"Your commandment is broad beyond measure" (Ps. 119:96)—it
is Torah as perceived in the upper worlds...

Mitzvot thus must be performed with speech, thought, action, and joy (meaning: one must expand oneself in greater
connection, until one arrives at joy). For when the Torah was
given at Sinai it was given through speech. And, of course, in
that moment there was not only speech but thought, for speech
comes from the world of thought. Thus, although Torah was
given in speech and thought, the aspect of action was left in
our hands. So when we perform *mitzvot*, we connect the action
aspect of the *mitzvah*—which takes place in the world of *asiah*,

or action—with the [realms] of speech and thought, the worlds of *yetzirah* and *briah*.

This is gestured at by the words, "[O maidens of Zion, go forth and gaze upon King Solomon wearing the crown that his mother gave him] on his wedding day [the day of his greatest joy]" (Song of Songs 3:11): This is the day of the giving of the Torah (Numbers Rabbah 12:8). What wedding happened that day? It means that there was a complete unification that day, for the world of *asiah* (the physical world of action) was raised up and connected to the world of *shmiah* (the conceptual world of hearing), which acts as a vessel to the world of *dibbur* (speech). Thus, the world of hearing contained both the world of speech along with the world of action. Through this, the lower realm of *asiah*, [the physical world in which we live], was unified with the upper realms.

And this is what is signified by [Moses's words to Pharaoh], "We will go three days in the desert" (Ex. 8:23): We will go into these three realms through receiving the Torah, which is given through speech.

The Maggid offers us a framework for approaching *mitzvot* not only as obligations or rote performances, but as meaningful moments. This should come as no surprise. While I have recited *kiddush* every Friday night since I was a young child, it is only in recent years that I have begun to take a moment before chanting the words to close my eyes, take a breath, and bring to mind my family, particularly my parents and my children—respectively, the people who taught me *kiddush* and those I taught to recite it. In doing so, I feel myself open up and become connected to what I have come to understand is a spiritual flow that weaves together generations across space and time. I feel a true sense of joy—not a superficial happiness, but a deep sensation of alignment and purpose.

So, too, when we take a moment to slow down, center, open up, and align with our intention before performing a *mitzvah*, we experience the moment not as simply the discharge of a responsibility but as a nexus point of unification. We feel ourselves linked with a whole network of associations—words, ideas, feelings, actions—of scores of generations who predate us and many more who will follow. We experience *ta'anug*, genuine joy.

Further, the Maggid reminds us that *mitzvot* lie not only in the realm of ritual. Rather, the Torah has the potential to touch every aspect of our lives, from the clothing we wear to the way we speak to others to how we conduct our business to how we play our roles as citizens in a democracy. When we do not look away from the suffering of our neighbors and fellow citizens, but rather take action to alleviate it; when we take action to ensure that the hungry are fed, the homeless housed, the vulnerable cared for; when we make choices to decrease the waste and pollution we generate—when we do these and so many more actions, we have the opportunity, through our learning and through our intention, to elevate them into holy acts of redemption.

So, too, by flying the flag and tending the fragile flame of our democracy—which are not *mitzvot* enumerated in the Torah, per se, but can nevertheless become sacred acts of meaning through our mindfulness and intention. May we cultivate these capacities as we repair our social fabric and work to bring about greater compassion, justice, and peace.

## Questions for Reflection and Conversation

- Have you had an experience like the Maggid describes, when you've performed a *mitzvah* with a real sense of presence, intention, and joy? If so, when was that? What happened? What was it like? Are there things that prevent you from having that experience more often? What might they be? How might you address them?

- Moses's words to Pharaoh, that the people would travel three days in the wilderness (and presumably return), can sometimes present a challenge because it seems like he's lying to Pharaoh. With this more spiritually-infused interpretation of the Maggid, how might you understand what Moses is saying to Pharaoh in the story?

## Ideas for Practice

Find a *mitzvah* you can focus on this week. It could be something like Shabbat *kiddush*, reciting a blessing before eating, or an ethical *mitzvah* like practicing mindful speech or honesty in your business dealings. Research and find the verse in the Torah where the *mitzvah* is articulated. Try to establish an intention for yourself with the *mitzvah*. Before you perform it, pause and expand your awareness. Notice what you feel, who is in your mind and what is in your heart. Allow your consciousness to expand to include people—ancestors, descendants, friends, role models—who share in the *mitzvah* with you. Hold these people in your mind as you perform the *mitzvah*. When you are finished, notice how you feel: perhaps more connected, aligned, and grounded. Try to do this practice several times this week.

# Bo:
# What Questions Do We Ask?

Several years ago I attended a workshop for public school teachers on a skill that was so obvious I was amazed it needed to be taught: How to help your students develop their own questions about their learning. Unsurprisingly, it turns out that when students develop their own questions about the material they're studying, they're more engaged and retain information longer. And yet, so many teachers have been schooled in "covering the material" and ensuring knowledge acquisition that they skip right over this basic element of the learning process and dive right into presenting content. In four hours, the workshop taught hundreds of teachers a simple technique for leading students through a process of question-generation.

This workshop was led by the Right Question Institute, whose founders, Dan Rothstein and Luz Santana, wrote a book on their approach. "The ability to ask questions may be taken for granted by highly educated people, just as asking questions as a democratic habit of mind may be taken for granted by people who have lived their entire lives in societies where they have the freedom to ask questions," they write. "But, the profound significance of being able to ask questions is not missed by people who have suffered from the absence of democracy. For example, Abraham Joshua Heschel, a rabbi and scholar who was a refugee from Nazi Germany, asserted at a White House Conference on Children and Youth in 1960 that in a democratic society we should be assessing our students less on their ability to answer our questions and more on their ability to ask their own questions."[35] Question-asking isn't only about better learning, argue Rothstein and Santana. It's also about democratic participation.

While Jews and Judaism are often described as unusually preoccupied with asking questions, my experience is that outside of attorneys and journalists most of us are not schooled in the skill of crafting questions. Not all questions are the same. Word choice, tone, context, the relationship of the asker to the asked—all of these matter to the shape and function of a question.

As noted in the introduction to this book, in this series of essays we are pursuing here a particular type of question—one which I've termed a Big Question, defined as a question that 1) matters to everyone and 2) that everyone can answer. Unlike Hard Questions (= matter to everyone but only some people can answer—specifically those who think they know enough

---

[35] Dan Rothstein and Luz Santana. *Make Just One Change: Teach Students to Ask Their Own Questions*. Cambridge: Harvard Education Press, 2011, 154.

about the question to talk about it), Big Questions lead not to debates about facts but to conversations about stories. They are questions that lead us to engage with our common humanity because they are questions we share by virtue of having bodies and living on the planet.

## The Questions of Seder Night

Questions are indeed central to Jewish life—and especially during the Passover Seder, which is described for the first time in Parashat Bo as the Israelites prepare to leave Egypt. "And it shall be when your child asks you in time to come, saying: 'What is this?' that you shall say unto him: By strength of hand the Divine brought us out from Egypt, from the house of bondage" (Ex. 13:14). This mention of asking, recapitulated in Deuteronomy 6:20, leads the rabbis of the Talmud to understand that the central commandment of the Seder—to tell the story of the Exodus—is to be performed *derekh she'ela uteshuva*, by means of question-and-answer. Thus, Pesachim 116a:

> The Sages taught: If his child is wise and knows how to inquire, his child asks him. And if he is not wise, his wife asks him. And if not [i.e., even his wife is not capable of asking or if he has no wife], he asks himself. And even if two Torah scholars who know the laws of Passover are sitting together [and there is no one else present to pose the questions], they ask each other.

In his encyclopedic codification of *halakha*, *Arukh HaShulchan*, Rabbi Yechiel Michel Epstein (1829-1908) summarizes the custom and the principle:

> After the recitation of "this is the bread of our affliction," the matzah is removed from the table. This was according to the custom of the time [i.e., the time of the ancient rabbis], for they had small tables, and would remove the table. Nowadays we cover the matzah with a napkin, and this is in place of taking away the table. This was also so that the children would ask, "Why are you taking away the table? We haven't eaten yet!" Immediately they would prepare the second cup of wine, so that the child would ask, "Why are you taking a second cup? We still haven't eaten!" ... And if the child does not have the sophistication to ask, the parent teaches them; and if they have no child someone else sitting at the table asks them. All this

because the Torah emphasized that remembering the Exodus on this night should be done by means of question-and-answer. Thus, even if there is no one to ask, one asks oneself and answers oneself.[36]

Why is question-asking so central? And beyond the formulaic, "How is this night different from all others?" what is the spiritual quality of question-asking and response we aspire to achieve—especially on Seder night, but at other times as well?

## Genuine Questions

The Piaseczner Rebbe, Rabbi Kalonymus Kalman Shapira (1889-1943), offers a creative approach to this question in a teaching for Passover in his work *Derekh HaMelekh*. In order to explore it, we first need to make a short digression into another area of *halakha* pertaining to the laws of borrowing. In Exodus 22:13, the Torah relates the following:

> When one borrows [an animal] from another and it dies or is injured, its owner not being with it, the borrower must make restitution.

The Talmud (Bava Metzia 95a) understands this verse to mean that, if the lender volunteered or was hired as a worker by the borrower along with the animal, the borrower is not liable for damages to or the death of the animal. However, if the borrower takes the animal first and only afterwards engages the owner as a worker—much less borrows the animal without the owner at all—then the borrower is on the hook even if the owner is standing right there at the time of the damage. The key, then, is that the borrower engages the owner as a worker or volunteer before borrowing the animal.

The Hebrew term for a borrower here is a *sho'el*, which also means "one who asks." (*She'eila* is a question.) This term, along with its *halakhic* contextual understanding, provides the basis for the *Derekh HaMelekh*'s exploration of asking questions on Seder night.

דרך המלך, פסח תרפ"ז

מה שבכלל צריכים לעבדו צריך כל איש בפרטיות להשתדל שיהיה
קרוב אליו לה' וה' אליו, והכל רק בהשתדלות ובעבודה, ואפילו
בפסח שד' מאיר את לבות ישראל יותר מכפי מצבם ולפי שרואים,

---

[36] *Arukh HaShulchan* 1:473:21

אבל הכל בדרך שאלה, ושאילה אם אינה בבעלים חייב על נזקה,
וצריכים להשתדל שיהיה שאילה בבעלים, שיהיה גם בעליו עמו.
כי כמו שרואים שיש איש שזכה לחכמה מד' מ"מ הוא נשאר איש
נמוך, ועוד בחכמתו הוא בבחינת חכמים המה להרע כן הוא בכל
דבר, רואים לפעמים איש מישראל מתפלל טוב בהתפעלות דחילו
ורחימו ולומד טוב מ"מ הוא שוכב בנמיכותו כמו שהיה, וזהו יען
שכל אלה רק בשאלה היו לו שד' השאילו, וכיון שלא הגביה את
עצמו ולא נתרומם בחי' ולו אנחנו וה' לנו שיהיה שאילה בבעלים,
רק נשאר רחוק מד' כמו הכתיב ח"ו ולא אנחנו, בכל דבר קל מן
יצה"ר נופל ח"ו וחייב בנזקו.

### Derekh HaMelekh Pesach 5687 (1927)

Although there is a general obligation to serve the Holy One, each of us, individually, must strive to be close to the Source, and for God to be close to us. All of this depends on effort and service. Even on Passover, when the Divine illuminates the hearts of Israel beyond our immediate circumstance or even what is visible to us—still this only comes about by means of questioning [*sheʼeila*]. And borrowing [*sheʼilah*] done without the owner's participation makes one liable for damage. We must therefore strive to make our *sheʼeilah* [asking] the kind done with the Owner, that the Owner should be with us.

For we see that there is the kind of person who has merited intelligence from the Infinite, but nevertheless remains on a rudimentary level of understanding. Moreover, with their wisdom they wind up doing wrong, and so it is with everything they do! Similarly, we sometimes witness a Jew who prays "well," energetically, with fear and love [of God], and who learns "well"—but nevertheless remains on the same low level. This is because they have undertaken their divine service as *sheʼelot*, merely asking the Divine to be a Lender [and not a participant]. Since they do not raise themselves up to the level of "we are God's," and "God is ours," which would be the level of borrowing an object along with the owner, they remain far from God, like what is written, "We are not God's."[37] In every small thing, the *yetzer hara*, the part of us that prevents us

---

[37] This line plays on a difference in the written and orally pronounced versions of Psalms 100:3 in which the word *lo* is written as לא, meaning 'we are not God's' but is read as לו, 'we are God's.'

from staying true to our truest intention and purpose, causes
us to stumble, and thereby be liable for the damage [we do
to ourself].

This is perhaps a more stern teaching from the Hasidic tradition than we
have examined up until now in our study, yet I would invite you to delve into
it. For our purposes, the Piaseczner is inviting us to explore what it means to
approach our spiritual lives as responses to true, genuine questions—where
we are connected to both the question and answer, to our own experience
and to the experience of the one we ask; not as rote performances, but as
something both simpler and deeper.

What does it mean that one who asks a question is also, in another sense,
a borrower? That our questions aren't simply perfunctory? When we wish
to borrow something, we humble ourselves. We recognize that whatever it
is we seek does not belong to us—otherwise why do we need to borrow it?
Not only that—in borrowing the item we also demonstrate that we do not
possess the means, or perhaps the will, to acquire it for ourselves. Rather we
make use of something that belongs to another and acknowledge that the
object isn't truly ours, that we are merely its custodian. So too with Torah,
and even with life itself: We are custodians of something that doesn't belong
to us. Questions asked from this posture of humility—not for the purpose of
ownership or mastery, but rather guided by our desire simply to be of service
to the Divine will—are deeper and more genuine.

Further, our aim in asking questions should be to keep the master with the
object—to illuminate the presence of the Divine in our lives and in the world,
not to separate our existence from it. This, I believe, is what the Piaseczner
means by suggesting that we seek to be *sho'alim*, question-asker/borrowers,
who also engage the owner of the animal. That is, we should strive to bring
God with us into the world and our lives through the questions we ask and
the way we ask them.

While this may seem esoteric at first, you might make it more concrete by
thinking about wise figures you have encountered in life or literature: Yoda,
Dumbledore, Hillel the Elder. Think of the generosity of their questions,
which are never used as weapons but rather as gentle but firm tools with
which we may non-judgmentally examine our experience. Think of children
and the earnestness with which they encounter a new discovery about life and
the world. The Piaseczner is inviting us to recover that kind of earnestness,
that quality of genuine curiosity and care, in the way we ask questions—of
ourselves, of others, of the world.

## Asking Our Own Questions

Writing a few decades after the Piaseczner, the German philosopher Hans-Georg Gadamer confronted the same malady. Anticipating Dan Rothstein and Luz Santana, Gadamer noticed the same failure in education and in our approach to knowledge—one which seems to be at the heart of much of modernity. "Understanding is always more than merely re-creating someone else's meaning," he wrote. Genuine questioning

> opens up possibilities of meaning, and thus what is meaningful passes into one's own thinking on the subject. Only in an inauthentic sense can we talk about understanding questions that one does not pose oneself—e.g., questions that are outdated or empty... To understand a question means to ask it. To understand meaning is to understand it as the answer to a question.[38]

Gadamer reminds us of a lesson deeply embedded in the story of the Exodus—particularly in the way the Jewish people have told the story year after year, century after century. While telling the story is central to our experience, telling it in response to a question is perhaps even more important, because that is when the story and its meaning is renewed within us. And as the Piaseczner teaches us, this is true not only with regard to Seder night, but at every moment throughout the year.

## Questions for Reflection and Conversation

- Think about the ways you encounter questions—ones you ask, ones you hear others ask. What kinds of questions do you notice? What contributes to some questions being particularly resonant or meaningful to you? What might make a question painful? What is it in the question, the asker, the context, and/or yourself that might contribute to your experience of the question?

- How do you feel about your own question-asking? When do the questions you ask open up space or close it down? When do your questions lead you to greater insight and deeper relationship?

---

[38] Gadamer, *Truth and Method*, 368.

- Are you able to formulate the question you'd really like to ask someone else, yourself, or God? What helps or hinders you from formulating it? And, once you've thought of the question, what helps or hinders you from asking it? Try to explore these questions without judgment, just noticing what you observe.

- How do you understand the teaching from *Derekh HaMelekh?* What do you think the Piaseczner means by equating genuine question-asking with borrowing an animal along with its owner?
- How do you understand Gadamer? What do you think he means when he says that "to understand meaning is to understand it as the answer to a question?"

## Ideas for Practice

This week try to focus on the quality of your question-asking, perhaps through a *tikkun middot* (personal growth) lens. As you are formulating a question, consider: What is driving my question right now? Is it genuine curiosity? Is it perhaps a drive to perform (i.e., look smart) in front of someone else? From the standpoint of *anavah*, or being a balanced self, is my asking a question taking up and/or creating a proper amount of space, or is it perhaps taking up, creating, or closing off too much?

If you choose to ask a question, try to be mindful of your tone and your word choice: Are you asking your question in a non-judgmental way? Again, is the way in which you ask the question opening up space for the person you're asking, or is it doing something else? Try to notice what happens and reflect on alternatives you might have.

This practice also need not only focus on others—it can also focus on yourself. As you ask yourself questions this week, whether in meditation or simply as part of your internal monologue, try to notice whether you are asking yourself questions compassionately, without judgment, and in a way that creates more space in your mind and heart.

# Beshallach:
# How Are We Silent?

My greatest public blunder as a musician came my freshman year of college. The orchestra was playing Tchaikovsky's Fourth Symphony, which opens with a dramatic, ominous brass fanfare in the trumpets and horns. Gradually the sound travels downward as the trombones are added and finally the tuba—that was me—enters to drop anchor. In the dress rehearsal I had screwed up counting the measures of rest before my entrance and came in one bar early, transforming a Vader-esque procession of fate into a clown car operation. I got a stern look from the conductor and, wearing my tuxedo that night, counted carefully—one, two, three, four, five. I took a big breath, pursed up my lips... and I still came in at the wrong place, this time in front of a thousand people. Oops. There's not much room to hide when you're a tuba player who comes in fortissimo at the wrong time.

That story illustrates something all skilled musicians learn, namely that silence is as important to music as sound. On a rudimentary level, one needs to play at the right time and not play at the wrong one. But of course, on a much deeper level, the interplay of silence and sound is, in fact, what makes music—and speech for that matter—both possible and meaningful. Like the ink and blank space that enable letters to come into existence, sound and silence dance with one another as we speak and sing and make music.

This observation comes to mind as we approach Parashat Beshallach, the centerpiece of which is the Song at the Sea. The Midrash observes, "From the time the Holy Blessed One created the world until the moment the Israelites stood at the Sea, we do not find anyone who sang to the Holy One other than Israel" (Shemot Rabbah 23:4). This is the longest poem or song (*shir* in Hebrew means both poem and song) in the Torah. The Song is so distinguishing that we refer to the Shabbat on which Parashat Beshallach is read as *Shabbat Shirah*. It is thus a good time to reflect not only on music, but on its deeper structure in sound and silence. Just as we asked a few weeks ago, *How do we cry out?* this week I'd like to reflect on the question, *How are we silent?*

## The Sound of Silence

To begin, I'd like to introduce Vladimir Jankélévitch, a 20th-century French moral philosopher who was Jewish and who also wrote philosophical works on music. In his book *Music and the Ineffable*, Jankélévitch explores a phenomenological approach to music, resisting the notion propounded primarily by German thinkers that music is a language. He rather invites us to put aside a search for meaning in music, and instead accept it for what it is.

In a chapter of the book devoted to "Music and Silence," Jankélévitch offers the following intriguing conundrum: Do we imagine the universe—and life—to be fundamentally silent and punctuated by noise, or fundamentally noisy and dotted by islands of silence? In the former, a human being, "as a creature of distractions, isolated himself on his little islet of sonority to beguile away the anguish of solitude and the silence that deforms being—like a traveler lost in the night, who talks and laughs as loudly as possible to persuade himself that he is not afraid, who believes that he has put death's phantoms to flight, thanks to this noisy protective screen." In a world in which silence punctuates noisiness, however, "silence is no longer analogous to nothingness, or a source of anguish, but is a haven where contemplation co-exists with total quiet."[39] Which is it—or, perhaps, which is it at this moment? Do we approach life as a dull, quiet, uneventful experience whose monotony is broken up by sound? Or, more likely in this technological age, do we feel like there is so much noise, and silence is a welcome respite?

In a certain sense the answer is immaterial. There is the same amount of noise as there is quiet. But Jankélévitch's beautiful question invites us to orient ourselves to the experience of sound and silence, to attend to the moments—like the opening of Beethoven's Ninth Symphony, or the beginning of Mahler's First—when the sound seems to come quietly out of nowhere, or like the end of Mahler's Ninth, where it fades into nothingness. When done well, there's a moment listening to Mahler's Ninth where one can exist in an ethereal state of suspended animation, not knowing whether the sound is still going or not. For Jankélévitch, such moments—and they exist all the time if we pay attention—are entry points to a different register of reality.

## Silence and the Divine

Rabbi Nachman of Breslov has many beautiful teachings about music, in particular about *niggun* or melody. But for our purposes I want to focus more on one of his teachings related to silence. In order to understand the teaching, we first need to study a Talmudic story about Moses and Rabbi Akiva (Menachot 29b):

---

[39] Vladimir Jankélévitch, *Music and the Ineffable*. trans. Carolyn Abbate. Princeton: Princeton University Press, 2003, 135.

Rabbi Judah said in the name of Rav: When Moses ascended on high, he found the Holy One sitting and affixing crowns to letters in the Torah. Moses asked, "Lord of the Universe, who hinders Your hand? [i.e., Who prevents you from revealing everything right now? Why do you have to affix crowns to the letters and leave something to be interpreted?]" God replied, "At the end of many generations, there will arise a man, Akiva ben Yoseph by name, who will infer an abundance of laws from each jot and tittle on these crowns."

"Lord of the universe," said Moses, "show him to me." God replied, "Turn around." Moses went and sat down behind eight rows [of Rabbi Akiba's disciples, and listened to their discourses on law]. Not being able to follow what they were saying, he was so distressed that he grew faint. But when they came to a certain subject, the disciples asked Rabbi Akiba, "Master, where did you learn this?" And Rabbi Akiba replied, "It is a law given to Moses at Sinai." Moses was reassured.

He returned to the Holy One and said, "Lord of the Universe, such a scholar will exist in the future, yet you give the Torah [not by his hand,] but by mine?" God replied, "Silence! Thus has it come to my mind." Then Moses said, "Lord of the Universe, you have shown me his Torah—now show me his reward." "Turn around," replied God. Moses turned around and saw Rabbi Akiba's flesh being weighed out in a meat market [after he had been put to death by the Roman government]. "Lord of the Universe," Moses said, "Such Torah, and such its reward?!" God replied, "Silence! Thus has it come to my mind."

This story is about theodicy—why bad things happen to good people. The punchline, invoked twice by God in response to Moses, is, on its surface, a statement about the limitations of language: God is telling Moses that there is a limit to what humans can understand, even humans as wise and spiritually attuned as he. Ultimately, the story seems to say, there is only so much we can know; God can't possibly reveal all of Godself.

Rebbe Nachman offers a brilliant and brief yet powerful reworking of this teaching:

**ליקוטי מוהר"ן 234:2**

כִּי הַמַּחֲשָׁבָה גְּבוֹהַּ מְאֹד, וּמִי שֶׁרוֹצֶה לְכָנֵס אֶל עוֹלַם הַמַּחֲשָׁבָה, צָרִיךְ לִשְׁתֹּק, וַאֲפִלּוּ אִם יְדַבֵּר אָז דִּבּוּר הַהָגוּן הוּא מַפְסִיד הַמַּחֲשָׁבָה, כִּי הַמַּחֲשָׁבָה הוּא דָבָר גְּבוֹהַּ מְאֹד, שֶׁאֲפִלּוּ דִּבּוּר הַהָגוּן מַפְסִידָהּ, וְזֶה בְּחִינַת (מנחות כט): שְׁתֹק, כָּךְ עָלָה בְּמַחֲשָׁבָה—שֶׁלַּעֲלוֹת אֶל הַמַּחֲשָׁבָה צָרִיךְ לִשְׁתֹּק, וַאֲפִלּוּ אִם יִשְׁתֹּק וְלֹא יְדַבֵּר כְּלָל, עִם כָּל זֶה יֵשׁ בִּלְבּוּלִים שֶׁמְּבַלְבְּלִין הַמַּחֲשָׁבָה וּמוֹנְעִין אוֹתָהּ, וְעַל זֶה צָרִיךְ טָהֳרַת הַמַּחֲשָׁבָה...

Likkutei Moharan 234:2

The realm of pure thought is very lofty and one who wishes to enter into it must be silent. Even if one speaks proper words, one loses the thought. This is an aspect of "Be silent—thus has it come to my mind, lit. 'thus has it arisen in thought before me.' For to ascend into thought one must be silent. And even if one is silent and doesn't speak at all, even so confusion and distraction enter into the mind and block access to the realm of thought. For this reason, one must purify one's thoughts...

In Rebbe Nachman's rendering, God's response to Moses in the Talmudic story becomes not a statement about the limits of human consciousness—or, at least, not only that—but an invitation to go further. In this rendering, silence becomes not an endpoint but a beginning; not the limit of thought through language but, in Mary Oliver's words, "the doorway into thanks, and a silence in which another voice may speak."

This kind of silence is familiar from mindfulness meditation practice. Like many others, my own initial experiences with silent meditation were challenging. The quiet of meditation felt like an absence, a distraction from what was really important in the world—the noise of emails and meetings and busy-ness. My mind rushed to fill in the space I was trying to create, and silent meditation for even a minute was exhausting. But with practice, and especially after my first retreat experience, my orientation gradually changed to the point where the silence became the space where I felt more at home. Meditation stopped being a chore and became something I couldn't get enough of. More than that, orienting myself around the quiet expanded my capacity to be in the noisy moments and not feel overwhelmed. Silence was no longer about absence, it was about presence—of myself with myself, of the Divine with me, and of me and the Source of Being with other people and Creation.

"It is silence that allows us to hear *another voice*," writes Jankélévitch, "a voice speaking *another language*, a voice that comes *from elsewhere*. This unknown tongue spoken by an unknown voice, this *vox ignota*, hides behind silence just as silence itself lurks behind the superficial noise of daily existence. Knowledge deepened by dialectics enables an individual who listens attentively to burrow through thick layers of noise to discover transparent strata of silence. And then, he or she will delve into the infinite within the depths of silence, to discover therein the most secret of all musics."[40]

This final observation from Jankélévitch helps us further imagine the tissue connecting silence and sound, the substructure and ultimate ground of a deeper reality of music. As Jankélévitch reminds us, we should not believe that we can only sense God's presence through silence. Making music together, singing, dancing, humming, praying—the infinite variety of things we can do together with sound—are powerful means for deepening our spiritual lives, both individually and, especially, in community. But as I learned in the orchestra many years ago, and the philosopher and Rebbe Nachman both remind us, the sounds we don't make, and the mindful silence that enables us to bring forth the sounds we do, are perhaps even more important.

### Questions for Reflection and Conversation

- Consider Jankélévitch's two orientations to life: as noisy and interrupted by silence, or as quiet and interrupted by noise. Does one of these resonate with you more than the other? Would your answer have been different at a different time in your life? Why or why not?

- There are different qualities of silence: Awkward, anxious, anticipatory, abundant, precious, to name a few. As you remember silences you've experienced, are there particular moments where the silence felt like it opened something up, expanded something in you, or helped you connect with something beyond yourself? What happened? What about the moment enabled that to occur? What about you allowed it to take place?

- What do you think Rebbe Nachman means when he says, "Even if one speaks proper words, one loses the thought"? What does it feel like when you are able to fully communicate what you're thinking? Or when you can't? What about when someone else can't put their thoughts into words? Does it frustrate you? How could you approach such moments with more compassion—for yourself or someone else?

---

[40] Ibid. 151.

## Ideas for Practice

This practice focuses on song—that is, the musical interludes between and containing moments of silence. It is based on the work of Rabbi Nechemia Polen, as adapted by IJS faculty Cantor Richard Cohn and Cantor Elizabeth Shammash.

- Choose a *niggun* or song you're going include in your practice.

- Sit quietly for three minutes, bringing attention to the natural arising of the breath as it comes and goes. (3 minutes)

- Listen to a recording of the niggun you're exploring today, remaining connected to breath as possible. Hum along, or sing on a comfortable vowel or niggun syllable, or sing with the words. When distractions arise, allow them to pass through. (up to 5 minutes)

- Sit quietly for three minutes, returning to the flow of breath. (3 minutes)

- Chant the niggun for five minutes, with or without the recording, or starting with the recording then continuing on your own. Feel the reverberation, the echo of your sound, your voice, God's voice—listen for God's voice! (5 minutes)

- Sit quietly for three minutes. Notice any sensation, vibrational quality, or awareness (physical or spiritual) that remain from the singing, including any connection you may be feeling to the text. Consider the possibility of journaling your reflections. (3 minutes, a little longer if journaling)

- Seal your practice with a blessing: *Baruch Atah Adonai, haBokher b'shirei zimrah*—"Blessed are You, Adonai, who chooses melodious song." (1 minute)

# Yitro:
# How Are We Connected?

Some of us are extroverted and thrive on the presence of other people. Others are more introverted and, after our gas tank is exhausted in the company of others, we feel a need go curl up inside some private space. And most of us live with some mixture of these dispositions. We oscillate between "I" and "We," between the need for us time and me time. Yet all of us, it seems, need some mixture of the two. As Aristotle observed, we are social creatures, hardwired for connection. And in the same breath, we also need solitude.

The opening scene of Parashat Yitro offers us a first reflection on the question of connection when the title character comes to visit Moses and observes him working so hard to judge the people's cases all day long.

> But Moses' father-in-law said to him, "It is not good the thing you are doing; you will surely wear yourself out, and these people as well. For the task is too heavy for you; you cannot do it alone."
> (Ex. 18:17-18)

Jethro's words in the first verse, "It is not good" evoke God's words in Genesis 2:18: "It is not good for Adam to be alone," not only because of the word choice, but because of the context. Like Adam, Moses here labors on his own, taking on a burden he cannot possibly carry without help. Commenting on Jethro's words *navol tibol,* "you will surely wear yourself out," Rashi colorfully elaborates: "You will surely become weary. Its meaning expresses the idea of withering, old French *flestre,* just as (Jer. 8:13) 'and the leaf is withered (נבל)'; (Is. 34:4) 'as the leaf withers (כנבל) from off the vine'—the meaning being that it becomes shriveled through heat and frost, its strength diminishes and it becomes, as it were, weary, and falls from off the vine." Alone, disconnected, overly-burdened, we become cut off from the vital nourishment of relationship, community, and human connection that we need to sustain ourselves. So, counsels Jethro, learn to share the burden—reconnect, Moses!

The main event of the Torah portion is of course the revelation at Mount Sinai, yet here too the question of connection is both present on the surface—this is, after all, a moment of connection between God and the world—and, if we plumb just a little deeper, even more expansive below it. Rabbi Mordechai Yosef Leiner of Izhbitz offers us a way into reflecting on the question of connection by means of some related concepts including limitation, concealment, incompleteness, contradiction, and imperfection:

**מי השילוח יתרו ה'**

אנכי ה' אלקיך. ולא נאמר אני, כי אילו היה כתיב אני, היה משמע
שגילה אז הקב"ה לישראל את כל אורו בשלימות ולא יוכלו אח"כ
להעמיק בדבריו, כי כבר גילה הכל, אך הכ"ף מורה שאינו בשלימות
רק דמות ודמיון הוא להאור שיגלה הקב"ה לעתיד, וכל מה שישיג
האדם יותר עמקות בד"ת יראה שעד עכשיו היה בחושך.

וע"ז מרמז היום והלילה, היום היינו שהש"י פותח שערי החכמה
לאדם והלילה היינו שלא ידמה האדם שהשיג הכל בשלימות,
כי כל מה שהשיג הוא כלילה נגד היום הבא אחריו וכן לעולם,
וממילא הכל הוא לילה נגד האור שיפתח הקב"ה לעתיד.

וזה שנסמך מאמר לא תעשה לך פסל ואיתא בזוה"ק (שמות פ"ז:)
משום דכתיב פסל לך ע"כ נאמר לא תעשה לך פסל ולא תעביד
לך אורייתא אוחרא. והענין בזה כי מלת פסל הוא דבר מחותך
במדה וקצב ובהשלמה בלי חסרון שום דבר בעולם:

וזאת אינו נמצא רק בתורת מרע"ה, אבל בשכל אנושי אין
באפשר לתקן דבר כזה בשלימות הגמור, כמו דאיתא (בגמ')[רות
רבה פרשה ג', ב'] שאמר ליה קיסר לר' יהושע בן חנניא גם אני
יכול לעשות תורה כמשה וגזר שלא יבערו אש ג' ימים ובתוך כן
ראה עשן יוצא מבית אחד והשיב לו הקיסר כי שר אחד חלה
והוכרח להתיר לו.

והאמנם כי גם אצלינו הדין ע"פ תורתנו הקדושה כי פקוח
נפש דוחה שבת, אך החילוק כי המחלל שבת ע"פ פקוח נפש אינו
מתנגד לתוה"ק, כי גם זאת נצטוינו שפקוח נפש ידחה שבת. וכן
בכל מקום שהוא עת לעשות לה' נרמז הציווי של הפרו תורתך ולכן
התורה כוללת כל ההרפתקאות שיעברו, ואורה מקיף כל האופנים
וכל ההתהוות שאפשר להתהוות, וזה אין בכח שום אדם לעשות,
וזה שמפרש בזוה"ק על לא תעשה לך פסל היינו במצות עשה, וכל
תמונה הוא במצות ל"ת, כי לא נגלה לאדם שום דבר עד תכליתו.

## Mei HaShiloach, Yitro 5

"I am (*Anochi*) *YHVH* your God". The text does not say ["I" as]
*"Ani,"* for if it had done so, it would have suggested that the Holy
Blessed One revealed all of the Divine light to Israel, in its fullness,
and that thereafter they would not have been able to go deeper in
God's words, for God had already revealed everything. Thus, the
*kaf* [distinguishing *ani* from *anochi*, which also means "I"] teaches
that it [the revelation] was not in its fullness, but rather an image,
a likeness of the light that God will reveal in the future. And all
that a person will grasp in going deeper in the words of Torah
will show that, even now, they are still in darkness.

Day and night suggest this reality. The day is when the Holy One opens the gates of wisdom to people. The night is so that the person will not think that one has grasped everything in its entirety. For all that we might have grasped is like the nighttime when compared to the daytime that will come afterwards. And so it always is. Thus, everything is nighttime in comparison to the light that God will open up in the future.

This is what is suggested by the connection the Zohar draws between the verse "Do not make an idol (*pesel*)" (Ex. 20:4) and [the later verse], 'Make for yourself (*p'sol l'kha*) two tablets like the first ones that you broke,' (Ex. 34:1, after the Sin of the Golden Calf, when Moses is instructed to make a new set of tablets). [The Zohar interprets this to mean] do not make Torah into something separate from you, something you don't know, and which was not taught to you by your teacher." The idea here is that the word *pesel* means something which is cut, delimited, finished and without anything missing.

But this is only found in the Torah of Moses. In human thought, nothing can be finished and made completely whole. As the Midrash (Ruth Rabbah 3:2) tells: Caesar said to Rabbi Joshua ben Hanania, "I am also able to make a Torah like Moses." And he decreed that no one light a fire for three days. But in those three days he saw smoke coming from a certain house. The Caesar was told that one of his ministers was ill, and he decided to allow [the minister to make the fire in his house]. Of course, in our holy Torah we have a similar rule, that saving a life outweighs Shabbat. But the difference here is that one who desecrates Shabbat to save a life does not transgress the holy Torah, because the commandment to do so is itself part of the Torah.

Likewise, in every place in which we invoke "When it is time to act for God," we have a hint [that it is also necessary and permissible to] "abrogate Your law [i.e., Torah]" (Ps. 119:12). Thus, the Torah contains within it all of its own future abrogations, and its light encompasses all contingencies and all circumstances that could possibly come to be. No human has the power to do this.

This is how the Zohar interprets "Do not make a *pesel*"—this refers to the positive commandments. "Or image"—this refers to the negative commandments. For nothing is revealed to any person in its entirety.

The Izhbitzer begins this teaching with a simple question: Why do the Ten

Commandments begin by God referring to Godself as *Anochi* rather than *Ani?* Both words mean the same thing and share the same letters, but the former contains an extra letter, *kaf.* Yet—or perhaps more accurately, therefore—that *kaf* is significant. *Kaf* at the beginning of a word in Hebrew signifies the comparative "like." With this understanding the Izhbitzer unpacks the presence of the *kaf* in God's self-reference as signaling that God is only revealing a likeness, a part, of the whole.

This notion grounds the rest of the teaching, leading us to lessons about the importance of human humility. Whenever we think we have grasped something, we can be mindful of the reality that we haven't actually done so. Why? Because even at the moment of God's revelation to the people of Israel at Mount Sinai God could not or would not reveal everything. How much more so in those moments of revelation we encounter in our lives—however much we think we may have grasped, there is always more to the story.

Yet the Izhbitzer goes further with this, commenting on the paradoxical nature of Torah itself. On the one hand, he observes, the Torah contains within it the principles for its own abrogation. Most famous among these is the rabbinic law that saving a life outweighs the laws of Shabbat and virtually any other commandment—and as Maimonides codifies, we do not ask other people to violate the rules of Shabbat for us in order to save a life, but rather whatever needs to be done should be carried out by "the scholars and sages of Israel" (Laws of Shabbat 2:3).

On the other hand, the Izhbitzer also seems to be saying that even when we think we understand something about Torah, we need to pause and reflect that we really don't fully understand that either! Torah itself is not something fixed, delimited, like a sculpture or an idol, and we must not allow it to be. Rather, our posture toward Torah, as toward everything, must be grounded in a humility that we do not possess the totality of knowledge. There is always another question to ask, another layer to uncover.

If that's the case, then it can potentially lead us to nihilism—nothing has any fixed meaning and therefore everything is meaningless. Yet here is where I would bring us back to connection, for it is the ground which steadies us and enables us to stand in this shifting reality. If our questioning is rooted in a steady sense of connectedness—to others, to creation, to the Divine—then it's hard to go down the path of nihilism. Like everything else in our lives—including ourselves—our relationships are constantly shifting. Yet through a grounding in connection, our relationships provide us the opportunity to recognize both the limits of our self-knowledge and the potential for greater awareness. We grow by having our thoughts, feelings, and perceptions reflected back to us through those with whom we are connected—and they through us. This is what the Izhbitzer means when he quotes the Zohar's admonition not to make the Torah something separate from us, fixed and delimited: rather we are connected with the Torah and with God—and like us and like the Divine, the Torah is growing and infinite and always in a state of becoming. That is the ground of our connection.

The contemporary writer and activist adrienne maree brown reflects on this dance of connection in her book *Emergent Strategy*. "Most of us are socialized toward *in*dependence—pulling ourselves up by our bootstraps, working on our own to develop, to survive, to win at life…" brown observes. Yet she advocates for a more organic mental image of life and society, one grounded in connection and interdependence: "The idea of interdependence is that we can meet each other's needs in a variety of ways, that we can truly lean on others and they can lean on us. It means we have to decentralize our idea of where solutions and decisions happen, where ideas come from."

brown continues:

> We have to embrace our complexity. We are complex. While many of us articulate a yearning for a more simple life, we continue practicing complexity as our evolutionary path. As I have deepened into a regular meditation practice, and regular retreat times, I have grown an appreciation for simplicity, while also understanding that I enjoy it as a visitation—that being in a complex life is actually intriguing and delicious to my system. And that I have to understand that it isn't just my own complexity at work, but everyone I am in relationship with, creating an abundance of connections, desires, interactions, and reactions.[41]

We are connected, whether we recognize it or not. We are implicated in each other's existence. If we can recognize and embrace that connection, if we can lean into the complexity within and between us, and if we can unlearn the habits that have led us to think we have to do the work alone rather than share the burden, we will be living a life that is more sustainable and more reflective of the nature of Torah and the Divine.

---

[41] adrienne marie brown, *Emergent Strategy: Shaping Change, Changing Worlds*. AK Press, 2017, 87-88. The simplicity to which brown refers, often experienced in meditation, is frequently used to mean "infinite," particularly when referring to the Divine. Yet the infinite in which we rest in meditation has no shape, and so is articulated through our engagement in complexity.

## Questions for Reflection and Conversation

- Has someone in your life played the role of Jethro for you? Have you encountered a time when you were feeling alone, overburdened, from taking on too much, and a friend or family member or colleague helped you find another path? What happened? How did it feel? What did you learn about yourself?

- How do you understand the Izhbitzer's teaching not to make an idol out of the Torah? Are there teachings or ideas or documents or people you idolize? What would it mean to treat them with greater elasticity, to open them up to questions or critique?

- adrienne maree brown outlines a dance we seemingly perform all the time as we toggle between complexity and simplicity. When do you find leaning into complexity to be helpful? When do you find it hard? When is it useful to simplify, and when do you find it unhelpful?

## Ideas for Practice

In meditation practice this week, consider bringing to mind a relationship of yours that has endured. See if you can bring to consciousness moments when the relationship has evolved, been tested, or been repaired. Try to notice the physical sensations that come up for you as you bring these different moments to mind. Stay connected to your breath, chair, cushion, or some other anchor as you practice and notice how that connection supports you as reflect on this relationship.

# Mishpatim:
# How Are We Free?

In her award-winning 2018 book, *The Obligated Self,* scholar Mara Benjamin observes that in the contemporary Western world, with its deep grounding in the idea of individual freedom, the experience of being a parent is perhaps the most common category through which many of us encounter the notion of obligation. To be a parent of a child—and, I would add, perhaps, to be the caregiving child for an ill or aging parent, or a foster-parent or otherwise committed mentor—is to live with a yoke of responsibility that trumps personal autonomy. Just think of the way that parental—and particularly maternal—obligations are portrayed in film or TV shows: to fail to live up to one's obligation to one's children is an act of profound failure and betrayal, even in a culture in which, under just about any other circumstance, we encourage people to follow their passions and dreams.

There is a midrash (Shabbat 88b) that Israel was coerced into accepting the Torah at Mount Sinai as God held the mountain over their heads. This might have nullified their obligation to Torah, since they agreed under duress. Yet the midrash explains that the people of Israel later accepted the Torah volitionally in the days of Ahashverosh (i.e., during the time of Esther). Commenting, Benjamin observes:

> The Israelites, at Sinai, could hardly be said to "accept" Torah. Only later can agency find a place: the "choice" that was in fact coerced is transformed when Israel chooses to affirm its earlier coercion as its desire. But this "coercion" of Israel at Sinai, in which the people stand under divine threat, also emphasizes obligation as a name for being always already in, bonded to, and responsive to a world... Torah, like gravity, allows free movement on the planet. Humans are creatures who come into existence in a world of constraint, as constrained beings. We are responsive to others and to a world we did not choose.[42]

Benjamin's book is an exploration of the ways in which the experience of being a mother (in her case, as she discusses, also a married lesbian and a mother both of a biological and an adopted child) can help us reflect on what it means to be obligated—particularly in an age when that term, once

---

[42] Mara H. Benjamin, *The Obligated Self: Maternal Subjectivity and Jewish Thought.* Bloomington: Indiana University Press, 2018, 15-16.

foundational to Jewish self-conception, can feel so foreign to so many of us. What does it mean to be obligated? And, inverting the question, what does it mean to be free? Especially in the context of the Exodus, the story of our leaving slavery for what we reflexively tell ourselves is freedom, how exactly are we free through this life of Torah?

### Doing Before Understanding?

This question receives further emphasis with the memorable conclusion of Parashat Mishpatim, when Moses performs a covenantal ceremony between God and the Israelites:

> Then Moses took the record of the covenant and read it aloud to the people. And they said, "All that YHVH has spoken we will do and we will understand." (Ex. 24:7)

The Italian commentator Obadiah Sforno (1475-1550) writes on this verse, the Israelites conveyed through this formulation—putting action before understanding—that they would listen to God's voice like *avadim*, servants. They would serve their master not to earn any reward, but simply because they are—in my words, via Benjamin—yoked in a relationship of obligation.

In his *Sefat Emet*, Rabbi Yehuda Leib Alter of Ger (1847-1905) invites us to delve further into this question via a reflection on the opening words of Parashat Mishpatim and this verse of *na'aseh v'nishma*, we will do and we will understand:

**שפת אמת, משפטים 1874**

ואלה המשפטים אשר תשים לפניהם אא"ז מו"ר ז"ל הגיד בשם הרב מפרשיסחא ז"ל שיהיו משפטי ה' קודם חיות האדם וזה לפניהם והוא ענין הקדמת נעשה לנשמע כו'. גם ברש"י ז"ל מה הראשונים מסיני כו'. ופרשנו עפ"י דברי מו"ז ז"ל שגם משפטי ה' אף שיש בהם טעמים. עכ"ז כל הטעמים ע"י רצונו ית' והוא העיקר. והטעמים נמשכים אחר רצונו. וז"ש שהם מסיני. אף שהשכל מבין שכך צריך להיות עכ"ז הכל ע"י שכך גזרה חכמתו ית'. וז"ש אתה כוננת מישרים פי' שע"י רצונו יתברך נעשו משפטיו ישרים וכל העולם מודים ומבינים שישר משפטיו שכל הדעת נמשך אחר רצון השי"ת כנ"ל. וכן צריך להיות ציווי השי"ת קודם לשכל האדם וזהו לפניהם כנ"ל.ובנ"י הקדימו נעשה לנשמע פי' שהי' חביב אצלם יותר מה שזוכין לעשות רצון עליון ממה שיבינו הטעם של המצוה. ועי"ז זכו שיבינו גם הטעמים כי מקודם ניתנו הדיברות

אח"כ המשפטים. וכ"כ מגיד דבריו הוא הנהגתו יתברך בלי הבנת
הטעמים אח"כ חוקיו ומשפטיו כו' וכן הוא בכל מצוה בפרטות
כמו שמקיים האדם בפשיטות בלי השגה כראוי רק שרוצה לקיים
מצות השי"ת זוכה אח"כ להבין הטעם. וז"ש רש"י ז"ל לא תעלה
על דעתך כו' ותמוה וכי מרע"ה אשר מסר נפשו בעבור ישראל
לא הי' חפץ להבין לבנ"י הטעמים. אך כי באמת העיקר לקיים
מצות השי"ת בלי הבנת הטעמים. רק שהשי"ת אמר שבנ"י זכו ע"י
הקדמת נעשה לנשמע שיבינו גם הטעמים כנ"ל:

**Sefat Emet, Mishpatim 1874**

"And these are the laws you shall place before them" (Ex. 21:1).
My grandfather and teacher said in the name of the Rebbe of
Peshischa [R. Simcha Bunim] that this means that one should
value the laws of the Holy One before even one's own life. This
is of a piece with the Israelites' commitment to live by the laws
(na'aseh) before saying they would understand them (nishma).

Additionally, Rashi interpreted "and these" to mean, "Just as
the Ten Commandments were given at Sinai, so too were the
rest of the commandments given at Sinai" (Rashi Ex. 21:1). We
have learned to interpret this according to my grandfather, that
mishpatim are to come "before" us [like hukim, which have no
rationale], even though they have a rationale.

Nevertheless, all the rationales themselves exist because of
the Divine will. And this is the essential thing—the rationales
flow from the will. This is what Rashi means that these mishpatim are from Sinai: Even though our rational thought understands that this is how the law needs to be, nevertheless it only
comes to be because of the decree of Divine wisdom. This is
what is meant by the verse, "It was You who established equity"
(Psalms 99:4)—that is, by means of God's will were these laws
made so clear and obvious that the entire world understands
them, because the consciousness which enables this sagacity
ultimately flows from the Divine will. Likewise, the command
of the Creator must come before human reasoning—this is the
meaning of "before them" as taught above.

The children of Israel said "we will do" before "we will understand"—that is, more precious to them than understanding
the reason for God's commandments was the opportunity to
do according to God's will. By means of this, they merited to

understand the reasons for the laws as well. First they received
the Ten Commandments and then the *mishpatim*.

As the Midrash interprets (Shemot Rabbah 30:9): "'God tells
God's word to Jacob, the divine decrees and laws to Israel'
(Psalms 147:19) [—this refers to the Ten Commandments, 'the
divine decrees and laws to Israel' (Ibid.)—this refers to the
*mishpatim*"]. I understand this to mean: 'God tells God's word'—
this signifies Divine guidance without any understanding of the
reasons. Afterward comes 'the decrees and laws,' [signifying
doing the commandment because we understand it]. This reality
applies to the details of every commandment: It is only when we
perform the commandment properly and simply, without any
desire to understand it but simply a desire to fulfill the word
of the Creator—only after this do we merit to understand the
reason.

Rashi teaches the following (Ex. 21:1): "God said to Moses:
It should not enter your mind to say, 'I shall teach them a section of the Torah or a single law twice or three times until they
know the text verbatim, but I shall not take the trouble to make
them understand the reason of each thing and its significance.
[Rather, you *should* teach them the reason for the law.]" This is
surprising—why would God need to tell Moses this, as Moses
devoted himself to Israel entirely? Wouldn't Moses have obviously wanted to teach the Israelites the reasons for the laws?
But the truth is that even more essential than understanding
the reasons for the commandments is their simple performance.
We can suggest that Rashi means that God informs Moses that
because they said, "We will do" before "We will understand,"
they merited that they would be able to understand the reasons
as well.

This is likely a challenging teaching on multiple levels. It is dense, packed
with associations and textual links between the Torah, Midrash, Talmud,
Rashi, and other Hasidic masters. And like many Hasidic teachings, it repeats
certain themes. But what may be most challenging about the *Sefat Emet* here
is the fundamental substance of what he has to say. Most centrally, the *Sefat
Emet* invites us to check our innate desire to know *why*: What are these laws
all about? What are they designed to do? As the Talmud and two thousand
years of Jewish legal discourse demonstrate, even the most pious Jews are
fascinated by questions of the meaning and purpose of laws we hold up as

divinely ordained. Yet the *Sefat Emet* suggests that the simple performance of the law is more important than achieving understanding of it. This alone would be difficult to accept. But, he goes beyond this. He claims that the ability to understand the law is itself only a further expression of divine will. The only path to understanding, he suggests, is through performance—and even when we achieve some understanding, that too only comes about because the Creator has willed it. Our understanding, and our will, are fully subsumed in the Divine intention and will.

## Freedom Through Obligation

We may experience this as a difficult stance to adopt. Yet here I would bring back Mara Benjamin and her notion of the obligation that we feel in our hearts and bodies when we are fully, absolutely, non-negotiably obligated to another human being. I think of my own experiences being awakened in the middle of the night by a sick child, or being interrupted in the middle of something I have deemed important by a child who needs food or a band-aid or a hug. I think of the experiences my wife had as a nursing mother of a newborn, when there was simply no question of individual autonomy or agency. I think of moments caring for my dying father in the hospital, when my brothers and I took turns sleeping in an uncomfortable chair so that one of us would be up with him through the night. In such moments, there is no reasoning that takes place. We don't think about why we're doing these things or whether they're the right things to do—we simply do them. Later we may reflect on why, and we may come to a deeper understanding of the meaning of our actions. But we can only really come to understand those actions, which are among the most meaningful of our lives, by going through them ourselves.

Okay, you may say—that's all well and good for those kinds of intense, intimate relationships between parents and children. But what does that have to do with making sure my animal doesn't harm someone (Ex. 21:28) or covering up a hole I've dug in my yard so that no one falls in it (21:33) or not oppressing the stranger (22:20) or resting on Shabbat (23:12)? I would suggest the *Sefat Emet* invites us to imagine what it might be like to feel the same kind of powerful, profoundly obligating force functioning in these commandments as we do when caring for someone for whom we are responsible, like a child or a parent. Could we open ourselves to experience the call to rest on Shabbat as powerfully as the call of a crying child? Could we feel the imperative to help those who are suffering and on the margins as strongly as the demand to care for a dying parent? What might that feel like?

In a study of Egyptian women who voluntarily left secular lives to embrace life under Islamic law, the late scholar Saba Mahmood presaged Mara Benjamin's exploration of freedom and obligation. Like Benjamin, Mahmood invited her western, university-educated readers to examine their presuppositions about the meaning of freedom and agency. How could these women leave behind lives of liberty to embrace subjection in a patriarchal system, many asked.

Yet Mahmood—herself a major scholar of anthropology at the University of Chicago and Berkeley—suggested that perhaps this was not the only—or even the most important—question to ask. Thus, we might also ask what we mean by freedom in the first place. What other values do we hold, often unconsciously or so in common with others, that we hardly recognize how they obligate us? When we do so, we may find it possible to embrace some notions of tradition, and the ancestors whose spirit it conveys, and open ourselves up to ways it can claim us: "Tradition... is not a set of symbols and idioms that justify present practices," writes Mahmood, "neither is it an unchanging set of cultural prescriptions that stand in contrast to what is changing, contemporary, or modern. Nor is it a historically fixed social structure. Rather, the past is the very ground through which the subjectivity and self-understanding of a tradition's adherents are constituted."[43] This is a different kind of freedom than we are perhaps used to thinking about, one from which we might learn and by which we might be enriched.

## Questions for Reflection and Conversation

- Mara Benjamin writes, "Humans are creatures who come into existence in a world of constraint, as constrained beings. We are responsive to others and to a world we did not choose." What do you think she means by this? Can you give examples (beyond parenthood)? Which, if any, do you sense as prominent in your life? Having reflected in this manner, how does Benjamin's statement resonate with you?

- The *Sefat Emet* writes, "It is only when we perform the commandment properly and simply, without any desire to understand it but simply a desire to fulfill the word of the Creator—only after this do we merit to understand the reason." How do you understand his message? In what ways have you found—if at all—that doing something first (without fully understanding it) reveals something you could not have known before?

---

[43] Saba Mahmood, *Politics of Piety: The Islamic Revival and the Feminist Subject*. Princeton: Princeton University Press, 2005, 115.

- What does it mean to perform a commandment properly and simply? Is this simply what you would expect from an ultra-Orthodox rebbe? What commandments do you sense that you already perform properly and simply? How—if at all—have you found your own need to fully understand before doing impeding you from doing anything? Are there times you're not only willing, but even excited, to simply jump in?

- Our Big Question for this week is, *How are we free?* How does reflecting on these questions illuminate aspects of freedom for you? Do you think of yourself as free? When, how, why or why not? Have you experienced perceiving greater levels of freedom through constraint or obligation?

## Ideas for Practice

As I referred to in this week's essay, one of the places we regularly encounter the tension between our idea of autonomy and the reality of obligation is when we are interrupted. As a *tikkun middot* (personal growth) practice this week, make a commitment to be mindful and present particularly at moments of interruption—when the phone rings, when someone comes in the room, when an email lands in your inbox. When the moment arises, practice *hitlamdut*—self-awareness and curiosity. Before you do anything else, give yourself the space to notice what is happening in your body—perhaps tension, frustration, or joy. Breathe and bring attention to what your body is telling you. Next, recognize the *bechira*, or choice, point: You have options for how to respond. What are they? You don't need to react. Instead, you can be mindful and present in how you respond to the interruption. *And:* As this week's teaching suggests, one of the things about *bechira* is that we don't always have it. Sometimes, even when we notice how we are feeling, we simply cannot, for whatever reason, make a different choice. That, too, is okay. Our aim through practice is to be mindful of what we are experiencing and doing as we are experiencing and doing it. And, having acknowledged the choices available to us—including the reality that we may not be able to make a choice—we can practice *teshuva*, returning to and aligning with our intention. We can attempt to enter our action with a full heart, embracing the freedom that comes not only from our own will, but from responding to the needs and realities of the moment as well.

# Terumah:
# What's Within Us?

Parashat Terumah begins a series of Torah portions recounting in pains-
taking detail the instructions for and construction of the *Mishkan*, the Tabernacle in the desert. In his 2008 book, *The Home We Build Together*, Rabbi
Jonathan Sacks poses a question many readers of these Torah portions have
wondered: Why is nearly 40 percent of the Book of Exodus devoted to this
telling and retelling? Doesn't the Exodus story reach its conclusion after the
crossing of the Sea? Or at Sinai? (These are, after all, where the film adapta-
tions usually stop.) What is all this here for?

Sacks answers, the lesson here is that "a nation—at least, the kind of nation
the Israelites were called on to become—is *created through the act of creation
itself*. Not all the miracles of Exodus combined, not the plagues, the division
of the sea, manna from heaven or water from a rock, not even the revelation
at Sinai itself, turned the Israelites into a nation. In commanding Moses to
get the people to make the Tabernacle, God was in effect saying, *To turn a
group of individuals into a covenantal nation, they must build something together.*"[44]

Additionally, Sacks observes, the *Mishkan* was a project of "orchestrated
diversity," with each Israelite bringing their own unique contribution—gold,
silver, bronze, jewels, fabric, skills, time. "The point is not what they gave,"
he writes, "but that each was valued equally… Because we are not the same,
we each have something unique to contribute, something only we can give."[45]

As inspiring as this teaching is, there is room to go further with it and
to ask: What effect is building the *Mishkan* meant to have beyond the collective on which Sacks focuses? What is it to mean for the individuals who
constitute that community? How is the work of building, and then living with
the *Mishkan*, intended to affect not only the ancient Israelites but, equally
as important, we their descendants today? How are we to understand the
meaning of "Build me a sanctuary and I will dwell among them?" What is
*Mishkan*-consciousness meant to arouse and shape in our inner life that will
enable this beloved community to take shape and flourish?

## The Capacity for Awareness: What We All Share

The Maggid of Kozhnitz (1737-1814) offers a teaching to orient us.

---

[44] Jonathan Sacks, *The Home We Build Together: Recreating Society*. New York: Continuum, 2009, 137.
[45] Ibid. 138.

עבודת ישראל תרומה
וזה שאמר למרע"ה ועשו לי מקדש פי' שתהיו אתם מקודשים
לשון מזומנים להב' ב"ה ואז ושכנתי בתוכם פי' בתוכם ממש בשיעורין
דלבא כשאתם תעבדו אותי רק בבחי' אשר אשפיע לכם אז יהיה מקום
משכני בקרבכם ממש.

Avodat Yisrael, Terumah

"And they shall make me a sanctuary that I may dwell among
them." We can understand this to mean that you are now sanctified, that is, specially appointed and invited for the blessed
Creator. [When you take this on, and live with this conscious-
ness], "I will dwell among them"—that is, literally "in them,"
in the chambers of their hearts. When you serve Me purely in
alignment with My essence that flows through you, then My
dwelling place will be literally within you.

For the Maggid, the *Mishkan* is a metaphor through which we can orient
our spiritual awareness. Recall that the Ark of the Covenant was placed at
the center of the Tabernacle, which was at the center of the Israelite camp
But, the Maggid suggests that the *Mishkan* exists not simply to arrange our
lives around the rules and regulations of the Torah, but to open up space
in our hearts. It is a calling to a life of capacious awareness of the Divine
working through us.

In his *Meor Eynayim*, Rabbi Menachem Nachum of Chernobyl (1730-
1797) invites us to explore this further, though in what may seem at first
like a tangent. The *Meor Eynayim* takes up the fact that Parashat Terumah
is always read in the first week of the Hebrew month of Adar, during which
we commemorate the death of Moses (7 Adar). He employs this fact to reflect on two of the aspects of Moses's life and character—*da'at* or awareness,
and humility—over an undertone of the themes of Terumah: the Divine
dwelling within the world and the equal share all Jews can claim in the life
of the Jewish people.

מאור עינים תרומה
וזהו משנכנס אדר מרבין בשמחה והוא תמוה דהא עיקר הנס היה
בי"ד ובט"ו בו ולמה התחילו בשמחה מתחלת החודש. אך דהנה
שמות החדשים עלו מבבל ויש טעם לכל השמות של החדשים
למה נקראים כך זה ניסן וזה אייר וכן כולם וטעם החודש אדר
למה נקרא כך הוא מפני שבחודש זה נרמז א' ד"ר רצה לומר א'
שהוא אלופו של עולם וכמו שכתוב אלוף נעורי אתה שכשם שאות

א' הוא ראשון לכל האותיות כך השם יתברך הוא ראשון לכל
הנמצאים וזהו ענין בחינת א' דר עם התחתונים שמשרה שכינתו
עם התחתונים.

והנה הרשע היה מפיל הגורל מיום ליום ומחודש לחודש לכלות
את עמינו בית ישראל בחודש אדר מפני שבז' באדר מת משה רבינו
ע"ה ולא ידע שבז' באדר נולד משה כמבואר בדברי רז"ל והענין
דאיתא בזוהר הקדוש אתפשטותא דמשה בכל דרא ודרא עד שיתין
רבוא דרי וזהו ענין בחינת הדעת שיש לכל אחד ואחד מישראל
להשיג בתורה והכל על ידי הדעת בחינת משה שהוא היה הדעת
של כל ישראל ויש לכל אחד ואחד ניצוץ דבר מה חלק מהדעת
של משה רבינו ע"ה בכדי שידע ויבין ויסיג כל אחד ואחד בתורה
כל חד וחד כפום שיעורא דיליה כפי בחינת משה שיש אצלו כך
הוא מבין ומשיג בתורתו.

ולכן אמרו רז"ל מאוד מאוד הוי שפל רוח בפני כל אדם והאיך
יצוו על זה חז"ל לכל אדם שעל כל אדם אמרו משנה זו לקיימה
והאיך יכול כל אדם לקיים זה הדבר הלא זה הוא אשר נשתבח
משה רבינו ע"ה במדה זו בתורה כמו שאמר הכתוב (במדבר י"ב, ג')
והאיש משה עניו מאוד מכל האדם גו' ואיך יזכה ילוד אשה אחר
זולתו לבוא למדריגה זו אך הענין הוא מכו שאמור שיש לכל אחד
ואחד מישראל בחינת משה והוא הדעת שלו ועל כן ציוו חז"ל
מאוד מאוד הוי שפל רוח כי מאחר שיש לך בחינת משה שהרי יש
לך דעת ואפילו אם הוא מעט מן המעט אף על פי כן הלא זה הוא
בחינת משה שיש לך אם כן איפוא זאת עשו גם אתה כמו משה
רבינו ע"ה להיות שפל רוח בחינת משה ואם גם זאת אין בך הלא
אמרו רז"ל כל אדם שאין בו דעת נבילה טובה הימנו ואם יש לך
אפילו מעט מן המעט תוכל לעשות כן להיות שפל רוח ועדיין אין
זה מדריגת משה עצמו כי במשה נאמר שזכה והשיג ענוה שהיה
לו השגה עצומה ונפלאה בזה.

והנה נאמר במשה רבינו ע"ה (דברים ל"ד, ו') ולא ידע איש את
קבורתו והוא על פי האמור שאתפשטותא דמשה בכל דרא ולזה
ענין בחינת משה הוא גנוז באדם הישראלי ולא ידע איש את
קברתו פירוש פירוש שלא ידעו היכן משה קבור וגנוז כי באמת הוא נגנז
ונקבר בדעת של כל אחד ואחד מישראל כאמור וזהו הוא שפל
בגיא פירוש שנגנז בחינת משה שהוא הדעת אצל מיש הוא שפל
בעינו כגיא ואינו מתגאה שהמתגאה הוא כאלו עובד עבודה זרה
ואין בו דעת בחינת משה וזה מול בית פעור רצה לומר שהדעת
גנוז אצל מי שהוא שפל בעיניו והוא מנגד והיפוך בית פעור
שהוא עבודה זרה שכל המתגאה כאלו עובד עבודה זרה אכן הענין
והשפלה הוא מנגד לדבר זה והפכו ממש שם הדעת האמיתי גנוז
וטמון:

Meor Eynayim, Terumah

[The Talmud teaches,] "When Adar enters we increase in joy" (Ta'anit 29a). This is a surprising statement, for the miracle of Purim happened on the 14th and 15th of Adar—so why would we increase our joy from the beginning of the month? But, understand: the names of the Hebrew months arose during the Jewish people's captivity in Babylon, and there is a reason for each name... Why is the month of Adar called Adar? Because this month gestures toward the message: "A' is *dar* ('א דר)"—that is to say, A', points to the *aluf* or chief of the cosmos... like the *aleph* which is the first of the letters—the Holy One is the first among all beings... In Adar, the Holy One, A', is *dar*, dwells among the lower creatures, and extending God's presence to dwell with them.

When Haman drew lots to determine on which day he would destroy our people, the House of Israel, he settled on Adar for [he knew] that Moses died on the 7th of Adar. But he did not know that Moses was also *born* on the 7th of Adar, as our Sages teach. And the Zohar further teaches that Moses's essence is found in every Jew in every generation. This is manifested in the capacity for awareness that every person has, which enables them to grasp the meaning of Torah. Awareness, *da'at*, is associated with Moses, who was the embodiment of awareness of all Israel. Every one of the people of Israel has a spark, a portion of Moses's awareness, that enables them to know and understand and grasp the meaning of Torah in their own unique way—as according to that aspect of Moses' they possess.

Therefore, our Sages taught that one should be exceedingly humble before every person. Yet how could the Sages have commanded this of everyone? Was it not said that Moses himself was "the humblest of all people?" How could the Sages expect the rest of us to live up to that standard? We can better understand when we remember that every Jew has an aspect of Moses in them—the capacity for awareness. Thus, when the Sages commanded that we should be exceedingly humble, they were saying to us: "You have this aspect of Moses, this capacity for awareness, planted within you! Even if it is in only the tiniest measure, nevertheless you have this aspect of Moses! If so, how can you access it? Be like Moses—be humble..."

It is also said of Moses that "no one knows his burial place" (Deut. 34:6). This aligns with our earlier teaching, that Moses's essence is found in every generation. That is, Moses is hidden within every Jew! "And no one knows his burial place"—that is, they do not know where Moses is buried and hidden, for in truth he is hidden and buried in the capacity for awareness held by every Jew. It is also said, "And God buried him in the valley [across from Beit Pe'or]" (ibid.)—that is, the Divine hid this aspect of Moses, this capacity for awareness, such that it becomes available when we make ourselves humble like a valley, and not prideful. For one who is prideful is like one who worships false gods and therefore likewise does not have the awareness of Moses. They are "across from Beit Pe'or," since *Peor* is also the name of a false god [and one who is haughty has made themself a false god]. One who is humble and low stands against/"across from" this and is able to access true consciousness.

## Humility as a Foundation of Community

Both the teaching of the Maggid of Kozhnitz and this teaching of the *Meor Eynayim* invite us to consider the ways in which we are equal by virtue of the fact that we are each uniquely endowed with Divine gifts—that is, we are all the same in the way we are special. The *Meor Eynayim* suggests that part of Moses lives on in each of us who are his spiritual descendants. We each have a capacity for *da'at,* expanded awareness, deepened consciousness, which was a hallmark of Moses. And in the same breath, realizing that notion leads us to another of Moses's distinguishing character traits: his humility. One might think that expanded consciousness might lead to pride or self-righteousness: "I have true awareness while you live in a realm of falsehood." But Moses, who our tradition teaches achieved a level of consciousness that no human before or since could reach, is described by the Torah as the most humble person who walked the earth. His consciousness led him not to think more of himself, but to realize his communion with others.

This of course is easier said than done. Once we think of ourselves as enlightened, it becomes easy, perhaps even inevitable, to look upon others as benighted. But this is precisely the work: To go deeper into our own consciousness and awareness and, in so doing, become closer to, less judgmental of, and more compassionate toward the other beings with whom we share the universe.

This perhaps offers another layer of understanding the work of building the *Mishkan* as a metaphor for building a community and a society, as Jonathan Sacks suggests. "The Tabernacle was built out of the differential contributions of the various groups and tribes," he writes. "It represented *orchestrated diversity*, or in social terms, integration without assimilation. That is the dignity of difference. Because we are not the same, we have something unique to contribute, something only we can give."[46] To live with this kind of consciousness requires not just a philosophical assertion, but ongoing practice. While espousing this vision is important, living it into being is hard work. The Hasidic masters above give us a guide to doing it.

## Questions for Reflection & Conversation

- Jonathan Sacks writes that "To turn a group of individuals into a covenantal nation, they must build something together." Have you ever been part of a joint effort that built a sense of community? When, how? Consider the project, the people doing the project, even yourself. Which of these—separately or together—helped bring about that sense of community? How did you recognize the emergence of that feeling?

- The Maggid of Kozhnitz offers a beautiful interpretation of God's words in the parasha: "When you serve Me purely according to My essence that flows through you, then My dwelling place will be literally within you." How do you understand his words? Have you ever experienced this kind of Divine flow? What did it feel like? If not, what do you imagine it might be like? How might experiencing that flow make you the *Mishkan*/a dwelling place for God?

- The *Meor Eynayim* exhorts us to be exceedingly humble. What does it mean to you to be humble? Can one be humble and still hold one's place in the world, stand up for oneself or others? How has your understanding of, and your expression of humility changed over time, if at all? What helps or hinders you from living out an appropriately balanced humility?

[46] Ibid.

## Ideas for Practice

The Mishnah memorably teaches, "Who is wise? One who learns from everyone." In light of the *Meor Eynayim*, we might also ask "Who is humble?" and respond in the same manner.

In my life, this maxim has been the basis of a life practice which has changed my relationship to others, and to myself. You might consider trying it this week. Take it upon yourself this week, at least once per day, to approach a conversation or interaction with the question, "What can I learn from this person?" Not only what can I learn from the moment about myself, but what can this person before me teach me and help me learn—for their sake, for my sake, for the sake of all others?

This is an enactment of the *Meor Eynayim*'s teaching that every one of us has a bit of Moses in them. So, operate as if that were true. How, if at all, do you sense this shifts the quality of the interaction? How does showing up with this mindset change how you feel about the other person and about yourself?

# Tetzaveh:
# How Do Our Hearts Break?

## The Heart of a Villain

The heart, perhaps, is not the first thing we think of when we think about Haman, the villain of the Purim story. Yet if we look closely, we find that Haman's heart is, in fact, a subtle but central factor in the story of Esther. Haman's heart is first mentioned after Esther invites him, with the King, to a feast. He is honored by the invitation, and the Megillah records, "That day Haman went out happy and lighthearted. But when Haman saw Mordecai in the palace gate, and Mordecai did not rise or even stir on his account, Haman was filled with rage at him" (Es. 5:9). Haman's heart is here the seat of his joy and his rage, his emotional center. He is easily pleased and just as easily angered, leading him to react with malice against not only Mordechai, but all of Mordechai's people.

Then, in the next chapter, the King is wondering what to do to honor Mordechai for having saved his life. Haman shows up and the King asks "'What should be done for a man whom the King desires to honor?' Haman said in his heart, 'Whom would the king desire to honor more than me?'" (Es. 6:6). Here Haman's heart drives him to make another hasty decision. Seduced by the prospect of yet more glory, he fails to ask the King the identity of this honoree, instead assuming that it will be himself, which of course only leads to further humiliation.

Finally, at the dramatic climax of the story, Haman's heart appears again when Esther tells the King that one of his advisers is plotting to destroy her people. The King responds in righteous indignation:

> Thereupon King Ahasuerus demanded of Queen Esther, "Who is he and where is he whose heart was so filled with pride that he thought to do such a thing?!" (Es. 7:5)

Esther of course responds that the man in question is Haman, whereupon the King orders him executed. In this case, it isn't so much a report of Haman's own heart as what the King *thought* of Haman's heart that brings about his ruin—namely that Haman's heart was full of itself, which, based on previous actions, is a pretty reasonable conclusion.

This notion, that the heart is a subtle but significant site of action in the Purim story, is perhaps refracted outward in Maimonides's understanding of the commandment to give gifts to the poor on Purim (Laws of Esther and Hannukah 2:17):

> It is preferable to spend more money on gifts to the poor than on one's Purim banquet and sending presents to one's friends. No joy is greater and more glorious than the joy of gladdening the hearts of the poor, the orphans, the widows, and the strangers. One who gladdens the heart of these un-happy people imitates the Divine, as it is written: "Thus says the high and lofty one who inhabits eternity, whose name is Holy: I dwell in the high and holy place, and also with those who are discouraged and humiliated, reviving the spirit of the discouraged, reviving the heart of the humiliated" (Isaiah 57:15).

Haman's prideful, angry, and seemingly closed-off heart leads ultimately to a perversion of law and ensuing violence and slaughter. Yet, hearts that are generous and open can help redress inequities, bring people on the margins of society to the center, and bring the Divine presence into the world.

## The Heart of the High Priest

The heart likewise plays a prominent role in Parashat Tetzaveh, particularly when the Torah describes the *hoshen misphat,* or breastpiece of judgment, and the *Urim v'Tumim,* both of which were to be placed over the heart of the High Priest: "Aaron shall carry the names of the sons of Israel on the breastpiece of judgment over his heart, when he enters the sanctuary, for remembrance before the Ineffable at all times. Inside the breastpiece of judgment you shall place the Urim and Tumim, so that they are over Aaron's heart when he comes before the Holy One. Thus Aaron shall carry the instrument of judgment for the Israelites over his heart before God at all times" (Ex. 28:29-30).

Rashi (on Ex. 28:30) explains that the word judgment (משפט) carries at least two possible meanings: "'And Aaron shall carry the judgment of the children of Israel'—the object by means of which they are judged and admonished whether they should do a particular thing or whether they should not do it. But according to the Midrashic statement (Zevachim 88b) that the breast-plate atoned for those who pervert justice, it was called "judgment" in allusion to the pardon thus given for perverse judgment." That is, the breastplate is understood both as an instrument of discerning the proper judgment for the people and as a means of atoning for the perversion of justice.

With these two interpretations in mind, Rabbi Chaim Tyrer of Tchernovitz (1740-1817) offers an explanation of the deeper meaning of this item of the High Priest's vestments:

**באר מים חיים, שמות, 28:29:1**

ונשא אהרן את שמות בני ישראל לזכרון לפני ה' וגו' ונשא אהרן את משפט בני ישראל על לבו לפני ה' וגו'. מעשה החשן פירשנוהו גם כן קצת בחיבורנו סידורו של שבת שם (בשורש הששי ענף ג') ואמנם שתי הנשיאות הללו שהזכיר הכתוב בשני הפסוקים האלו הוא גם כן כאשר פירשנו במעשה האפוד למעלה לומר כי נשיאה אחת היה לזכרון לפני ה' שיזכור ה' בזכות השבטים וישמור זכותם לבניהם אחריהם לכפרה על עוון עוות הדין כמאמר חז"ל (זבחים שם) ועוות הדין עוון גדול הוא למאוד כמאמר חז"ל (אבות ה', י"א) חרב בא לעולם על עינוי הדין ועל עוות הדין וכו', ועל כן היה הזכרון שלפני ה' מכפר מהדברים האלה.

ואך להגין עליהם מכל וכל נשא אהרן את משפט בני ישראל על לבו שהוא היה בבחינת לב בני ישראל כי נבחר מתוך בני ישראל כלומר מאמצעות בני ישראל והוא בחינת הלב הממוצע בהגוף, כי כבר נודע שכל ישראל גוף אחד הם כמו אדם אחד ויש בהם שישנם בבחינת הראש ועל כן נקראים ראשי בני ישראל ויש בבחינת עינים הנקראים עיני העדה וכן כל האברים, ועיין בדברי האר"י ז"ל בליקוטי תורה (קדושים מצות ואהבת לרעך). ואהרן היה בבחינת הלב ועל כן נשא אהרן את משפט בני ישראל על לבו כלומר לפי שהוא היה בבחינת לב בני ישראל היה צריך לשאת אותם להגין עליהם ולהצילם מכל רע

כי ידוע אשר הכאב מכל האברים מגיע קודם אל הלב ועל כן היה הוא המרגיש תחילה בכאב ישראל ומבקש רחמים עליהם וכיפר עליהם להמתיק הדין מעליהם ולברכם בברכת כהנים. וכן כל כהן גדול שעמד אחריו היה הכל בבחינה זו, לכפר על ישראל בכח עצמיותם ונשא את משפטם שהיא בחינת משפט הדין והיסורין על לבו לכפר עליהם תמיד לפני ה'.

Be'er Mayim Hayim, Ex. 28:29:1

In these two verses (Ex. 28:29-30) the Torah refers to two different instances of Aaron "carrying." These two acts of carrying are related. One serves as a memorial before the Holy One, that God should remember the merit of the people's ancestors and safeguard that merit for their descendants, to serve as a means of atonement for them for the sin of perverting justice. Our Sages teach, "The perversion of justice is a very great sin," (Babylonian Talmud Zevachim 88b and Shabbat 33a); "The

sword comes to the world because of the delay of judgment
and the perversion of judgment" (Avot 5:8). [The] memorial
[of the High Priest's breastpiece] before the Holy One atoned
for these things.

But to protect them from all adversity, Aaron carried the
judgment on his heart—for Aaron represented the heart of
the Children of Israel, as he was chosen from among them.
He was lifted up from the center of the Children of Israel,
just like the heart which is at the center of the body. For we
hold that all of Israel is one body, like a person. There are
those among them who embody the aspect of the head, and
they are thus referred to as "the heads of the children of
Israel," and there those who embody the eyes and are called
"the eyes of the people," and so forth. Aaron embodied the
heart, and thus he carried the judgment of the people on his
heart. That is, because he embodied the heart, he [like the
heart] bore them [in toto], to protect them and rescue them
from every ill.

For just as pain in any part of the body is first sensed by
the heart, so too Aaron was the first to sense pain among
the Israelites. He requested mercy for them and atoned for
them to reduce the pain of judgment on them, and he blessed
them with the priestly blessing. So, too, for every High Priest
who followed after him—they atoned for Israel by means of
their very selves, carrying the burden of the judgments and
the afflictions [of Israel] on their hearts, in order always to
atone for them before the Divine.

For the *Be'er*, the placement of the breastplate and the *Urim v'Tumim*
over the heart opens up a connection between judgment, justice, and the
feeling dimensions of human experience. His observation that pain in the
body is first sensed not in the mind, with an intellectual awareness, but
in the heart, invites further exploration. As we know from mindfulness
practice, wise judgment is not ultimately rooted only in our minds but,
indeed, stems from the entirety of our embodied selves. Our physical and
emotional pain affect our capacity for good judgment and right action just
as much as our clear thinking. Yet often times we have to bring consciousness to that reality. We may need to remember to eat or move, or to bring
loving attention to discomfort or soreness or stiffness or any of the many
other ways our bodies and inner lives might come to be out of balance or

alignment. Aaron's carrying of these sacred objects over his heart is meant to symbolize and enact this reality, perhaps reminding the judges of Israel, and the rest of us, of the link between heart, body, and mind.

## The Heart of Democracy

With the advent of democratic systems of government, every citizen holds a piece of the sovereign, and thus it is not only the hearts of our official leaders that matter, but all of our hearts. No one has written more movingly or powerfully on the heart of democratic citizenship than Parker Palmer:

> If you hold your knowledge of self and world wholeheartedly, your heart will at times get broken by loss, failure, defeat, betrayal, or death. What happens next in you and the world around you depends on *how* your heart breaks. If it breaks *apart* into a thousand pieces, the result may be anger, depression, and disengagement. If it breaks *open* into greater capacity to hold the complexities and contradictions of human experience, the result may be new life. The heart is what makes us human—and politics, which is the use of power to order our life together, is a profoundly human enterprise. Politics in the hands of those whose hearts have been broken open, not apart, helps us hold our differences creatively and use our power courageously for the sake of a more equitable, just, and compassionate world.[47]

The Book of Esther, which is always read in close proximity to Parashat Tetzaveh, has been described frequently as the book of the Bible most instructive for political life in a multiethnic society in which Jews are a powerful minority. With that in mind, we can come full circle and think about the various hearts we have examined here: Haman's heart, which seems to break apart into pride, envy, and rage; Aaron's heart, which feels the pain of the people and transmutes that pain into forgiveness; and Palmer's human heart of democracy. The Torah, as interpreted by the *Be'er Mayim Chaim*, invites and even demands of us to practice, so that we develop hearts that break open with compassion, rather than clench up with fear and anger. "Be of the disciples of Aaron," teaches Hillel the Elder, "loving peace and pursuing peace, loving human beings and drawing them close to the Torah" (Avot

---

[47] Parker J. Palmer, *Healing the Heart of Democracy: The Courage to Create a Politics Worthy of the Human Heart*. San Francisco: Jossey-Bass, 2011, 18.

1:12). The heart of Aaron is what enables him to be an emblem of peace. The invitation and charge to the rest of us is to grow our hearts to do the same.

## Questions for Conversation & Reflection

- The *Be'er* writes that "pain in any part of the body is first sensed by the heart." In your own words, what do you think he means? Does this resonate with your own experience? When? How? What kind of pain registers first in your heart?

- Following the Talmud, the *Be'er* suggests that the reason Aaron carried these items over his heart was to atone for the sin of perverting judgment. In your own experience, how have you noticed that your physical, emotional, and spiritual states affect your capacity to make wise judgments? Have you ever had a moment when bringing attention to some of these non-cognitive aspects of your life helped you to make a better judgment? Has ignoring them contributed to judgments you regretted? What happened and what did you notice?

- Parker Palmer writes about two types of heartbreak—breaking apart into a downward spiral and breaking open in a way that, as he puts it, "may result in new life." Have you experienced either or both of these types of heartbreak? What happened? What helped or hindered your ability to make the experience one of breaking the heart open rather than apart?

## Ideas for Practice

During the first year of the Covid-19 pandemic my colleague Rabbi Jonathan Slater created a wonderful podcast entitled "Open My Heart: Living Jewish Prayer." Each of the over 50 episodes featured a guest presenter who shared an element of their personal practice that helped them deepen their experience of *tefillah*, prayer. The invitation for this week is to choose an episode of the podcast and try out the practice described there. All of them are outstanding and can be found here: https://podcasts.apple.com/us/podcast/open-my-heart-living-jewish-prayer/id1542085651.

If you need a recommendation, perhaps consider episode 13, which features Rabbi Amy Eilberg sharing a meditation practice built on the words of the Priestly Blessing.

# Ki Tissa: How Do We Understand?

In his early 20th-century opera, *Moses und Aron*, Austrian-Jewish composer Arnold Schoenberg created a midrash on the story of the *Mishkan* and the Golden Calf. Schoenberg's libretto emphasizes the different ways the brothers relate to and represent language: Moses, who describes himself as "not a man of words" and "of uncircumcised lips," struggles with the need the people have for both linguistic and physical representations of an abstract deity. Aaron, on the other hand, is a priest, a man of the people, gifted with language, ritual, and the world of the senses. This passage is representative:

> Aaron: Chosen is this folk, thus to love one great god ever and ever, with a thousand times more devotion than all other earthly peoples for their many godly beings. Not be seen, not imagined. Folk chosen by the only one, can you worship what you dare not even conceive?
> Moses: Dare not?! Not conceived because unseen, can never be measured, everlasting, eternal, because ever present, and almighty. The one God is almighty.

Aaron understands the people's need to see something, to put it into human categories of sense and language, in order to experience it. Moses, by contrast, recognizes in that need a danger of limiting God, of making God in our image rather than the other way round.

This of course is a central tension of the series of Torah portions that encompasses both the building of the *Mishkan* and, jarringly in Parashat Ki Tissa, Israel's cardinal sin of idolatry in worshipping the Golden Calf. What do human beings need in order to understand the divine? What of the divine essence is lost in the effort to understand? And not only vis-à-vis God, but even other human beings: What is lost in translation, and what is gained? What standard of purity do we maintain, and what accommodations to human limitations are we willing to forgive? These are the stakes between Schoenberg's Moses and Aaron.

## Understanding and Forgiveness

This last theme of forgiveness is another central theme of the Torah portion. After the Golden Calf episode, Moses intercedes on behalf of the people to seek forgiveness from God who, in turn, teaches Moses a formula to recite—a set of words that over time became the centerpiece of Jewish liturgy during the High Holiday season in general and on Yom Kippur in particular. These are known as the Thirteen Attributes [*middot*] of Divine Mercy, and are enumerated in Exodus 34:6-7: "The Holy One passed before him [Moses] and proclaimed: 'YHWH, YHWH, the Divine, compassionate and gracious, slow to anger, abounding in kindness and faithfulness, extending kindness to the thousandth generation, forgiving iniquity, transgression, and sin.'" Commenting on this passage, the Talmudic sage Rabbi Yohanan offers the following midrash: "The Holy Blessed One wrapped Godself in a prayer shawl like a prayer leader and showed Moses the structure of the order of the prayer. God said: 'Whenever the Jewish people sin, let them act before Me in accordance with this order and I will forgive them'" (Rosh Hashanah 17b).

In a brilliant and intricate passage, Rabbi Levi Yitzchak of Berditchev (1740-1809) fuses together the themes of forgiveness, physical limitation, and the limitations and possibilities of language. He does so by means of drawing a parallel between the Thirteen Attributes [*middot*] of Divine Mercy and another collection of thirteen *middot:* the hermeneutical, or interpretive, principles [also called *middot*] of the second-century Sage Rabbi Ishmael ben Elisha. While these principles may not be as well known to us as the attributes of mercy, Levi Yitzchak's readers would have been familiar with them (indeed, these principles are recited as part of the daily morning liturgy in many communities). Knowing Rabbi Ishmael's thirteen principles is not necessary for following the passage, as we will explain the particular principles to which he refers in turn.

**קדושת לוי כי תשא יד-טז**

ויעבור ה' על פניו ויקרא כו' (שמות לה, ו). עיין ברש"י מלמד שנתעטף הקדוש ברוך הוא כשליח צבור. הנה אמר אדוני מורי ורבי מורינו הרב ר' דוב בער, כי שלש עשרה מדות שהתורה נדרשת בהן אחת הם עם הי"ג מדות אלו, ומדת קל וחומר הוא מדת אל, ומדת רחום הוא גזירה שוה, כי הכלל כאשר העשיר מרחם על העני אז צריך העשיר להשוות עצמו ולדבק עצמו בצער העני ובדחקות העני כדי לרחם על העני על ידי זה שמשוה עצמו לעני ובזה הוא רחמנות מן העשיר על העני ונמצא אז העשיר והעני הוא בשוה. וכן הוא כביכול אצל הבורא יתברך כנאמר (תהלים צא, טו) עמו אנכי בצרה, וזהו רחום גזירה שוה כנ"ל:

או יבואר, ויעבור ה' על פניו ויקרא כו'. והענין הוא, בוודאי אין הקדוש ברוך הוא בא בטרוניא עם בריותיו וישראל הם העיקר כמו שכתוב (בראשית רבה א) בראשית בשביל ישראל שנקראו ראשית. ואם היה השם יתברך דן לפי רוממות מדריגתם בעולמות העליונים וודאי

אי אפשר שיתקיימו אפילו שעה אחד בעולם, כי בוודאי שורש
נשמתם מחויב להיות מקודשים וטהורים מאד בכל מיני טהרה אך
כי אין צדיק כו', ובפרט אם היה רוצה לדון לפי מדותיו הקדושים
העליונים ולפי קדושתו הגדולה אשר הם צריכים לדמות צורה
ליוצרה שנקראו בנים למקום ובן של מלך צריך להתנהג בנימוסי
אביו אך על ידי שמרחם הבורא יתברך על ברואיו שמדת רחום
היא גזירה שוה שמשתלשל מחשבתו להעולמות עליונים ומסתכל
בהם ודן אותם כפי עולמות החומרים, כי רחום אותיות חומר ואז
בודאי מעורר רחמים עליהם כמו העשיר מסתכל בשפלות העני
וצערו ומשתלשל מחשבתו בו להסתכל בו אז מרחם עליו ונותן לו
כל צרכו. כך בהבורא יתברך שמו מתלבש מחשבתו בתוך הלבושים
בעולמות התחתונים ומרחם עלינו:

וזהו הרמז ויעבור, שעובר כביכול מפנימיות קדושתו והשתלשל
מחשבתו כביכול בתוך המדות המצומצמות בתוך העולמות ולבושים
שלנו אז ויקרא ה' ה' שנתמלא רחמים וחמלה וחנינה. וזהו הרמז
ברבותינו זכרונם לברכה שנתעטף הקדוש ברוך הוא, דהיינו כנ"ל
במדות ולבושים שלנו. וזהו ויעבור ה' על פניו, דפניו היינו עצם
התפשטות בהירתו בלי לבוש רק כל זה הוא מדה כנגד מדה אם
אנו עם קדוש רוצים להעלות מחשבותינו מתוך הלבושים רק לדבק
בשורשו עילת העילות ואם אנו חס ושלום הולכין ממדות שלנו אז
השם יתברך גם כן הולך ממדות שלו כביכול. וזהו שאמרו חכמינו
זכרונם לברכה אם אתם עושים לפני כסדר הזה כמו שאני עושה
וזהו לפני אזי אני גם כן אלך ממדות שלי לשלכם. וזהו גם כן הרמז
אני לדודי ודודי לי, ומובן מאליו ודו"ק:

### Kedushat Levi, Ki Tissa 14-16

My Master and teacher Rabbi Dov Baer (the Maggid of Mezritch) taught that the thirteen interpretive principles [*middot*]
through which the Torah is interpreted are identical with the
thirteen attributes [*middot*] of Divine mercy. For instance, the
interpretive principle of *kal v'chomer*, or *a fortiori* inference [i.e.,
"If one scoop of ice cream is tasty, then two scoops of ice cream
are obviously tasty"] is identical with the [Divine] attribute of
*El*. Likewise the [Divine] attribute of *rahum*, compassion, is
identified with the principle of *gezera shava* [deciding a case
based on an identical word in another case]. In general, when
one who is wealthy is compassionate toward one who is poor,
the wealthy person must identify with the poor one, connecting
with their pain and marginalization. In doing so, the wealthy
person and the poor person find their common humanity. We

can imagine that this is how the Divine relates to us, as the book of Psalms states, "I will be with him in moments of trouble" (Ps. 91:15). This is how the *middah* of compassion is the same as the *middah* of *gezera shava*.

Another interpretation: The Holy Blessed One does not deal tyrannically with His/Her/Their creations. The people of Israel is particularly central within creation, as the midrash (Bereshit Rabbah 1) teaches: "'In the Beginning'—meaning, for the sake of that which is the beginning, i.e., Israel, who are referred to as *reishit*, or first." If the Holy One were to judge them [Israel] according to the exalted nature of their being "first", it would be impossible for them to continue to exist for even a moment in the created world. The roots of their souls are planted in levels of holiness and purity, yet [as embodied people] they, like everyone else, cannot help but make mistakes. In particular, if God wished to judge by means of God's holy attributes, then accordingly Israel would be bound to follow the model of its Creator: Israel is referred to as *banim*, children of the Divine, and children of the king must conduct themselves with royal manners. Yet the Creator has compassion on His/Her/Their creations. The attribute of compassion (*rahum*) is the hermeneutical principle of *gezera shava*, meaning that the Divine connects the Divine thought to the upper realms, takes cognizance of them, and judges them according to the standard of the physical world. The word *rahum* (רחום) is made up of the same letters as *chomer* (חומר), the word for physical matter. In this manner God awakens God's compassion on Israel, like the wealthy person who looks upon the degradation and pain of the poor person and connects their thought to the latter, so that they may truly see them. The wealthy person then has compassion for them and gives them whatever they need. So, too, the thoughts of the Blessed Creator inhabit the lower worlds, comprehending them, and so God has compassion on us.

This is hinted at in the word *Vaya'avor*, "And God passed by." That is, God passes, as it were, from God's inward-facing holiness, extending the Divine mind to inhabit the limitations of our worlds and our embodied existence. Then: "And God called, 'YHWH! YHWH!'" That is, God was filled with compassion, mercy, and grace.[48] And this is what is hinted at the teaching of our Sages that the Holy Blessed One wore a tallit: that is, [God inhabited] the attributes and human limitations of our world. Further, this is what is meant by, "And the Holy One passed before his [Moses's] face," for the face displays a person's pure essence without any garb. All of this is measure for measure: If we, the Holy People, wish to raise up our thoughts from the dimensions of this world, we need cling to our roots on high alone. But if we, God forbid, [do not seek to live up to our exalted status, but] behave according to our own, this-worldly understanding, so too will the Creator behave according to the Creator's own attributes. This is what the Sages meant when they taught, "If you perform this order [that is, recite these thirteen attributes of compassion] **before** Me," that is, as I am [as I passed "before" Moses, displaying my full being], then I will likewise act towards you according to My attributes. This is likewise hinted at in the verse, "I am my beloved's and my beloved is mine" (Song of Songs 6:3).

This is an exceptionally rich interpretation. By juxtaposing the attributes of mercy with the interpretive principles of the Torah, Levi Yitzchak invites us to reflect on the ways in which the limitations of our human world—both physical and conceptual—intersect with questions of purity and impurity, perfection and imperfection. In his telling, the presence of the Divine in human life inherently involves an ongoing negotiation. God, as it were, must limit Godself in order to accommodate the dimensions and limits of the world (i.e., God is willing to connect emotionally to our human condition). Further, the interpretation of Torah, which is what enables it to live and breathe in the world and in our lives, and constitutes the means by which we discern the Divine will, is bound up with and even identical to the process of forgiveness (i.e., the thirteen *middot* of interpretation are identical to the thirteen *middot* of God's compassion). Putting the pieces together, we can summarize by saying that the translation of the infinite potential of divinity into human terms rests upon accommodation, which in turn rests upon forgiveness.

## Forgiveness, Understanding, and Relationship

We likely know this from our own experience of trying to communicate a

---

[48] In Jewish mystical teaching, YHVH is associated with Divine compassion—in contrast to God's name of Elohim, which is associated with judgment.

thought to another person—trying to find just the right words, tone, gesture, or other expression to convey our meaning. Think of how many times you may have said, "I'm sorry if that didn't land the way I intended," or "Forgive me—let me rephrase." (And if this is true in person, *kal v'chomer*, even more so is it true online!) Communication involves constant acts of forgiveness as we grope for the right expression and, inevitably, come up short or wind up doing unintended harm. Likewise, on the receiving end of a message, as we seek to understand our conversation partner, we both seek and offer forgiveness for the limitations in our understanding. We ask, "I didn't quite get that. Could you try explaining again?" We might be distracted and not giving our full attention, or we might presume bad intentions instead of giving the benefit of the doubt. Levi Yitzchak helps us to see that achieving understanding in communication is not only a lofty conceptual notion, but a manifestation of the presence of the divine in our own lives and language. The same acts of micro-forgiveness that allow language to function, and that allow Torah to be continually refreshed, also enable the relationship expressed through that language to endure.

Schoenberg intuited this in his depiction of Moses and Aaron. The tension between Moses's commitment to the pristine revelation and Aaron's under-standing that the people needed language and forms through which to relate to the Divine had the potential to break apart the people even more than it did (in the form of a civil war that killed 3,000 people). Yet ultimately the crisis was resolved through forgiveness—God's forgiveness of the people, Moses's re-engagement with them, and Moses ultimately inducting his brother as the High Priest. The Midrash relates,

> Israel says before God, "Who will give you to me like a brother for me?" (Song of Songs 8:1). We find that all brothers [in the To-rah] hate each other: Cain hated Abel... Ishmael hated Isaac... Esau hated Jacob... Joseph's brothers hated Joseph. So about which brothers is Israel asking when it asks God to behave with her like a brother? Like Moses and Aaron, as it is said, "How pleasant it is when brothers dwell together" (Ps. 133:1), for they dearly loved one another. At the moment Moses took the mantle of kingship and Aaron the mantle of the priesthood, they did not hate one another, but rather each was happy for the other's achievement. (Tanhuma Shemot 27:27)

At the end of the day, the two brothers were, it seems, committed to relating to one another. On the basis of that commitment, they found a way to accommodate and forgive one another and achieve some understanding—embodying the ongoing processes of forgiveness necessary for all of us to live in the world with each other, with the Divine, and with ourselves.

## Questions for Reflection & Conversation

- In explaining how the process of Divine empathy and self-limitation works, the Kedushat Levi twice invokes the metaphor of a rich person standing in the shoes, as it were, of a poor person, writing "the wealthy person must identify with the poor one, connecting with their pain and marginalization." Why do you think he chooses this particular metaphor? What is the nature of this relationship: in terms of power, in terms of self-image, in terms of attitude of one toward the other? What do you experience as you consider this image? Do you experience it as inviting, challenging, or something else? Is there another such image that you might employ to communicate the same interpersonal interaction and shift in self-regard?
- Schoenberg draws a (perhaps overly) sharp distinction between Moses, who in his rendering reflects commitment to pure thought, and Aaron, who embodies accommodation to human needs of language and physicality. Are you more drawn to one or the other of these personas? Do you find it a helpful dichotomy for explaining elements of your own life? How so (or not)?

- The Midrash Tanhuma cites Moses and Aaron with approval as unique among the brothers featured in the Torah. In your own life, are there people—whether siblings or friends or colleagues—with whom you have had profound disagreements while maintaining a bond of commitment and relationship? What about each of you enabled that relationship to work? How did you accommodate one another? How did you communicate that enabled the relationship to endure? Or, if the relationship needed to end, is anything about that experience reflected in this week's texts?

## Ideas for Practice

Many groups and organizations have developed communication norms or agreements that are intended to help them maintain a space that enables participants to be vulnerable with one another and take risks in order to achieve greater self-understanding and understanding in the minds of others. Below are guidelines developed by the Institute for Jewish Spirituality entitled "How we make for safety." Read them, and as you do consider how, if at all, you might enact some of these practices in an important relationship. Consider sharing them with the other person and making a shared intention to act with them in mind. What do you notice about the quality of your communication? Of the relationship? Of your level of trust and ability to understand and be understood?

- Presume and extend welcome. It is almost always challenging, in one way or another, to be part of a group. Good news: there is no "inside" and no "outside" to this group! Be aware, though, of such sensitivities in ourselves and in each other.

- Know that there is genuine freedom in this circle. We do not engage in "forced sharing." Every invitation to speak and participate is just that: an invitation. Passing or staying quiet is perfectly acceptable.

- We do not engage in "fixing, advising, saving or correcting" (Parker Palmer). Each of us is here to refine our ability to listen to the still, small voice inside. Trust that we will all find our own way.

- Give your full attention to the person speaking, whether in a small group or the group as a whole. Do not engage in side conversations. Use "I" statements when speaking. Be aware of how much space you are taking up.

- Respect difference. We are a truly diverse group. Notice judgment and practice experiencing it with compassion rather than conviction. (Remind yourself that other people are not failed attempts at being you!) Cultivate curiosity.

- Each person in the circle commits to both conventional and "double" confidentiality. Conventional confidentiality means that we do not speak to anyone outside the group about what is shared in this group. "Double" confidentiality means that when a person shares a confidence that we sense makes them vulnerable, we do not raise the issue again with that person or anyone else in the group, without the invitation of the person in question.

# Vayakhel-Pikudei: How Do We Work?

## Defining Work Through Shabbat

Concluding a rather long hibernation period after the opening verses of the Torah, Shabbat reappears to become a frequently-repeated theme of the Book of Exodus. It is mentioned in connection with the Mannah (ch. 16), the Ten Commandments (ch. 20), and the Ritual Decalogue (ch. 23). Significantly, Shabbat also forms the frame for the Torah's discussion of the construction of the *Mishkan*. God's instructions for building the *Mishkan* conclude with a commandment about Shabbat (Ex. 31:12-17), and in mirror fashion, the Torah's account of the actual building, which comprises the double-parashah of Vayakhel-Pikudei, begins with a discussion of Shabbat (35:1-3).

This framing seems quite deliberate. Rashi, quoting the midrash Mekhilta, teaches, "God intentionally told them about the prohibition regarding Shabbat before the command about the building of the *Mishkan* in order to teach that it [erecting the *Mishkan*] does not (supersede) keeping Shabbat" (Rashi, Ex. 35:2). One might have thought that the holy work of building the *Mishkan* was so important that it overrides Shabbat. The commandment comes to teach that it doesn't.

On another level, we might also observe, as traditional commentators and biblical critics alike have done, that the Torah's language in narrating the construction of the *Mishkan* is strikingly reminiscent of the opening chapters of Genesis. Instead of God doing and making and creating, now it is human beings who engage in the labor. And instead of God completing the work of Creation (Gen. 2:1-2), it is Moses who completes the work of building the *Mishkan* (Ex. 40:33). All of this suggests that the building of the *Mishkan* is a reciprocal gesture of creative labor, a way in which human beings enact our status as images of God.

The rabbis of the Talmud observed these parallels and derived from the work involved in building the *Mishkan* a whole system for identifying creative labor: The work prohibited on Shabbat is derived from the work of building the Tabernacle. The various processes involved in making fabric (required for Aaron's garments and the substance of the tent) or planting and harvesting wheat to ultimately bake bread (for the sacramental bread) or carrying (the poles) or writing (numbers on the poles) or building or hammering—in all the rabbis identified 39 categories of work involved in making the *Mishkan*, and from those categories they were able to determine what actions were prohibited on Shabbat.

## What Should Work Be?

But there's an inverse to this teaching as well. We should be concerned
not only with what is prohibited on Shabbat, but what our labor should look
like the other six days of the week. This is also a lesson we learn from the
*Mishkan*, elaborated beautifully in this passage from the Piaseczner Rebbe,
Rabbi Kalonymus Kalmash Shapira's *Aish Kodesh*:

**ספר אש קודש - פרשת ויקהל**

ויקהל משה את כל עדת ישראל ויאמר אליהם אלה הדברים אשר
צוה ד' לעשות אותם. ששת ימים תעשה מלאכה וביום השביעי
יהיה לכם קודש שבת שבתון לד' כל העושה בו מלאכה יומת
(שמות לה, א-ב):

ונודע הדיוק בספרים קדושים (עי' אור החיים שמות לא, טו, ותולדות
יעקב יוסף פר' וארא ד"ה ששת) למה הוצרך הכתוב לצוות על הששת
ימים תעשה מלאכה הא זאת מעצמם יעשו, ורק על השבת היה
צריך להם לצוות:

ואפשר לומר כי הגמרא (שבת ע. ושם צז: וברש"י שם) דורשת מאלה
הדברים מספר הל"ט מלאכות, דברים תרי, הדברים ג', אלה
בגמטריא ל"ו הרי ל"ט. כי הענין שדורשים הגמטריא מאותיות
התורה הוא מפני שאין כתב התורה להבדיל כשאר הכתבים
שבעולם, בכולם העיקר רק המכוון והמחשבה אשר בהם, אך כיון
שאי אפשר לכתוב את המחשבה כמו שהיא, לכן עושים אותיות
שהם רק רמזים אשר הסכימו לעשות, ובהם בונים תיבות לרמז
בהם על המחשבה והמכוון שרוצים, והאותיות רק רמזים בהסכמה
הם כנאמר לעיל, כי מה שהסכימו לעשות אות זה, היו יכולים
להסכים לעשותו אות אחר:

לא כן הם אותיות התורה הקדושה כל אות דוקא כמו שהוא
הוא ולא היה יכול להיות בצורה אחרת, ולא א' ב' ולא ב' א',
מפני שלא בלבד מחשבת ושכל התורה אשר בהם קודש, רק גם
הכלים והגופים היינו האותיות קדושות הן, הקדושה גם אל הכלים
התפשטה, וכשמתפשטת יותר אז גם מילואי האותיות מתמלאים
בקדושה, ולא האותיות בלבד רק גם הגימטריא קודש וגם חשבון
האותיות מאור התורה שלמדין מהם:

והנה נודע מזוהר הק' (ח"ג צד:) החילוק בין שבת ליום טוב, שיום
טוב הוא מקרא קודש שקוראים את הקודש ומזמנים אותו, ושבת
הוא בעצמו קודש, כמו שכתוב (שמות לא, יד) "כי קודש הוא לכם".
וגם זאת רואין שבשבת אין מצוה לעצמה - כמו בראש השנה
השופר, ביום הכפורים הה' עינוים, בסוכות הסוכה ודי מינים וכו' -
רק בזה שאין עושין מלאכה שעושין בששת ימי המעשה:

כי השבת גם מן ימי החול עושה קדושה, ועוד זאת שגם אל'
ששת ימי המעשה קדושת השבת נמשכת כנודע עד יום ד' מקבלים
משבת העבר, ומן יום ד' ואילך מן השבת הבא (פסחים קו.) היינו שגם
הגופים מתקדשים בשבת וגם ימי החול מתקדשים:
וזה אלמלי היו ישראל משמרים ב' שבתות מיד היו נגאלים (שבת
קיח:), לפי הנאמר לעיל שבת אחד - השבת, והב' השבת שבימי
החול, שנמשך להם קדושת שבת:
"ששת ימים תעשה מלאכה וכו' יהיה לכם קודש שבת שבתון", ב'
שבתות כנאמר לעיל, מפני שגם בששת ימי החול תמשכו הקדושה,
לכן באזהרה זו רמזה התורה כל הל"ט מלאכות בגימטריא, לרמז
(שכיון) שהכל נתקדש, עד שגם הגמטריא קדושה וגם ממנה תצא
תורה:

### Aish Kodesh, Vayakhel 5700 (1940)

Moses then convoked [the whole Israelite community and said
to them:] "These are the things that *YHVH* has commanded
you to do. Six days shall you do work, and the seventh day will
be holy for you, a day of solemn rest to the Holy One." (Ex.
35:1-2) Our holy books ask: Why did the text feel it necessary to
command labor on the six days—we would do this of our own
accord [without being commanded to work!]? It would appear
that we only needed to be commanded not to work on Shabbat.

One possible solution: The Talmud (Shabbat 70a) interprets
from *"eleh ha-devarim"* ("these are the things") the number
39 as the number of *avot melacha*, forbidden labors: *devarim*
(plural, suggesting two things), *ha-devarim* (the direct object,
*ha*, the, suggests one thing), and *eleh* (אלה) in *gematria* is 36:
thus 39. The basis of the notion of *gematria* is that the text of
the Torah is not like any other texts: In other texts, the essence is the intentional communication of the thought within
them. Since it is impossible to write thought in its true form,
the authors make letters—which are only symbols, agreed-
upon conventions—and from these they construct words to
symbolize the thought intended by the author. The letters are
only agreed-upon symbols, for just as [one culture] has agreed
that this letter will represent *this*, it could just as easily have
agreed upon another letter [for the same purpose].

But this is not so with the letters of the holy Torah, for every
letter in the Torah is precisely as it was meant to be; it would
have been impossible for it to be in any other form—*aleph*

could not be *bet*, and *bet* could not be *aleph*. For it is not only the thought and wisdom of the Torah which are holy, but holiness extends to the bodies [forming the words, communicating thought]—that is, the letters—as well. The holiness spreads even further, such that even the way we *spell* the names of the letters is holy. And not only the letters, but the *gematria*, too, is holy: even the calculus of the letters [which emerge] teach us of the light of Torah.

The Zohar (3:94 Emor) has made known the distinction between Shabbat and festivals (Yom Tov): Yom Tov is a *mikra kodesh*, a time *called* "holy", when we call out to the holy and invite it into our presence. But Shabbat is holy in and of itself, as the verse states, "For it is holy unto you" (Ex. 31:14). Further, we see that Shabbat has no *mitzvah* performance of its own— as we have with the shofar on Rosh Hashanah, for example, or the five afflictions of Yom Kippur, or the sukkah and four species of Sukkot, etc. Rather, the only observance we have is that we do not do the *melacha*, the labor, that we do on the six days of the workweek. For Shabbat makes holiness out of the six days of work. Moreover, the holiness of Shabbat extends into the six days of work, as it is taught that until Wednesday [i.e., midweek] we receive [spiritual energy from] the Shabbat of the previous week, and from Wednesday onward from the Shabbat to come. Thus, our bodies are made holy on Shabbat, and the days of work are made holy, too.

This is an expression of the notion (Shabbat 118b) that "If Israel would only keep two Shabbatot, they would be immediately redeemed." According to what we have said, the first Shabbat in this statement is Shabbat itself, while the second is the Shabbat within the days of the week, to which the holiness of Shabbat extends. "Six days shall you do work, and the seventh day will be holy for you, *shabbat shabbaton*, a day of solemn rest." Two Shabbatot are mentioned in the verse because the holiness of Shabbat extends into the workweek. In this manner, the Torah hints at all 39 labors through *gematria*, to teach indirectly that all can be made holy, even the *gematria*, and from it will emerge Torah.

The *Aish Kodesh* here weaves together two large themes: the relationship of Shabbat and the workweek on the one hand and a particular sensibility regarding the nature of the text and language of the Torah. Related to our starting point about work, Rabbi Shapira opens up an inversion of the corpus of prohibitions the rabbis derived from the construction of the *Mishkan*: It isn't only that such work is proscribed on Shabbat—it's also that our work during the workweek exists in relationship to the holiness and wholeness of Shabbat. Here the *Aish Kodesh* would seem to be elaborating on the halakhic, or Jewish legal concept, that the work proscribed on Shabbat is *melekhet makhshevet*. This is a phrase taken from Ex. 35:33 to describe the craftsmanship of Bezalel in building the *Mishkan*, but deployed by the Rabbis in a more literal sense to mean "purposeful work," or "work with intention." Only work that is done intentionally, with full awareness, is, according to the rabbis, biblically prohibited on Shabbat.[49] With the help of the *Aish Kodesh*, we can turn this around: If work prohibited on Shabbat is intentional, purposeful work, then by inference our work during the week is also supposed to be intentional and purposeful. This, I would suggest, is what he means (or could mean, at any rate) in saying that the holiness of Shabbat extends into and suffuses the workweek. "Six days shall you do work" is not a throwaway line—it is rather as much a part of the commandment as "and on the seventh you shall rest."

The *Aish Kodesh* links this understanding of holiness and work to his point about language. Often, we relate to language as instrumental. Words can change their meanings through changing social convention. That can be a depressing reality to consider because it means that, on some level, we are never able to fully communicate—to other people, to ourselves—the depth of our experience, what we truly feel and mean. But Rabbi Shapira invites us to consider approaching the language of Torah with a sense of the possibility of wholeness: Present in the language of Torah, whether because it is ontologically that way or because we agree to approach it as such, is the possibility for a far deeper, richer level of meaning and integration—the same kind of integration we experience through the completion we may sense on Shabbat and through the fulfilling work we perform during the workweek. Both hold the possibility for wholeness, and indeed wholeness is really only achievable through the braiding together of Shabbat and the workweek, rest and creativity, stillness and action, silence and speech.

In a recent book of reflections on everyday words, the contemporary writer

---

[49] See, for instance, Maimonides's Laws of Shabbat 1:9: "One who intended to pluck black figs but plucked [green] figs, or intended to first pluck figs and then grapes but the matter was switched and he plucked grapes first and then figs, is exempt. Even though he plucked all that he thought, since he did not pluck [them] in the order that he thought, he is exempt—as he did it without intention. For the Torah only prohibits thought-out work (*melekhet makhshevet*)."

and poet David Whyte offers an evocative meditation on the word *work*:

> To reduce work in our societal imagination merely to competi-
> tion, and to the act of beating the competition, is to condemn
> our societies, our communities and our individual lives to
> imaginative poverty of the very worst kind. In the real world
> it is also an isolating approach that closes off the possibilities
> of cooperation and conversation across scientific boundaries
> and artful borders. In the mystery of real contact and of real
> creativity, as in the lover's embrace, there is no abstract other
> and no competition. With the right work, the right relation-
> ship to that work and the mystery of what is continually being
> revealed to us through our endeavors, we find a home in the
> world that eventually does not need debilitating stress, does not
> need our exhausted will and does not need enormous amounts
> of outside energy constantly fed in to sustain it.[50]

I would suggest that Whyte here evokes a similar relationship to work as
the *Aish Kodesh*, one in which we are not separated from our labor, where we
do work without purpose. As Exodus reminds us, the work of our lives is
meant to be building a *Mishkan*. In everything we do we have the opportunity
to make a sanctuary for the Divine, to realize the life force flowing through
us and connecting us with the other beings of the universe. That was God's
work at the time of Creation—work from which God rested on the very first
Shabbat; and it is our reciprocal work throughout our lives, work from which
we rest on Shabbat every week. It is not only in resting that we emulate the
Divine—it is also in our work.

## Questions for Reflection & Conversation

- When have you felt most alive in your work? What was it about
  you at that time which enabled this feeling? What was it about
  the work? What, if anything, might prevent you from experiencing that sensation of alignment between soul and work on a more
  regular basis?

- In your experience, has meaningful, purposeful work during the
  week made Shabbat more meaningful for you? When, how, why

---

[50] David Whyte, *Consolations: The Solace, Nourishment and Underlying Meaning of Everyday Words*. Many Rivers Press, 2014, 244-245.

or why not? The Piaseczner suggests that Shabbat extends holiness into the week that follows it, yet is also made more holy by our intentional work during the week. Does this change how you understand—and might experience—Shabbat in your life?

- Can you paraphrase the *Aish Kodesh's* point about the language of Torah? What do you think he means when saying, "For it is not only the thought and wisdom of the Torah which are holy, but holiness extends to the bodies [forming the words, communicating thought]—that is, the letters—as well"? How do you imagine that "divine thought and wisdom" is present in every aspect of Torah? Have you ever seen this play out in a manner that was meaningful for you? Is this a useful idea for you—why or why not?

## Ideas for Practice

This week, consider keeping a journal. Each day, spend a few minutes completing the sentence, "Through my work today I made the Divine visible in the world when I _____." Write about what happened, what you did, what others may have done, what you noticed, how you felt. It could come through a conversation, a moment in a relationship, something you do with your hands or your body, something you make, something you give, space you help to hold or to make for others... See if each day you can notice a way in which your work, however you understand it, is purposeful, intentional, and holy.

# Vayikra: Whose Voice Do You Hear?

Readers of a certain age (I include myself) will likely remember the expression, "Tune in next time," or "stay tuned," from old radio and TV shows. It was another way of saying, "Come back here for the next part of the story." With the advent of cable TV and digital radio, much less Netflix and iTunes, "tune in" has been replaced by "stream." Yet it's worth recalling the origins of the expression: A signal was broadcast at a certain frequency and you, the radio or TV user, aligned the receiver on your set to receive that frequency and translate it into sound and/or pictures. Achieving that alignment was "tuning in," that is, getting things tuned up and in sync.

Getting the alignment right wasn't always easy. Depending on the sun or the clouds or the rain or even the wind that day, it could be easier or harder to get a clear picture. Or, in a car radio, depending on the distance one was from the transmitter, or if you were among tall buildings, or going under a bridge, the signal might be more difficult to receive. Some readers may even recall moving the "rabbit ears" of the television antenna ever so slightly while a relative sat on the couch saying, "Almost... a little to the left... Perfect—stay right there!" at which point one might even wind up literally standing in that place, as any deviation from the spot might affect the quality of the picture.

This process of tuning in became a wonderful metaphor for spiritual teachers, and for our purposes I'm bringing it back. The Divine voice is likened to the transmitter, always broadcasting a signal, while human beings are compared with the receiver, always needing to be tuned in to the voice. In particular, the Book of Leviticus that we begin this week offers one of the most sustained opportunities in the Torah for reflecting on the intimate voice of the Divine that resides within us, and the sometimes quite subtle movements of body, mind, and spirit necessary to hear it.

Rabbi Menachem Nachum of Chernobyl (d. 1797) offers us a teaching on the very first word of the book, which provides its name in Hebrew, *Vayikra*.

המאור עיניים, ויקרא

ויקרא אל משה וידבר ה' אליו מאוהל מועד וגו' ויש להבין
שמתחלה סתם ויקרא ולא פירש מי קרא ואחר כך פירש וידבר ה'
אליו, הנה העניין הוא שהשם יתברך הוציאנו ממצרים ונתן לנו תיכף
מצות פסח ומילה ואחר כך קרע לנו את הים ואחר כך הוליכנו
במדבר בעמוד ענן יומם ובעמוד אש לילה ואחר כך נתן לנו את
התורה ואחר כך צוה לעשות משכן כאמור (שמות כ"ה, ח') ועשו לי
מקדש ושכנתי בתוכם בתוכו לא נאמר כו' כמשל מי שהיה מעולם
במקום חושך ולא ראה אור מימיו אם היו מוציאין אותו פתאום

לאויר העולם לא היה יכול לסבול האור ולכן צריך להראות לו
בהדרגה שמתחלה עושין לו סדק קטן שיכול לראות משם מעט אור
ואחר כך מרחיבין לו הסדק עד שנעשה חלון ואחר כך מוציאין אותו
לאויר העולם ומראין לו האור כך ישראל במצרים היו משוקעים
בנ' שערי טומאה ואלו היה מראה להמתיקף זיו שכינתו לא היו
יכולין לסבול לכן הוצרכו לכל הדרגות הנ"ל ועיקר התכליתהיה
ועשו לי מקדש ושכנתי בתוכם וגו':

והנה אמרו רז"ל המהלך במקום סכנה מתפלל תפלה קצרה
בכל פרשת העבור יהיו צרכיהם לפניך וקא מפרש בגמרא אפילו
בשעה שהם פורשין לעבירה יהיוצרכיהם גלוים לפניך העניו הוא
שהבורא ברוך הוא מצומצם אצל כל אחד מישראל ואפילו אצל
רשע גדול יש אצלו עדיין הבורא יתברך והראיה שלכל רשע באים
לוהרהורים תשובה דהיינו שהקב"ה קורא אותו בעצמו ואומר שוב
אלי רק שאינו מבינשהשם יתברך קורא אותו:

וזהו ויקרא אל משה א(ל)"ף זעירא דהיינו שהשם יתברך
שהוא אלופו של עולם הוא מצומצם אצל כל אחד מישראל וקורא
אותו לשוב דהיינו הרהורי תשובהשבאים לו רק מפני שאינו מבין
שזה קורא אותו השם יתברך ב"ה לכן כתיב ויקרא סתם. אבל
כשמבין שזה קורא אותו השם יתברך לשוב מדרכו הרעה והוא
משיבעצמו אל הבורא יתברך אז אחר כך וידבר ה' אליו מאוהל
מועד לאמר דהיינו כשבא לעשות איזה עבירה והקב"ה מונע אותו
על ידי איזה סיבה שלא יוכל לעשות העבירה הרי הוא כמו שמדבר
אליו שובה אלי עד מתי תלך אחר הבליך וזהושאמרו רז"ל מתפלל
תפלה קצרה לקצר הקליפות הושע השם את עמך את וכו' אפילו
בשעה שהם פורשים לעבירה כו' וזהו שאמרו רז"ל תפשו הקב"ה
לירבעם חזור בך היינו בשעה שהיה בוגד שהיה עומד ומקריב
לעבודה זרה והוכיח אותו הנביא ורצה לשלוח יד בו ותיבש ידו
ולא יהיה יכול לעבוד עבודה זרה והיינו כמושאמר הקב"ה חזור
בך דהיינו במה שמנע ממנו כו':

## Meor Einayim, Vayikra

"And S/He/They called to Moses, and the Holy One spoke to
Moses from the Tent of Meeting, saying" (Lev. 1:1). Why does
the text begin by referring to God indirectly, with the third
person pronoun, without making clear who was calling out,
and only afterward clarifying that it was God?

The Divine brought us out of Egypt and immediately gave
us the commandments of Passover and circumcision, and soon
after split the sea for us, and after that brought us through
the wilderness with a pillar of cloud by day and a pillar of fire

by night, then gave us the Torah, yet [despite all that,] commanded us to construct the Tabernacle as the Torah states, "And they shall make me a sanctuary and I will dwell among them" (Ex. 25:8). It does not say, "And I will dwell in it," [rather it says, "I will dwell in them"—for the temple of God is the human, and from there it spreads to the Tabernacle.[51]]

The following parable may help: Consider one who lived where it was always dark, and had never seen light. If they were suddenly taken out into the sunlight, they would not be able to endure it. Instead, they would need light revealed to them little by little—first a crack in the window shade to let in just a little bit of light, then gradually wider and wider until the whole window was revealed, and then finally out into the world to see all the light. This was the situation for Israel in Egypt, who were mired in the lowest levels of impurity. If the Holy One had immediately revealed the entire brightness of the Divine presence, they would not have been able to take it. Instead, they required all of these stages [of revelation] leading to the ultimate goal: "Make me a sanctuary that I may dwell among/in them."

Our Sages taught (Mishnah Brachot 4:4): "Rabbi Yehoshua says: One who cannot recite a complete prayer because they are walking in a place of danger, recites a brief prayer and says: Redeem, Lord, Your people, the remnant of Israel, at every transition [parashat ha'ibur]. May their needs be before You. Blessed are You, God, Who listens to prayer." The Talmud (Brachot 29b) understands this to mean, "Even when they violate [ovrim] the commandments of the Torah, may all of their needs be before You." The notion here is that the Blessed Creator is present in every Jew. The Blessed Creator is present even in a very wicked person. The proof of this is that every wicked person still has stirrings of return and repentance within them—this is the Holy Blessed One personally calling out to them saying, "Come back to me." But they do not understand that it is the Holy One calling them.

In the written Torah, "And He called," Vayikra, is written with the letter aleph in small superscript. This is the Holy One, the aluf, or chief, of the cosmos, who is found in every

---

[51] Alshich Ex. 31:13:6

person and calls to them to return. We hear these murmurings of return, but we do not understand that it is the Holy One calling to us. This is why the verse states, "And s/he/they called to Moses" [using a pronoun and not a proper name]. But when we do understand that it is the Holy One calling to us, and we return from our incorrect ways and turn back to the Blessed Creator, then: "And the Holy One spoke to him from the Tent of Meeting saying." That is, when we come to do something not aligned with our best intention, and the Holy Blessed One prevents us from doing so by whatever means, it is like the Divine is saying to us, "Return to me! How long will you follow these unbecoming ways of living?" This is what the Sages of the Talmud meant in their instruction to say a short prayer [*tefillah ketzarah*]—that is, to prune away [*lekatzer*] the things that block us from our truest selves. Likewise, the Sages taught (Sanhedrin 102a) that the Holy Blessed One grabbed hold of the wicked King Jeroboam and said to him, "Turn away, and you and I and the son of Yishai will stroll together in the Garden of Eden." That is, this took place when Jeroboam was rebelling (I Kings 13), offering sacrifices to idols, and the prophet was rebuking him. In his anger, Jeroboam wanted to seize the rebuker. He reached out his arm to do so, but the arm became stiff, which made it impossible for him to offer any more sacrifices. All of this was as if the Holy Blessed One were saying to him, "Turn away!"

The heart of this teaching rests on the notion that the Divine is within each of us and that, as such, the Divine voice is within us too—we just need to tune in to hear it. For the *Meor Einayim* this reality is reflected in the special way the word *vayikra* is written in the Torah, with the last letter *aleph* appearing almost as a small footnote. That *aleph* represents the Divine residing within us, even when we may not be aware of it. The voice of the Divine is constantly broadcasting, calling out to us.

Perhaps most strikingly, the *Meor Einayim* situates this reality as the ultimate destination of the process of the Exodus. Rather than freedom from oppression at the Red Sea or even receiving the Torah at Mount Sinai, it is living with the awareness that we, ourselves, are the dwelling place of the Divine that constitutes the true purpose of all that has preceded it. All of the pyrotechnics in Egypt and at Sinai, the commandments of Shabbat and Manna and the rest of the Torah—all of it is in fact to prepare us to do the most important, yet finest work of all: to make our own hearts the sanctuary for the Holy One. Thus, God's voice is not outside us but is, instead, right inside—perhaps quite deep inside, but there. To hear it may initially require some gross movements (changing the channel of our behavior, as it were), but ultimately it comes down to some finer, subtler gestures: adjusting the rabbit ears a touch to the left or the right; standing just so. If we can attune ourselves to that voice, we can tune in to the broadcast emanating from our own hearts.

## Questions for Reflection & Conversation

- Have you ever had a moment when you were able to hear a voice deep within that you identified as something spiritual calling out to you? What happened? Was it pleasant, unpleasant, or something else? What was happening to you in the moment and/or what might you have done for yourself that perhaps enabled that voice to be heard?

- The *Meor Einayim* suggests that even people who commit truly wicked acts have this Divine voice calling to them from within. How does this notion sit with you? Do you find it inviting, challenging, or something else? If you agree, how does it affect the way you live your life? If you disagree, why?

- What do you find helps you to "tune in" to your inner voice? What hinders you from doing so? What is one step you can take to remove a hindrance and improve your ability to listen for that voice?

## Ideas for Practice

Consider a question you have about a choice of action to take. It may be about how to deal with an interpersonal situation. It may be about a career, professional, or work-related choice. It may be simply: how can I be my best self?

Situate yourself for meditation. Sit in a posture of dignity and ease, where you will be able to remain still and focused for a period of time. Bring your attention to the sensations of the body: where you come into contact with your seat; the sensation of the air or clothing against skin; the subtle sensations of the body—tingling, vibration or the like. Allow your attention to settle in the sensation of the breath moving in and out of the body.

In this posture of ease, bring to mind the question, choice, or quandary you are facing. Feel the sensation of uncertainty, of curiosity, of hopefulness, of fear—whatever is true for you. Allow those feelings to rest, without judgment, in your body, heart, and mind.

Express, internally, an intention for this period of meditation, perhaps something like: May the best outcome for this situation be revealed to me. Or: May I come to sense clarity in this situation. Or: May the truth that I know about what to do become evident to me.

Let go of thinking about this intention, and simply sit in meditation May the quiet in which you rest, and the intention you have set, attune you to a voice of truth for you. And, if not, you have not failed. You have meditated and set an intention. Who knows when the "answer" will be revealed?

# Tzav—Shabbat Hagadol:
# How Is This Night Different?

In most years, Parashat Tzav coincides with Shabbat HaGadol, the Shabbat immediately preceding Passover, which culminates a series of special Shabbatot. Before the month of Adar started, we observed Shabbat Shekalim, which served as a reminder of the collection in ancient times of the annual contributions used to fund the Temple in Jerusalem. Before Purim we observed Shabbat Zakhor, when we fulfill the commandment to remember what the Amalekites did to our ancestors after they left Egypt. Before the start of Nisan, we marked Shabbat Parah, a recollection of how our ancestors ritually prepared themselves for the Passover sacrifice. And two weeks ago, we observed Shabbat HaChodesh, marking the beginning of Nisan, the month of our redemption.

The series, and the drumbeat of anticipation and preparation that it signals, comes to a conclusion this week with Shabbat HaGadol, the Shabbat immediately preceding Passover, after which our attention shifts to the Seder and the days that follow. Yet the series of Shabbatot itself also invites us to consider the ways in which Shabbat and Pesach are related, and how the two interact. Beyond this, it invites us into related but distinct registers of reflection, particularly on the ways in which we nurture and experience liberation and redemption.

## Shabbat & Pesach, God & Nature, and Us

In his *Sefat Emet*, Rabbi Yehuda Leib Alter of Ger (1847-1905) frequently discusses Shabbat and its unique place in Jewish consciousness. Writing on Shabbat HaGadol 1889, he offered the following reflection on the relationship between Shabbat and Pesach:

שפת אמת, ב"ה מפ' אחרי שבת הגדול
בענין שבת הגדול שהי' שורש הגאולה ביום השבת. כי הגאולה
היא למעלה מסדר הטבע. שיש הנהגה עפ"י הטבע והשי"ת בחר
לבנ"י ההנהגה שלמעלה מהטבע. והוא הנהגתו בש"ק. כי בימי
המעשה הוא ע"י צמצומים בעשי' ובטבע וע"י מלאכים. ובש"ק
הוא הנהגה עליונה.
ויצ"מ הי' ע"י הקב"ה בעצמו אני ולא מלאך. והוא בחי' השבת.
לכן פסח נק' ג"כ שבת. לכן ש"ק הוא זכר ליצ"מ כדכ' וזכרת כי
עבד היית כו' ויוציאך כו' ביד חזקה על כן צוך כו' לעשות כו'
השבת. פי' כי הקב"ה הי' יכול לגאול את בנ"י בדרך הטבע ג"כ.

אך רצה למסור לנו הנהגה עליונה מאתו בעצמו והוא עדות כי
הנהגת השבת מיוחד לנו.

וע״ז אומרים אלו לא הוציא הקב״ה כו׳ הרי אנו ובנינו כו׳. ופי׳
מהר״ל ז״ל כי אם לא הי׳ הגאולה ע״י הקב״ה בעצמו הרי אנו
משועבדין ע״ש. והוא כנ״ל. שע״י שהיה בהנהגה עליונה שהוא
למעלה מהטבע והזמן.

א״כ לעולם יש זכר ליצ״מ. כי מה שהוא במקרה ועפ״י טבע
הוא בזמן ומקום ידוע. אבל יצ״מ שהי׳ מהקב״ה וב״ש בעצמו הוא
בכל הזמנים ובכל המקומות כנ״ל:

### Sefat Emet, Shabbat Hagadol

The roots of redemption are planted within Shabbat. For redemption takes place beyond nature. There is a guiding force
that happens through nature, but the Holy One opted to lead
Israel by supernatural means—this is how the Holy One behaves with us on the holy Shabbat. During the workweek, the
Divine consents to work through the physical world and the
laws of nature, indirectly. But on Shabbat God works with us
in a higher dimension [i.e., beyond nature].

The Holy Blessed One personally effectuated the Exodus
from Egypt, [as the Haggadah interprets], "I and not an angel."
This is an aspect of Shabbat. Thus, Passover is also called Shabbat.[52] Meaning: The Holy Blessed One could have redeemed
Israel by natural means. But the Divine wished to give us a
higher form of guidance from God's very self. This is how
God engages with us on Shabbat [beyond nature], which is
ours alone.

Thus, we say [in the Haggadah], "If the Holy Blessed One
had not redeemed us, we, our children, and our children's children would still be slaves to Pharaoh in Egypt." The Maharal
of Prague[53] interpreted this to mean: if God had not brought
about the Exodus "personally," directly, we would, even now,
still be slaves. And this accords with what we have taught here,

---

[52] This is a reference to Leviticus 23:15: "And from the day on which you bring the
sheaf of elevation offering—the day after the Sabbath—you shall count off seven weeks.
They must be complete." The verse itself refers to the counting of the Omer period,
which begins on the second night of Passover and continues until Shavuot. The Talmud
(Menachot 65b) infers from this that "the Sabbath" referred to in the verse therefore
does not refer to Shabbat, but to the first day of Passover.

[53] Rabbi Judah Loew (d. 1609)

that the Holy One led Israel by means of a higher form—one beyond the natural order of space and time.

If so, then there is always a remembrance of the Exodus from Egypt, for whatever takes place in the natural world happens in a certain time and place. But the Exodus from Egypt, which was performed by the Holy Blessed One Godself, is present to us in every time and every place.

The *Sefat Emet* seems to be elaborating on Shabbat as a nexus point of two narratives, two consciousnesses. In the first, Shabbat is *zekher l'ma'aseh bereshit*, a remembrance of the creation of the world. On Shabbat we step out of the artifice of the world that separates us from its divine roots: God created the world—and nature—and Shabbat points us back to the Divine and all which is "beyond nature." In the process, we are able to return to ourselves, to one another, and to the Divine in a restorative way. In the second consciousness, Shabbat is *zekher l'yetzi'at mitzrayim*, a remembrance of the Exodus from Egypt. In parallel fashion to the Creation-oriented consciousness, this Exodus orientation invites us to step out of the ways in which we may be enslaved to things other than the truest reality, to re-embrace our status as creations in the Divine image. In our liberation, we connect intimately with our true nature, which is "beyond nature." These two consciousnesses are ultimately one: Shabbat is a practice of freedom to return to our deepest self.

Yet Pesach adds an additional dimension, a heightened focus to this practice of Shabbat. While every Shabbat invites us to cultivate and live in this liberatory consciousness, Pesach—referred to as *haShabbat, the* Sabbath—calls us to attune ourselves even more to this theme. On Pesach we are invited to reflect in a singular way on the reality that it was not some accident of history that enabled us to be free—or, indeed, that enables any of us to be truly free. Rather, our freedom comes through realizing that the Divine indeed works in and through us, while holding out an image, an aspiration, for that which is beyond nature (the social and societal conventions we experience as "natural"). When we can genuinely sense that, we can embrace our own liberation—and work for the liberation of others. That is the miracle of Pesach, the bread that all of us who are hungry are invited to come and eat.

## From Inner to Outer Liberation

This is resonant with a message in much contemporary work that links mindfulness and liberation. Zen priest and activist Rev. angel Kyodo Williams, for instance, talks about the relationship of inner, personal liberation and outer, or political freedom:

> Understanding that part of our capacity to make change outside in a way that's actually generative comes from having done work inside so we can actually have empowerment that doesn't have to do with external conditions. We actually have models for it on a grand scale. All people admire Nelson Mandela for his refusal to be imprisoned in his own being, which enabled him to come out of prison after twenty-eight years, which then gave room for a level of change to happen on a social level... We have to commit to our own liberation regardless of what happens outside. And paradoxically, that gives way to change happening outside.[54]

Pesach is an invitation to, perhaps even a demand for, just this kind of inner work. From our search for *hametz* to our noticing how *this* night, this moment, is different from all others, to the stories we tell and the reflections we engage in so that we may genuinely see ourselves leaving Egypt *right now*, Pesach is an opportunity to bring renewed and deeper attention to our truest nature as liberated beings—aware of our own freedom and, in love and compassion, helping all beings to realize theirs.

## Questions for Reflection & Conversation

- The *Sefat Emet* writes, "During the workweek, the Divine consents to work through the physical world and the laws of nature, indirectly. But on Shabbat God works with us in a higher dimension." How would you paraphrase this in your own words? Have you ever had a sense of the Divine working with or through you in a different way on Shabbat? When? How so? What did you do, if anything, to nurture such an experience? If this way that God works "in a higher dimension" is "beyond nature" do you sense that it is even possible to attain this experience through your own efforts? If so, how? If not, why not?

- Rev. angel Kyodo Williams writes, "We have to commit to our own liberation regardless of what happens outside. And paradoxi-

---

[54] angel Kyodo williams, Rod Owens and Jasmine Syedullah. *Radical Dharma: Talking Race, Love, and Liberation.* North Atlantic Books, 2016, 53.

cally, that gives way to change happening outside." How does this passage land with you? Do you find it inviting, challenging, or something else? Why or why not?

- Do you find yourself drawn more toward a notion of Shabbat as a remembrance of Creation, or as a remembrance of the Exodus? How do you understand the difference between the two? If, as the *Sefat Emet* suggests, Passover brings a special focus to a quality of Shabbat present every week—or even in every moment—how would you describe that special focus? What is the special opportunity of Passover?

## Ideas for Practice

There is no shortage of good Jewish meditations and mindfulness practices for Seder night. Yet we sometimes focus on the Seder so much that we may overlook the preparatory work that comes before it, especially at a spot that is this nexus of creation, oppression, and liberation: the kitchen. For many people (certainly for me!), cleaning and preparing the kitchen for Passover is a daunting task—and that's *before* we even get to cooking all the food! Sometimes we can be overwhelmed by it, and we undertake both the preparation and the cooking in a mindless, begrudging, even angry state of mind.

So, here's a practice from my IJS colleague Rabbi Myriam Klotz. Before beginning the preparations in the kitchen—or, really, anytime—allow yourself to sit in your kitchen. You might sit on a chair or on the floor. You might be alone or with a partner or other family member. Allow yourself to find a dignified posture. Perhaps soften your gaze or close your eyes. Find an anchor in your breath, a point of contact between your body and the chair or floor, or in a sound. Sit for a couple of minutes and allow your mind to settle, however much it may. Then, when you're ready, open your eyes and look around slowly, taking in the kitchen without judgment. Notice what's here. Notice what emotions are present. Then, when you're ready, close your eyes or soften your gaze again with an intention to enter into the work of Pesach with compassion—for yourself, for your loved ones, for your community, for all beings. Perhaps allow yourself to feel the presence of ancestors who may have engaged in this same work of cleaning and cooking and liberating. See if you can extend compassion to them as well. Consider how this kitchen, however you may be in it, might be a place of liberation.

Try to sit for 18 minutes total—the amount of time in which matzah is required to be baked, from the moment the flour touches water.

# Shemini: How Do We Develop Wisdom?

You may recall the essay from Parashat Vayetzei, in which I cited a letter from the Six Nations to the colonial governments of Virginia and Maryland after the French and Indian War. The Native Americans politely passed on the colonists' invitation to send their sons to the College of William and Mary because, in their view, their young men would learn nothing of value to them and in fact come back less useful than when they left. Having spent most of my adult life as a student and professional in and around American higher education, I don't necessarily have quite so low an opinion of universities. I do think there's an important dimension of much discussion about higher education that's missing—one which those Native American leaders pointed to, namely wisdom.

Wisdom is different than intelligence or skill. It is not something one masters through book knowledge or degrees, or even through the critical thinking required to write a doctoral dissertation. Wisdom is as much about attitude and disposition as it is about intelligence. It is about developing, as King Solomon prayed for while a young man (I Kings 3:9), a "listening heart." It is typically associated with age, but as Solomon's example shows, it can also be developed even while young.

## Wisdom & Youth

How do we develop wisdom? And are the dimensions of age and experience part of the answer? These are our questions this week, as we look at the story of Nadav and Avihu. These two sons of Aaron make an unauthorized incense offering shortly after the consecration of the *Mishkan* and tragically die as a result. What wisdom did they lack—and what wisdom might they have to teach us?

We begin with a teaching of Rabbi Mordechai Yosef Leiner of Izhbitz (1801-1854) in his *Mei HaShiloach*:

**מי השילוח א, שמיני**

ויהי ביום השמיני וכו'. ויקחו בני אהרן נדב ואביהוא וכו'. ענין מיתת נדב ואביהוא הוא ע"פ מה דאיתא (באבות) (תמיד ל"ב.) איזהו חכם הרואה את הנולד. הענין בזה אף שנאמר (דברים י"ח, י"ג) תמים תהיה עם ה' אלקיך ונתפרש שם שלא ירבה להתחכם, אך רואה את הנולד הוא, בזה המעשה עצמה שהוא עושה יחקור ויתבונן אם המעשה והרצון הזה הוא מבורר שיהיה קיים כן לעולמי עד אפילו לעוה"ב.

וענין קטורת הוא כדאיתא בזוה"ק (במדבר קנ"א:) מאי קטורת קטירא
דכולא, היינו שהש"י הוא תוך כל המעשים שנעשו מבריאת העולם
ועד סופו, ובלתי רצונו לא יעשה שום דבר, וע"ז מורה ענין קטורת
כמו שנתבאר בפ' תצוה [ד"ה ועשית].

ובאמת כפי מה שהאדם מקרב עצמו לה', כן זוכה להתגלות
אור ה' מבלי לבושים שהם גדרים וסייגים, כי באור הברור, שם לא
נמצא שום סייג ואיסור, ושם כל מעשה האדם מבוררים שהם לה'.
וזהו ענין קטורת שהיה סוד ואסור להתחכם בזה, כי רק ר' עקיבא
ירד בשלום (חגיגה י"ד:)

וזה שנאמר (ויקרא ט"ז,א') בקרבתם לפני ה' וימותו, שהיו מקרבים
עצמם לה' והסתכלו בעומק הצפון ורצו לעמוד על בירור התנהגות
הש"י, ולזה הטעם על לא צוה אותם הוא מרכא כפולא, היינו שכל
כך בער בלבם אהבת ה' עד שמסרו נפשם, כי מרכא היא לשון רך
שלבם נתרכך, וכפולא היינו כפול ברוב טובה אשר לא צוה הש"י.

ולפי שהיו צעירים לימים ולא אנסיבי ולא אתכללו במשה
ואהרן כדאיתא בזוה"ק (שמות ל"ז:), ולא נטלו עצה, ולזה הפלוגתא
(בגמ') חד אמר שתויי יין היו היינו שיש לטעון על קרבותם שהיתה
ח"ו מקלות ראש, או שהיתה כוונתם שיוסר מהם עול הגדרים כמו
שנתבאר, וגם מאמר המדרש שהיו מחוסרי בגדים ומה היו חסרים
המעיל (ויקרא רבה פרשה כ',ו') אף שהמעיל אינו רק לכהן גדול רק הם
הכניסו עצמם למקום שהיו צריכים למעיל, והבן

## Mei HaShiloach, Shemeni 1

The death of Nadav and Avihu can be understood by the Talmudic teaching, "Who is wise? One who has foresight" (Tamid 32a). This teaching in the same spirit as [the commandment], "Be wholehearted with the Holy One" (Deut. 18:13), which is understood to mean, [Accept whatever comes to pass and do not seek to control the future].[55] So how is having foresight praiseworthy? It is that in *this action*, the action you do *right now*, you should investigate and reflect whether your action and desire are clearly aligned in such a way that they will stand the test of time, even unto the world to come.

The Zohar teaches that the incense offered in the *Mishkan* binds everything together. This signifies that the Divine is within everything that has taken place since the Creation of the World, and so also to its very end; nothing takes place that is not the will of the Creator.

---

[55] The *Mei HaShiloach* seems to be referring to Rashi's interpretation of the verse in Deuteronomy. Our translation follows Rashi's comment there.

To the degree a person offers themselves to the Divine, they will merit revelation of the Divine light without any obstruction—without hedges and fences.[56] For in the refined light one perceives no barrier, no prohibition. And in that light one sees that all one's actions are for the sake of the Divine. This is reflected in the incense, which is a fundamental mystery and about which it is forbidden to reason. For only Rabbi Akiva returned intact from his encounter with fundamental mystery.[57]

[Now we can understand what happened to Nadav and Avihu.] The Torah relates that "they came before the Holy One and died" (Lev. 16:1)—that is, they drew close to the Holy One, looked into the hidden depths and wished to understand, with clarity, the ways of the Divine in the world. This is the reason that the words "did not command them" (לא צוה אתם/ lo tzivah otam) are notated with the unique cantillation mark mercha kefula—namely, the love of the Divine burned so intensely in their hearts that they gave up their lives: the מרכא/ mercha denotes that their hearts were רך/rach, soft; כפולא/kefula signifies that they were כפול/kaful, wrapped in God's great goodness—but precisely that depth of goodness which we are commanded not to investigate.

[The mistaken behavior of] Nadav and Avihu [arose because they] were young and inexperienced (N.B. literally "unmarried") and did not apprentice themselves to Moses and Aaron or take their advice. In this light the Sages disagreed: One interpretation is that they were drunk—meaning that their drawing near to God was done in a state of frivolity, God forbid; [the other holds] that they wished to remove from themselves the yoke of the legal fences, as we explained above. And the Midrash deepens this point when teaching that when they brought their offering, they were not wearing the High Priest's robe. Yet would they have needed the High Priest's robe, as they were not the High Priest? [Rather the midrash comes to

---

[56] Hedges and fences also a refer to common rabbinic language used to describe the nature of law, e.g., "Make a fence for the Torah" (Avot 1:1).

[57] This is a reference to the Talmudic passage on Hagiga 14b that teaches that four Sages entered the Pardes (literally orchard, but here meaning the mystical realms): Ben Azzai, Ben Zoma, Elisha ben Abuya, and Rabbi Akiva. Of these, only Rabbi Akiva returned intact.

teach that] they brought themselves to such a spiritual state
that they should have worn the robe.

The first part of this teaching rests on a reminder that Nadav and Avihu
specifically brought an offering of incense, which, according to rabbinic
teaching, was one of the great mysteries of the Temple. This observation
leads the Izhbitzer to gesture at a level of reality within which there are no
contradictions—no fences, no hedges, no obstructions. At that mysterious
level, it seems, difference dissolves into a Divine unity and all is one. For the
Izhbitzer, that level is where one finds ultimate truth—hence his assertion,
which is fundamental to his theology, that "nothing takes place which is
not the will of the Creator." At the deepest level of mystery, beyond human
comprehension, nothing exists apart from the Divine.

That, of course, could lead the Izhbitzer to claim that Nadav and Avihu
in fact did right—for, in light of such a recognition, how could we even say
wrong exists? They were simply doing God's will! Yet he doesn't go that far.
Rather, he follows Rabbinic tradition in judging that Nadav and Avihu did
something wrong. In his eyes, while their impulse to experience ultimate
unity was well-intentioned, it was immature—and manifestly dangerous.
This brings us back to his opening point about foresight, which is one of the
key messages for us: "In *this action*, the action you do *right now*, you should
investigate and reflect whether your action and desire are clearly aligned
in such a way that they will stand the test of time, even unto the world to
come." This was what Nadav and Avihu could or would not do. If they had
been older, had some more experience, humbled themselves more before their
elders—then they would, perhaps, have had more perspective with which to
evaluate their actions and realize that they would not stand the test of time;
that however well-intentioned they were, something was off. However much
their hearts told them this was the right thing to do in the moment, that
missing dose of maturity would have helped them see that they were literally
playing with fire and about to get fatally burned.

It is important to note that the Izhbitzer does not come down hard on
Nadav and Avihu (and indeed, in other places in his commentary, he shows
a profound sympathy for the energetic, unbounded spirituality of youth). At
the same time that he conforms to the interpretive tradition that sees them
as having done something rash and wrong, he also holds up what he reads
as their noble intentions. In doing so, I believe he invites us into a reflection about truth, impulsiveness, humility, learning, wisdom, maturity. For
many of us, there is unquestionably something lost as we grow up, as our
prefrontal cortexes finally come to completion and we develop the capac-

ity of foresight—spontaneity, exuberance. I can certainly think of things I did in my youth (or that I see my own children do now) and judge now as, well, dangerous and pretty stupid. I imagine you might be able to do so, too. They were often moments of transgression, when I didn't pay attention to boundaries—or when boundaries simply seemed to fade away. Yet in that unboundedness, those were also delightful, amazing, memorable moments of discovery and living! Would I rather I hadn't taken wild risks I took in my youth? Would you? (I hasten to add: There is a crucial ethical difference between unbounded and potentially foolish moments of youth where the victim is oneself, and moments that involve inflicting physical, sexual, or profound emotional harm on others. In this exploration I am dealing only with the former category.)

## Wisdom as a Conversation Between Generations

The Native American poet Duane Niatum opens his poem, "Consulting an Elder Poet on Writing an Anti-War Poem," which he dedicated to his teacher, the poet Elizabeth Bishop, this way:

> One day you said to me,
> "there's nothing you can do,"
> and recited Auden's line:
> "Poetry makes nothing happen."

Niatum closes the poem this way:

> Fifteen cobalt-blue years later,
> I must ask myself, if the dust
> and rubble of each new war
> that settles in our bones
> and deadens a generation,
> are little more than negatives
> of the Kennedys, King and Lennon,
> has less weight than what
> we felt the day the Apollo spaceship
> landed on the moon,
> and Auden's line is true,
> then why did you til your last breath,
> sing into your ruin?[58]

[58] Duane Niatum, "Consulting an Elder Poet on an Anti-War Poem." *Drawings of*

Niatum points us toward one additional dimension of this question of foresight, maturity, spontaneity, and wisdom, which is its fundamentally intergenerational nature. Recall that the midrash the Izhbitzer cites mentions that one of the reasons for Nadav and Avihu's demise was that they were not in relationship with their elders, their father Aaron and their uncle Moses. That would seem to be a failure of both the students and the teachers. Yet it also reflects a reality about the difficulty of forming and sustaining the intergenerational relationships through which wisdom is developed and realized. As Parker Palmer writes, "Truth is an eternal conversation about things that matter, conducted with passion and discipline."[59]

Youth, the Torah seems to remind us here, has a vital role to play of enabling fresh vision, in raising the question, *Why not?* which is as essential to wisdom as the question, *Why?* Age likewise needs to listen to it—not only in a political sense, but in an experiential one as well. We might hear in this the idea of beginner's mind, our capacity to see things afresh even when we are laden with experience. The lesson of Nadav and Avihu is thus not simply a sermon about the rash behavior of youth, but about the truth they sought and the responsibility of elders to make space for the truth of their questions to be heard, in order that wisdom may continue to develop and live.

### Questions for Reflection & Conversation

- Who is one older person with whom you had direct contact who modeled wisdom for you when you were a younger person? Are there things about them that you try to emulate? What are they? Were there things about yourself that enabled your relationship with them to cultivate wisdom within you? What were they?

- How are you—or how might you hope to be—an elder who creates space for wisdom to emerge in relationship with younger people? Are there elements of being a wise elder that come more naturally to you? Are there elements you find harder? What makes them easier or harder for you?

- The Izhbitzer describes foresight—which, for our purposes, we might also call wisdom—this way: "In *this action*, the action you do *right now*, you should investigate and reflect whether your

---

*the Song Animals: New and Collected Poems.* 1991.
    [59] Palmer, *The Courage to Teach*, 130.

action and desire are clearly aligned in such a way that they will stand the test of time, even unto the world to come." Does this resonate with you? How does this definition land with you? Do you agree? How do you understand what he means by invoking "the world to come?" If you would amend or alter his words, how would you do so and why?

### Ideas for Practice

As a journaling exercise for yourself this week, consider writing a letter exchange with your younger self. You can start from your position now, as an older person writing to a younger you, or feel welcome to start as your youthful self, writing to your older self. As preparation, the following may be helpful.

- Consider your older self, meeting your younger self. Allow whatever images of that younger self you carry to come to mind and heart. Are there "iconic" photos you recall, or specific events that come to mind? What feelings arise in response to these images and memories? Even if there is pain associated with some of these earlier moments, open your heart to hold them—and so your younger self—with love.

  Turn to this younger self, and say: "Oh, (insert your name). How much fun you had! You took such joy in X / you were so enamored of Y / you dedicated yourself to Z. You had such hope/courage/passion."

  Bring those memories, and your appreciation of them fully to heart and mind. Really enjoy them. Feel your love for that younger self. Now, tell that self how those experiences are still alive in you—or how they are no longer, and why—or how they are no longer, and how you feel about that.

  It may be that your response to those memories emerges thus: "Oh, (insert your name)! How careless you were—or you took such risks—or you hid yourself so much. How sad/lonely/discouraged you were."

  Bring those memories, and your awareness of their painfulness fully to heart and mind. Really take them in. Feel your compassion for that younger self. Now, tell that self how those experiences are still alive in you—or how they are no longer, and why—or how they are no longer, and how you feel about that. How, if at all, did you grow from those experiences? Can you look back on your younger self and say: "It got better"?

Listen deeply for whatever else may emerge.

- Consider your younger self meeting your older self. Try to recall how you imagined your future life would unfold. How did you think things would work out for you? Is the work that you are doing, the relationships you have had (or haven't had), what you imagined? Recall what you thought the world you were growing into would become.

  Turn to your older self and say: "Oh, (insert your name)! When I look ahead there are so many possibilities; there are so many options for me; there is so much I want to do. How did I become you? What part of me now is still alive in you? What did you learn from me? Does anything I'm doing really matter in the end, to you?"

  Feel your yearning, your anxiety, your curiosity. Tell your future self what you wish might persist, which parts of yourself you cherish now. Explain how you know, deep down, that some of your "foolishness" back then was not "really you." Open up to the possibility that back then you really didn't know anything about yourself, and were flailing about for hope and clarity.

  Ask your future self for help. "What shall I hold on to? What can I let go of? What can I do to undo shame, to lift up honor, to live freely? Help me find my way."

  Listen deeply for whatever may emerge.

# Tazria-Metzora:
# What Does Nature Mean To Us?

## Spirituality & The Natural World

Here's a fascinating nugget from a recent major study about Americans' spiritual lives sponsored by the Fetzer Institute: 63 percent of Americans said that they frequently feel touched by the beauty of creation. That's nearly two-thirds of Americans who say they have some kind of moving relationship with the created world. When the results are filtered by respondents' description of themselves as "spiritual and religious," "spiritual only," "religious only," and "neither spiritual nor religious," the results are striking: 74 percent of "spiritual and religious" people say they feel touched by the beauty of creation frequently, while 63 percent of "neither spiritual nor religious" people say they never do.[60]

This suggests a strong correlation between the degree to which Americans understand themselves as spiritual people and the frequency with which they relate to the created world with a sense of appreciation for its beauty—and responsibility. The survey authors note, "the more a person feels accountable to a higher power for their impact on others and the natural environment, the more likely they are to believe community and civic action is important, and engage in community, civic, and political behaviors themselves… Expectedly, most people who do not believe in a higher power do not feel accountable to one for their impact on others or the natural environment."[61] (They also note that there are people who believe in a higher power but don't feel responsible for the natural environment.)

When do we feel connected to the natural world? How does that connection deepen our awareness of and relationship with the divine life force? And how does a life of Torah and *mitzvot* both depend on and contribute to such an awareness and relationship?

## Spirituality & Embodiment

Parashat Tazria invites a reflection on these questions for several reasons. First, it comes immediately on the heels of the conclusion of Parashat Shemini, which detailed the commandments about animals which are permitted

[60] The Fetzer Institute. *What Does Spirituality Mean to Us? A Study of Spirituality in the United States*. Kalamazoo: The Fetzer Institute, 2020, 54.
[61] Ibid. 87

and forbidden to eat. Second, like the book of Leviticus in general, Parashat
Tazria speaks to us as embodied beings, part of nature and yet also distinct
from it. As Nehemia Polen teaches, "Leviticus offers an alternative way of
knowing, an embodied spirituality that highlights space, demonstrative gesture, and gift-giving as touchstones of religious life. Rather than assuming
the betterment of the human condition will take place by means of education
and the promulgation of ideas, it relies on proximity and access to a locus of
transformative energy and spiritual power to effect positive change. It avoids
the didactic voice so common elsewhere in Judaism and instead celebrates
immersive action."[62] In other words, from the very embodied actions of the
sacrifices and rituals to the physicality of the commandments about sexuality and the sabbatical year, Leviticus is grounded in *gashmiyut,* the material
nature of the world, even as it offers us ways to imbue that *gashmiyut* with
*ruchnyiut,* spiritual reality.

In his *Maor VaShemesh,* Rabbi Kalonymus Kalman Epstein (1751-1823)
develops an interpretation of the opening verses of Parashat Tazria that helps
us reflect more deeply on the connections between the physical and spiritual
dimensions of our lives as beings who are part of the larger creation. He
does so by noting the connection between the concluding verses of Parashat
Shemini and the opening verses of our parasha. He will then draw our attention to the vision of the prophet Ezekiel and use it to further explain the
spiritual connections that emerge through our embodiment.

**מאור ושמש תזריע**

עוד בפסוק הנ"ל אל משה לאמר גו' אשה כי תזריע וילדה
זכר כו' מדרש והובא ברש"י ז"ל אמר ר' שמלאי כשם שיצירתו
של אדם אחר כל בהמה חיה ועוף במעשה בראשית כך תורתו
נתפרשה אחר תורת בהמה חיה ועוף אף שדברי המדרש הלז
נראים פשוטים יש לנו דברים בגו [לפרשו עפ"י רמז וסוד ונקדים
לבאר סמיכת הפרשיות מה שסיימה הפרשה הקודמת זאת תורת
הבהמה והעוף וכל נפש החיה הרמשת במים ולכל נפש השורצת
על הארץ להבדיל בין הטמא ובין הטהור ובין החיה הנאכלת ובין
החיה אשר לא תאכל הדקדוקים רבו מפני מה נאמר וזאת תורת
הבהמה והעוף ולא נאמר ביניהם חיה רק כאמר בפ"ע וכל נפש
החיה הרומשת במים ולא נאמר נפש חיה הרומשת על הארץ ומה
הוציאה מן הכלל כי אח"כ נאמר ולכל נפש השורצת על הארץ

---

[62] Nehemia Polen, "Touches of Intimacy: Leviticus, Sacred Presence, Torah's Center." Green, Arthur and Ariel Evan (eds) Mayse. *A New Hasidism: Branches.* Jewish Publication Society, 2019, 44.

ולא נאמר נפש החיה גם מה שנאמר בזו הסדרה כל מקום החיה
כמו כל נפש החיה ובין החיה הנאכלת ובין החיה אשר לא תאכל
כולה נאמר החיה בה' ידיעה מה ששייך הה"א ומה הודיע לנו בה
גם בתחילת הפרשה נאמר דברו אל בני ישראל לאמר זאת החיה
אשר תאכלו מכל הבהמה אשר על הארץ ומדרש רבותינו ידוע
ללמד שבהמה בכלל חיה ועדיין יש ללמוד מה בשנותו את טעמו
דווקא כאן ללמד שהבהמה בכלל חיה הול"ל במקום אחר]

ונראה לי לפרש כי ידוע דכל דבר שהוא בעולם התחתון יש לו
שורש מלמעלה כי כל עשב יש לו כוכב הממונה עליו מלאך שאומר
לו גדל כמו כן דומם צח"ם הכל נשרש בעולמות עליוניות וכל דבר
אשר יש לו נפש חיה כמו בהמות חיות ועופות המה בשרשם בחיות
הקודש שבמרכבה הקדושה וע"י האדם העוסק בתורה ומצות ה'
יתברך הוא מדבק ומקשר הכל למעלה בשורשו וממשיך השפעה
וחיות מעילא לתתא לכל דבר ודבר באכילת הצדיק שהוא אוכל
מאכליו בקדושה ובטהרה מדבק כל דבר בשורשו כל מאכל ומאכל
בשורש השייך לאותו מאכל

וזהו שאמר הכתוב ביחזקאל ומתוכה דמות ארבע חיות וזה
מראיהן דמות אדם להנה ועוד נאמר שם ודמות פניהם פני אדם
ופני ארי' אל הימין לארבעתם ופני שור מהשמאל לארבעתן ופני
נשר לארבעתן ופי' רש"י מפני מה נאמר דמות אדם להנה הא כמו
כן היה דמות ארי' ושור ונשר ופי' רש"י מפני שדמות אדם הוא
דמות יעקב אבינו הוא החשוב שבכולם מפני כן אמר דמות אדם
להנה

ועפ"י דברינו ידויק על נכון כי כל נפש החיוני' אשר על הארץ
כמו הבהמות וחיות ועופות המה בשרשם בחיות הקודש שלמעלה
כמו החיות בשורש ארי' שבמרכבה והבהמות בשורש שור שבמרכבה
ועופות בשורש נשר שבמרכבה והכל הוא נשרש למעלה ע"י האדם
המקשר הכל למעלה זהו שנאמר דמות אדם להנה וזהו שנאמר
ופני ארי' אל הימין כי ארי' הוא הגבור שבחיות והוא מדת גבורה
ע"כ הוא בימין שהוא במדת אברהם אבינו מדת החסד להיות נכלל
הגבורה בחסד ויהיה כולו רחמים ופני השור לשמאל אף שמדת
השור הוא ג"כ גבורה שהוא הגבור שבבהמות אעפ"כ אין מדתו
מדת גבורה כמו מדת ארי' ע"כ אף בשמאל נוכל להמתיק מדת
השור ופני נשר הוא מדת יעקב שהוא רחמים גמורים והכל נמתקים
ע"י הצדיק שממתיק ומקשר הכל למעלה לשרשו וממשיך ההשפעה
מעילא לתתא מהחיות הקדושות וזהו שנאמר דמות אדם להנה
והנה למעלה במרכבה נקראים הכל חיות אף דמות השור והנשר
נקראים חיות כמש"ה ומתוכה דמות ארבע חיות

ומשם בארה הוא הביאור הפסוק שלפנינו וזאת החיה אשר
תאכלו מכל הבהמה אשר על הארץ ר"ל באם תאכלו מאכלכם רק

בקדושה ובטהרה אז אף הבהמות וארציות היינו מהגשמיות נעשה
קדושה ונדבק הכל למעלה בחיות הקודש וזהו הבהמה בכלל חיה
היינו שאף הגשמיות נדבק בחיות וקדושות של מעלה וזהו שאמר
הכתוב זאת תורת הבהמה והעוף הבהמה הוא השור שבמרכבה
והעוף שהוא הנשר שבמרכבה שהמה למעלה רחמים גמורים וכל
נפש החיה הרומשת במים חיה הוא בדמות ארי' שבמרכבה שהוא
נמתק במים שהוא מדת החסד לאברהם ולזה כתיב "בה' הידועה
היא החיה הידועה שבמרכבה הקדושה ולכל נפש השורצת על
הארץ ר"ל כל הארציות והגשמיות אדם הצדיק מדבק הכל למעלה
בחיות הקודש שבמרכבה להבדיל בין הטמא ובין הטהור ובין החיה
הנאכלת ובין החיה אשר לא תאכל ובין החיה הנאכלת ר"ל אותם
החיות אשר נאכלים למטה ובכללם גם הבהמות ועופות הנקראים
ג"כ חיות למעלה הכל נדבק למעלה
נמצא נזכרים בפרשה של מעלה שלשה החיות שבמרכבה היינו
דמות ארי' ושור ונשר לכך נאמר אח"כ אשה כי תזריע זהו תורת
אדם הוא החיה הרביעי שבמרכבה החשוב שבהחיות הנ"ל כמו
שאמר הכתוב דמות אדם להנה שהכל נקשר למעלה ע"י האדם
הצדיק וזה ודברי ר' שמלאי כשם שיצירתו של אדם אחר כל בהמה
חיה ועוף במעשה בראשית ר"ל במרכבה הקדושה הכל נמתק ע"י
האדם הצדיק כך תורתו נתפרשה אחר תורת בהמה חיה ועוף ר"ל
שכל בהמות חיות ועופות נדבק למעלה ע"י תורת אדם הצדיק
המדבק הכל למעלה וממשיך השפעה מעילא לתתא והבן.

**Maor VaShemesh, Tazria**

In his comment on the opening verse of the Torah portion,
Rashi brings the following midrash: "Rabbi Simlai said: Just
as the creation of human beings comes after the creation of all
the animals and birds in the Torah's account of the creation
of the world, so too the teaching [Torah] pertaining to the
humans come after the teaching [Torah] about the animals
and birds." While this midrash seems straightforward enough
on its surface, there is more to explore on the deeper levels…

It is known that everything in the lower worlds has a root
in the upper realms; "Every blade of grass has a star appointed
for it, an angel that urges it, 'Grow!'" (Genesis Rabbah 10:6). So,
too, with all created things: everything is rooted in the upper
worlds. Everything that has a living soul, such as animals and
birds, are, in their essence, rooted in the holy life force that
emanates from the holy beings in the Divine chariot. Human
beings, who engage in the Holy One's Torah and *mitzvot*,

draw everything near, connecting it to its spiritual root, and bringing the flow of life energy from above to each and every thing below. With every piece of food a righteous person eats in holiness and purity, they connect each thing to its respective divine root.

The prophet Ezekiel describes his vision of the Divine chariot thus: "In the center of it were the figures of four creatures. And this was their appearance: They had the figures of human beings" (Ez. 1:5). But the prophet also says, "Each of them had a human face [at the front]; each of the four had the face of a lion on the right; each of the four had the face of an ox on the left; and each of the four had the face of an eagle [at the back]" (Ez. 1:10). Rashi explains [the seeming contradiction between the verses] thus: "The face of the human was that of Jacob our Ancestor and was the most important of all four of the faces." For this reason, [verse 5] stated "they had the appearance of human beings."

Based on what we have said, we can gain a more precise understanding of this passage. Every living being on the Earth, such as the animals and birds, has its root in a holy life force in the upper realms: wild animals (*chayot*) are rooted in the lion of the Divine chariot; domesticated animals (*behemot*) have their roots in the ox on the chariot; birds are rooted in the eagle; and the roots of all of them are connected upward by means of the human. This is why Ezekiel first refers to only the human [in verse 5]... All the beings in the chariot above are referred to as *chayot*, as the verse states, "In the center of it were the figures of four creatures (*chayot*)."

From this we can interpret the verse before us: "And these are the creatures (*Chaya*) you may eat from among all the land animals (*behemot*) on the earth" (Lev. 11:2). The verse means to say: If you take care to eat your food in a state of holiness and purity, then even your animal nature (*behemiyut*) will be made holy—and everything in the world will likewise be connected upwards to its holy life force...

We find that in the closing section of Parashat Shemini three of the creatures from the vision of Ezekiel are mentioned: The lion, the ox, and the eagle. Thus, immediately afterward, [our parasha opens with] "When a woman gives birth" (Lev. 12:2). This is the teaching [Torah] of humanity, the fourth of the creatures on the Divine chariot and the most significant among them. This reflects that it is the righteous human, the *tzaddik,* who connects everything upward. And thus we can interpret the words of Rabbi Simlai: "Just as the creation of the human comes after that of all the birds and animals,"—that is, in the holy Divine chariot it is the human, the *tzaddik,* who sweetens judgment—"so the Torah of the human is taught after that of the birds and animals"—that is, the birds and animals are connected upward by means of the Torah of the *tzaddik,* who connects everything upward and causes the Divine flow to emanate from the upper to the lower realms.

## Mind, Body, Spirit and the Planet

It may be tempting to intellectualize the *Maor VaShemesh*'s understanding of unification, to say that through our consciousness and our language we humans make meaning of the world and, in so doing, elevate it to its source. This is akin to the influential approach of the Modern Orthodox leader Rabbi Joseph Soloveitchik, who described the scene of "halakhic man" coming across the scene of a brook bubbling quietly: "He already possesses a fixed, a priori relationship with this real phenomenon: the complex laws regarding the halakhic construct of a spring. The spring is fit for the immersion of a *zav* (a man with a discharge); it may serve as *mei hatat* (waters of expiation); it purifies with flowing water..." Soloveitchik compares Halakhic Man to "a mathematician who fashions an ideal world and then uses it for the purpose of establishing a relationship between it and the real world." People learn and develop theories and then apply them to the created universe: "*Halakhah,* which was received from God, consists in creating an ideal world and cognizing the relationship between that ideal world and our concrete environment." For Soloveitchik, there is a qualitative difference between physical, intellectual, and spiritual domains.[63]

Yet the *Maor VaShemesh* is, I believe, saying something quite different. Meaning is not only or even primarily an intellectual enterprise, and it does not begin with cognition. Rather, it begins with opening ourselves to a different kind of awareness about our relationship with creation. It is less about being fluent in the sophisticated linguistic universe of a thought system like *halakha* (which is an enormous legal-ethical corpus spanning millennia) and much more about a simpler yet deeper way of approaching life and our place in it. Rather than standing over-and-against nature, the *Tzaddik* stands amidst, as a part of, creation. The connections that the *Tzaddik* (who can

---

[63] Joseph B. Soloveitchik, (trans. Lawrence Kaplan). *Halakhic Man.* Philadelphia: Jewish Publication Society, 1983, 20-21.

be us) makes between the natural world and the heavenly realms are made through nothing more or less than a profound awareness of interconnectedness and mutuality—an awareness the *Tzaddik* nurtures and sustains from moment to moment. Indeed, all that cogitating, while beautiful, can become a barrier to such a relationship. Thus it is no coincidence that contemplative practice is grounded so deeply in stillness and silence.

It goes without saying that our species' relationship with the created world has reached a crisis point. The modern view, by which human beings stood apart from the rest of the created world and subdued it in order to remold it to suit our aims and desires, has run its tragic course. Through the traumas of severe weather, drought, pandemic, and other consequences of human-induced climate change, we have re-learned the lesson that we are a fragile part of the created world—with exceptional power to do both good and harm. Like our future, our present—this very moment—rests on our capacity and willingness to nurture a wiser kind of consciousness. This is the invitation and possibility of Jewish spiritual practice.

## Questions for Reflection & Conversation

- The Fetzer Institute study asked respondents the question, "How often do you feel touched by the beauty of creation?"[64] Answer options were: Frequently, Some Days, Once in a While, or Never. What would you answer? What leads you to answer that way?

- The *Maor VaShemesh* writes, "With every piece of food a righteous person eats in holiness and purity, they connect each thing to its respective divine root." What do you think he means by this? Does this description resonate with you? Why or why not? Do you find eating to be a spiritual act? Do you think it should be? If so, what might you do to make your eating more of a spiritual experience? If not, why not?

- Are there other *mitzvot* or rituals besides eating that you find nurture your relationship with the created world? Sukkah might be one. *Tashlikh* could be another. How might you nurture your awareness in order to experience less obvious examples as moments of connection with creation?

---

[64] This question was originally developed as part of the Daily Spiritual Experience Scale by Lynn Underwood: http://www.dsescale.org.

## Ideas for Practice

The Raisin Meditation is a classic basic mindfulness practice. This version has been adapted from The Greater Good Science Center.

1. Holding: First, take a raisin and hold it in the palm of your hand or between your finger and thumb.
2. Seeing: Take time to really focus on it; gaze at the raisin with care and full attention—imagine that you've just dropped in from Mars and have never seen an object like this before in your life. Let your eyes explore every part of it, examining the highlights where the light shines, the darker hollows, the folds and ridges, and any asymmetries or unique features.
3. Touching: Turn the raisin over between your fingers, exploring its texture. Maybe do this with your eyes closed if that enhances your sense of touch.
4. Smelling: Hold the raisin under your nose. With each inhalation, take in any smell, aroma, or fragrance that may arise. As you do this, notice anything interesting that may be happening in your mouth or stomach.
5. Placing: Now slowly bring the raisin up to your lips, noticing how your hand and arm know exactly how and where to position it.
6. Notice any sensations of wonder or gratitude within you. With awareness and intention, recite the blessing for eating a raisin:

בָּרוּךְ אַתָּה יְיָ, אֱלֹהֵינוּ מֶלֶךְ הָעוֹלָם בּוֹרֵא פְּרִי הָעֵץ.

Blessed are You, Sovereign of the Universe,
who creates the fruit of the tree.

7.
8. Gently place the raisin in your mouth; without chewing, noticing how it gets into your mouth in the first place. Spend a few moments focusing on the sensations of having it in your mouth, exploring it with your tongue.
9. Tasting: When you are ready, prepare to chew the raisin, noticing how and where it needs to be for chewing. Then, very consciously, take one or two bites into it and notice what happens in the aftermath, experiencing any waves of taste that emanate from it as you continue chewing. Without swallowing yet, notice the bare sensations of taste and texture in your

mouth and how these may change over time, moment by moment. Also pay attention to any changes in the object itself.

10. Swallowing: When you feel ready to swallow the raisin, see if you can first detect the intention to swallow as it comes up, so that even this is experienced consciously before you actually swallow the raisin.

11. Following: See if you can feel what is left of the raisin moving down into your stomach, and sense how your body as
a whole is feeling after you have completed this exercise.

12. Consider: the raisin was once in your hand, separate from you.
Now it is in your stomach. Is the raisin "you" now? Was it "not
you" when you held it in your hand? Where did that raisin come
from to be in your hand, and where does it go once it is in you?
What is the connection between the "you" who has consumed
the raisin, the raisin that you consumed, the place from which
it came, the soil from which it grew, the rain which watered
it, the sun which shone on it (and dried it)? How might the
consciousness you have of this connection "raise" the raisin to
its root? How might the consciousness you have of raising the
raisin to its root raise you as well? How, if at all, do you imagine this consciousness changes you, and then the world?

13. With awareness and intention, say the short blessing that may be recited after eating any food:

בָּרוּךְ אַתָּה ה' אֱלֹהֵינוּ מֶלֶךְ הָעוֹלָם, בּוֹרֵא נְפָשׁוֹת רַבּוֹת וְחֶסְרוֹנָן עַל
כָּל מַה שֶׁבָּרָאתָ לְהַחֲיוֹת בָּהֶם נֶפֶשׁ כָּל חַי, בָּרוּךְ חֵי הָעוֹלָמִים.

Blessed are You, Sovereign of the Universe, who creates a
myriad of creatures and their needs; and for all that you have
created that sustains the life of every living thing. Blessed is
the life force of all worlds.

# Acharei Mot-Kedoshim:
# What Does Holiness Mean To Us?

In her classic 1966 study *Purity and Danger*, anthropologist Mary Douglas observed the dialectical nature of the word *kadosh*, holy. On the one hand, Douglas noted, holiness connotes separateness: "Holiness is the attribute of the Godhead. Its root means 'set apart.'"[65] To be holy is to be different, special, separate. It is, as Rashi comments, to be *perushim*, to separate ourselves from forbidden things and unclean thoughts (Rashi, Lev. 19:2). On the other hand, Douglas notes, "Granted that its root means separateness, the next idea that emerges is of the Holy as wholeness and completeness."[66] As so much of Leviticus teaches us, that which is holy is that which is whole: only animals that are unblemished may be sacrificed and eaten; priests who have physical imperfections may not serve; people who come into contact with death must undergo a ritual of purification. Holiness in this sense follows more closely the impulse of other sages who quote the Talmud: "Sanctify yourself within that which is permitted to you" (Yevamot 20a). Separation is just the first move; a second move, gesturing toward completion, is implied in the meaning of holiness.

Much as these definitions of holiness are important, I have long found them insufficient. Too frequently in my experience this kind of discussion of holiness leads us toward externalizing holiness and focusing on boundary policing. We focus so much on what is and isn't kosher, what is or isn't pure, or even on the attempt to experience holiness through acts of completion. This tight focus leads us to miss some more latent dimensions of holiness that are right in front of us—within us, between us, available to us if only we take the time to look, see, feel, and behold. It is this additional sense of holiness that I'd like to explore this week.

## An Expansive Holiness

We'll focus again on a teaching of the *Maor VaShemesh*, Rabbi Kalonymus Kalman Epstein (1751-1823), which comments on a statement of Rabbi Dov Ber, the Maggid of Mezritch (originally of Rovno, d. 1772). It will help us open up a more capacious understanding of holiness by understanding its link with *chochma*, or wisdom.

---

[65] Mary Douglas, *Purity and Danger: An Analysis of the Concepts of Pollution and Taboo*. Routledge, 1966, 50.
[66] Ibid. 52.

**מאור ושמש קדושים**

או יאמר קדושים תהיו וגו'. כי שמעתי פירוש המדרש שכתב קדושים תהיו יכול כמוני תלמוד לומר כי קדוש אני ה' קדושתי למעלה מקדושתכם. שמעתי בימי נעורי פירוש בשם הרב המפורסם מורנו הרב בער מראוונ זצוק"ל קדושתי למעלה רצה לומר הקדושה של הקב"ה למעלה, היא מקדושתכם רצה לומר שבני ישראל גורמים למעלה קדושה בכביכול על ידי מעשיהם הטובים, וזהו קדושתי למעלה היא מקדושתכם שאתם מקדשים עצמיכם למטה, כך שמעתי ודברי פי חכם חן:

ונראה לתת סעד לדבריו הקדושים להבין מעט יותר דבריו הקדושים, דהנה הקב"ה ברא כל העולמות כולם בחכמה כמו שנאמר (תהלים קד, כד) כולם בחכמה עשית מלאה הארץ קנינך, והפירוש הוא כך כי כי ספירת החכמה היא ראשונה לעולמות, כי כתר אי אפשר לדבר בו כלל וכלל כידוע מספרי האר"י ז"ל, והחכמה היא נשמת כל העולמות עד נקודה תחתונה שבתהומות הארץ, וכל מי שרוצה לבוא להשגות אלהות ישיג חכמת אלהותו יתברך שמו מכל הברואים שבעולם ואפילו מבריה קטנה שבקטנות שבעולם יוכל לראות ממנו חכמת אלהותו יתברך שמו. וממילא כשיסתכל האדם בחכמת אלהות שבכל הברואים שבעולם, שכולם בחכמת אלהותו נבראו והם חיים וקיימים בחכמתו יתברך שמו שנתן חיות להיות להם קיום בעולם, ועל ידי זה יוכל לבוא לחכמה עילאה להיות דבוק בהחכמה עילאה ולמשוך משם כל השפעות טובות, דהיינו פלאות החכמה כי משם באה כל השפעות טובות חיי בני ומזוני, כי החכמה תחיה וגו' (קהלת ז, יב):

נמצא כשאדם חוקר ודורש ומבקש מציאות אלהותו יתברך שמו ורואה שהכל דבוק בחכמה, ומקשר חכמה תתאה בחכמה עילאה ועושה יחוד גדול בכל העולמות כנ"ל זה הוא הצדיק אשר חלק לו ה' שכל ובינה לקשר גם נשמת בני אדם בהבורא ברוך הוא, כי הוא דבוק בחכמה. נמצא נקרא הוא כמו נשמה לעם בני ישראל, כמו כביכול בחכמתו הוא נשמת כל העולמות כן הצדיק הנ"ל הוא נשמת בני ישראל, כי הוא מחיה אותם בתורתו ושכלותו לקרבם לעבודתו יתברך שמו להתלהב הלבבות להבורא יתברך שמו:

וזהו ידוע שתיבת קדוש נקרא חכמה כידוע מזוה"ק (ח"ב קכא.), וזהו פירוש קדושים תהיו רצה לומר שתהיו דבוקים במדת החכמה ותהיו אתם חיות של ישראל למשוך להם כל השפעות טובות וגם שכל לעבודת הבורא ברוך הוא, כי קדוש אני רצה לומר כמו שאני במדת החכמה שנקרא קדוש בראתי כל העולמות כמאמר הכתוב כולם בחכמה עשית והוא חיות כל העולמות, כן תהיו גם אתם קדושים רצה לומר תהיו דבוקים בחכמה שנקרא קדוש ותהיו אתם חיות של כל העולמות למשוך השפעות טובות מלמעלה למטה.

וזהו פירוש דברי קדוש מורנו הרב בער הנ"ל קדושתי למעלה
מקדושתכם, כשתהיו דבוקים בהחכמה תפעלו יחודים וקדושות
גדולות בכל העולמות ותהיה נחת רוח לפני מי שאמר והיה העולם:

### Maor Vashemesh, Kedoshim

"You shall be holy." The midrash (Lev. Rabbah 24:9) comments
here, "One might have thought the Holy One meant to say that
we are to be holy in the same manner as the Infinite is holy. But
the rest of the verse states, 'for I, your God, am holy.' Which
is to say, my holiness transcends yours." As a youth I heard
an interpretation of this midrash in the name of the famous
teacher Rabbi [Dov] Ber of Rovno: "My holiness transcends
yours" means to say: to the extent that the Holy Blessed One
is transcendent, it is so through Israel's holiness. The children
of Israel bring about holiness in the heavenly realms by means
of their good deeds. That is, the holiness of the Divine is made
transcendent through our holiness, when we do holy things
in our world.

I would like to expand a bit on these holy words in order to
understand them more deeply. The Holy Blessed One created
all the worlds with *chochma*, as the verse states (Psalms 104:24),
"How many are the things You have made, O Creator; You
have made them all with wisdom *(chochma)*; the earth is full
of Your creations." We explain this as follows: The *sefira*, or
Divine emanation, known as *Chochma*, is the first of the worlds
(since of *Keter*, the highest of the worlds, it is impossible to say
anything, as is known from the writings of the Holy Rabbi
Isaac Luria, the Ari). *Chochma* is the soul of all the worlds, even
unto the tiniest speck at the lowest point of the deepest depths.
Anyone who seeks to come to an understanding of the Divine
must grasp the wisdom of Divinity in every part of the created
universe. Even in the very tiniest creation in the world one
can see evidence of the wisdom/*chochma* of the Divine. Thus,
when one casts one's gaze upon the Divine *chochma*/wisdom
present in every part of the universe—all created through that
*chochma*—and beholds that they live and are sustained through
that *chochma* (for the Holy One gives them life force that they
may exist)—then one can arrive at *chochma* itself. One can cling
to it and draw from it the flow of Divine goodness, that is, the
wonders of *chochma*/wisdom, from which we are blessed with

life, children, and food: "for *chochma* preserves the life of one who possesses it" (Ecclesiastes 7:12).

We thus find that when a person investigates and researches and seeks to find the nature of Divine reality, they see that everything is connected to *chochma* and thus they connect the *chochma* of the lower world to the *chochma* of the upper realms. In doing so, they bring about a great unification. This is the work of the *tzaddik*, the truly righteous person, to whom the Divine has apportioned insight and understanding by which they connect the souls of people with the Blessed Creator, for the *tzaddik* clings to *chochma*. For this reason, the *tzaddik* is like the soul of the people of Israel, just as, on another level, the Holy One, by means of Its *chochma*, is the soul of all the worlds. The *tzaddik* is the soul of the people of Israel: sustaining Israel with Torah and insight in order that they might increase their service of the Divine, warmed by their love of the Holy Creator.

The word *Kadosh* (holy) is synonymous with *Chochma*.[67] This, then, is the meaning of "*Kedoshim tihyu*, You shall be holy": You shall cling to the *middah* of *chochma*, and you shall be the life force of Israel, drawing forth the flow of Divine goodness and putting all in the service of the Divine. "For I am Holy:" that is, just as I created all the worlds through *chochma*, which is called *kadosh* and which is the life force of all worlds, so, too, will you be *kedoshim*, suffused with *chochma/kedusha* and, thus, likewise the life force of all worlds as you draw the flow of Divine goodness from the upper realms to the lower. This, then, is the meaning of the teaching of our Rebbe Ber, that "My holiness is made transcendent through your holiness": When you attach yourself to *chochma*, you shall bring about unification and great holiness in all the worlds [upper and lower] and this will be a source of joy before the One Who Spoke and the World Came to Be.

---

[67] This is a mystical reference to a teaching in the Talmud (Shabbat 31a): "Reish Lakish said: What is the meaning of the verse: 'And the faith of your times shall be a strength of salvation, wisdom, and knowledge, the fear of the Lord is his treasure' (Isaiah 33:6)? Faith = the order of *Zera'im*, Seeds, in the Mishna. Your times = *Moed*, the order of Festivals. Strength = is the order of *Nashim*, Women. Salvations = is the order of *Nezikin*, Damages. Wisdom = the order of *Kodashim*, Consecrated Items. Knowledge = the order of *Teharot*, Purity. And 'the fear of the Lord is his treasure.'"

The way both the Maggid and the *Maor VaShemesh* approach holiness is a refreshing change from the emphasis on separation in so many other commentaries. We find holiness not only, or perhaps even primarily, through making sure things are separated between good and bad, pure and impure, kosher and unkosher. Rather, and most importantly, we bring holiness into the world through opening ourselves to witness and experience the profound wisdom of Creation and the Creator. We can go through our whole lives making sure we do everything just right by the books, following the rules very punctiliously. But unless we open our hearts in this way, and enable ourselves to connect the holiness of the created world with that of the worlds that exist beyond our physical senses, we're unlikely to experience a genuine sense of wholeness. Without that sense of profound interconnection, our conception of holiness remains limited, brittle, and dry. With it, our appreciation of holiness takes on new life. Accessing holiness becomes less a project rooted in the fear of contamination, and more in the love of connecting, relating, weaving together. It ceases to be grounded in the anxiety of incompletion, instead becoming rooted in the profound joy of recognizing and experiencing the wholeness of the universe and our lives within it.

## Holiness and Death

Hovering over this double parsha of Acharei Mot-Kedoshim, and in many ways framing our discussion of holiness, is death. It is right there in the name of the parasha: Acharei Mot, *after the death* of Nadav and Avihu, Aaron's sons. As Douglas observes, "Death presents a challenge to any metaphysical system."[68] For the rabbis, death is *avi avot hatuma*, the greatest of all sources of impurity. Outside the prescribed parameters of sacrifice, death is prohibited from the *Mishkan*. The *kohanim*, who embody holiness, are prohibited from contact with dead bodies other than their closest relatives, while the High Priest is categorically prohibited from contact with any dead body. For these and other reasons, death is often presented in Jewish thought as the ultimate form of separation, the barrier between corporeal, finite human beings and an infinite Divinity that is the source of all life. It stands then, seemingly, as the antithesis of holiness.

Yet our teaching this week might open up other ways of relating to death—not, perhaps, as something dirty and unclean to be kept at arm's length, but as yet one more site of chochma/Wisdom, with its own latent holiness and its own difficult and often painful dynamics. The work of the poet May

[68] Douglas 174.

Sarton (1912-1995) comes to mind, particularly her poem, "All Souls,"[69] which describes the holiness we may experience through connection with those who are no longer physically and temporally present but whose voices penetrate through our own, weaving and braiding with them. Darkness and light, Sarton reminds us, are not static, absolute categories but constantly changing, intermingling, like so many other supposed binaries—pure and impure, alive and dead, Divine and human.

*Kedoshim tihyu*, the Torah exhorts and invites us: We shall be holy—through chochma, true wisdom, which can help us exist within and beyond these binaries, enable us to connect heaven and earth, and in so doing witness and make manifest the holiness of the Holy One.

### For Reflection & Conversation

- The Maggid of Mezritch teaches, "The children of Israel bring about holiness in the heavenly realms by means of their good deeds. That is, the holiness of the Divine is made transcendent through our holiness, when we do holy things in our world." In your own words, what does this mean? Does it ring true with your own experience? Why or why not?

- How do you understand the link between *chochma*/wisdom and *kedusha*/holiness? Do you perceive a natural connection between the two? How might equating the two change your understanding of what wisdom is? Of what holiness is?

- May Sarton describes a reality in which the voices of people who are no longer living find expression through our own voices. How does this resonate with your own experience of loss, perhaps your relationship with a loved one who is no longer living? How is it challenging? How is it empowering? How might it illuminate your understanding of holiness as interconnection?

### Ideas for Practice

Springtime, when Parashat Acharei-Mot is always read in the northern hemisphere, can be a wonderful time to cultivate a wisdom/holiness consciousness through a walk, attending to the a natural world. It can be a walk

---

[69] May Sarton, "All Souls." *Harper's* November 1957.

through a nature preserve or park, or even just a conscious and mindful stroll through your neighborhood.

Make an intention to walk slowly and to simply notice what is in the natural world. You aren't in a rush to get anywhere. Rather, your purpose is to allow your senses to be awake to the *chochma*/wisdom of the natural world and to mindfully recognize that *chochma*/wisdom.

Try to use all the senses you have available to you: What do hear? What do you see? Smell? Feel? Taste? Know?

What happens if you look up? What about if you look down? What if you bring your attention to something very small? What do you notice?

Where do you see life? Where do you behold death and decay?

What sensations do you notice arising in your body as you walk, stop, and pay attention? What feelings are coming up?

What happens if you give yourself the time not to rush but rather to appreciate the wisdom and holiness of the world?

# Emor: How Does Time Move In Us?

There's a quotation attributed to Albert Einstein that runs, "The only reason for time is so that everything doesn't happen at once." It's a cute statement that, of course, belies Einstein's much deeper intuition: that time is relative, a construction of our finite embodied existence but not, in any absolute sense, true. As Einstein's theory suggests, time depends on the speed at which we're moving. Beings moving at different speeds not only experience time differently, but even physically manifest time at different rates. Time really is in our heads.

During the first year of the Covid-19 pandemic, like many others I found my relationship with time changed. Certain things slowed down as I remained almost permanently in my house without travel or events to punctuate the days and weeks. In the build-up to the 2020 presidential election, the inauguration, and the rollout of vaccines, time couldn't move quickly enough. And yet, I was also consistently amazed at how quickly it felt that a week would go by, that another Shabbat would arrive, that my children continued to grow, that the seasons came and went.

Rashi's very first comment on the Torah reminds us that time is foundational to much of Jewish life. Why did the Torah begin with Creation, he asks, instead of with the first commandment God gives to Moses and Aaron in Egypt: "This month shall be for you the first of the months" (Ex. 12:2)? Time is how we order our hours, days, weeks, months, years, and even longer cycles like jubilees. It is how we count everything from the days from birth until a *brit milah* (8) to how many days we mourn our dead (7 days, 1 month, 1 year) to how long we wait between eating meat and milk (1, 3, or 6 hours, according to various customs documented in Jewish legal codes).

Yet all of this focus on time—which, let's also remember, has some unique particularities since the advent of the clock—can, like so many other things, be both a help and a hindrance in our spiritual mission to be *avdei Hashem*, servants of the Divine. While paying attention to time enables us to delimit and make sense of the world and our experience, it can also become a taskmaster, shifting our focus away from our feelings and inner sensations outward toward performance and productivity. So, for instance, not making people fast unnecessarily is surely an expression of compassion. But when the question "Did we end Yom Kippur on time?" becomes more important than "Did we discern the presence of the Infinite today?" we should probably investigate our relationship with time, and whether it's really doing the work for us we want it to do.

## In and Out of Time

Parashat Emor details Jewish sacred time. "Speak to the children of Israel," God commands Moses, "and say to them: These are My fixed times, the fixed times of YHVH, which you shall proclaim as sacred occasions" (Lev. 23:2). The Torah then enumerates the sacrifices to be offered on Shabbat, Pesach, the Omer, Shavuot, Rosh Hashanah, Yom Kippur, and Sukkot, concluding with the words, "So Moses declared to the Israelites the set times of YHVH" (Lev. 23:44). Thus, the parasha provides us an opportunity to reflect on questions of time: What is it? How do we experience it? And how might we both inhabit it as humans and transcend it—inasmuch as we are suffused with the Divine?

Our guide for this exploration is Rabbi Elimelech Weisblum of Lizhensk (1717-1787) in his *Noam Elimelech:*

**נועם אלימלך אמר ו:א**

דבר אל בני ישראל כו' אלה הם מועדי. דהנה השי"ת ב"ה הוא למעלה מן הזמן, שבו ית' אין לתת בו זמן כלל כידוע, וכבר כתבתי דהעולמות נקראים מועדים לשון זמן ומועד, לפי שאצל העולמות שייך לשון זמן שהם תחת הזמן, והנה ידוע דהנהגת העולמות הוא ע"י שם הוי"ה ב"ה הנותן חיות ושפע להעולמות, וזהו "דבר אל בני ישראל מועדי ה'" פי' העולמות הנקראים מועד, הם מתנהגים ע"י שם הוי"ה ב"ה, המשפיע בהם בכח הא"ס ב"ה.

אכן אחר "אשר תקראו אתם מקראי קדש" פי' ע"י שאתם תקראו אותיות התורה בקדושה ובטהרה, אתם מעלים את העולמות אל מדריגות גדולים שנשפעים ע"י הא"ס ב"ה בכבודו, כי האותיות התורה שהאדם מדבר ומקרב עצמו להבורא ב"ה, אז עושה יחוד בכל העולמות, ולזה נצטוינו לקרות בתורה בשבתות ובמועדים לייחד העולמות ולהעלותם, ולמלמד אותנו הכתוב איך שנבוא למדריגה זו להעלות העולמות, "ששת ימים תעשה מלאכה" פי' כשתעסוק באיזה מלאכה, אל תכניס כל מחשבתך במלאכה, רק שתעסוק בה דרך עראי והמלאכה תעשה מאליה, כן תתנהג כל ששת ימי המעשה, "וביום השביעי שבת שבתון" שתקדש עצמך כ"כ שע"י השבת שאתה שומר למטה, תתקן את השבת העליון שיהא שבתון שבת שלם, "שבת היא לה' בכל מושבותיכם" פי' בכל מקום שאתם יושבים, יהא ניכר ונראה הקדושה והאור של השבת, הן בבית הן בחוץ, בכל מקום יאיר ויזהיר האור של השבת קודש בכח קדושתכם הגדולה.

או יאמר דבר אל בני ישראל ואמרת אליהם מועדי ד' כו' אלה הם מועדי. י"ל על כפל הלשון, דהנה השי"ת ב"ה נתן לנו המועדות שהם זמן שמחה ותענוג לנו, והשי"ת ב"ה עיקר תענוגו ושמחתו

הוא כאשר אנחנו מתנהגים בקדושה במחשבות טהורות, וזהו "אלה
מועדי ה'" שנתן לנו השי"ת למועד ולשמחה, "אשר תקראו אותם
מקראי קדש" פי' כאשר תקראו אותם בקדושה וטהרה, אז "אלה
מועדי" פי' היא שמחתי ותענוגי, ואמר הכתוב הראיה לזה שהעיקר
הוא המחשבה הקדושה, שהרי "ששת ימים תעשה מלאכה" פי'
המלאכה נעשית מאליה, ולא פועל ידך עשתה המלאכה כ"א ע"י
הבורא ב"ה, ואעפ"י שהמלאכה אפילו בחול נעשית ע"י הבורא
ב"ה, אעפ"כ ייחשב לכם השביתה שאתם שובתים בשבת ממלאכה
למצוה כאילו אתם שובתים ממלאכה ממש מחמת מצות שבת, וזהו
"ולא תעשו מלאכה" שהכתוב תולה המלאכה בכם.

Noam Elimelech, Emor 6:1
"Speak to the Israelite people and say to them: These are My
fixed times, the fixed times of YHVH, which you shall proclaim as sacred occasions." (Lev. 23:2). The Holy Blessed One
is beyond all time and space. And as I have written elsewhere,
the lower worlds are referred to as *mo'adim*, sacred occasions,
as the worlds are limited in dimension, just as the *mo'adim*
take place at specific times and seasons. Yet also recall that the
workings of the various levels of reality take place through the
Divine name HVYH [N.B. *Havaya* = Being = a permutation
of YHVH], which gives life and the flow of energy through
all the worlds. This, then, is the meaning of "Speak to the
children of Israel... proclaim the *mo'adim*/sacred occasions":
Let them know that all levels of reality, referred to as *mo'ed*, are
conducted through the name HVYH, which pours through
them from the power of the Infinite.

Yet now we must understand that it is "you [i.e., we people]
who proclaim the fixed times of YHVH." When you read
[N.B. *likro* in Hebrew means both to read and to proclaim]
the letters of the Torah in holiness and purity, you raise up the
lower worlds to the great heights which are infused directly
by the Infinite. For by means of the letters of the Torah that a
person speaks, they bring themself close to the Blessed Creator
and thereby unify all the worlds. For this reason, we are commanded to read from the Torah on Shabbat and holidays, so
that we may unify the lower worlds and elevate them. The text
teaches us how to come to this level, to lift up the lower worlds:
"On six days may work be done" (Lev. 23:3). That is, when you
engage in work, do not allow all your consciousness to enter

the work. Rather, see your own involvement as passing, and recognize that the work happens of its own accord. Conduct yourselves this way all six days of the workweek. "But on the seventh day there shall be a Shabbat of Shabbats, a sacred occasion" (Lev. 23:3)"—that is, sanctify yourselves to such a degree that by means of the Shabbat you observe in the lower worlds you cause the Shabbat in the upper realms to be a complete Shabbat. "It shall be a Shabbat of the LORD throughout your settlements"—in every place you dwell, enable the light and sanctity of Shabbat to be discernable and recognizable, inside and outside; in every place let the light of the holy Shabbat shine through your great holiness.

Another interpretation, which explains the repetition in the verse, "These are My fixed times, the fixed times of YHVH, which you shall proclaim as sacred occasions." The Holy One gave us the holidays as times of joy and delight. The essence of God's own joy and delight is when we conduct ourselves with holiness and purity of consciousness. This, then, is the meaning of, "These are the fixed times of YHVH," which YHVH gave us for festive celebration, "that you will proclaim as sacred occasions,"—when you proclaim them in holiness and purity, then "these are My appointed times," that is, they become My own joy and delight. And the text further proves this notion that the essence of God's joy is in our purity and holiness of consciousness: "Six days shall work be done"—that is, the work is done of its own accord, not through the actions of your hands. Rather, the work is accomplished by means of the Blessed Creator. Now even though work is actually done by the Creator on the weekdays, when you arrive at Shabbat and rest from work, nevertheless your rest will be considered a full *mitzvah* of refraining from work, as if you are truly resting from work on account of the commandment of Shabbat. Thus, "*You* shall do no work."

Let's unpack this teaching one paragraph at a time. In the first section, the *Noam Elimelech* distinguishes between the Divine essence, *Ein Sof*—Infinite, without end—and the lower worlds (*sefirot*) that exist with some sense of limitation. Because there are limits to those worlds—not only physical limits, but limits of consciousness, thought, imagination, etc.—there are dimensions to them, including time. Yet what animates these lower worlds, including the ones we inhabit, is the life force that ultimately emanates from the Infinite, which, R. Elimelech reminds us, is beyond time and space.

In the second paragraph, we come to appreciate that through our language—specifically through the language of the Torah—we recognize the reality of the Infinite that animates the finite world; we testify to it, and we imbue it with meaning and holiness, lifting it up from the mundane into something precious. This is especially true on Shabbat, which happens not seasonally but every week. Since the Infinite is the animating life force of the universe, we should strive to be conscious of the illusion that it is we who do work. It isn't us; rather it's the Divine making things happen in the world. But when, every seven days, we demarcate a special zone of time to cease from our illusory (i.e., time-bound) labor and behold the genuine reality of the cosmos, we bring consciousness of the Source of Life into the reality of these lower worlds. In the final paragraph, R. Elimelech reinforces his point from the previous one, emphasizing that the holidays, including Shabbat, are vehicles for a refinement of consciousness through bearing witness to the divinity that animates our reality.

## Transcending Time

The development of the clock led to the externalization of time. Since then, and particularly in the last number of decades, our relationship with time has become more and more debilitating. "Time is money" is the watchword of our capitalist society. We measure our minutes and hours in terms of productivity, and then we try to compensate with "quality time"—as though our other time is something less. We kill time, we save time, we bide our time. We give ourselves time or we take time. We fill hours and days. All of these phrases, so common we barely stop to notice them, reflect the ways that time, like money, has taken on a life of its own in our culture. It has become an idol we serve, much of the time without even noticing that we're doing so.

Yet our souls are awake, and at certain moments they break through, crying out to us, "What are you doing? Are you here, or are you thinking about where you want to be in five minutes, or where you were an hour ago?" Our souls want us to be present, in this moment, as that is how we remember our intimate connection with the Divine. When we hear the small voice inside us that beckons us to look up from the computer, to stop doomscrolling on our phone, and notice the person sitting with us, or even simply to feel the breeze gently caressing our face—what we actually hear in these moments is the voice of the Infinite animating life force that calls us to step out of time and just *be*.

That voice is always there. Shabbat and the holidays, and by extension the even more frequent time-established sacred moments of the day—moments of prayer, blessing, performing *mitzvot*—are, paradoxically, vehicles for us to step outside of time. They are standing invitations for us to be right here, right now, with nowhere else to go and nothing else to do. This is the paradox: We have to make time to transcend time. And having done that, our perspective may be reset, our relationship with time may be renewed, and we may come to recognize the Divine presence working its way through us.

## Questions for Reflection & Conversation

- Can you, in your own words, paraphrase *Noam Elimelech*'s teaching? How does he distinguish between the Infinite and the finitude or limitation of the world we inhabit? What are the implications for the role that sacred times play in our lives as he presents it?

- How do you understand *Noam Elimelech*'s paradoxical point about work and Shabbat: we think we are working, but God actually fulfills our efforts, and Shabbat reveals that to us? If you were able to internalize this attitude toward your work, how might it affect your attitude toward it? How might you experience the movement from work to rest/relaxation and back again?

- In your own experience, have you found Shabbat and holidays to be moments when you are able to step out of time and connect with a broader sense of vitality/life force? If yes, when? Describe the experience. What, if anything, makes that consciousness possible for you in those moments, but not others? If not, can you imagine what it might be like, and what you might be able to do (or stop doing) in order to help facilitate it?

## Ideas for Practice

Here is a guided 20-minute audio meditation by my teacher and colleague, Rabbi Sheila Peltz Weinberg, which focuses on developing a Shabbat consciousness.[70] This meditation does not, of course, need to be done only on Shabbat—it is available and potentially helpful anytime, just like Shabbat itself.

---

[70] https://tinyurl.com/mrxj8du5

- If we look through the lens of Shabbat at ourselves, our world, and our lives, Shabbat is the harvest. It is the receiving. Shabbat is rest, repose, reflection, completion in the ongoing creative process. We recite the Shabbat prayer, *Yismechu B'malechutecha*—Let us rejoice in your realm, in your *malchut*.

- *Malchut* means kingdom or realm and in Jewish mysticism is identified with Shabbat.

- "Let us rejoice in the *malchut* of *malchut*." Let us rejoice in being present, right here—in being present to this moment.

- Please sit in a way that is both comfortable and alert. Allow your eyes to close, softly. Or keep them open and unfocused. Start to feel the natural rhythm of your breath.

- Take a few deep breaths at first and then just notice how the breath comes in naturally. Let yourself become quiet and present.

- Feel how your breathing moves gently and how its movement can be sensed throughout your whole body. Let yourself rest in this moment. Rest in the natural peace and ease of the mind and body.

- You might want to smile and open yourself in acceptance of the *shefa*, the divine flow of light, the abundance that fills and surrounds us.

- Sitting is bowing to this moment of existence, to the natural radiance of your heart, the natural beauty that is right here and right now. If you forget, that is a signal that you have remembered. When you remember that you have forgotten, you are remembering.

- Accept this moment as an expression of *shlemut*, shalom, wholeness. Receive the Shabbat.

- Bow to the radiance that is you.

# Behar-Bechukotai: What Do We Own?

Years ago, as a teen or young adult, I remember walking to shul one Shabbat morning, contemplating the world and looking at houses and buildings and parks, when it hit me how absurd real estate is. The notion that we can delimit some parcel of earth, control access to and use of it, value it, buy it, sell it, rent it—it's one of the most extraordinary legal fictions we humans have conceived of. Because I have a deed to my house (and let's be honest: For many more years, it's still going to be the bank's house), I can order people who I don't want there to leave. And if they don't leave, I can call in armed police officers to enforce my ownership rights. Within my property, I have an extraordinary degree of control. Yes, I have to obtain permits if I want to make major modifications, but I can plant and grow flowers and herbs and vegetables; I can cut down things that are growing; I can let my dog run free in the backyard. I am lord of the manor on my little plot in Skokie, Illinois.

This doesn't only apply to real estate, of course. It also applies to movable property and to currency, to money itself. Like real estate, we—individually and collectively—think of the things we own and the money in our bank accounts as *ours*, with the force of law to back them up. As Lynne Twist writes in her book, *The Soul of Money*, "From the very beginning, money was invented to facilitate the sharing and exchanging of goods and services... Now, rather than relating to money as a tool we created and control, we have come to relate to money as if it is a fact of nature, a force to be reckoned with."[71] Like real estate, a legal fiction that has taken on a reality of its own, money has likewise become a genie out of the bottle. In both cases, the conceptual creation of human beings has become our master.

And yet: my body is of no greater value than the person I can exclude from my property. That person is just as much an image of the Divine as I am. The Divine presence resides just as much within them as it does me. Their fragility, their vulnerability to pain, illness, and suffering ultimately is the same as mine, even if I may, by virtue of my socioeconomic status, be somewhat more insulated from the vicissitudes of life. And their capacity for goodness, for caring, for smiling is likewise the same as mine—infinite.

How have we gotten so far from this reality? And what might we do about it?

---

[71] Lynne Twist, *The Soul of Money: Transforming Your Relationship with Money and Life*. W. W. Norton, 2017, 8.

## "For the Earth is Mine"

Parashat Behar anticipates all of this and offers a corrective through the Sabbatical and Jubilee years. Every seven years we are to observe a Shabbat for the land, to relinquish our control (and, in the time of the Bible, to set our indentured servants free). Every 50 years we are to celebrate a Jubilee, entirely relinquishing our claim on the land, pulling the veil off the illusion of land ownership by returning buildings and plots of which we have taken possession to their original owners. In the retelling of the Sabbatical year practice in Deuteronomy, where it is referred to as Shemitah, we also forgive debts every seven years, (re)awakening from the dream in which money is a real thing. All of this, the Torah clearly says, is so that we may know that we are but "strangers and sojourners" with the Divine upon the earth, and that ultimately the land, like all our possessions, does not belong to us, but to the Creator (Lev. 25:23).

In his *Sefat Emet*, Rabbi Yehuda Leib Alter of Ger (1870-1905) offers a deeper reflection on both the theology and phenomenology of this illusion of ownership and the spiritual intention of the institution of Shemitah.

**שפת אמת בהר תרל"ה**

ברש"י מה ענין שמיטה אצל הר סיני כו' מה שמיטה כו' אף כל המצות כו'. ומדתלינהו בשמיטה. משמע שהיא מצוה שכל המצות תלוין בה. כמו שבת דשקולה נגד כל המצות וע"י מצוה זו מקיימין כל המצות. וכתיב כי תבואו כו' שהקב"ה נתן א"כ לבנ"י וסוף הכוונה כדי שבאמצעיות בנ"י יתמשכו כל הדברים להקב"ה. וגם רצון בנ"י להיות שולטין על הכל צריך ג"כ על כוונה זו כדי לבטל עצמם וכל התלוין בהם להקב"ה. וז"ש ושבתה הארץ שאחר שזכו בנ"י בארץ כנען ישבתו בשמיטה לבטל עבודת הארץ בעבור הש"י. וכמו שמצינו באדם דכ"ז דמשועבד לאחר א"י לקבל עמ"ש כדאיתא בזוה"ק האי עול לא שריא במאן דכפות באחרא. לכן הוציאנו המקום ב"ה ממצרים. ויש להוסיף עוד כי צריך להיות מקודם עול ושיעבוד אחר. ואח"כ כשפורק ממנו עול זה זוכה לקבל עמ"ש. וכן הוא באדם שמשועבד ת"י היצה"ר בתחילת שנותיו כנודע. וכמו כן הארץ הי' מקודם ת"י כנען אח"כ נפדית ונכנסת ברשות ישראל. ואח"ז צריך לצאת גם משיעבוד בנ"י להיות רק תחת רשות הקב"ה בעצמו. ודבר זה נוהג בכל הדברים והנבראים והבן. ועיקר מצות שבת ושמיטה היא להעיד על שהקב"ה מקיים הנבראים בכל עת מחדש. כמאמר אומר ועושה פי' לבד המציאות שהמציא יש מאין רק שנותן בהם כח חדש תמיד. וכמו כן בבחי' תורה ומצות שנתן לבנ"י ג"כ נוהג דבר זה שנותן תמיד כח והארה

בלב איש ישראל לקבל התורה ולקיים המצות. ולכן כפי בירור
התחדשות הזאת שבנ"י מבררין. כמו כן זוכין לתורה. כי חידוש
העולם הי' הקדמה לנתינת התורה וכן לדורות ג"כ כנ"ל:

Sefat Emet, Behar 5635

Rashi comments, "What does the Sabbatical year have to do
with Mount Sinai that the Torah felt compelled to expressly
state where it was commanded? Weren't all commandments
given on Sinai? Rather, the statement is intended to suggest the
following comparison: Just as the general rules and minute details of Shemitah were ordained on Mount Sinai, so, too were
all commandments with their general rules and their minute
details ordained on Mount Sinai." Yet the Torah pins all of this
on Shemitah, which suggests that all the other commandments
depend upon it, like Shabbat, which is equivalent in weight to
all the other commandments put together and through which
all the other commandments are upheld.

The Torah continues, "When you come to the land..." The
Holy Blessed One gave the land of Canaan to the Children
of Israel. The ultimate intention of this was that the Israelites would, through life on the land, connect everything to
the Holy Blessed One. The desire of the Israelites, to direct
everything, for this same purpose: that they would subdue
themselves so that they, and all that depended on them, would
be devoted to the Holy Blessed One. This is why the Torah
commands, "And the land will rest." That is, after the Israelites
proved themselves worthy in the land of Canaan, they would
rest throughout the Sabbatical year, setting aside the work of
the land for the sake of the Holy One.

It's like what we find in our human experience: Anyone
who is in the service of another is unable to accept the yoke of
the Divine sovereignty at the same time, as the Zohar teaches:
"The yoke may not come to rest upon one who is indentured to
another" (Zohar 3:108a:9). This is why the Holy One took us out
from Egypt. But we may add to this: one must experience the
yoke of serving another, to then know what it means to cast
off that original yoke and thus become capable of accepting
the yoke of Divine sovereignty.

The same dynamic applies to an individual—in this case,
one who is under the rule of the evil inclination in their youth.

Likewise, the land was, early on, under the rule of Canaan and only afterward was redeemed and came into the possession of Israel. Yet even after this, the land must move from under the servitude of the Israelites and come into the sole possession of the Holy Blessed One. And, just as this applies to the Land, so too does it apply to everything in Creation.

The essence of both Shabbat and Shemitah is to testify that the Holy Blessed One sustains all beings anew in every moment, as we say [in our liturgy], "The Divine *speaks* and *does*"—that is, besides the reality that the Creator brought everything into being through speech, creating existence out of nothingness, the Divine likewise continually gives new energy to creation. This reality obtains with regard to the Torah and the commandments which the Divine gave to the Children of Israel—that is, the Holy One continuously grants power and illumination within the heart of every Jew so they may receive the Torah and enact the *mitzvot*. Therefore, the degree to which they are clear about this continual renewal is likewise the degree to which they merit the Torah. For the renewal of the world was a precondition for the giving of the Torah—as it continues to be ever since.

For the *Sefat Emet*, the practice of the Sabbatical year is both a precondition and an outgrowth of the more familiar Shabbat consciousness which is so central to our weekly and even day-to-day existence. It is outgrowth in the sense that, just as the practice of Shabbat enables us to stay awake to the reality that the Creator is constantly renewing creation—from week to week, from day to day, from moment to moment—the Shemitah cycle awakens us to that same consciousness, only on a larger scale of time, space, and community. By not working the land for an entire year, we mirror the weekly practice of not cooking on Shabbat—we must surrender. For that period, whether Shabbat or the Shemitah year, we must live entirely on what God provides for us or what we have prepared for ourselves beforehand.

Yet Shemitah is also a precondition for Shabbat consciousness, according to the *Sefat Emet*. That is, in order to re-experience Shabbat as a time of freedom—a memorial to the Exodus from Egypt—we have to first reawaken to our consciousness of the Holy One's constant re-creation and re-animation of the world. And in that sense, letting go of our fiction of ownership is something we have to do all the time, not just every seven years. We do this in mindfulness meditation all the time: This breath is not ours—in fact, we're not even breathing it. Instead, we are *being breathed*, as air is forced in and out of our bodies, whether or not we think we're controlling the process. The *Sefat Emet* suggests that we must cultivate this awareness of holding and letting go—with each breath, each moment, each day, week, year, and Shemitah cycle. Through that awareness, through that letting go, we grow deeper in our awareness of the Divine and our vocation as *avdei Hashem*, servants of the Holy One.

## A Different Kind of Consciousness

In his book, *Decolonizing Wealth*, Native American philanthropy professional Edgar Villanueva says this about the advent of the phenomenon of colonization: "The concept of colonization followed the trend that seems to have begun when humans first became farmers and began managing, controlling, and 'owning' other forms of life." According to Villanueva, colonization "required that humans think of themselves as separate from the rest of the natural world"—which both enabled people to travel from their native land to other places and then to treat both the land and the people living on it as resources to be exploited. By contrast, Villanueva writes, an indigenous worldview is one "which seeks not to own or control, but to coexist with and steward the land and nonhuman forms of life.'"[72]

As the very publication of Villanueva's book suggests, we are living in a moment when questions about land, money, inequality, and power are very much at the center of our national and global debates. Yet what the *Sefat Emet* reminds us is that these are not simply questions of policy—they are fundamentally about our spiritual orientation to life and the world. Policy prescriptions for more just, equitable, and sustainable approaches to wealth are profoundly necessary, but they aren't sufficient. As Shemitah, like Shabbat, reminds us, true transformation will come about only when we cultivate a different kind of consciousness, one in which we live not as separate from the earth, one another, and the Creator, but as profoundly interconnected and interwoven with each other.

---

[72] Edgar Villaneueva, *Decolonizing Wealth: Indigenous Wisdom to Heal Divides and Restore Balance*. Berrett-Kohler, 2018, 22. David Graeber and David Wengrow's book, *The Dawn of Everything*, interrogates some of these assumptions in important ways. For our purposes here, Villanueva's basic point about our relationship with the earth and its inhabitants is still vital and rings true.

## Questions For Reflection & Conversation

- The *Sefat Emet* concludes by saying, "the renewal of the world was a precondition for the giving of the Torah—as it continues to be ever since." I've offered an interpretation of this. In your own words, what do you think that means? How is the world renewed before the giving of the Torah? How do Shabbat and Shemitah contribute to that renewal?

- Edgar Villanueva contrasts colonialism with indigenous thinking by saying the former (which he views negatively) relies on a worldview that sees the individual as separate from the rest of the world, while the latter (which he views positively) sees individuals as interwoven with all other beings and elements of creation. Is this your experience of "ownership" of property, or control of things? When do you sense yourself as separate from the rest of the world (if at all), and when interwoven? Would you want to internalize Villanueva's worldview? Why or why not?

- Think about your own relationship with money and property. How do you feel regarding your need for money, or your desire for things/property? When do you experience anxiety or constriction around money/finances, and when do you feel expansive? How have you engaged your spiritual practices to help to keep them in perspective, if at all? How might you grow in your relationship to money and property?

## Ideas for Practice

A key element of the *Sefat Emet's* teaching is the concept of *ol malchut shamayim*, the self-abnegation that enables us to accept Divine sovereignty. My colleague Rabbi Jordan Bendat-Appell teaches a prayer practice of accepting the yoke of Heaven. This week, consider listening to this practice and engaging in it as a means of enacting the values of Shabbat and Shemitah into your daily routine. You can listen to the practice, and find a transcript, here: https://www.jewishspirituality.org/what-are-we-the-redemptive-power-of-prayer/.

# Bemidbar: Do You Count?

Ever since I encountered it years ago, I periodically find myself thinking of Bertholt Brecht's poem, "A Bed for the Night." The poem is about a man who goes out every night on the corner of 26th and Broadway to ask passers-by to give lodging to homeless people. It's a good thing, Brecht says—we can help individuals to be warm for a night, we can ensure they are protected from the elements. But, he reminds us, our one little act won't really change the world. It won't change the larger systems that bring about homelessness or hunger. We can do some good, but we can't change everything with our individual righteous action.

My mind goes to this poem when I think about individual cases of suffering that I witness or confront: A person begging for money or food, or in need of health care they can't afford, or unable to access the many bureaucratic systems of modern society, from banking to the internet to education to voter registration. My own compassion and sense of responsibility moves me to try to help them. And yet my thinking mind knows that this will not solve the larger systemic problems they confront. "A few people have a bed for the night... But it won't change the world... It will not shorten the age of exploitation."

The poem, like my experience, lives in a toggle between the specific, infinitely valuable image of God in front of me, a person who has a name and a story, and the larger, faceless category of "homeless" or "hungry" or "society's most vulnerable." I can do something about the first—give them something tangible, call them by their name, notice them. But for the latter, which is abstract, which lacks a specific name but rather exists as numbers and charts and statistics—not so much. Even as I try to bring attention to *this* person, *this* manifestation of the Divine presence, I think of the larger systems and the many others who also have faces and names but who, in the abstract, are simply the poor and suffering.

## Names and Numbers

It is this tension between the specific, named, human with a face and the general, quantified category without one, that animates much of the Book of Numbers. The book derives its name from the multiple censuses that take place in it: The first happens in our parasha this week, while another occurs 40 years later in Parashat Pinchas. In both cases, the counting seems intended to prepare the Israelites for their corporate life—as a military, as a nation—in the Land of Canaan, a transition that requires a significant degree of self-effacement and assimilation into a whole. Furthermore, the counting, and the larger questions of incorporation into a collective entity it both enacts and represents, also marks another kind of transition, from a founding generation that directly experienced the Exodus from Egypt to a new generation that will now have to negotiate the complexities of memory and tradition as they confront the realities of their own time and place.

In the Book of Numbers, for the first time a generation of Jews begins to ask, How do we remember the Exodus? How do we remain in a genuine relationship with the Divine and the Torah that was revealed to our ancestors, even as we encounter the circumstances of our own time and place which are both similar and different from theirs? How do we carry the abstract concept of "Jewish tradition" with us and live ourselves into it, and it into us? The abstraction from individual names and faces to the numbers of a corporate entity—this is the transition of the Book of Numbers.

Rabbi Tzadok haKohen Rabinowitz (1823-1900) offers a reflection on this theme in his *Pri Tzadik*. He elaborates on the counting that takes place in Parashat Bemidbar as well as the repetitive nature of the princely offerings in Parashat Naso, and invites us to approach them with fresh eyes.

**פרי צדיק במדבר ג:ב**

וזה הענין אחר שנזכר מפקד כל שבט כתבה התורה ויהי כל פקודי בני ישראל וגו' ויהיו כל הפקודים וגו' ובכל מקום מקשה בגמ' מנינא ל"ל. ולמה כתבה התורה סך הכולל הלא כל אחד יכול לחשוב כלל המספר כשיצרף יחד מספרי השבטים. וכן נשנה אחר כך המספר בפרשת הדגלים כשנחשבו כל שבט עם נשיאו וכן מספר כל דגל. ואחר כך נשנה עוד מספר סך כל הדגלים ובתורה אין אף אות אחת מיותר כש"כ פרשיות שלימות. אך באמת מצינו כעין זה בפ' קרבנות הנשיאים שנשנה בכל נשיא קרבנו וגו' אף שקרבן כל נשיא שוה והל"ל וכן הקריב נשיא שבט פלוני. וכן כ' אחר כך פ' שלימה זאת חנוכת המזבח וגו' סך כלל הקרבנות. ונראה שזה היה קשה להמ"ר ודרש (במדרש רבה י"ג וי"ד) רמזים שונים לכל שבט ושבט. והיינו שאף שהקרבן היה שוה מ"מ היה לכל אחד מהנשיאים כונה מיוחדת בקרבנו. וכן אחר כך בסך הכולל כל קרבנות הנשיאים דרש שם רמזים אחרים. והיינו כשיצטרפו כל המספרים מהקרבנות היה בזה מכוון אחר. וכן העניין כאן. הרמב"ן ז"ל הקשה למה הוצרך המספר ולמה נכתב בתורה וכ' ואולי להודיעם חסדו שבשבעים נפש ירדו מצרימה והנה הם כחול הים. אך יקשה הא במצרים היו הרבה יותר שלא עלו רק א' מחמשה או א' מחמשים או א' מחמש מאות (תנחומא בשלח א') והיה אז יותר הרבה ולא נפקדו. אך עיקר המכוון של המספר היה לנשיאות ראשם עדמ"ש (אבות פ"ד) אין לך

אדם שאין לו שעה כו' והיינו שכל א' מישראל באותו שעה ובאותו
ענין הוא הגדול מכל ישראל וכן חבירו בשעה אחרת. והיינו מפני
שכל א' מישראל יש לו חלק בתורה אות או חלק מאות אשר
בחוסר אותו האות או חלק ממנו הס"ת פסול. וזה היה ענין חיילין
דאורייתא אשר פקד משה לידע בכל שבט איך כל נפש ונפש מיוחד
בקדושתו ובתורתו בחיילין דאורייתא. וזה שנשנה הלשונות שנרמזו
לענינים שונים בכל שבט. די"ב שבטים כנגד י"ב חדשים וי"ב מזלות
וי"ב צרופי הוי"ה (תנחומא ויחי ט"ו) ויעקב אבינו ע"ה נתן לכל שבט
ברכתו ואחר כך כללן יחד כמש"נ איש אשר כברכתו ברך אותם
וזה הענין שנפקד כל שבט בפרט כל אחד בחיילין דאורייתא וכן
על ידי אהרן לידע חיילין דמשכנא.

Pri Tzadik, Bemidbar 3:2

...After the Torah recounts the tally of each tribe, it then summarizes: "These are those that were counted... and the total
count was..." (Num. 1:44-45). The Talmud asks, Why does the
Torah need to report the accounting? Why does the Torah
need to write the total number? Everyone could simply add
up the count of each tribe all together! Furthermore, the text
repeats the tally as it recounts the host arrayed around each
tribal flag [in chapter 2]. And, like the earlier section, here too
the Torah adds up the total of each tribe by its flag (Num. 2:32).
Given that the Torah contains no extraneous letters, much
less entire sections, we are left to wonder: what is the meaning here?

Truth be told, we have a similar question in the case of the
offerings of each of the tribal leaders (ch. 7), in which the offering of each leader is recounted in detail, even though all
of them made exactly the same offering. To economize, the
Torah simply could have said, "Thus brought the leader of
Tribe X." Moreover, after the completion of all of the leaders'
offerings, the Torah likewise offers a summation: "This was
the dedication of the altar" (Num. 7:44-49), which includes a
total of all the offerings.

It would appear that this bothered the authors of Midrash
Rabbah (Numbers Rabbah 13:7-14:12), who interpreted different
meanings related to each tribe's offering. That is, even though
the offering itself was the same from tribe to tribe, nevertheless
each tribal leader brought his offering with a unique intention.
Then, further, in the summative paragraph, the Midrash like-

wise interpreted different meanings. That is, when the total numbers of the offerings were added up, a new intention could be discerned. So, too, in our case [of the two counts of the people].

Ramban (Nachmanides) asks, Why did the Torah need to make this count? He answers that perhaps that the Torah wished to remind the Israelites of God's great love for them—that they went down to Egypt with 70 souls and now, here they are, as numerous as the sands of the sea. Yet we still find a difficulty with this interpretation, as there were many more Israelites who did not come up out of Egypt. [According to various interpretations] only one of five (or possibly one of fifty, or even one of five hundred) actually came out. There were many more, then, in Egypt, yet they were not counted!

Rather, the essential intent of this counting was to raise up their heads in the spirit of the Mishnah that states, "Every person has their time, and every thing has its place" (Avot 4:3). That is, every Jew has a moment wherein they are greater than all their fellows, and likewise for their friend at another moment. This is because each member of Israel has a share in the Torah—a letter, or a section of a letter—and without that letter or section, the Torah scroll [i.e., the totality of Israel] is not fit for ritual use.

This is related to the notion of the Troops of Torah[73] that Moses counted in order to know, within each tribe, the unique holiness and teaching of each and every person. This is why the language is repeated, in order to hint at these differing meanings within each tribe. For the twelve tribes correspond to the twelve months, the twelve signs of the zodiac, and the twelve permutations of Y-H-V-H. [Similarly, we see that when] Jacob blessed each of the tribal ancestors individually, he then blessed them as one, as the Torah says, "All these were the tribes of Israel, twelve in number, and this is what their father said to them as he bade them farewell, addressing to each a parting word appropriate to him" (Gen. 49:28). In our

---

[73] See Zohar 3:117:b (Pritzker Edition, trans. Daniel Matt): "Once the Torah and the Dwelling were established, the Blessed Holy One wished to count the forces of the Torah—how many troops of Torah there were, and how many troops of the Dwelling... And all were as one, inseparable from each other, all corresponding to the pattern above; for Torah and Dwelling do not separate from one another and proceed as one."

case, Moses counted the people tribe by tribe as members of the Host of the Torah, and Aaron counted them as members of the Host of the *Mishkan*.

Reb Tzadok's question is straightforward enough: Why all the repetition? And why, in particular, all the repetition of numbers? And his answer, likewise, is simple and elegant, an elaboration of the phrase the Torah itself uses to describe the counting, *bemispar shemot*, literally "the number of their names" (Num. 1:2): Each counting is an invitation to recognize some different facet of the uniqueness of each member of the host—if we can embrace it as such.

## Repetition, Numbers, and Meaning

That, of course, is the rub. Turning people into numbers can both promote equity between images of the Divine (think of Medicare) yet simultaneously erase the uniqueness of each of those images (again, think of Medicare). Likewise, turning experiences and memories into codified rituals, with prescribed times and measures for their performance, can likewise drain them of their meaning (think of bad prayer experiences)—or not (think, perhaps, of good prayer experiences). As Reb Tzadok suggests, the mere fact that something with a unique name and identity has now been accounted as part of a larger corporate identity does not, in and of itself, drain it of meaning—it just means that, perhaps, we need to pay more attention. If we can bring our awareness to the unique features of our experience in *this* moment, *this* encounter, we can touch the reality that this moment is anything but monotonous. It, like us, is created anew right now.

This challenge is particularly pronounced when we are not dealing with objects or things or rituals, but with people. While the presence of the Creator is latent throughout Creation, it is specially so in human beings, images of the Divine. And thus the attention we bring to our encounters—with *this* person, in *this* moment—is of particular importance. Indeed, we might see our mindfulness practice vis-à-vis things and objects as a kind of practice to prepare us for encounters with other humans and with ourselves, when the Divine presence is most visible. Of all our acts of counting, it is the way we count people that matters most.

In my earlier life I was a classical musician, and this challenge is one that many classical musicians encounter: How to make these pieces, which we have heard and played dozens of times before, come alive again in *this* performance, for *this* audience? Writing of the development of form in Western music, the French philosopher Vladimir Jankélévitch offers a response to this challenge very much in the spirit of Reb Tzadok's reflection on Bemidbar:

> Hearing again, playing again, become modes whereby to discover, interminably, new relationships or subtle correspondences, beauty kept secret or hidden intuitions. The polyphonic superimposition of several independent voices that are nonetheless arranged in accord with one another, the multivocal ambiguity that results, the innuendos and allusions that accumulate in these superimposed levels, the unsaid things that they conceal like hidden treasure—in these no doubt there is a source of inexhaustible pleasure.[74]

In our contemporary culture the new and novel are so much more valued than the old and traditional. Yet it is from the old—whether rituals or people—that we learn wisdom, and through tradition, and the people and communities that convey it, that we live into the life and lives of a larger people. If we are open to it, if we can bring our awareness to it, we find that our names are already written in our people's book.

## Questions for Reflection and Conversation

- Reb Tzadok haKohen writes, "Each member of Israel has a share in the Torah—a letter, or a section of a letter—and without that letter or section, the Torah scroll [i.e., the totality of Israel] is not fit for ritual use." In your own words, try to paraphrase this statement. What, if anything, about it do you find inviting? What, if anything, do you find challenging?

- Thinking about your relationship with Jewish ritual, when, if ever, have you struggled because you experienced it as routine? When, if ever, have you experienced something positive precisely *because of* its routine nature? In either case, was there anything about you (rather than people or things beyond your control) that may have contributed to how you experienced the ritual? If so, what? If not, how might you consider approaching a ritualized moment differently so as to experience it differently?

---

[74] Jankélévitch, *Music and the Ineffable*, 24-25.

## Ideas for Practice

Parashat Bemidbar is always read in the waning days of the Omer period. In these final days of the Omer, consider engaging in a practice to bring greater awareness and presence to the act of counting each day. You might try this practice, which comes by way of my colleague Rabbi Sam Feinsmith:

> Begin by sitting with the breath—but with less focus on maintaining concentration and more attention to what makes each breath precious and unique, an event that never happened before and will never happen again. Try to enact an intention of recognizing the way the breath connects you with the whole of existence, the entire field of energy and vitality that surrounds us. Now, count your breaths—but don't count them sequentially. Instead, count each breath as *Echad,* one. Do this for three to four minutes. Then, when you are ready, bring your attention to counting this unique day of the Omer—this day which never was before and never will be again, and which is yet part of a continuum of days connecting the liberation from slavery in Egypt with the acceptance of Divine sovereignty at Sinai.

# Naso: How Do We Read?

In her 2020 book *Just Us: An American Conversation*, African American poet, MacArthur fellow, and Yale University professor Claudia Rankine offers an exceptionally honest and unique take on race, race relations, and the ways we exist as individuals within larger histories, narratives, and forces beyond our control. Mixing personal essays with research, statistics, and artistic photographs, Rankine creates a space within the pages of her book in which people of all backgrounds and identities can listen to her, explore the complexities of race and contemporary American identity, and engage themselves with compassion on the route to a much broader and richer sense of awareness.

Poet that she is, Rankine begins the book with a poem, the penultimate stanza of which asks, urgently,

> What is it we want to keep conscious, to stay known, even
> as we say, each in our own way, I so love I know I shrink I'm
> asked I'm also I react I smell I feel I think I've been told I
> remember I see I didn't I thought I felt I failed I suspect I was
> doing I'm sure I read I needed I wouldn't I was I should've I
> felt I could've I never I'm sure I ask...
>
> You say and I say but what
> is it we are telling, what is it
>
> we are wanting to know about here?[75]

As I read this, I hear breathlessness in Rankine's voice as she grasps for a sense of grounding as she, a Black woman who teaches at a bastion of privilege (my own alma mater), attempts to engage herself and others in a deep and nuanced reflection about identity, race, and language. So often when thinking or talking about race, Rankine suggests, language feels insufficient. Rankine gestures at the sensation that even when she, or someone next to whom she is sitting on an airplane, may want to have a conversation with the very best of intentions, it frequently feels like she or they stick their foot in their mouth, that the language of both thought and speech is inadequate for the complexity and nuance of the task: "What is it we are telling, what is it we are wanting to know about here?"

---

[75] Claudia Rankine, *Just Us: An American Conversation*. Graywolf Press, 2020, 11.

## Reading and Being Read

Reading Rankine as an Ashkenazi, male, straight rabbi with ordination from an Orthodox rabbinical school, I am struck by the evocations her writing prompts in me, which are many. One way I understand the problem Rankine is dealing with is to see it as a problem of reading: How do we—we humans, whatever other "we"s we are part of—read other people, or ourselves? How do we interpret their physical presence, their speech patterns, their written words, their intention? How do we narrate them in our own minds, and how do we articulate them in our own words? In my mind, these become, essentially, variants of the question, How do we read? How do we make meaning, and how is meaning made for us?

My mind is further taken to the Hasidic tradition, and in particular to the *Meor Einayim* of Rabbi Menachem Nachum of Chernobyl. (And here, with the help of my colleague Rabbi Myriam Klotz, I imagine Claudia Rankine and the Chernobyler seated next to each other on an airplane, having a conversation, which is a wonderful scene to imagine.) In his first comment on Parashat Naso, the *Meor Einayim* explores this question by means of a Hasidic take on the opening words of the parasha: *Naso et rosh b'nei Gershon*, "Count the heads of the descendants of Gershon," one of the sons of Levi (Num. 4:22).

מאור עינים נשא

וידבר ה' אל משה לאמר נשא את ראש בני גרשון גם הם לבית
אבותם למשפחותם וגו'. וצריך להבין מהו לאמר, בשלמא במצות
שייך לאמר שהפירוש הוא לאמר לישראל, אבל כאן היה למשה
לבדו, ועוד שהתורה היא נצחיית ושייכת בכל זמן, דאם לא כן
היה ח"ו רק סיפורי מעשים שהיו בזמן קדום, ואם כן למה נקראת
תורה מלשון הוראת דרך שהיא מורה ומלמדת אותנו דרך ה', ומה
הוראת דרך יש כאן.

והנה כתיב ולדבקה בו ודרשו רז"ל איך אפשר לדבקה בהשם
יתברך, והלא אש אוכלה הוא, וכתיב בזוה"ק אשא אכלא כל אשין
דעלמא, ואם כן איך אפשר לבשר ודם לדבק באלהי כזה, אלא
הדבק במדותיו מה הוא רחום אף אתה רחום וכו'. וצריך להבין
מה תירץ לו על קושייתו, הן אמת שבמדותיו יכולים לדבק אבל
בפסוק נאמר ולדבקה בו.

אך האמת הוא שהשם יתברך נתן לנו התורה כדי שיוכל האדם
לדבק בהשם יתברך, כי איך היה אפשר להאדם שהוא בעל גבול
ותכלית, לדבק בהשם יתברך שהוא בלתי בעל תכלית שאין לו
תחלה ולא תכלה, ולכן לנו השם יתברך התורה וצמצם כביכול
עצמו בתורתינו הקדושה, כדי שבדבקנו בהתורה הרי הוא דבוק

בהשם יתברך השוכן בתוך התורה. וזהו מאמר רז"ל הדבק במדותיו,
פי' בהתורה שהתורה נדרשת בשלש עשרה מדות דהיינו מקל וחומר
ומג"ש וכו', והן הן עצמם הי"ג מדות רחום וחנון גו', וכשידבק
בהתורה הרי הוא דבוק בהשם יתברך השוכן בתוך התורה.

והנה לפ"ז היה נקל מאוד לאדם לדבק בהשם יתברך, דהיינו
בדבקו באותיות התורה ותפלה שהם היכלות להבורא ב"ה השוכן
בתוכם, אך יש מחשבות זרות שבאים ומבלבלים אותו בעת
עסקו בתורה ותפלה, והנה מה עושים לזה צריך לשאול בעצת
התורה, שהתורה נותנת לנו עצה בזה, דהנה צריך להבין מהו ענין
המחשבות זרות, הלא הם אותיות שנפלו, שכל שום מחשבה א"א
להיות בלא אותיות, והמחשבות זרות הם גם כן אותיות רק שנפלו
מחמת מעשיו גופיה, ולכן כשבא לדבק בהשם יתברך הם באין גם
כן שיעלה אותן, אבל אין המחשבות זרות באה ח"ו לבלבל אותו,
וצריך להעלות אותם לשרשם.

וזהו שמלמדת אותנו התורה הקדושה בדברים הנעימים נשא
את ראש, ר"ל שתתנשא ותגביה א"ת הם הכ"ב אותיות שמא' ועד
תי"ו, תגביה אותם אל הראש וראשון שהוא הבורא יתברך, שכל
תיבות התורה והתפלה הכל המה צירופי אותיות, כשמצטרפין
אותיות ו' י' ד' ב' ר' נעשה תיבת וידבר, וכן כל התיבות הכל המה
צירופי אותיות, וצריך להעלות האותיות לשרשם, ואם תעשה
כן, אז בני גרשון, הם האותיות שנפלו ונתגרשו, גם הם יעלו
לבית אבותם, הם אברהם שהוא מדת החסד והאהבה, ופחד יצחק
שהוא מדת יראה, וישראל אשר בך אתפאר היא מדת התפארת,
דהיינו כשלומד ומתפלל ביראה ואהבה ולפאר ליוצרו על שם
כבוד מלכותו, אז מתעלים האותיות של למעלה אל האבות כנ"ל
למשפחותם לדביקותם כמו (שמואל א ב', ל"ו) ספחיני נא וגו'.

אך איך עושים כל הנ"ל פירש לנו שלמה הע"ה (קהלת ט', י') כל
אשר תמצא ידך לעשות, ר"ל כל דבר שתרצה לעשות רצון השם
יתברך, בכחך עשה, צריך לעשות בכח דהיינו כשמשים כל כחו
וחיותו בתוך האותיות התורה ותפלה בזה מעלה אותם לשרשם
אל הבורא יתברך שמו:

**Meor Einayim, Naso**

"And the Holy One spoke to Moses saying (*leimor*), 'Count [lit.
'raise up'] the heads of the sons of Gershon as well, according to
their ancestral houses and their families." We must understand
why the word *leimor*, literally "to say," is here. When the Holy
One gives Moses a commandment for the Israelites, it makes
sense that "to say" means [that Moses is] *to say* that commandment to the rest of the Israelites. But here the instruction is

only to Moses. Furthermore, the Torah is eternal, a bearer of meaning in every era—if it were not so, these would just be stories about events from a time long ago. Why then would we call it "Torah," from the word *hora'ah*, instruction? The Torah guides and teaches us the ways of the Holy One. But what is the instruction for us in this commandment?

In Deuteronomy 11:22 we are instructed to "walk in God's ways and hold fast to the Divine." Our Sages asked, How is it possible to hold fast to the Blessed Ineffable One, for is not the Divine described as a 'consuming fire' (Deut. 4:24)? The Zohar comments that this consuming fire consumed all the fires in the world. If so, how is it possible for a creature of flesh and blood to cleave to such Divinity?! Rather, the Sages respond, we are to hold fast to the virtues of the Holy One: Just as God is compassionate, so you should be compassionate, etc.[76] Yet we must understand how this solves the original question: for while one can certainly hold fast to the qualities of the Divine, the verse itself commands us to hold fast to the Holy One, and not only to the Holy One's attributes.

The truth is that the Blessed Ineffable One gave us the Torah in order that humans would be able to cling to the Holy One. For how would it be possible for a person, who is subject to the limits of space and time, to hold fast to the Ineffable, Who is unlimited, without beginning or end? Therefore, the Holy One gave us the Torah and contracted Him/Her/Theirself, as it were, within our holy Torah, so that, through our drawing near to the Torah, we would draw near to the Divine Who dwells within it. This is what the Sages meant by instructing us to "hold fast," i.e., to emulate the attributes of the Divine—that is, we are to follow the Torah, which is interpreted, classically, through the thirteen hermeneutical principles [of Rabbi Ishmael], which are identical with the 13 attributes of Divine Compassion. When we cleave to the Torah, we draw close to the Divine Who dwells within the Torah.

Accordingly, it is quite simple for a person to cleave to the Blessed Ineffable One—by means of the letters of the Torah and of prayer, for they are palaces of the Creator Who resides within them. Yet foreign thoughts come to us and confuse us in

---

[76] See Shabbat 133b.

the moments when we are engaged in Torah and prayer. What are we to do when that happens? We must seek counsel in the Torah itself, for the Torah gives us advice. We must investigate to understand: what are these foreign thoughts? They are nothing other than letters which have fallen, for no thought may come to be without letters. Foreign thoughts are thus also letters, but they have fallen from their holy status because of our worldly actions. Therefore, when we come to cling to the Holy One, the foreign thoughts come along as well, in order that we may raise them up. But the foreign thoughts do not come to us, God forbid, to confuse us—rather, we must raise them up to their roots.

This is what the holy Torah comes to teach us through the lovely words, *naso* et *rosh*, "lift up the head" (Num. 4:22). It means to say, lift up and elevate et, את, the 22 letters of the Hebrew alphabet from a*leph* to t*av*. Raise them up to the *rosh*, the head, which is *rishon*, the Origin—the Blessed Creator. For all the words of the Torah and of prayer are combinations of letters. When we combine the letters *vav, yod, dalet, bet, reish*, we make the word *vayidaber*, And God spoke. All words are combinations of letters and we must raise them up to their source. And if we do this, then *b'nei Gershon*, which are letters that fell and were *nitgarshu*, sent away—they likewise will be raised up to *beit avotam*, the house of their Ancestors: Abraham, who is the virtue of *Hesed* (loving connection) and love; Isaac, who is the virtue of awe; and Israel, the virtue of *tiferet*, splendorous balance. When we study and pray with awe and love in order to bring beauty to the Creator, we raise up the letters to their ancestral source, "to their family."

Yet how do we do all this? King Solomon has taught us: "Whatever you wish to do, do with all your power" (Eccl. 9:10). That is, Whatever you wish to do in accordance with the will of the Divine, Do with all your power. That is, you must recognize your full potential and power, and put all your effort and life force into the letters of the Torah and prayer. In this manner you will raise them up to their source, to the Blessed Creator.

In this classic teaching, the *Meor Einayim* invites us into a profound reflection on the nature of language and our question about the nature of reading.

He takes as a starting point that human beings live in and through language, which is subject to the possibilities and limitations of the other dimensions in which we exist, namely space and time. Language is always approximate, partial, never fully expressive of the totality of the reality we perceive, much less the reality that exists beyond our everyday perception. Likewise, he takes as a given the Torah's statement that the nature of the Divine is that it is "a consuming fire," something that exists beyond all sense, all limits. And yet, the paradoxical, miraculous reality is that we can come to know the Divine—and not only the Divine attributes—through the very letters and words of our holy texts. Each letter, he writes, is a "palace of the Creator who resides within" it. Each act of reading therefore holds the possibility of communing with the Holy One.

In philosophical terms, this is a beautiful idea. But what does it mean in practice? To begin with, we have to start with the orientation that language, and in particular the language of the Torah, is more than a mechanical enterprise. It is a practice that leads us beyond being merely a bearer of meaning. And it reminds us that meaning is a miraculous thing. The very fact that you can read these words and understand me; that you can share them with a friend and have a conversation about them; that they can open up associations and reflections and new thoughts and sensations—don't overlook how utterly amazing, precious, and mind-blowing that is! If we can approach our texts with this orientation, we're already well on our way to the kind of experience the *Meor Einayim* describes.

Beyond this, I would suggest, lies a next move, which is to extend this kind of charitable or loving orientation—an orientation that lives into the notion that the world does indeed have meaning for us when we open our eyes to look—not only to texts, but to the people who live in and through those texts. In the words of R. Tzadok of Lublin whom we studied last week, each of us is in a letter in the Torah scroll of the Jewish people. Thus, when we approach a text, we might approach it as we do a person—with wonder, reverence, awe, possibility; and when we approach a person, we might approach them as we do such a sacred text. (This is something to consider the next time you are standing in the presence of a Torah scroll in synagogue and even offer it a kiss.) To read a text is to read a person; to read a person is to read a text.

And when "foreign thoughts" of anger, fear, jealousy, suspicion, degradation, or snarkiness enter our minds is precisely the moment when we can pay heed to the *Meor Einayim* and practice *hitlamdut*. Whether in response to a text—from a book to a Facebook post—or a person—from a family member to a member of a political party toward whom we find it hard to be charitable—we can ask ourselves, "How might I, in this moment, raise the letters of my own thoughts, speech, actions, and feelings up to their holy roots?" In doing so, we can create more space between stimulus and response, recognize the options before us, and, hopefully, choose one that elevates the fallen letters to their original source in goodness.

## A Hermeneutics of Faith

In academic-theological parlance, we might refer to this as a kind of hermeneutics of faith rather than a hermeneutics of suspicion. Rather than approaching our interlocutors, and ourselves, cynically as (only) under the influence of a false consciousness, we might approach ourselves and others as (also and equally) manifestations of the Divine in the world, full of possibility, meaning, and a latent capacity for goodness. Holding ourselves and others in this reality opens us to a deeper mode of reading—of both texts and people. Through this, our language, our experience, and our relationships may be continuously renewed, and our posture toward ourselves and others may be softened by compassion.

In her poem "what if" from which we quoted at the beginning of this essay, Claudia Rankine offers these words by way of conclusion:

> What if what I want from you is new, newly made
> a new sentence in response to all my questions,
> a swerve in our relation and the words that carry us,
> the care that carries. I am here, without the shrug,
> attempting to understand how what I want
> and what I want from you run parallel—
> justice and the openings for just us.[77]

As the *Meor Einayim* shows us, our reading of both texts and people can be, in every encounter and every moment, an opportunity to create "a swerve in our relation and the words that carry us." If we take the time to cultivate our capacity to approach our reading of texts and people (and people-texts?) with openness, curiosity, wonder, and empathy, we can make space for the Divine to become manifest, for the letters of our lives to be restored to their holy roots.

---

[77] Rankine, 11.

## Questions for Reflection & Conversation

- The *Meor Einayim* says, "When we study and pray with awe and love in order to bring beauty to the Creator, we raise up the letters to their ancestral source, 'to their family.'" Have you ever had an experience of reading a text this way? If yes, describe how you felt. What dimensions of the experience—you, the text, the person or people with whom you may have been reading it, the place in which you were reading—contributed to your experience, and how so? If you have not had such an experience, what do you imagine it might feel like, and how might you put yourself in a position to experience it?

- When the *Meor Einayim* discusses "foreign thoughts" that come to us in moments of study or prayer, what do you think that means? Do you find that you have 'foreign thoughts' during your own periods of focused attention or practice? If so, what do you do when they come to you? What does it mean to you to raise them up and return them to their source?

- When Claudia Rankine says that she seeks, "a swerve in our relation and the words that carry us," what do you think she means? How do words carry us? How might changing the meaning of those words change our relations? And who might the "us" in the line refer to? Given Rankine's sustained focus on race relations in her book, how do you understand this stanza of her poem, and how might it apply in your own life and spiritual practice?

## Ideas for Practice

An essential component of cultivating a more charitable form of reading people and texts is the practice of *hitlamdut,* self-awareness. Here are two small but important practices for bringing greater self-awareness to your day-to-day activities this week:

- Option one:

  Choose a small, routine practice in your life from which to learn from each day. For example: brushing your teeth. The goal is not to brush your teeth better, or to judge yourself if you skip brushing your teeth one night, but to learn something from the experience of how you brush your teeth each day. See what you can notice by slowing down, paying attention, and being mindful of the many movements and sensations involved in this mundane practice.

- Option two:

  Choose to learn something from the small acts of others, at least one time a day. This can be from the same person, or from different people. Again, the goal is not to judge anyone for their behavior, but to observe and learn from it. For example, you might choose to learn from observing the security guard at a building you frequent, or the barista at a coffee shop, or the way a neighbor or coworker or another person conducts themselves. What can you observe in yourself as you notice them?

# Beha'alotcha: What Do We Want?

Parashat Beha'alotcha marks the end of an era. For nearly a full year, ever since chapter 19 of Exodus—that is, for the second half of that book, the entirety of the book of Leviticus, and the first ten chapters of the book of Numbers—the Israelites have been camped at the foot of Mount Sinai, first to experience revelation and then to build the *Mishkan*. Dramatically, the Torah announces, "In the second year, on the twentieth day of the second month, the cloud lifted from the Tabernacle of the Pact and the Israelites set out on their journeys from the wilderness of Sinai" (Num. 10:11-12).

On a spiritual high from the last year, we expect that the Israelites will live in close alignment with the Divine will. And, for a time, it seems that they do. *Al-pi Adonai*, at the word of the Holy One, the Torah says, the Israelites camped and broke camp. In the six verses between Num. 9:18-23 the Torah repeats the phrase *al-pi Adonai* eight times, as if to drive home the synchronicity between the people and the Divine.

And then, of course, everything falls apart beginning in chapter 11, when the people begin to complain. From here on, the book of Numbers takes on a decidedly different feeling as the people and God grow increasingly impatient with one another. Plagues, fires, snakes, and more quail than anyone has ever eaten are among a host of maladies that beset the people. It is as though there are parallel stories being told here—one of a state of blissful union, the other of bitter distrust and dysfunction.

## Desiring Something Else

In describing the heart of Numbers, contemporary Bible scholar Avivah Zornberg draws on French psychoanalyst Jacques Lacan's term *juissance*, which she defines as "a primordial, infinite desire."[78] She writes,

> The wilderness experience, with Sinai at its heart, represents both death and life. This is the place of passionate love, of the *juissance* that floods the gates of perception. It is also a terrible and inconceivable place, where being-with-God—or containing God-within-them—endangers their being. The Revelation at Sinai is *instantly* followed by its backlash, the Golden Calf. And even after the Tabernacle has been built in their midst, with God at its heart, a profound ambivalence makes them

---

[78] Avivah Gottlieb Zornberg, *Bewilderments: Reflections on the Book of Numbers.* Schocken, 2015, 70.

*turn away* from Sinai—from the unfathomable "heart of the mystery" that might forever change them.[79]

Zornberg locates much of this ambivalence, this tension, in the issue of desire, which takes center stage in Parashat Beha'alotcha, particularly in this memorable passage:

> The riffraff in their midst felt a gluttonous craving; and then the Israelites wept and said, "If only we had meat to eat! We remember the fish that we used to eat free in Egypt, the cucumbers, the melons, the leeks, the onions, and the garlic. Now our gullets are shriveled. There is nothing at all! Nothing but this manna to look to!" (Num. 11:4-6)

The people here are presented in their most human, and perhaps most tragic, light. The manna, which the Torah goes on to remind us was a miraculous food in every respect, has become "nothing." They are unable, or unwilling, to acknowledge the Divine goodness present in their midst, and, driven by their sensual desires, they complain loudly.

## Human Desire, Divine Will

Commenting on this passage, Rabbi Yehuda Leib Alter of Ger (1847-1905) offers the following lesson in his *Sefat Emet*.

שפת אמת בהעלותך תרל"ג

עשה רצונו כרצונך כו'. הוא עצה לתקן הרצון כפי מה שאדם
מדבק כל רצונו וחשקו במצוה ומעשה טוב. מתדבק הרצון בקדושת
השי"ת ועי"ז אין יכול להתפרד אח"כ אף שיש לו רצונות אחרים
ג"כ. כי הקדושה שומרת הרצון שלא יתקלקל ויוכל עי"ז להעלות
כל הרצונות להשי"ת. כי צריך אדם להאמין כי כל מה שיש רצונות
אחרים בעולם הם לטובה. ושעי"ז יכול להיות רצון אמת לעבודת
השי"ת. וכשאדם לומד ק"ו מרצונות אחרים איך לעשות רצונו
ית' כראוי עי"ז מעלה כל הרצונות אשר לא טובים המה להשי"ת.
ואפשר ז"ש התאוו תאוה שהי' חסר להם התאוה. כי היו רחוקים
מתאוות גשמיות. לכך היו חסרים תאוה טובה. ולכן התאוו תאוה.
ונחשב לחטא כי השי"ת רצה שיהיו המה באופן אחר. ואנחנו ע"י
אמונה צריכין לקרב כל הרצונות להשי"ת שיהי' נעשה רצון אחד
להשי"ת מכל אלו הרצונות:

---

[79] Ibid. 88

Sefat Emet, Beha'alotcha 5633 (1873)

"[Rabban Gamaliel, the son of Rabbi Judah HaNasi used to say...] do God's will as though it were your will, [so that God will do your will as though it were God's. Set aside your will in the face of God's will, so that God may set aside the will of others for the sake of your will]" (Avot 2:4). This teaching advises us to rectify our will to the degree that we pour our entire will and longing into every *mitzvah* and good deed. If we bind our will or desire to the holiness of the Blessed Ineffable One, then our desire will never be separated afterwards—even if we have other wants, for the holiness ensures that our will shall not be degraded. By means of this, we will be able to raise up all our wants to the Blessed Ineffable One. We must have faith that all seemingly extraneous desires (which do not appear to be God's will) are still for the good. This will permit us to cultivate a true desire to serve God. And, even more so, when we extrapolate from these other wants how to properly fulfill God's will, then, by means of this, we will raise all our negative wants up to the Blessed Ineffable One.

This is a possible understanding of *hit'avu ta'ava* (Num. 11:4) lit. "had a desire for desire," the people experienced some craving—that is, [contrary to the traditional understanding that the people were overcome by desire,] rather, they lacked desire itself. For at this point the people were far from physical desires—and thus they lacked positive desires as well. Therefore, *hit'avu ta'ava*, "they desired desire." Their desire was considered a sin [as it led them from their heights to the material world, and not vice versa], since God wanted them to engage in the world in a different manner. And we, by means of faith, must bring near all our wants and desires to the Blessed Ineffable One, such that out of all of these many wills will be forged a single will.

The *Sefat Emet* begins with what, to its audience, would be a well-known teaching from the Mishnah in *Pirkei Avot*. On its surface, this Mishnah presents a straightforward lesson: We should align our individual will with God's will. Yet the *Sefat Emet* senses that there is much more here if we dig a little deeper: Where exactly does our will end and God's will begin? What does the Mishnah mean in saying that God will do our will if we align ourselves with God's will? If we are created by the Divine, then how do we even have independent wills in the first place? How does this mysterious complex of will, want, and desire actually work?

It goes on to suggest that, if we can achieve a level of *devekut*, cleaving or clinging to the Divine, then it becomes impossible for our own desire to be separated from the will of the Holy One. We will be able to sanctify even our seemingly bad desires. (While this is a powerful teaching, it almost goes without saying that it also opens a door to serious ethical problems by justifying abusive or violent behavior. We'll come back to that in a moment.)

Then the *Sefat Emet* links this Mishnaic teaching with the episode from Parashat Beha'alotcha when the Torah describes the people with the words *hit'avu ta'ava*, traditionally rendered as "were overcome by desire," but translated more literally as "desired desire." Having experienced the otherworldliness of Sinai, he suggests, the people were in essence disconnected from their sensual, human desires. And now they desired desire itself. The Holy One intended that the people would be able to direct their worldly urges toward their Divine purpose. But they failed in that, instead thinking they were, or should be, cut off from worldly desire rather than channeling it. The lesson for us comes through a life of faithful commitment to Torah. If we can live faithfully in accordance with the Torah, concludes the *Sefat Emet*, we become capable of experiencing a complete, wholesome sense of alignment with the Divine, elevating our impulses, urges, yearnings, and desires to a holy purpose.

Yet how do we do that? How do we align what it is we want, and what the Divine wants of us? I would suggest that the *Sefat Emet* is pointing toward the cultivation of an enlightened awareness, one that is cognizant of our human desires, is able to acknowledge them and bring them to serve holy purposes by means of *Emunah*, a committed, disciplined relationship with the voice of Divinity available to us within. It is when we react rather than respond, when we do not make the time or space to cultivate more expansive and attuned habits of mind-heart, that we are most prone to unthinkingly following our desires—which can result in regretful actions or, worse, abusive behavior.

## The Discipline of Desire

Avivah Zornberg quotes Rashi on Numbers 11:10, who comments that, when the Torah says the people were "weeping in their families," it really means that they were crying over the prohibition of incest. "Incestuous desire is, essentially, a desire for a *desire-free* life," writes Zornberg. "In fantasy, family love is a resource that can be exploited without effort. One need never yearn for *jouissance*, for that dangerous and intoxicating fire. But once incest is forbidden, sexuality becomes a force bound by prohibitions. In that moment, desire is born. A partner has to be sought from beyond the family group... Gaps must be bridged, language shaped to frame laws, conventions, a network, a fretting, through which the fire of *jouissance* may shine."[80]

With this comment, Zornberg, via Rashi, brings us bracingly to ground, dealing with some of the most elemental and basic conflict that can occur between drives and conventions (and one of the epicenters of Freudian psychology). Indeed, the taboo of incest is so deeply ingrained in us that you may well have squirmed a bit reading the last paragraph (I squirmed as I wrote it). Yet Zornberg's larger question, like that of the *Sefat Emet*, is how we live into the unbounded desire of the Divine that lives within us while simultaneously living within the very bounded life we live as creatures of flesh and blood, time, and language.

In my own meditation practice, I have come to appreciate how every breath is a process of the building and release of tension. When I breathe in, I first experience pleasure. As I continue breathing and my lungs fill up, I start to feel a bit of tension, even a little anxiousness to begin breathing out. Then I experience that outbreath, at first, as pleasurable. But by the time I reach the end of the breath, I feel a tiny urge of desperation to start breathing in again. And on and on it goes—this continuous cycle of anticipation, desire, fulfillment, release, anxiety, over and over again, tens of thousands of times a day, millions of times a year. It is hard-wired into us, this process of desire and fulfillment.

Yet that same practice helps me to be mindful of my many other desires, to recognize and name them. And when I am able to bring quiet attention to my mind-heart, I find I can also hear other desires, other wills, speaking—not only the ones my body articulates to me, but desires that come from a place within and beyond me. They come to me through words of Torah and *tefillah*, prayer—words I sense were spoken at Sinai and which, in our tradition, the Divine Teacher continues to call out from that holy place every moment of every day. By cultivating my own mindfulness and channeling my attention through the words of Jewish tradition, I find I am able, in my own way, to experience what I hope is a healthy sense of alignment with the Divine will.

### Questions for Reflection & Conversation

- A central line in the teaching of the *Sefat Emet* is this: "If your will cleaves to the holiness of the Blessed Ineffable One, then by

---

[80] Ibid. 73.

means of this you cannot be separated afterwards—even if you have other wants, for the holiness ensures that the Divine will shall not be degraded." Try to paraphrase this teaching. What do you think the *Sefat Emet* means by "you cannot be separated?" From whom or what can you not be separated? And how do you interpret the statement that the holiness to which we cleave ensures that the Divine will cannot be degraded?

- Do you experience tension between what you sense as your own desire and that of the Divine? If yes, how do you navigate that tension? If not, what do you think keeps that tension from coming up?

- Avivah Zornberg writes that "a profound ambivalence makes [the people] turn away from Sinai—from the unfathomable 'heart of the mystery' that might forever change them." This description of the *midbar*, the wilderness, is evocative of other moments in life when we, too, might sense such an "ambivalence." What does it evoke in you? Is there an experience or sensation in your own life when you felt you were encountering "the unfathomable heart of mystery"? If so, how were you either pushed or pulled, attracted or repelled? What happened next?

## Ideas for Practice

The R.A.I.N. practice (Recognize, Accept, Investigate, Non-Identify) has proven to be a useful approach for many people in dealing with conflicting or difficult emotions or sensations—or, in our case, with a sense of conflict around our various and conflicting wants and desires. This meditation, created by my teacher and colleague Rabbi Nancy Flam, guides you through it. This week, consider spending time with this practice as a way of working through competing drives or desires en route to cultivating a greater sense of alignment between your own will and what you sense as that of the Divine. Gently close or lower your eyes.

Remember, R.A.I.N is an acronym that stands for R - recognize, A - accept, I - investigate, N - non-identify. We will start with the breath. If you find during any of the four stages that you feel overwhelmed by the difficult emotion you're working with, you can always go back to one of the prior stages and start again or go back to your breath as a kind of home base.

Settle into a posture that, like Jacob's ladder, is firmly planted and simultaneously reaching toward heaven. Set a *kavannah*—an intention—to mindfully turn toward difficult emotions rather than recoiling from them. Now, let's spend a moment anchoring our attention to the breath, allowing ourselves to be breathed. Note the freshness of the breath as it arises anew from moment to moment. When the mind pulls your attention away, gently return your attention to the breath. This will help you become more attentive to the body, which will be important for our practice of working with difficult emotions. Let's turn to the breath now.

When you feel somewhat settled and relaxed, move toward the dark cloud: call to mind an experience you've had with a difficult emotion such as anger, indignation, anxiety, lust, greed, sadness, or something else. It doesn't have to be the most intense difficult emotion. It could be a smallish irritant. Try to really imagine yourself in the situation that elicited your feelings. The first step is to recognize the emotion. Is it anger, hatred, jealousy, lust, greed, anxiety, sadness, or something else? Simply say to yourself, "Ah, yes, this is anger, etc." Spend some time recognizing the difficult emotion.

Next, practice acceptance. Note if there is any resistance to the emotion, strong or subtle. Are you in an adversarial relationship with the emotion? How does that resistance exacerbate the intensity of your suffering? Can you accept your resistance? What happens if you soften your whole body, relaxing your attention into the difficult emotion with a sense of balanced acceptance: "Ah, yes, this is anger. This is really what's going on right now. I don't like it. But it's OK." Apply that practice of acceptance during the next minute.

Now we investigate the emotion. How do you know you're feeling anger or some other emotions? What's happening in your body that clues you into what you're feeling? Where in your body do you feel the emotion? What sensations accompany it? Are those sensations pleasant, unpleasant, or neutral? What thoughts or stories bubble up in the mind along with the sensations in the body? Is any of this permanent? Spend the next minute finding out.

Now we practice non-identification. If you fix your attention on these sensations and thoughts, are they permanent or impermanent? Are they "you" or "yours," or is it more accurate to say that they are moving through you like a river of sensation and energy? Do you find you say to yourself "I'm angry" or "I'm sad" or "I'm scared"? Can you shift your orientation to saying "anger is present" or "sadness is present" or "fear is arising?" How does doing so shift your relationship with sensations and thoughts? Take the next minute and practice non-identification.

When the time you allotted for this meditation practice is complete, close your meditation by bringing your attention back to the breath, gently open your eyes and return your awareness to the room.

# Shlach Lecha: How Do We Think?

In the essay in Parashat Vaera, I referred to 20th-century psychologist Jerome Bruner, who discusses how we make meaning. I applied his teaching particularly to ritualized acts like *mitzvot*. I want to return to Bruner, specifically a point he makes about the power of institutions in shaping our thought: "Experience in and memory of the social world are powerfully structured not only by deeply internalized and narrativized conceptions of folk psychology but also by the historically rooted institutions that a culture elaborates to support and enforce them." As an example, Bruner cites F. Scott Fitzgerald's story "The Rich Boy" (1926), which begins with the observation, "Let me tell you about the very rich. They are different from you and me." Bruner observes that this is "not just because they have fortunes: they are *seen* as different, and, indeed, act accordingly." As another example, Bruner refers to established scientific evidence of gender bias. He concludes by saying, "The very structure of our lexicon, while it may not force us to code human events in a particular way, certainly predisposes us to be culturally canonical."[81]

Language, whether the unspoken language of thought, the communicated language of speech and writing, or the embodied language of social comportment, relies on, generates, and exists in tension with all sorts of rules and codes. We learn these conventions primarily through osmosis (perhaps more accurately mimesis) as we listen to language being used, observe the way people interact, and so forth. That is, we primarily pick up language unconsciously.

Precisely because that process is unconscious, all kinds of structural biases creep in and shape our thoughts—whether the gender bias Bruner mentions, the structuring attitudes toward wealth alluded to by Fitzgerald, or a host of other kinds of unconscious influences having to do with race, gender, sexuality, nationality, religion, education level... The list is fairly endless.

## Disrupting Unconscious Thought

Parashat *Shlach Lecha* invites us to reflect on how we may fall victim to these unconscious forces. "We looked like grasshoppers to ourselves, and so we must have looked" to the inhabitants of the land, report the spies after the reconnoitering of the land of Canaan (Num. 13:33). Where did they get this idea? What prior attitudes may have been at work, shaping their self-conception and their projection of that self-conception onto the inhabitants

---

[81] Bruner, *Acts of Meaning*, 57-58.

of the land? Likewise, what might it have been in Caleb and Joshua that enabled them not to fall victim to this narrative, and instead to believe in their own agency?

Seemingly as a direct response to the episode of the spies, the very last paragraph of the parasha includes the commandment to make *tzitzit*, fringes on the corners of our garments. We are to look at them and, thereby, remember the role of the Holy One in bringing us out from Egypt. Whereas the spies were commanded *la-tur*, to scout out the land (Num. 13:2, 16, 17, 21), the *mitzvah* of *tzitzit* instructs us to look at the fringes and remember the *mitzvot*, "so that you do not follow [*lo toturu*] after your heart and eyes in your lustful urge" (Num. 15:39). That is, in looking at the *tzitzit* and remembering the Exodus, we are, it seems, meant to disrupt the normal conventions of our conditioning—just as God disrupted the political and moral order by performing the act of redemption itself.

Building on this theme, Rabbi Levi Yitzchak of Berditchev offers the following short reflection on the last line of the parasha.

קדושת לוי שלח

אני ה' אלהיכם אשר הוצאתי אתכם וכו' אני ה' אלהיכם (במדבר טו, מא). כפל. הכלל, כי אדם צריך תמיד להעלות על מחשבתו שכל דבוריו ומחשבותיו ותנועותיו עושים רושם למעלה ולכך צריך האדם לשמור כל מחשבותיו ותנועותיו ודיבוריו בידאת ה' כיון שכל תנועותיו עושים רושם למעלה וזה הוא כלל גדול בעבדות הבורא שצריך האדם להעלות על מחשבתו שכל תנועותיו עושים רושם למעלה, כי השם יתברך יודע מחשבות בני אדם ומשגיח תמיד בהשגחה פרטיות על כל דרכי בני אדם, וזה העיקר עבדות האדם שאדם יעלה על מחשבתו שהשם יתברך משגיח עליו על דרכיו. וזהו אני ה' אלהיכם אשר הוצאתי אתכם מארץ מצרים, ותעלה על מחשבתך אני ה' אלהיכם, אני משגיח תמיד על כל דרכיך:

Kedushat Levi, Shlach

"I YHVH am your God, who brought you out of the land of Egypt to be your God: I, YHVH, am your God." (Num. 15:41) Why the repetition?

We take it as an established general principle that we must constantly bring to mind that all our words, thoughts, and movements [in this world] make an imprint in the celestial world above. Therefore, we must attend carefully to all our thoughts, movements, and words with profound awareness

of their awesome potential, since every action carries cosmic
significance.

This is, in fact, a guiding value in our service of the Creator.
For the Blessed Ineffable One is conscious of human thought
and continually watches over and cares about all the ways [we
act and live]. Practicing with this awareness is the essence of
our service [of the Divine]—to be constantly aware that the
Blessed Ineffable One watches over us and our ways [and is
impacted by them].

This [then is the significance of the repeated phrases in our
verse]: "I am YHVH your God who brought you out of the
land of Egypt"—bring to mind always that "I am YHVH your
God"—I constantly watch over all your ways.

For the *Kedushat Levi*, our unconscious, unthinking thoughts, impulses,
and drives are Egypt. The commandment of *zechirat yetziat mitzrayim*, remembering the Exodus from Egypt, is not only about remembering the
historical event of the Exodus, but, in each and every moment, bringing
mindful awareness to our thoughts, words, and actions. In bringing that attention and awareness to our inner lives, we continually re-enact the Exodus.

But beyond this, it is not *we* who take ourselves out—rather, it is the Divine. Just as the Holy One took our ancestors out of Egypt, so too, in every
moment in which we bring mindful awareness to our thoughts, words, and
deeds, the Holy One is bringing us, personally, out of Egypt. This is what
the *Kedushat Levi* means by referring to *hashgacha pratit*, or individual Divine
providence—less that God looks out for us like a guardian angel and more
that the Redeemer is continually working through us to enable us to become
free from the Egypt of our lesser thoughts and impulses.

Thus the *Kedushat Levi* reads the full verse to say: 1) "I am YHVH your
God who brought you out of the land of Egypt"—and thus, when you bring
mindful awareness to each moment, I am working through you to liberate
you anew;" and 2) "I am YHVH your God"—when we live out this kind
of awareness, and with the concomitant awe that every thought, word, and
action matters in the most profound sense, then the Divine is made manifest
in our own lives and in the world.

One of the elements of the *Kedushat Levi* I find most striking is the language of *roshem*, or imprint. Like other Hasidic masters, R. Levi Yitzchak
offers us the image of our own lives and actions leaving a trace, a footprint,
in another stratum of reality. Returning to Jerome Bruner, there seems here
to be an inversion. The institutional forces of language—and the forces that

contribute to the creation and sustenance of that language—leave their imprint on us subconsciously as we "pick up" the words and cues of a culture,
and we then reinscribe their imprint by using them. In the *Kedushat Levi's*
teaching however, it is *we,* even on an individual level, who leave an imprint
on the upper worlds.

Within this inversion, I would suggest, lies an invitation, even a call,
to Jewish mindfulness as a vital form of protest against oppressive forces
(=*mitzrayim*). In her book *The Inner Work of Racial Justice,* legal scholar Rhonda Magee discusses how our individual practice can, and indeed must, be
brought to bear in service of upending the kinds of unconscious bias that is
hard-wired into us, our language, and much of our society. In doing so, she
echoes the *Kedushat Levi.*

> When stressed out, or when operating on automatic pilot, we
> often retreat into the ways in which we have been trained. We
> read cues that we have associated with race, cues that intersect
> race with gender, sexual orientation, and other forms of iden-
> tification. In ways that range from unconscious to blatantly
> obvious, we all read and rely on such cues...
>
> If we see ourselves as separate, hard-bound, and apart from
> other humans in essential ways (as many people do), then the
> subtle but life-shaping trainings of race make our hyperindi-
> vidualized identities seem all the more real. Ideas about race
> reinforce our tendency not only to see ourselves as separate
> from others in profound ways, but also to group others along
> the lines of demarcation that we have been taught to see. We
> are each and all engaged, to one degree or another, in race-
> making or "doing" race—the processes and practices by and
> through which racialization happens. In many and various
> ways, we each participate in the activities by which the idea
> of race remains strong, and the practices of racism remain
> relational. We do this in subtle, fleeting moments—in deci-
> sions such as where we will live, from whom we will learn,
> and so on—that set us on one road and all but foreclose others.
> Whether we are black, white, brown, yellow, or red, we are
> caught up in racecraft.
>
> And yet, if we can see more clearly through the lenses of
> awareness, we recognize that while we are trained for division
> in so many ways, we are also inherently capable of experienc-
> ing connection with one another. Becoming more aware of

our own racecraft, our own subtle racial predispositions and predictions, is a step toward increasing our capacity for doing just that. Noticing that we are sometimes guilty of micro-aggressions is another step in the right direction. Practicing mindful awareness of these aspects of our conditioning and habits of the mind helps us to know what we are up against *within ourselves* as we seek to make change in the world.[82]

The thing we are "up against within ourselves" we might call our own Egypt. In bringing mindful awareness to our thoughts, words, and actions, we are, with the aid of the Creator, liberating ourselves from Egypt once again—and again and again. Through an accumulation of countless acts of liberation, we might just invite others into doing the same, thereby helping to liberate them. And if enough of us live into this kind of consciousness, the systems and languages of oppression may finally be upended.

Those countless acts of liberation come about not through simply good intentions, but through practice. Remembering the Exodus from Egypt is the stated purpose for numerous *mitzvot*—embodied practices and disciplines—ranging from observing Shabbat to the Passover seder to, in Parashat Shlach, affixing and beholding the *tzitzit* on the corners of our garments. Through an exquisite range of such practices, the Torah invites us to practice a more liberatory awareness, to re-enact the Exodus in every moment of every day.

### Questions for Reflection and Conversation

- The *Kedushat Levi* says, "The Blessed Ineffable One is conscious of human thought and continually watches over and cares about all the ways [we act and live]." How do you understand this—if you do at all? What does it mean to you, if anything, that "God watches over and cares" about you and your behavior? Do you find this idea comforting, challenging, inviting, repelling, or something else? Why or why not?

- Both *Kedushat Levi* and Magee point us to a practice of constant awareness. Is this something with which you are familiar? Is it a practice to which you aspire? When, how, why or why not?

- When, if ever, have you encountered a moment or incident in

---

[82] Magee, *The Inner Work of Racial Justice*, 133-134.

which you became more aware or conscious of some unconscious impulses, biases, or assumptions? What happened? What was it about you in that moment that enabled that awareness to come about? What was it about the other people or the setting in which the incident took place that helped it to happen? Can you imagine that this might have been a moment of the Divine working through you? Play with that image; let it bring its own force to bear. How might allowing this conception of Divine-human interaction affect how you behave in the future? Would you want to cultivate this experience? If so, what might you have to do (practices, intentional communities of awareness and action, reading and talking, etc.)?

## Ideas for Practice

This week, if you have access to one, consider wearing a tallit and including Num. 15:37-40 in your prayer practice. (This paragraph, which contains the commandment to wear *tzitzit*, fringes, on the corners of our garments, is the third paragraph of the *Shema* in the traditional liturgy.)

Spend time in meditation before reciting the words.

Bring your attention to the tactile sensation of the *tzitzit* in your fingers, perhaps with your eyes closed. Observe the sensations that arise.

Then, open your eyes and bring a gentle, loving, and attention-filled gaze to the *tzitzit*, bringing to mind the words of the Torah, "That shall be your fringe; look at it and recall all the commandments of the Divine and observe them, so that you do not follow your heart and eyes in your lustful urge" (Num. 15:39). Again, observe what sensations—physical, mental, emotional—arise for you.

As you prepare to recite Num. 15:41 ("I YHVH am your God, who brought you out of the land of Egypt to be your God: I, the YHVH your God"), make an intention to open your awareness to unconscious thoughts, urges, and impulses. Investigate: Might any of these constitute an inner Egypt for you? How might becoming aware of them lead to your own exodus? What might that feel like?

Try to sit with this awareness for several minutes before offering a gentle kiss to the *tzitzit* in your hand and letting them go.

# Korach: How Do We Disagree?

There may be no question more pressing for us as a society than this one: How do we disagree? From state legislatures to Twitter, from college campuses to family dinner tables, we seem to be suffering from our inability to sit with discomfort and difference. It appears we have developed a dangerous cultural habit of trying to eliminate ideas, attitudes, and people who trigger emotional distress.

I hasten to add that I'm not making a judgment on whether that distress is real or justified. If one of my children says they're hurting, I accept that they're hurting until they say they aren't. I don't judge for them the extent of their pain. I trust they'll figure that out and articulate it on their own. And I extend the same courtesy to people who aren't my children—which is to say, the rest of the world.

As important, I understand my role and responsibility as a parent to be to help my children develop the capacity to manage their suffering—of course, to avoid unnecessary pain; but also to accept that living means bearing the slings and arrows of existence, which are simply a part of life. In every moment we are dying and being reborn, experiencing both pleasant and unpleasant sensations. My own Jewish mindfulness practice is an exercise in being aware of and responding mindfully to my own calling as an *eved Hashem*, a servant of the Divine, in the moment—and not following mindlessly after the longings of my eyes and heart, in the concluding words of last week's parasha. I aim to live this way not only for myself, but as an example for my children—and, by extension, for my students and the rest of the world.

Yet it is one thing to do that internally, responding to my own inner voice. It is another to do it in response to the voices and words and actions of other people—not an unrelated thing, but still a different kind of endeavor. When the stimuli involve other people, the response, in my experience, becomes more complex. How do I sit with the discomfort someone else may be causing me because of their opinions or views? Likewise, how do I sit with the discomfort that someone else experiences because of my words, actions, or beliefs? How do I avoid being triggered, and instead respond wisely? And not only within myself: How do I, as a family member, a neighbor, a citizen, a leader, hold a civic space in which others can do the same, a space of dialogue and productive disagreement?

## Korach: Unheavenly Disputes

These questions come to mind in reading Parashat Korach, which in the

Rabbinic imagination becomes the paradigmatic example of unhealthy disagreement:

> **Pirkei Avot 5:17**
> Every argument that is [for the sake of] heaven is destined to
> prove constructive. But if it is not [for the sake of] heaven—it
> is not destined to prove constructive. What [is an example of an
> argument for the sake of] heaven? The argument of Hillel and
> Shammai. What [is an example of an argument not for the sake
> of] heaven? The argument of Korach and all of his followers.

Commenting on this passage, the 15th-century Italian commentator Rabbi
Obadiah of Bartenura writes:

> [Regarding] the controversy which is for the sake of Heaven,
> the purpose and aim is to arrive at the truth, and this [process]
> proves constructive, as it is said, "from a disagreement the truth
> will be revealed." This was revealed in the disputes between
> Hillel and Shammai, [as in the end it was determined] that the
> law was like the school of Hillel.[83] And regarding a controversy
> which is not for the sake of Heaven, its purpose is to achieve
> power and for the love of victory, and its end will be destruc-
> tive. This is as we find in the dispute of Korach and his band,
> as their aim and end-goal was a lust for honor and power—just
> the opposite.

That is straightforward enough, yet it still leaves us asking, What are the
actual habits and practices of mind, body, and soul that you or I or we might
cultivate that would enable us to sit with the internal discomfort and distress
that arise when we're in a disagreement, much less a public one like those of
Hillel and Shammai or Korach and Moses?

To answer this, we'll look to a teaching from Rabbi Nachman of Breslov

---

[83] See Babylonian Talmud Eruvin 13b: "Rav Abba quoting Samuel said: For three
years the School of Shammai and the School of Hillel disagreed. One said, 'The law
is according to us,' and the other said, 'The law is according to us.' At last a voice from
heaven went forth and said, 'Both these and these are the words of the Living God.' If
so, how is it that the School of Hillel merited that the law is determined according to
them? Because they were at ease. They were humble. They studied their own words and
the words of the School of Shammai. And not only this—they mentioned the words of
the School of Shammai before their own."

(1772-1810) which emphasizes the central role of awareness, *da'at,* in cultivating productive disagreement and peace on the intrapersonal, interpersonal, and communal levels.

ליקוטי מוהר"ן נו:ח

כִּי הַשָּׁלוֹם תָּלוּי בְּדַעַת וְכַנַ"ל. וּמַחֲלֹקֶת הוּא הֵפֶךְ הַדַּעַת. אַךְ יֵשׁ
מַחֲלֹקֶת שֶׁהוּא לְשֵׁם שָׁמַיִם, שֶׁהוּא בֶּאֱמֶת דַּעַת גָּדוֹל מְאֹד, יוֹתֵר מֵהַדַּעַת
שֶׁל שָׁלוֹם, כִּי בֶּאֱמֶת זֶה הַמַּחֲלֹקֶת הִיא אַהֲבָה וְשָׁלוֹם גָּדוֹל, כְּמוֹ שֶׁאָמְרוּ
חֲכָמֵינוּ זִכְרוֹנָם לִבְרָכָה (קידושין ל:): אֶת וָהֵב בְּסוּפָה—לֹא זָזוּ מִשָּׁם עַד
שֶׁנַּעֲשׂוּ אוֹהֲבִים זֶה לָזֶה. וְזֶה שֶׁאָמְרוּ רַבּוֹתֵינוּ זִכְרוֹנָם לִבְרָכָה (אבות פ"ה):
מַחֲלֹקֶת שֶׁהִיא לְשֵׁם שָׁמַיִם סוֹפָה לְהִתְקַיֵּם; הַיְנוּ שֶׁבֶּאֱמֶת הִיא אַהֲבָה
כַּנַ"ל. וְזֶה: סוֹפָה לְהִתְקַיֵּם, בְּחִינַת אַהֲבָה, כְּמוֹ שֶׁכָּתוּב (במדבר כ"א:י"ד):
אֶת וָהֵב בְּסוּפָה כַּנַ"ל.

וְזֶה בְּחִינַת מֹשֶׁה, כִּי מֹשֶׁה הוּא בְּחִינַת הַדַּעַת, שֶׁהוּא בְּחִינַת
מַחֲלֹקֶת לְשֵׁם שָׁמַיִם. וְעַל כֵּן מֹשֶׁה הוּא רָאשֵׁי-תֵבוֹת מַחֲלוֹקֶת שַׁמַּאי
הִלֵּל, שֶׁהֵם בְּחִינַת מַחֲלֹקֶת לְשֵׁם שָׁמַיִם.

וְעַל כֵּן הָיָה גְּאֻלַת מִצְרַיִם עַל-יְדֵי מֹשֶׁה, כִּי עִקַּר הַגְּאֻלָּה—עַל-יְדֵי
הַדַּעַת, כְּמוֹ שֶׁכָּתוּב (שמות ט"ז:ו') וִידַעְתֶּם כִּי ה' הוֹצִיא אֶתְכֶם וְכוּ'
(ויקרא כ"ג:מ"ג) לְמַעַן יֵדְעוּ וְכוּ'.

וְזֶה שֶׁכָּתוּב בַּזֹּהַר הַקָּדוֹשׁ (תצוה דף קפג:) כִּי מַצָּה הִיא אַסְוָתָא, כִּי
מַצָּה, שֶׁהִיא בְּחִינַת מַחֲלֹקֶת לְשֵׁם שָׁמַיִם, בְּחִינַת דַּעַת, בְּחִינַת שָׁלוֹם
כַּנַ"ל, הוּא רְפוּאָה. כִּי שָׁלוֹם הוּא רְפוּאָה, כְּמוֹ שֶׁכָּתוּב (ישעיהו נ"ז:י"ט):
שָׁלוֹם שָׁלוֹם לָרָחוֹק וְלַקָּרוֹב אָמַר ה' וּרְפָאתִיו; כִּי עִקַּר הַחוֹלְאַת, חַס
וְשָׁלוֹם, הוּא מֵחֲמַת הֶעְדֵּר הַשָּׁלוֹם, הַיְנוּ מַחֲלֹקֶת הַיְסוֹדוֹת, שֶׁיְסוֹד
אֶחָד מִתְגַּבֵּר עַל חֲבֵרוֹ, וְשָׁלוֹם הוּא רְפוּאָה.

וְזֶה שֶׁנִּקְרָא מַצָּה לֶחֶם עֹנִי (דברים ט"ז:ג'), כִּי אֵין עָנִי אֶלָּא מִן הַדַּעַת
(נדרים מא), וְזֶה בְּחִינַת חוּלָה, כְּמוֹ שֶׁכָּתוּב (שמואל-ב יג): מַדּוּעַ אַתָּה
כָּכָה דַּל בֶּן הַמֶּלֶךְ, וּמַצָּה הִיא אַסְוָתָא כַּנַ"ל, וְזֶה לֶחֶם עֹנִי, שֶׁהוּא
רְפוּאָה לְהָעָנִי כַּנַ"ל:

**Likkutei Moharan 56:8**
Peace is dependent upon awareness [*da'at*]… while dispute is the opposite of awareness. Nevertheless, there is dispute that is for the sake of Heaven, which in truth is expansive awareness, even greater than the awareness that is the foundation of peace. For in fact, such dispute expresses great love and peace, as our Sages, of blessed memory, said (Kiddushin 30b): *"et vaHeV be'Sufah"* (Numbers 21:14)—"they [those in dispute for the sake of Heaven] do not move from there [where they are engaged in dispute] until they become *oHaVim* (lovers). [And, do not read the next word as *be'Sufah,* the place called Sufah, but *be'Sofah,* at its conclusion]."

This is the meaning of what our Sages, of blessed memory, said:
"Dispute that is for the sake of Heaven, will in *Sofah* (the end)
prove constructive" (Avot 5:17), as it is truly an expression of love
(as we said). This dispute will prove constructive as it is grounded
in the dimension of love, as it is written, *"et vaHeV be'SuFaH,"*
as explained above.[84]

This corresponds to Moses, because Moses is the aspect of
*awareness*, which [as we suggest above] is tied to *machloket* (dispute) for the sake of Heaven. Thus, [Moses=] *MoSheH* is an
acrostic for *Machloket Shamai Hillel*, the ongoing disagreement
between Shammai and Hillel, for they embodied/enacted the
form of dispute for the sake of Heaven.[85]

The redemption from Egypt therefore came through Moses,
because the essence of redemption is through awareness, as it
is written, "and you will be aware of YHVH who took you out
of Egypt" (Exodus 16:6); "You shall live in booths seven days; all
citizens in Israel shall live in booths, in order that future generations may live with the awareness that I made the Israelite people
live in booths when I brought them out of the land of Egypt, I
the LORD your God." (Leviticus 23:42-43) …

Now, it is written in the holy Zohar (II, 183b): "matzah is a
remedy." For matzah participates in the nexus of dispute for the
sake of Heaven/awareness/peace… and is a cure. This is because
peace is a cure, as it is written (Isaiah 57:19), "Peace, peace, to
the far and the near—says God—and I will heal them." For
in the main, illness, Heaven forbid, stems from an absence of
peace—i.e., dispute among the [four foundational humors, or]
elements, when one of the elements overpowers another. But
peace is a cure.

But matzah is called "poor person's bread." [It represents
dispute for the sake of Heaven, yet] poverty can be considered
the lack of *awareness* (Nedarim 41a). This is then reflected in a sick
person, as it is written (2 Samuel 13:4), "Why are you so poor [of
spirit], O prince?" But matzah, [which represents dispute for the
sake of Heaven], is a remedy [for impoverished awareness], as

---

[84] Rebbe Nachman is engaging in a wordplay here: the letters H and V (ה and ב) in
the word *vahev* also appear in *ahava*, love. We have capitalized these letters here to help
illuminate the teaching.

[85] Again, this is a wordplay: the Sh and H (ש and ה) in Moses's name signal, respectively, Shammai and Hillel.

explained above. This is the meaning of "poor person's bread": it is a cure for poverty [of awareness], as explained above.

Within this rich web of interrelated concepts, Rebbe Nachman weaves together the notions of awareness, dispute, and peace through the symbols of Moses and matzah, and through the centrality of these latter two to the Exodus from Egypt. Perhaps most important for us, he draws our attention to the connection between *da'at*, or mindful awareness, and *machloket l'shem shamayim*, dispute for the sake of heaven. Whereas *machloket*, or dispute, that is not for the sake of heaven is grounded in a lack of awareness, *machloket* that comes from a place of mindful awareness is both ultimately destined to prove constructive (as per the Mishnah) and is the basis of *shalom*, wholeness and peace.

In the concluding paragraphs, Rebbe Nachman suggests this is true not only interpersonally, but intrapersonally as well: When we are not whole with ourselves, when we do not practice mindful awareness [that is, cultivate our capacity of *da'at*] within our own lived experience, then we become party to, as it were, a *machloket*, a dispute with our own nature—between the elements within us. That can lead to spiritual illness (and perhaps other forms of illness too). By contrast, when we cultivate our capacity for *da'at*, we help ourselves to better manage the impulses, drives, urges and thoughts that make up our inner life, leading to greater peace within our own heart-minds and, in turn, within the larger collectivities of which we are part.

## Practice for Transformation in the Age of Information

This lesson, about the vital link between inner spiritual work and communal peacemaking, is one we would do well to lift up much more in our communal and societal discourse today. The advent of social media, in particular, has given a bullhorn and a forum to those who shout rather than listen, who react rather than respond, who seek to divide and label people rather than embrace and dignify people. In turn, those who are not party to the debate often seem to feel pressured to pick a side, rather than sustain a more deliberative and contemplative way of engaging with fellow images of the Divine. Facebook—to say nothing of Twitter—is not generally a space for *machloket l'shem shamayim*.

Yet even, or perhaps precisely in these spaces, we would do well to take Rebbe Nachman to heart. What might it look like if we brought our practice to bear on our civic lives—as they play out in social media and other spheres? For me, Jewish mindfulness practice has helped me not to be triggered by words and images I might initially find shocking or inflammatory. By cultivating my capacity for *da'at*, I find I've developed a spiritual muscle that allows me to first notice the sensations arising in my body, in my gut, in my heart, and to gently inquire of myself, "What is it I'm feeling right now? Where is that feeling coming from?" In doing so, I sometimes notice that I'm sensing a kind of internalized pressure to pick a side, to proclaim my solidarity. I give myself the time and space to listen to my own body and heart-mind, and to discern whether the impulse I'm feeling is coming from a place of truth, the Divine voice within, or perhaps from somewhere else.

Having brought my awareness to these sensations and these deeper questions, I next turn to questions about what action I might take: If I respond, why am I doing so? What's motivating me? Will my response generate more heat or more light? Is it grounded in compassion, or in something else? Will it make the *Shekhina*, the Divine presence, more recognizable? What might be other implications of my responding right now? If this really is so important, what might be other ways I might engage that could help others develop their own awareness and contribute to greater *shleimut*/wholeness in themselves and the world?

Again, my awareness in this practice is not limited to cognitive or intellectual faculties. More often than not, I find my own body aids in my awareness about how my answers are or aren't in alignment with my deeper sense of the Divine call. If I land on a proposed course of action and my gut is still saying to me, "This isn't quite right," I listen to that—because it's most often another way I experience the Holy One calling to me. When, at last, my body is at peace with an idea for speech or action, I find I'm able to express myself in ways that bring greater peace to the conversation.

I don't claim to have any particular wisdom, of course—far from it. This is not some radically new concept; indeed, it is radically old, as old as Shammai and Hillel. But in a culture that values the new, the immediate, the loud, and the snarky, that thrives on dividing and disconnecting us from ourselves and one another—a culture, in short, of *machloket lo l'shem shamayim*, disputes not for the sake of heaven—we are called to respond with *da'at*, with expansive mindful awareness, in order to nurture *shalom* in ourselves and in the world.

## Questions for Reflection & Conversation

- Rebbe Nachman invokes the following Talmudic teaching: "Those in dispute for the sake of Heaven do not move from where they are engaged in dispute until they become lovers." In your own words, what do you think this teaching means? How do you understand the process of remaining in dispute leading to love? What kind of love is being referred to here? Do you have any experience in your own life with this kind of disagreement? If so, what about you, your interlocutor, and the moment contributed to the outcome? How does this help you to understand Rebbe Nachman's teaching?

- In your own experience, does cultivating your capacity for *da'at/* mindful awareness contribute to your ability to sit with the discomfort of disagreement? If so, what is it about this practice that helps you? If not, why?

- Are there areas of your life in which you might want to bring more mindfulness practice to your approach to disagreements—work, family, social media, religious or community associations, something else? How might you do that? How might you employ your mindfulness practice to support you in bringing more mindfulness to these situations?

## Ideas for Practice

This meditation practice by my colleague Rabbi Myriam Klotz invites us to cultivate our awareness not only in our minds, but in our bodies as well, through noticing the sensations that come to us through our senses. Consider trying this practice this week to perhaps develop some added dimensions of *da'at* that can aid in your capacity to be present with uncomfortable emotions and sensations that arise—in disagreements or in any other part of life.

As you find your location for this practice, notice your body settling into the chair or the couch, or whatever structure it is that supports you. Bring awareness to the sensations along the back of your body, where the body and the chair, cushion, or other structure come together. Feel the pressure and the solidness of that chair as it holds your bottom, perhaps the lower back, legs.

Bring your awareness down toward the feet. Allow the toes to move and wiggle a little bit and just feel as you notice them bare or inside your shoes or socks. Notice and feel the movement in your toes, aliveness in your feet. Notice what sensations come to be as you move and wiggle your toes, and then let your feet settle. Let them rest on the floor. Feel the soles of the feet making contact with what is underneath them.

As you settle into your practice, sustain your awareness in this body, in its aliveness, noticing sensations as they come and they go, and the various senses of this body. If you have the ability of sight, notice what you see with your eyes. Notice qualities of light and darkness, of colors, of shapes. Just notice, and let them pass before your eyes as you look around. When you're ready, you can let your eyes close.

If you have the capacity of hearing, turn your attention now to sound. Notice yourself hearing any sounds that may be in this room where you are, or outside of the room, outside of this building. Just notice sound coming and going, its volume, its tenor, its sharpness or softness, muffled or clear. What do you notice that you hear right now? Again, focus on the practice of noticing what it is as what the body is perceiving and experiencing in this moment. Cultivate mindful presence. Land right here, where we are. Sit with this awareness for several minutes.

Now bring awareness to the quality of touch, of sensations. Notice how clothing may feel against the outer skin of the body. Rub a finger gently against whatever clothing may be on your legs. Just notice that. You can notice the quality or temperature of air against skin. Is it cool or warm? Dry, moist? Any scent or smell that may be in the air that you perceive through the sense of smell.

And now, with closed eyes, allowing your body to rest in a position of relative comfort, begin to let your mind's eye move through the body, noticing areas that might feel comfortable or pleasant and noting areas that might feel less comfortable and not so pleasant. Is there an itch? See if you can notice an itch and perhaps not fulfill the need to scratch. Just notice. Or if there's an area of tightness, perhaps just notice that. Notice what it feels like to be with that slight unpleasant sensation.

Then bring attention to the nostrils, where breath moves in and out of the body. Begin to bring your attention to that breath. Follow it in your mind's eye. As it proceeds down into the chest, into the belly. And then, as it leaves, follow that journey out. Notice the inner abdominal wall, the inside of the belly expanding with the next in-breath, perhaps very slightly, the chest rising. Notice how the breath leaves your body. The slight movements, the inner belly, the lungs, the chest.

For the next little bit of time, continue to track the breath moving in the body, paying attention to whatever sensations or subtle movements come and go with the breath.

If you notice your mind begin to wander, as it will, simply bring your attention back and place it again in the body with any prominent sensation that may be happening now. Then let the breath resume as the centerpiece of your awareness.

This body filling and emptying of the breath. Just pay attention for one more cycle of in-breath and out-breath. As you complete that out-breath, you can let the eyes open. Complete the practice.

# Hukkat: How Do We Rebuke?

Like many other people, one of the most difficult things for me to do is give negative feedback. Whether at work, at home, or in public, I routinely run into internal fears when the situation invites pointing out to someone else what's wrong with their behavior. I'm worried about how they'll feel, about the conflict that is likely to be generated, about seeming judgmental or self-righteous. The thought of rebuking someone often feels icky.

At the same time, as I have gotten older, I've come to appreciate hearing negative feedback about myself because I've learned how essential it is for me to grow. As a parent and a leader, I've also developed a deeper appreciation for the reality that my critical feedback, and even occasional strong rebuke, is necessary for the good of my family or the group or organization I lead. Sometimes, without being aware of it, we test the boundaries of acceptable behavior—and at those times, I have found it is important not only for me, but for other members of the group and for the organization as a whole, for me to firmly draw a line and say, "That's out of bounds."

How do we give critical or negative feedback? How do we acknowledge the powerful emotions that may be at play—within ourselves, the object of our feedback, and other observers or members of a group? And, most importantly, how do we offer critique and rebuke in ways that lift up the Divine presence, rather than diminish it?

## Kind Words and Harsh Words

"Listen, you rebels! Shall we get water out of this rock?" Moses says angrily to the people in Parashat Hukkat. He then proceeds to strike the rock and indeed brings forth water, but in the process violates God's instruction to speak to the rock. As a result, God decrees that Moses will not enter the Promised Land, "because you did not trust Me enough to affirm My sanctity in the sight of the Israelite people." (Num. 20:10-12)

Classical commentators have long struggled to understand the nature of Moses's failure here that it merited such a significant consequence. Rashi's (1040-1105) explanation focuses on the opportunity for spiritual education that Moses seems to have missed:

Rashi on Numbers 20:12:2

To SANCTIFY ME—For had you spoken to the rock and it then brought forth water I would have been sanctified before the whole congregation, for they would have said: Consider that

this rock, which cannot speak and cannot hear and needs no
sustenance, yet it fulfils the bidding of the Omnipresent God!
How much more should we do so?

Ramban (Nachmanides, 1194-1270) takes a different approach, following Maimonides and emphasizing that Moses's anger provided a poor moral
example to his followers:

### Ramban on Parashat Hukkat
Maimonides understands [Moses's sin] to be that he inclined
to anger when he said, "Listen, you rebels!" God held him to a
high standard, for when someone of Moses's station gets angry
with the Israelites when it is not appropriate to be angry, and
any situation similar to that where such behavior would be
considered a desecration of the Divine Name, everyone looks
to him and learns from his words and actions.

Commenting on both of these commentaries, Rabbi Levi Yitzchak of
Berditchev (1740-1809) offers a lesson on rebuke, and particularly on giving
it from either a place of anger or a place of love.

קדושת לוי, במדבר, חקת ד'

ודברתם אל הסלע לעיניהם גו' יען לא האמנתם בי להקדישני לעיני
בני ישראל (במדבר כ, ז-יב). הנה רש"י והרמב"ן חולקים בחטא של
משה אחד מפרש על שאמר לישראל שמעו נאכר', ואחד מפרש
על שהכה את הסלע. והנראה שטעם אחד הוא, כי זה גרם זה.
והנה יש שני בחינות במוכיח שמוכיח את ישראל שיעשו רצון
הבורא ברוך הוא. אחד, שמוכיח בדברים טובים, דהיינו שאומר
לכל איש ישראל גודל מעלתו ומקום מקור מחצב נשמתו אשר
באמת נשמת ישראל חצובה למעלה מכסא כבוד וגודל הנחת רוח
אשר להבורא יתברך כביכול ממצות כל איש ישראל וגודל השמחה
אשר בכל העולמות בעשות איש ישראל מצות הבורא בזה ובזה
התוכחה מטה את לב בני ישראל לעשות רצון הבורא ברוך הוא
לקבל כל איש מישראל עול מלכות שמים עליו.
ויש שמוכיח את ישראל בדברים קשים ובדברי ביושים עד שהם
מוכרחים לעשות רצון הבורא. והחילוק שביניהם, זה שמוכיח את
ישראל בטוב מעלה את נשמת ישראל למעלה למעלה ומספר
תמיד בצדקת ובגדולת ישראל כמה גדול כוחם למעלה וראוי הוא
להיות מנהיג על ישראל. וזה שמוכיח את ישראל בדברים קשים
אינו בבחינה הזאת.

והנה זה שמוכיח את ישראל בטוב ומספר תמיד בגדולת ישראל
וצדקתם אז כל הדברים הנבראים בעולם צריכין לעשות מעצמם
הרצון של ישראל לדבר שנבראו, דהיינו בשביל ישראל. אבל אם
אינו מספר ומעלה צדקת ישראל אז צריך להכריח כל הנברא
בהכרח גדול לעשות מה שנברא, דהיינו לעשות רצון ישראל.
והנה משה אמר בכאן שמעו נא המורים, הוכיח את ישראל בדברים
קשים ולכך הוצרך להכות את הסלע לעשות מה שנברא, כי אילו
היה מעלה את ישראל כנ"ל, וכמו שהיה כוונת הקדוש ברוך הוא
ודברת אל הסלע, כי אז היה מדבר אל הסלע אתה שנבראת בשביל
ישראל והם במעלה גדולה צריך אתה לעשות מה שנבראת, דהיינו
להוציא מים לישראל. אבל עתה שהוכיח את ישראל בדברים קשים
שמעו נא כו', הוצרך להכות את הסלע לעשות רצון ישראל, ונמצא
זה גרם את זה וטעם אחד הוא.
וזהו הרמז יען לא האמנתם בי להקדישני לעיני בני ישראל, כי זה
שמוכיח את ישראל בטוב יכול גם הוא להשיג את העם זה השכל.
וזה הרמז להקדישני לעיני בני ישראל, כמאמר חכמינו ז"ל עיני
עדה, חכמי עדה שגם הם ישיגו זה השכל:

## Kedushat Levi, Hukkat 4

"And speak to the rock in their sight … For you did not show
faith in me to sanctify me before the children of Israel."

Rashi and Ramban disagree about Moses' sin: One explains
that Moses said to Israel, "Listen you rebels!" and one says that
it is because he hit the rock. It would appear that they are really one and the same explanation, for one leads to the other.

For there are two types of people who rebuke Israel to do
the will of the Holy Blessed Creator. The first is the one who
rebukes with good words, telling each person of the greatness
of their high station, and the source from which their soul was
chiseled—for, in truth, the soul of a Jew is formed on high,
from the Throne of Glory—and the great pleasure that God
derives from the performance of each and every *mitzvah* by
each and every Jew, and the happiness that occurs in all the
worlds when a Jew performs the command of the Creator. In
this manner, this person inclines the heart of the children of
Israel to do the will of the Creator, for each to take on the yoke
of Divine Sovereignty.

But there is also the one who rebukes Israel with harsh
words, with shaming words, compelling them to do God's
will. The difference between them? The one who rebukes Israel

with good lifts up the soul of Israel, higher and higher. They constantly speak of the righteousness and greatness of Israel, of how great their power is to ascend in the supernal realms. This one is fit to be a leader of Israel. But the one who rebukes Israel with harsh words is not like this.

The one who rebukes with goodness and speaks constantly of their righteousness and greatness—as a result of this, every part of creation must, *ipso facto,* do the will of Israel and perform that for which it was created: for the sake of [the people] Israel. But if one does not speak this way, one will be required to use great force to get creation to fulfill its purpose, which, in the supernal realms, is aligned with Israel's will.

Thus when Moses says here, "Listen you rebels!" he rebukes Israel with harsh words. Therefore, he must strike the rock in order to get it to fulfill its purpose. If he had exalted Israel as we have described, which is what God wants, and spoken to the rock, he would have said something like: "You that were created for Israel, who are so exalted, you must fulfill your purpose, namely to give forth water for Israel." But because he rebuked Israel with harsh words, he had to strike the rock to make it do the will of Israel. And thus we see that one kind of behavior causes the other, and in this manner the two explanations are one.

This is hinted at in the words of the verse, "For you did not have faith in me, to sanctify me in the eyes of the children of Israel:" One who rebukes Israel through goodness is able to bring the people to a greater level of insight. This is suggested by "to sanctify me in the eyes of the children of Israel," as our Sages taught: the eyes of the people are its wise ones. If Moses had acted with kindness, then the whole of the people would have come to this insight as well.

The *Kedushat Levi* invites us to explore some of the inner-life dimensions of this difficult question of negative feedback, critique and rebuke. When we speak harshly to others, it seems to suggest, we start down a path that evokes and perhaps even leads to physical violence. Since Moses started out by speaking harshly to the people, he inevitably wound up needing to hit the rock—and it is both parts of the action, the speech and the hitting which came as a result, that constitute his failure. Speech and action are linked, and in this case, he suggests, harsh words led to harsh action.

By contrast, had Moses rebuked the people lovingly, by reminding them of the Divine Presence within, between, and amongst them, he wouldn't have needed to hit the rock—his words would have sufficed. Powerful speech, which is both grounded in and expressive of the loving connection that binds us, the material world, and the Divine together, would ultimately be the means of bringing forth water from the rock.

Of course, this is easier said than done—even for Moses, and all the more so for us. When we are tired, angry, and stressed, we are more easily triggered, and our anger becomes more liable to flare up. That's precisely why we practice mindfulness, so that we can be more aware of what's happening in our minds, hearts, and bodies and become more intentional in choosing our response, rather than reacting out of base emotions. But the Berditchever helps us understand that there's even more to it than this: It is not only a matter of managing our emotions, but also of living in harmony and alignment with the Divine call within us. When R. Levi Yitzchak speaks of the link between rebuking with good words and the rest of creation performing its intended purpose, I understand him to mean that rebuking with good words helps us live in alignment with our own deepest nature. And when we are aligned with our own purpose, the rest of the world can be too. If we aren't, then neither is the rest of the world.

## Human Dignity and Divine Dignity

A useful related concept in this discussion is dignity. God's statement to Moses that, "you did not have faith in me, to sanctify me in the eyes of the children of Israel" could be understood to say that God felt as though God's dignity werereviolated. Harvard University scholar Donna Hicks observes how the honoring or violation of dignity is central to how we deliver and receive critique and rebuke:

> The wounds we inflict on one another during a breakdown of a relationship are not only painful, but also often humiliating. Whoever said, "Sticks and stones will break my bones, but words can never hurt me" got it wrong. Words can be used as weapons to psychologically annihilate people's dignity—their sense of value and worth. It's like aiming for the heart when you want to physically destroy someone. Words that take aim at dignity can inflict pain that is devastating. But unlike a physical injury, there are no broken bones, no blood, no obvious sign of a wound. The pain that results from interactions

that violate dignity remain invisible, causing people to suffer silently…

The emotional volatility of having our dignity honored or violated cannot be overstated. When people feel that their value and worth are recognized in their relationships, they experience a sense of well-being that enables them to grow and flourish. If, by contrast, their dignity is routinely injured, relationships are experienced as a source of pain and suffering.[86]

In this final paragraph, Hicks echoes R. Levi Yitzchak. When we can offer critique in a way that enhances human dignity, that speaks in kind words, that builds and raises up rather than humiliates and tears down, it isn't just a virtuous social-psychological circle we set in motion. The "sense of well-being that enables them to grow and flourish" brought about by dignity-affirming words is, in the *Kedushat Levi*, the alignment of the deepest workings of the universe with our own essence and that of the Creator.

## Questions for Conversation and Reflection

- Consider this passage from the *Kedushat Levi*: "The one who rebukes with goodness and speaks constantly of their righteousness and greatness—as a result of this, every part of creation must, *ipso facto*, do the will of Israel and perform that for which it was created: for the sake of [the people] Israel. But if one does not speak this way, one will be required to use great force to get creation to fulfill its purpose, which, in the supernal realms, is aligned with Israel's will." What do you think this means? Do you understand it to suggest that the natural laws of the universe literally "do the will of Israel?" If so, how does that work? If not, how do you explain what the text is getting at?

- Can you identify a moment in your own life when you received the kind of loving, dignity-affirming critique that Hicks and the *Kedushat Levi* speak of? What did it feel like—pleasant, unpleasant, or something else? Were you able to receive it lovingly in the moment, or did it take time? How did receiving this sort of critique change your behavior, but, perhaps more importantly, your

---

[86] Donna Hicks, *Leading with Dignity: How to Create a Culture That Brings Out the Best in People.* New Haven: Yale University Press, 2018, 23-24.

sense of self in the world? How did you behave following this sort of critique?

- Would you say it is relatively easy, or relatively hard, for you to offer critique in this way? What are some of the things that make it so? Is this something you work on as part of your spiritual practice? If so, what are some ways you do so? If not, is it something you'd like to try doing?

## Ideas for Practice

The following practice suggestions were originally offered by my colleague Rabbi Marc Margolius as part of his series, *Pitchei HaLevavot:* Heart Openings.

- In the heat of this season, try to find a *kabbalah*, or commitment, to "chill yourself" internally when you face a situation which might agitate or stir you up. You might look for a stone or rock to represent the rock struck by Moses: a rock to keep in your pocket and hold, or to keep on your desk, as a reminder to breathe, to notice internal agitation, and to allow it to pass before speaking or acting.

- Find or compose your own focus phrase which can bring your attention to any feelings of resentment or anger: examples might be, "may I be with these feelings," "these, too, shall pass," or "may You lead me beside still waters."

- "Rise above events that are inconsequential—both bad and good— for they are not worth disturbing your calmness of soul" (Rabbi Menachem Mendel Lefin of Satanov, *Cheshbon ha-Nefesh*). This week, see if you can identify small, daily situations which tend to "stir you up," and identify which you would consider "consequential" (worth attending to) and which are inconsequential (not really worth attending to). You might silently "label" these experiences as they arise, "filing" them as appropriate.

# Balak: How Does God Work?

One of the most challenging aspects of theology for many people is the notion of a personal God: a divine being who has a personality, who has relationships, who thinks and talks and acts like a person. As children, we tend to understand the Torah this way, and indeed there are many parts of the Torah that, in their surface reading, present God like this. God regrets making human beings and brings about the flood. God makes promises to the matriarchs and patriarchs. God rescues the Israelites from the Egyptians. God rewards and punishes. This mental image of God can be challenging for modern readers.

One of the reasons the idea of a personal God can be so hard for us as moderns is that we are schooled to rule out supernatural causes for anything. We are taught that history is reducible to economic causes (there was a bread shortage which brought about a revolution) or scientific causes (there was a drought which caused a bread shortage which brought about a revolution). But to ascribe actions to God (God caused a drought which caused a bread shortage which brought about a revolution) is a bridge too far. And this is to say nothing of the problem of theodicy: If God is present in these moments, why is God seemingly absent at others? Jews, perhaps more than anyone, have had to confront this question.

And not only on the collective historical level. Many folks find it challenging to accept the idea that God might be active in their life. God doesn't cause babies to be made and born—science has told us how that happens. And God doesn't cause people to fall in love or fortuitous business dealings to happen or healing from illness to come about. All these things can be explained just as well, if not better, without God.

Yet I'd like to suggest that we might reconsider the word "cause." For as much as scientism has taught us about what doesn't cause many things (i.e., a supernatural being hurling lightning bolts), it has also taught us that causation is exceptionally hard to pin down because the universe—much less the human mind—is so exceptionally complex. What did cause that drought that led to the bread shortage? Probably a whole bunch of things. And what did cause this couple to find each other and decide to spend their life together? Also, probably a whole bunch of things. And what really caused you to decide to read this essay right now? Again, probably a whole bunch of things.

One of the capacities we cultivate through Jewish mindfulness practice is to maintain a broader awareness of the many complex forces at play in any given moment. No moment is reducible to a single cause, just as no person—including ourselves—is reducible to a single label. When we practice deeper, more expansive, awareness, we often find that there are many things going on at the same time—and, beneath that, we may become aware of other stirrings, deeper undertows, gently but firmly pulling or beckoning to us. I'd like to suggest that this might be a way we can think differently about God.

## How Does God Change Balaam's Speech?

To help us get there, we can turn to a teaching on Parashat Balak from the *Ma'or VaShemesh* of Rabbi Kalonymus Kalman Halevi Epstein (1753-1825). In this passage he is commenting on Balaam's statement that, even if he were to be paid a handsome amount of gold and silver, he would be compelled to say whatever words God puts in his mouth.

מאור ושמש, בלק ד'

"ויען בלעם ויאמר אל עבדי בלק אם יתן לי בלק מלא ביתו כסף וזהב לא אוכל לעבור את פי ה' אלהי לעשות קטנה או גדולה." ויש להתבונן מה לשון "בית"? מה מדה הוא בית מלא זהב? וכי דרך למדוד בבתים כסף וזהב? הול"ל "כלים מלאים כסף וזהב" או "כיסים מלאים כסף וזהב"! ותו קשה הדיקדק הנ"ל: מאי "לעשות קטנה או גדולה"? הול"ל "לעשות טובה או רעה" כאשר אמר לבלק "הלא אל מלאכיך אשר שלחת לאמר אם יתן לי בלק כו' לא אוכל לעשות טובה או רעה מלבי". מה הוא "קטנה או גדולה"? איזה דבר קטן או גדול? וצריכא למודעי.

ונראה ע"ד הנ"ל דהענין הוא כך דהקב"ה ברא את העולם, וברא את העולם עפ"י טבע. והנה האומות העולם סוברים שהעולם כמנהגו נוהג, אבל אנחנו קבלנו מהאבות העולם, אפילו קודם מתן תורה, שהעולם מתנהג עפ"י השגחה פרטיות, לשלם לאיש כמעשיהו. והראייה מדור אנוש שהציף שליש העולם, ובדור המבול ששטף את כל העולם, וישאר אך נח הצדיק ובניו. וגם מהפיכת סדום, אשר הפך ה' באפו ובחמתו. והצדיקים ממשיכים את "ההויות" לתוך "הטבע", שהיא בגימטריא "אלהים", ומיחדים הכל. כי "ה' הוא האלהים". והרשעים מפרידין ומאבדין את העולם, לפי שהולכים אחרי הטבע לבד, ומפרידים השם "הויה מהטבע שהוא גימ' "אלהים. ובעו"ה בזמן הגלות, כביכול, אין השם שלם, כי יש פירוד בין י"ה לחצי שם האחרון כידוע. והצדיקים כל כוונתם שמיחדין במחשבתם השם הוי"ה לשם "אלהים שהוא "הטבע. ובזה הם מקיימים העולם וממשיכים "ההויות ממקור הרחמים, מי"ג ת"ד עילאה, לתוך "הטבע שהוא גימ' "אלהים, ומיחדים השמות "ה' הוא אלקים", ומקטנים השם "אלהים" לעשותו שם אלהי כנ"ל. כידוע, כי שם "אלהי" הוא לבוש הנשמה, ומסתיר אותה ממקטריגים

כמאמרינו בכל יום מה שתיקנו לנו חז"ל: "אלהי נשמה שנתת בי
כו'", וממשיכים שמות "ההוי"ה" משלשה שמות "ההוי"ה", שהוא
מקור הי"ג ת"ד עילאה, שהמה נקראו "גדלות המוחין". ועי"ז
מקטינים השם "אלהים" וכאמור.

והנה בלעם הרשע ימ"ש כל רצונו היה להפוך, למשוך אחרי
הטבע ולעשות פירוד בשם הוי' חלילה. כאשר נעשה פירוד
בעו"ה אח"כ בזמן הגלות, ונעשה כביכול השם קטן ש"כל הנשמה
תהלל י"ה" דייקא. די לעולם להשתמש בשתי אותיות מהשם
עד ביאת הגואל בב"א. לזה היה ג"כ כל כוונת בלעם הרשע
לעשות כביכול השם של רחמים קטן, ולהגדיל שם "אלהים" שיהיה
חלילה התגברות הדינין ר"ל. והשי"ת ברוב רחמיו מפיר עצת גוים
הניא מחשבות עמים, ובע"כ שם רסן בפי בלעם הרשע שיהיה
מוכרח לברכם ולמשוך רחמים גדולים ממקור עליון. כידוע, לא קם
בישראל כמשה, אבל באו"ה קם ומנו בלעם, והם ברכות עליונות
עד למאד.

ונבוא אל ביאור הפסוק "ויען בלעם ויאמר אל עבדי בלק
אם יתן לי בלק מלא ביתו כו'". ר"ל המילוי של בית הוא ת"י
והוא בגימטריא "כישף". וזהו "מלא ביתו" דייקא: ביתו של בלק
לא יוכל "לעבור את פי ה' אלהי לעשות קטנה או גדולה": ר"ל
כנ"ל, "לעשות קטנה", היינו לעשות השם "הויה" קטנה, להפרידו
חלילה. "או גדולה": ר"ל להגדיל שם אלהים, שהוא מקור הדינים
והגבורות, לפי שאין בידו כלל. וזהו שאמר "לא אוכל לעבור את
פי ה' 'אלהי'": ר"ל שלא יוכל "לעבור את פי ה' וכו'", היינו שם
"הויה", להקטינו חלילה, "אלהי", ר"ל שם "אלהי" שהוא לבוש
הנשמות ומסתירו מהדינים. אינני יכול לעבור להגדולות, ולעשותו
גדול, שיהיה "אלהים" שהוא התגבורת הדינים ר"ל. כי לא יוכל
לעבור כלל, לפי שמוכרח הי' מאת ית"ש ויהיה שם הוי"ה שלם,
שהוא שם רחמים. ושם "אלהים" יהיה בקטנות, היינו "אלהי"
ורחמים, עלינו ועל כל ישראל.

Ma'or VaShemesh, Balak 4

"Balaam replied to Balak's officials, 'Though Balak were to give me his house full of silver and gold, I could not do anything, big or little, contrary to the command of the YHVH my God'" (Num. 22:18). We need to investigate to understand: Why does Balaam speak of a house here? And what is the measure of a house full of gold [or silver]? Is this any recognizable form to measure silver and gold? If anything, we might speak in familiar terms, of, for instance, vessels full of silver and gold, or sacks full of silver and gold. Further, why does Balaam

speak of doing a "large or small thing?" Shouldn't he instead
say, "to do good or evil," as he says to Balak [in a parallel pas-
sage]: "Though Balak were to give me his house full of silver
and gold, I could not of my own accord do anything good or
bad contrary to the YHVH'S command. What YHVH says,
that I must say" (Num. 24:13). What does he mean, then, when
our verse says: "big or little"? What big or little thing? This
all requires study.

It appears from what we have said that the notion here is as
follows: The Holy Blessed One created the universe according
to the laws of nature. The nations of the world reason that the
world goes of its own accord. But we have received the tradition
from our ancient ancestors, even before the giving of the Torah, that the world has been conducted through Divine providence... The righteous connect the supernatural life force with
the natural world [ha-teva] which, in Gematria, is numerically
equivalent to Elohim [both equal 86], and thereby they unify
everything. For "YHVH is HaElohim" (I Kings 18:39). Yet, the
wicked separate and destroy the world, for they conduct themselves only according to the natural order—separating YHVH
from Elohim. In our era of exile, the Divine name is, as it were,
even more incomplete, as even YH and VH are separated. The
sole intention of the righteous is to sustain the world by uniting,
through their thoughts, YHVH with Elohim (which is nature).
Through this, they connect the life force that flows from the
source of compassion—the 13 supernal attributes of compassion—into the natural world (which in Gematria is Elohim),
and thereby unify the names YHVH and Elohim. Likewise,
they shorten the name Elohim into Elohai, for this name garbs
the soul, protecting it from those who would attack it. That is
why we say [in the morning prayers] every day, according to
our Sages, "Elohai, my God, the soul you have implanted with
me [is protected and therefore pure] ..."

The wicked Balaam's consuming desire was the opposite: to
make everything follow after the natural order, and to cause
a rupture within the Divine Name... Balaam's intention was
(as if it were possible) to make the Divine name of compassion (YHVH) small and to magnify the name Elohim, which
would (as if it were possible) enable negative forces to triumph.
The Blessed Ineffable One, in the fullness of Divine compas-

sion, overturns such thoughts. The Divine placed a restraint in Balaam's mouth, against his will, forcing him to bless Israel and to draw forth great compassion from its source on high... and these were the very highest blessings.

Now we can return to explaining our verse, "Balaam replied to Balak's officials, 'Though Balak were to give me his house full of silver and gold, I could not do anything, big or little, contrary to the command of the YHVH my God.'" The grammatic essence of *bayit* is *taf-yud*, which in Gematria is 410 and equivalent to *kishuf*, sorcery. The *bayit*, the magical "home (i.e., sorcery)," of Balak is unable to overcome the word of "YHVH-*Elohai*" to do small or large—that is, to make small, to shrink YHVH, or to do large, that is, to enlarge *Elohim*, the source of negative forces—for nothing was in his control. This is what he meant in saying, "I am unable to transgress the word of YHVH-*Elohai*." That is, he was unable to transgress the word of YHVH—to make it smaller—*Elohai*, the name that enclothes and protects the soul. "I am unable to make the name *Elohim* larger," to allow negative forces to overcome compassion, for it is established by the Blessed Ineffable One that the name YHVH (the Name of compassion) should be complete, so that compassion should predominate, and that the name *Elohim* should be diminished—made into *Elohai*—so that compassion will prevail on us and all Israel.

There are, in my reading, two essential parts to this teaching of *Ma'or VaShemesh*. The first is his (seemingly polemical) contention that there is something not only wrong, but even destructive, in reducing our understanding of the natural world to just the laws of nature or scientific causes. He invites us to consider and engage with the vitality, the aliveness, in everything which exists in a manner beyond the "natural." It may not be "super-natural," but it is a step beyond complete (or completely satisfying) scientific explanation. When we ignore that "force" in everything, and treat the world merely as "natural," we empty the world of its numinous, even divine, quality. Emptying the world of a such a sense of a Creator who is constantly present, actively imbuing it with spiritual vitality, we perform, he contends, a kind of violence against Divinity itself. We split off Divinity from the natural world, exiling the Divine from nature, and even from its own internal unity. In the process, we contribute to our own exile by bringing *dinim*, negative forces, the more severe, judgmental aspect of reality, into greater prominence. In other words, by promoting disconnection, or even by failing to cultivate a lived awareness of our interconnection with the world, we allow division to take root in our own spirits, in the collective, and within God.

The second part of this teaching comes in the last paragraph, which, building on this first point, suggests that the fundamental Divine force at work in the world seeks connection. Though Balaam seeks to speak words of curse (separation), God turns them into words of blessing (connection)—not only because God cares about Israel, but because God's own nature is to enable loving connection (*Hesed, Rachamim,* love) to predominate over disconnection (*Din,* judgment, negative forces). The Divine senses that something terrible is about to happen and intervenes to change the story. Alternatively, the tendency toward unification is more powerful than that of separation, thereby overcoming Balaam's intention, compelling even him to speak words of connection.

### Mindfulness Practice: Attuning to the Divine Voice

How does this work, exactly? Some of us may feel uncomfortable accepting a personal God who actively intervenes in history in a very clear, identifiable, supernatural way. Yet, I think there is nevertheless considerable room to consider subtler forms of Divine presence in this story and, indeed, in our own lives. In my own Jewish mindfulness practice, I find that taking the time to deepen my awareness—to slow down, to listen to the stirrings of my body and heart, opening, ultimately, to the still, small voice within—inevitably leads me to greater compassion and interconnection with creation, with other people, and with the Divine. Of course, that may be because I set an intention to cultivate those traits and engage in practice to develop them. But where does that intention come from? It isn't simply because I "naturally" want to be a nice guy, or that I am even "naturally" so. After all, being open, connected, and compassionate feels good. But it is also true that sometimes a really clever put-down, or some other demonstration of power over another, can feel good, too. No, the stirring toward compassion and connection comes from someplace, or something, else besides pleasure or some "natural" process.

That stirring comes from someplace deeper, a place that, through my practice, I tap into and from which I draw forth energy. I especially feel that place around my eyes, in my jaw, in my heart, and in my belly. When I soften my gaze, release my jaw muscles, open up my heart, and let go of the tightness in my belly, I begin to experience a warmth, a sense of fullness, connection, and compassion. I feel judgmentalism becoming smaller, and a calling to love growing bigger. I sit with this sensation, feeling it grow within me. I experience this as growing in connection, where I, the world, and the Divine come together as one.

Now, is that just me, or is there something else at work? Certainly, there are good scientific explanations for the sensations I'm describing. Yet for me it is far more powerful, and frankly rings truer, to understand this phenomenon as the Divine working in and through me. The stirring I feel toward connection and compassion is "YHVH-*Elohai*:" "the Ineffable One" whom I know as "my God," and whom I sense through my body.

Perhaps we can imagine that Balaam experienced something along these lines. Perhaps, preparing to curse the people, Balaam entered a meditative state. And perhaps in that practice his body-heart-mind became attuned to the compassionate Divine voice within him. Perhaps, despite his original intention to do harm, his practice brought into his awareness a calling to connection and compassion. And then, inexorably, ineluctably, and from a place of deep truth, he was led to offer words of blessing rather than words of curse.

Perhaps. Or perhaps not. But if you, like me, have trouble—for whatever reason—with an uncomplicated version of a personal God, perhaps this way of understanding how the Divine worked through Balaam opens a window into how the Divine may work in your own life. Perhaps it's worth a try.

## Questions for Reflection & Conversation

- The *Ma'or VaShemesh* writes, "We have received the tradition from our ancient ancestors, even before the giving of the Torah, that the world has been conducted through Divine providence." He then goes on to say that "the righteous connect the supernatural life force with the natural world…unify[ing] everything." What is the difference between "Divine providence" and "the world goes of its own accord?" Why would it matter to God, or to Divine Providence, if people focused on the world working solely by natural, scientific rules? How do you understand the role of the righteous in counteracting/contradicting the latter view? What is the work of the *tzaddikim* (the righteous), as you understand it, in this lesson?

- When, if at all, have you felt/do you feel the Divine working through you? What was that experience like? Are there things you do to actively cultivate it? Are there things about this experience that make you uncomfortable, confused, or are otherwise difficult for you?

- How do you feel talking about your relationship with the Creator/ God/the Divine/the Holy One? Are there people around with whom you feel more comfortable having this conversation? Who, when, and what supports this? And, if not, why do you think this may be so? What might move you to feel able to speak of this, despite your sense of discomfort?

## Ideas for Practice

My colleague Rabbi Jonathan Slater offers the following ideas for practice in connection with this week's question, *How does God work?*

We might "translate" the Divine Name YHVH as "Life Unfolding." Divinity is present in the world in each moment, as existence unfolds in its infinite ways. Consider some, or all, of the following as practices through which you might cultivate a deeper capacity to connect whatever seems "natural" to this sense of Life Unfolding:

- Sit with a bowl of yogurt, or ice cream, or your favorite food. Take a bit of it in a spoon, and slowly put it in your mouth. Allow its flavor to fill your mouth. Take in every sensation. All of the different taste/flavor receptors in your mouth are firing. What else is going on? How might the whole cascade of experience be the presence of Life Unfolding?

- Weather (and bugs) permitting, sit outdoors at dawn/early morning or dusk. Allow your vision to open to a diffuse, unfocused gaze. Allow your sense of hearing to expand to take in all the sounds that surround you. Notice—without naming or labeling— all that you hear. Take in the world as it awakens or moves toward sleep (and the night). How might all that comes to your ear, all that you hear, be an expression of Life Unfolding?

- Walking on the street, or sitting at a red light in your car, observe all the people around you doing whatever they are doing. They exist separate from you; yet, you observe them, and so are connected with them. Moreover, your behavior will have an impact on them. How might this moment of non-verbal, non-physical interaction be an expression of—and an experience of—Life Unfolding?

# Pinchas: When Are We Unified?

In one of his first major popular works, *The Dignity of Difference*, the late British Chief Rabbi Jonathan Sacks took up the questions of universalism and particularism, multiculturalism and diversity, that had reached the center of social conversation in the mid-1990s, and which took on new urgency following the tragic, fractious events of September 11, 2001. In the book, Sacks made a forceful argument, which he would repeat countless times in his subsequent writings, in favor of a particularism that leads to universalism. We learn to love people in general, Sacks argued, by loving particular people, not the other way round.

Importantly, Sacks did not advocate a focus on Jewish particularism at the expense of the world. Just as he embodied in his own public life, first as Chief Rabbi and also later as a member of the House of Lords, Sacks saw the particulars of Jewish life—Jewish language, the Jewish calendar, the Jewish textual tradition, Jewish ritual—as a home in which Jews learn how to be part of a larger community. The aim, he suggested, was that Jews, and by extension all people, would be "secure in one's home, yet moved by the beauty of foreign places, knowing they are someone else's home, not mine, but still part of the glory of the world that is ours." For Sacks, having this sense of identity within one's own home enables one to understand their life as part of a larger whole of humanity and Creation. "Those who are confident in their faith," he wrote, "are not threatened but enlarged by the different faith of others." Writing in the wake of 9/11, he concluded, "In the midst of our multiple insecurities, we need that confidence now."[87]

The question at the root of Sacks' book, and of much of his larger oeuvre, has to do with the seeming tension between uniformity and diversity, wholeness and division. In an increasingly global, interconnected world, how do we hold up and embrace the manifold diverse expressions of humanness and Creation on the one hand, even as we, on the other, stay rooted in a sense of interconnection and sacred relationship by virtue of our shared identity as dwellers on planet Earth? In recent years, these questions have taken on increasing urgency on a socio-political level—and on a personal one as well. How might our Jewish spiritual practice help us hold them and live within them in a healthy, wise, and mindful way?

---

[87] Jonathan Sacks, *The Dignity of Difference: How to Avoid the Clash of Civilizations*. Continuum, 2003, 65-66.

## Shabbat and the Workweek, Evening and Morning

To help us explore this question, we turn to the Maggid of Kozhnitz, Rabbi Yisroel Hopstein (1737–1814), in his *Avodat Yisrael*, and specifically a comment on the Shabbat sacrifice outlined in Parashat Pinchas.

עבודת ישראל, פנחס

עולת שבת בשבתו וגו'. דאיתא בזוה"ק לית מלכא בלא מטרוניתא. והוא הענין כי אין מלך בלא עם, וכביכול אין נקרא בשם מלך ואינו מתענג כי אם בעת עבודת ישראל עמו והם עולים אליו. נמצא מה שישראל שובתים למטה ועולים בשבת במוסף הם עולים בשבתו כביכול שהוא שורש השבת והתענוג. על עולת התמיד, פירוש שעל פי היחודים שאנו עושים כל ימות השבוע ועושים הכנה לקדושה, על זה עולה בשבת ומצטרף היחוד דחול להעלות בשבת היחוד יותר ויותר:

ואגב אשמיעך מה שנראה לפי עניות דעתי בנוסח התפלה מ"ש רז"ל אשרינו שאנו משכימים ומעריבים ערב ובוקר ואומרים פעמים בכל יום שמע ישראל וכו'. דלכאורה מלת ערב ובוקר מיותרים והיה די באמרנו משכימים ומעריבים, אלא על פי מ"ש האר"י ז"ל כי היחוד נעשה בבוקר ונכלל מדת לילה ביום ובלילה בשעת היחוד נכלל מדת יום בלילה כנודע ליו"ח. וזהו פירוש שאנו משכימים ערב ובוקר, דהיינו שאנו מיחדים בהשכמה מדת ערב במדת בוקר, וכן מעריבים להיפך מדת בוקר במדת ערב והבן:

Avodat Yisrael, Pinchas 4

"A burnt offering for every Sabbath, [in addition to the regular burnt offering and its libation]" (Num. 28:10). The Zohar teaches: "There is no King without a Queen." This is related to the teaching, "There is no King without a people." Thus, it would appear that the Divine is only called "Sovereign" and only receives delight when Israel, the Holy One's people, offer their service and so ascend to God. Thus, when Israel cease from labor below on Shabbat, and then rise up through the additional Musaf service, they ascend through the Holy One's Shabbat (as it were), as ultimately the Holy One is the root of Shabbat and its delight. "In addition to the regular burnt offering:" by means of the *yichudim* [mystical unifications in every dimension] that we bring about during the workweek, we prepare for holiness. Through this preparation, we ascend on Shabbat, and connect the unifications of the workweek, so that on Shabbat we can raise them up higher and higher.

Along the way, let me share with you something of what I perceive in our prayers. The Sages wrote: "Happy are we that we get up and go to sleep, morning and evening, saying, twice each day, 'Hear O Israel [*YHVH* is our God, *YHVH* is One].'" Now, in this formulation the phrase "morning and evening" is superfluous; it would have been sufficient simply to say, "we get up and go to sleep." But the AR"I [Rabbi Isaac Luria, 1534-1572] taught that the unification we bring about in the morning must incorporate the quality of the evening in the daytime. And at night, when we enact that unification, the quality of day is incorporated in night. This is the sense, then, of "we get up [and go to sleep] evening and morning:" we unify at our arising the quality of "night" in the day, and at evening we do the opposite, incorporating the quality of day in that of nighttime. Understand.

At the heart of this teaching lies a conundrum: We confront, simultaneously and repeatedly from moment to moment, a complex reality in which we are both part and whole, discrete and united, uniquely us and yet inseparable from everything. In our spiritual practice we often set an intention of counteracting our sense of *pizur hanefesh,* disunity of the spirit. We do so to experience a sense of centeredness and wholeness in ourselves, in all of Creation, and in the continuous life of the Infinite and Ineffable. As we sit in stillness and allow our awareness to expand, we seek to unify the disparate sensations and movements of our bodies, hearts, and minds, to uncover the Divine that is part of us, of which we are part, and which is present in everything. As the *Avodat Yisrael* teaches here, Shabbat is one of the foundational practices by which we do this, bringing the various unifications we perform during the workweek—the acts of gathering, centering, experiencing wholeness—into their original register of primordial wholeness. For me, that practice enables an experience of renewed interconnection with myself, my family, other people, and the world, and, in the same breath, not only interconnection, but communion.

Yet in the second paragraph, I think the *Avodat Yisrael* is gesturing toward the simultaneous reality that we live in a world of time and space, a world of limitation, in which there is, alongside the mystical reality of unity, another reality of distinctiveness. Day is not night, sky is not land, you are not me, God is not me—even when, as explained above, God is the ultimate reality of all these things, too. Just as both night and day are worthy of their own blessings, so are you, so am I, so is the Divine. As the AR"I teaches, our practice enables us to both honor the distinctiveness of each time of day—and, by extension, every other facet of Creation (night and day are just the first). This leads up to the culminating bi-reality of the workweek and Shabbat—which completes the Creation process—through which we actively remember that both are rooted in the same Divine origin. We do this particularly by being aware that the edges of what we perceive as distinct entities are not really edges: When precisely does day begin and night end? Where does my body end and the chair or the air or the earth begin? Bringing awareness to moments and sites of transition helps us both to honor the integrity within each entity, and to recognize a larger integrity in which borders of separation dissolve.

This, I suggest, is something we might discern from the *Avodat Yisrael's* cryptic *"v'haven,"* "understand," with which he closes his short commentary here. *Haven* points us toward *binah*, the *sefirah*, or aspect of the Divine, in which a larger, *both/and* consciousness is rooted. For all of his emphasis on unification (*yichud* in Hebrew), we might understand that term only partially to express this paradoxical reality, which might better be captured in the term *shleimut*, wholeness (from which we derive *shalom*). I find this to be true in my own experience: When I put my focus on oneness and unification, I find it can produce a pressure of its own, as if to say that if I don't achieve a sensation of unity—within myself, in my relationship to the Jewish people, in my relationship with humanity, the world, the Divine—I am somehow failing. Yet if I shift my focus to inhabiting a sense of wholeness, that pressure is lessened. Instead, my awareness can take in my own sense of unique identity and integrity and, simultaneously, the sense that I am part of an infinite whole.

## Wholeness in Self, Wholeness in Society

I find this orientation can be helpful as well in approaching the vital questions of diversity that are always present in a democratic society, and which have become especially pronounced in recent years. As contemporary political theorist Danielle Allen observes, "A speaker cannot use the word 'one' to mean multiplicity, but the word 'whole' entails just that."[88] Beings are diverse and multiform, and humans particularly so in their cultural and personal expressions of self. To make space for this diversity, and to avoid

---

[88] Danielle Allen, *Talking to Strangers: Anxieties of Citizenship Since Brown v. Board of Education*. Chicago: University of Chicago Press, 2009, 17.

subsuming them under a homogenizing label, wholeness, rather than one-ness, is a more fruitful conceptual foundation. Allen goes on to discuss the importance of this shift from oneness or united (think, for instance, of the motto emblazoned on American currency, *e pluribus unum*) to wholeness for contemporary social-political life: "The effort to make the people 'one' cultivates in the citizenry a desire for homogeneity, for that is the aspiration taught to citizens by the meaning of the word 'one,' itself. In contrast, an effort to make the people 'whole' might cultivate an aspiration to coherence and integrity of a consolidated but complex, intricate, and differentiated body."[89]

Allen's work helps us draw a link between our personal spiritual work of *tikkun hanefesh* and our social-political spiritual work of *tikkun ha'olam*. The orientation we bring to our inner life is interwoven with and gives shape to our orientation to our outer life. Seeking *shleimut* within and among our inner many selves, we learn to witness, embrace, and celebrate the many diverse others in the world, and of the world, as an expression of *shleimut* as well. To embrace the diversity and multiplicity of Creation, and of the many communities and publics of which we are each a part, cultivating our capacity to be aware of and embrace difference—within ourselves and oth-ers—is essential. This is the invitation of every Shabbat, every evening, every morning, every moment.

## Questions for Reflection & Conversation

- *Avodat Yisrael* writes, "By means of the *yichudim* [mystical uni-fications in every dimension] that we bring about during the workweek, we prepare for holiness. Through this preparation, we ascend on Shabbat, and connect the unifications of the workweek, so that on Shabbat we can raise them up higher and higher." Are there ways you prepare spiritually for Shabbat? What do they include? Do you find spiritual preparation for Shabbat to be a challenge? If so, why? Are there things you might do to deepen your awareness of your activities (and spiritual practice) during the week as preparation for Shabbat?
- In your own practice, how do you relate to the paradox of both be-ing distinctively *you* and, simultaneously, a part of the infinite? Do you find one or the other to be more pleasant or appealing? More difficult or uncomfortable? When, how, why or why not?
- Danielle Allen points us to a distinction between oneness and

---

[89] Ibid.

wholeness, or *achdut* and *shleimut*, in Hebrew. Do you find one or
the other of these terms to be more inviting or more challenging
as a spiritual orientation? If so, why?

## Ideas for Practice

This week, consider making a *kabbalah*, a commitment, to notice and hold
in your attention a perspective of wholeness. You may find it in any variety
of places, but here are a few to guide you:

- Consider a twist on an old exercise you may have learned as a
  child (I remember first encountering it as a proposed way to stop
  hiccups) of bringing your pinky fingers as close together as possible without touching. (The actual hiccup cure came when an older
  brother would, after a period of silence, shout really loud to "scare
  the hiccups out of me." Pay attention to the sensation. Where do
  you notice one finger ending and the other beginning? What happens if you shift your perspective, and no longer see them as two
  fingers, but as (mirroring) parts of one body? What happens if
  you try it with someone else? What do you notice? How does the
  experience help you reflect on oneness and wholeness?
- Try a mindful eating exercise. As you bring food into your mouth,
  try to notice the sensations of each stage of the process: crossing
  the threshold of your lips, chewing with your teeth, tasting on
  your tongue, swallowing and traveling down the esophagus, land-
  ing in the stomach. At what point is the food separate from you?
  At what point does it become you?
- In the spirit of the *Avodat Yisrael*, make an intention to prepare for
  Shabbat each day this week. At least once a day, try to set aside
  something—an item of food, something you want to read, a picture you intend to look at, a prayer you wish to spend time with—
  and, with intention, say, "I'm setting this aside for Shabbat." Try
  to notice the bodily sensation and emotions that arise as you do
  this. What are they? Do they change as you get closer to Shabbat?
  Does it affect how you sense time during the week? Does it give
  you a different appreciation for *this* day, *this* moment? How, when,
  why or why not?

# Matot-Masei: What Does the Time Call For?

A few years ago, I made a vow not to eat meat on weekdays. There were a number of reasons for my decision, among them a personal, moral abhorrence of industrialized slaughter and a desire to be more economical and healthier in my lifestyle. But the biggest reason was climate change—or, more accurately, my awareness of the impact of industrial animal farming in driving climate change and my sense of obligation to my children and their descendants. On the list of things we can personally do to be better stewards of the planet, ending our consumption of meat is at or near the top. I decided that I didn't want to have to say to my kids (and, God-willing, grandchildren) that I didn't take some of the meaningful steps I could have taken to stop the world they will inherit from becoming uninhabitable.

There have been occasions when I've finished some meat leftovers on a Tuesday that otherwise might go bad—and I think that's a reasonable exception to make (after all, why waste even more food?). And, following the example of Abraham Isaac Hakohen Kook, the first Ashkenazi Chief Rabbi of British Palestine, and in an effort to maintain *shalom bayit*, or peace in the home, I enjoy eating meat on Shabbat and holidays. But, overall, I'm happy to say that I've remained true to my commitment. And having made that commitment, and stated it publicly to my family, I feel a sense of ongoing obligation—to them, to myself, to the planet, to the Creator.

Of course, despite my own small gesture, climate change shows no signs of slowing down or abating anytime soon. But what if it did? Might I loosen my self-imposed restriction? Might I one day decide I could eat meat—grass-fed, free-range, painlessly slaughtered—on Wednesday *as well as* Shabbat? Or, having developed this new practice, might I continue with it despite the change in the original conditions that led me to make my vow in the first place?

To extrapolate up one notch: My vow is a vow for now. But might I decide it needs to be a vow for all time? When does my decision shift from being situational to becoming absolute? How do I, or we, determine that the time we're living in is a special period that calls for special practices, and how do we determine if or how that period has ended, or shifted into another? How do we know what the time calls for?

### Zeh HaDavar: This is the Thing

The issue of vows is the first subject of Parashat Matot: "If a person makes a vow to YHVH or takes an oath imposing an obligation on themselves, they shall not break their pledge; they must carry out all that has crossed their lips" (Num. 30:3). The Torah and later rabbinic commentaries assume that there are specific formulas and designs of vow- and oath-taking—ones under which my own vow, or contemporary versions of vows, would technically not fall. But the spirit of the Torah here lies in the tension between, on the one hand, the expectation that the promises we make are sacrosanct ("they must carry out all that has crossed their lips") and, on the other, the reality that circumstances change. In some cases, that's because we have imperfect information: If we had known then what we know now, we wouldn't have made the vow. In other cases, it's because reality changes, and the conditions in which it might be sustained no longer apply. Thus, a vow, if held unswervingly and without attention to our lived experience, rather than bringing us closer to Divine service, can drive us further away from it. Time changes, and, because we are creatures who live in time, so do we.

Rabbi Mordechai Yosef Leiner of Izhbitz (1801-1854) explores these themes of vows, time, and change in a comment on Parashat Matot in his *Mei HaShilo'ach*. His teaching builds on an ancient commentary, which Rashi also brings, that notes the specific language used in Parashat Matot: "*Zeh HaDavar*, This is the thing that YHVH has commanded" (Num. 30:2). This is a different formulation than that used by later prophets, who generally preface their words by saying, "Thus says YHVH." What does it mean that Moses can say, seemingly more emphatically and specifically, "This is the thing YHVH has commanded?"

**מי השילוח מטות**

וידבר משה אל ראשי המטות לבני ישראל לאמר זה הדבר וכו'. (בגמ') (ספרי מטות ב') כל הנביאים נתנבאו בכה הוסיף עליהם משה שנתנבא בזה הדבר.

ודבר זה לא היה נוהג אלא בדור הזה, והוא כי כל הנביאים היה שליחותם לישראל במאמר נביאתם כפי העת והזמן וכפי כח השגתם כן התנבאו, ועלה ברוח נביאתם אשר דבר דבר נבואה הלז יהיה קיים לעולמי עד, אך באמת נמצא שנוים כפי ערך דור ודור, וע"ז הוסיף עליהם משרע"ה להתנבאות בזה הדבר, היינו שהוא השיג כל דבר לפי שעתו ומקומו והבין כי הנבואה אינה רק לזמן ולאחר זמן יחפוץ הקב"ה בענין אחר,

ולכן בפרשת נדרים נאמר זה הדבר אף שהוא נוהג לדורות כדיליף בגמ' (בבא בתרא ק"כ:) משחוטי חוץ, אעפ"כ נאמר זה הדבר, כי הנודר מדבר הוא לפי ערך השגתו שדבר הזה ירע לו לעבודת ה' וגם שאין בדבר הזה שום טובה, ולכן נאמר זה הדבר שצריך האדם להבין כי לא נאסר לו רק לזמן, והש"י יוכל ליתן לו כח

לקבל כל הטובות שבעולם ולא ינתק מעבודת הש"י.

**Mei HaShilo'ach, Matot**
"Moses spoke to the heads of the tribes of the children of Israel,
saying, 'This is the thing that YHVH has commanded'" (Num.
30:2). [The Sifrei comments,] All the prophets prophesied using the word *koh*, 'Thus says YHVH.' Moses exceeded this to
prophesy using the formulation, *Zeh HaDavar*, "This is the
thing YHVH has commanded."

*This thing* only applied to *this generation*. That is, the mission
of each of the prophets to Israel—the words they prophesied—
were according to their time and era, and according to their
own capacity for understanding. It arose in them, according to
their spirit of prophecy, [believing] that their prophetic words
would be for all time. But the truth is that differences can be
found between each generation.

It was in this sense that Moses exceeded them, namely to
prophesy using the language *Zeh HaDavar*, this is the thing.
That is, Moses grasped each thing according to its time and
place. He understood that the prophecy [he was giving at the
time] was only for that specific time, and that after that time
had passed the Holy Blessed One would inspire a different
prophecy.

So, this section of the Torah dealing with vows is introduced with the words, *Zeh HaDavar*, This is God's word—
even though the Sages taught that this law [regarding vows] is
[to be] observed even in subsequent generations. Rather, [*Zeh
HaDavar* teaches us something else in this context]: One who
makes a vow to abstain from something acts according to their
own understanding, namely that this thing will be detrimental
to them in their service of YHVH, and further, that there is
nothing good [for them] in this thing [from which they abstain].
Thus, the Torah uses the language *Zeh HaDavar* [to teach that]
one must understand that the thing [from which one vows to
abstain] is only forbidden to them for a particular time. After
all, the Blessed Ineffable One has the ability to grant them the
capacity [despite their personal judgment or feeling] to receive
all the goodness of the world, without, as a consequence, also
being cut off from the service of the Creator.

The Izhbitzer here offers a reflection not only on vows, but on speech and time, permanence and impermanence. Where the later prophets of Israel thought they were speaking to an audience not only of their own time but all time, Moses had the insight to recognize that his words were, primarily, for the people of his own time and place. They were not permanent objects but, rather, things of the moment. He was, it seems, more modest, more human, more present in the present. This the Izhbitzer infers from the Midrashic gloss on the idiom *Zeh HaDavar*, this is the thing/word *(davar* means both word and thing in Hebrew)—this, right here and now, the word that connects you and me, is the word of the Divine.

The Izhbitzer proceeds to locate this observation in the context of vow-making, and here he speaks to the experience we might have as individuals in making oaths and promises. When we swear that we will not partake of something, we are, says the Izhbitzer, acting from our limited understanding of the time, place, and circumstances we're in at that moment. In the moment, we think that our current conditions will be for all time, so we make a commitment that projects forward in time—even though we can't know what reality will look like in the future. There is, he suggests, a certain hubris in doing so. In arrogating to ourselves the determination that we know what will be good and right for us in the future, we wind up cutting ourselves off from the fullness of Creation in the present, in the time in which we are right now. It is not I, but the Holy One, who truly knows.

## Being Present in the Present

In my own experience, I find that sometimes I rush to make a promise—not so often to abstain from something, the way the Izhbitzer discusses, as to take on a commitment. Throughout my life, I have tended to overcommit, taking on too many projects—and too many promises—and inevitably putting myself in a situation where I needed to violate my word, let someone down and thereby erode trust, and consequently judge myself harshly. Through mindfulness practice, I've noticed that in recent years this tendency has diminished. Perhaps that's because I've developed more of a capacity to put some space between stimulus and response, allowing myself more time to think for a moment about whether or not taking on a new commitment that will extend forward in time is really the wisest course of action.

Yet where did the impetus to commit so quickly come from in the first place? On reflection, I think it was largely driven by my discomfort being present in the present. I didn't want to sit with making a decision, with thinking it through, and with the anxiety that decision-making, and the many potential futures that unfold from the present, would bring about. I would rather simply commit and have the decision, the future, and the stress of the moment, over with. I hear in the Izhbitzer a loving lesson that my impatience to sit with the discomfort of the present led me to an unmindful arrogation of the future to myself, taking on an unwise commitment I would not be able to keep. When I rush into such decisions, I'm living neither in my own time nor in the future; I'm cutting myself off from the goodness of Creation, which is only truly available in the moment we have right now.

According to the Izhbitzer, Moses's greatness was his ability to be with what is in the moment (his episode of impatience at the rock notwithstanding—the exception that proves the rule). *Zeh HaDavar*—this is the thing, where we are right here and now. This is the time that is real for us, not the past or the future. We can't know what will be true in the future, and so predicating our happiness and all of our plans on that supposed time to come will lead to unhappiness. Instead, being present with what is allows us to be flexible, adaptive, welcoming, and curious. Our practice is an exercise in being present in the present, of making a space for the Divine to dwell within us. When we can be with ourselves in the moment—that is when we the Holy One can enter our hearts.

## Questions for Reflection & Conversation

- Consider your own approach to promise-making. Are there situations or relationships in which you find you are quicker to promise? What do you sense motivates that? Has your approach to commitment-making changed over time? How? Do you perceive it has gotten more mindful, less mindful? What helps and hinders your ability to make wise commitments?

- The Izhbitzer writes, "The Blessed Ineffable One has the ability to grant them the capacity to receive all the goodness of the world, without, as a consequence, also being cut off from the service of the Creator." When, if ever, have you experienced this sense of "all the goodness of the world"? What did it feel like? How, if at all, do you sense that it came from your full service of the Creator? Did you need to deny yourself something in order to experience it? Did you need to nudge yourself toward something new, more, different in order to experience it? What did you need to say *no* to, and what did you need to say *yes* to, in order for the experience to occur?

## Ideas for Practice

This week, consider setting an intention to be present in the moment when you have a commitment to make. It could be a small commitment (going out for ice cream one night) or a bigger one (taking on a volunteer responsibility, or making a lifestyle change you've been contemplating).

- Try to notice when you sensed you are called to make the commitment.

- Then, practice *hitlamdut,* bringing your awareness to what is working within you at the moment. What different forces, sensations, or voices are present for you?

- Then, notice the *bechira* points, the options you have before you (if they still exist—it could be, of course, that you cannot avoid this commitment right now). What might be your wisest, most skillful response that aligns with your intentions?

- Give yourself time—you don't need to rush. Check out how your various options feel within you.

- Then, when you have discerned the choice that is most aligned with your intention, practice *teshuva,* coming back to balance and wholeness. Internalize your decision—to commit, to not commit, or something else—to know that it is now consistent with your intention.

# Devarim: What Do We Say?

In her bestselling historical exploration of death and meaning during and after the American Civil War, former Harvard University president and professor of history Drew Gilpin Faust offers a reflection on the work of Emily Dickinson. "Marked by discontinuities," Faust observes, "her poems were assailed after their posthumous publication by critics who deplored their travesties of grammar and syntax. But contemporary critics see in these attributes the embodiment of Dickinson's doubts about the foundations of understanding and coherence." Faust quotes Hebrew University English professor Shira Wolosky, who contends that Dickinson's poems challenge "the whole question of linguistic meaning and of meaning in general." Faust concludes, "This is a crisis of language and epistemology as much as one of eschatology; it is about not just whether there is a God and whether we can know him [sic] but whether we can know or communicate anything at all."[90]

Like Faust's Dickinson, whose broken language emerged out of the trauma of the Civil War, Parashat Devarim begins a period in which the very notion of language, meaning, knowledge, and the Divine is particularly present in the Jewish calendar, just before the 9th of Av, the day on which the first and second *batei mikdash* (temples in Jerusalem) were destroyed in ancient times. Tisha b'Av is the culmination of a period of three weeks of intensifying suffering that began on the 17th of Tammuz, a day which marks, among other things, Moses's breaking of the first set of stone tablets on which were written the Ten Commandments in his anger at the people over the sin of the Golden Calf. This period, which reaches its climax on Tisha b'Av, is a moment when Jewish language is uniquely broken, as it were.

One of the day's most remarkable features (according to the *Shulchan Arukh*, the authoritative code of Jewish law from the sixteenth century) is that one is not to greet others on Tisha b'Av, nor should one study Torah or Talmud (except for passages related to the collective trauma of the day). That is, the language we normally associate with Jewish life, the language of Torah and of welcome and blessing, is absent on Tisha b'Av. Even schoolchildren, *tinokot shel beit rabban*, whose very breath the Talmud describes as sustaining the world, are quiet on the day, so deep is the trauma and, as a result, so absent is language.[91] We simply don't have the words on this day.

---

[90] Drew Gilpin Faust, *This Republic of Suffering: Death and the American Civil War.* Vintage Books, 2008, 208.

[91] See Babylonian Talmud Shabbat 119b and *Shulchan Arukh Orach Hayim 554:1*

## "A Man of Words"

Devarim, the name of the parasha and of the fifth and final book of the
Torah, means "words," taken from the opening line of the book: "These are
the words that Moses spoke to all Israel on the other side of the Jordan." In
one of the poetic twists of the Jewish calendar, we read this parasha just
before the Ninth of Av every year. Just when our language is most broken,
when our words are most impoverished, we begin a book whose very title
connotes language and meaning.

Additionally, and unlike the four books of the Torah that precede it, this
is a book spoken by Moses. Given that earlier in the Torah Moses describes
himself as "of uncircumcised lips" (Ex. 6:12) and, even more directly, "not an
*ish devarim*/a man of words" (Ex. 4:10), it is surprising that now, at the end of
his life, not only is Moses a man of words—he has a whole book full of them!
This seeming disjuncture has invited generations of readers to reflect on the
deeper meaning of Moses's relationship with speech and language, and what
that relationship conveys about his relationship with the Divine. Coming as
it does at this low point on the Jewish calendar, it opens up further reflection
on these questions for all of us.

In his nine-volume work *Shem MiShmuel*, the Sochatchover Rebbe, Rabbi
Shmuel Bornsztain (1855-1926), explores this question of Moses's speech.
He begins by referencing an earlier teacher, Rabbi Judah Loew of Prague (d.
1609, known as the Maharal).

שם משמואל, דברים, א

הנה כבר כתבנו פ' חקת בשם המהר"ל ז"ל שהכבידות פה לא הי'
גרעון למשה רק באשר שכח הדיבור בא מכח הרכבת גוף ונפש,
שהבהמה ותינוק באשר אין להם כח הנפש וכן הנפש לבדה, אינן
יכולין לדבר, וע"כ מרע"ה באשר היתה נפשו נבדלת איננה מוטבעת
בהגוף ע"כ הי' כבד פה. וכתבנו שם שמאחר שזכה לתורה ונזדכך
גופו יותר ממה"ש ע"כ לא הי' גרעון להנפש להתאחד עם הגוף,
וע"י כן נשלם אצלו כח הדיבור עי"ש,

והנה במ"ש מהר"ל והנפש לבדה אין לה כח הדיבור לכאורה
יקשה ממעשיות שהובא בש"ס שהמתים מספרים זה את זה וכן
הרוחות מספרות זו את זו וכמו כן מצינו במה"ש וקרא זה אל זה,
[והנה ממה"ש אין קושיא כל כך, דאיתא בס' שערי אורה שגם
במלאכים יש גוף ונפש אך לא כגופים של בני אדם כי הגוף שלהם
ג"כ רוחני] אבל הפי' הפשוט שאף שהנפש בעצמה יש לה הדיבור
הוא רק נשמע לנפש כמותו, וכן מה"ש זה אל זה, וע"כ תרגם
המתרגם וקרא זא"ז ומקבלין דין מן דין,

ודיבור של מה"ש אל בנ"א הוא באחת משתי אלה, או שהשומע
הוא נביא ובעת נביאותו נפשו מובדלת מהגוף ונתבטל כח חושי
הגוף כמ"ש הרמב"ם, ושוב שומע הדיבור בחלקי נפשו לבד, או
שהמלאך מתלבש בלבוש גוף כעניין המלאכים הנראים לבני אדם
וכמ"ש הרמב"ן:

ולפי"ז י"ל שכל דור המדבר באשר הי' דור דיעה ואחר שקיבלו
את התורה נעשו כמ"ש בפדר"א, והיו במדריגות הנפשיי, ע"כ היו
יכולין לקבל הדיבור ממשה אף אם לא הי' לשונו מתרפא, ועיקר
הראי' שנתרפא לשונו הוא ממה שדור באי הארץ היו יכולין לקבל
הדיבור ממנו וזו ספר משנה תורה:

### Shem MiShmuel, Dvarim 1

...The Maharal of Prague writes that Moses's speech impediment did not diminish him. Rather, the capacity for speech comes from the combination of the soul and the body. An animal or a baby, inasmuch as their capacity of soul is not yet implanted in their body, but so too, a soul independent [of the body], all are unable to speak. Thus, in the case of Moses, whose soul was separated and not implanted within his body, speaking was difficult for him... But once Moses merited to receive the Torah, through which his body was further purified beyond the ministering angels, it was no loss to his soul to be united with his body. Through this [unification of body and soul] the capacity for speech was completed within him.

Yet we can raise a difficulty with the Maharal's teaching that the soul, when it is separated from the body, lacks the capacity for speech. For the Talmud brings stories of the dead speaking with one another and spirits talking to each other. Likewise, we find that the ministering angels "call this one to this one."[92] (In the case of the ministering angels it is not so much of a difficulty, as we find in the book *Sha'arei Orah* that angels do have both bodies and souls. Their bodies are not like human bodies, but are instead spiritual bodies.) The simplest answer is that, even when the soul is separate from the body it still has the capacity of speech—but its speech can only be heard by another soul like it. Similarly with the ministering angels who call one to the other: the Targum translates that passage as "they receive one from the other."

---

[92] See Isaiah 6:3 and the *kedusha* recited as part of the daily *Amidah*, for instance.

When angels speak with humans, then, their speech was one of these two types: a) that the one hearing was a prophet, and at the moment of their prophecy their soul was separated from their body and their sensory capacities were completely transcended, as Maimonides teaches, and thus they heard only through their soul aspect; or b) the angel was dressed in the garb of a human body, as when an angel appears to people (such is the position of Nachmanides).

On this basis, we can answer as follows: The entire generation of the wilderness was a generation of [special] awareness. After they received the Torah, they became like angels (as taught in Pirkei d'Rebbe Eliezer) and attained the level of the spirit. Thus, they were able to receive the Divine word from Moses, even though his own power of speech [comprised of body-and-soul] was not yet whole. Yet we find proof that this transformation ultimately took place from the fact that the generation that entered the land [now listening to him, and not the generation of the wilderness, who had died off] were able to receive the Divine word from him: the book of Deuteronomy.

One way of understanding the *Shem MiShmuel's* commentary is as a response to the question, How can we, who are limited in time, space, and understanding, relate to the infinite and ineffable Divine, which has no limits in any dimension? More specifically, how is it that Moses, the generation that stood at Sinai, and then subsequent generations, have the capacity to hear and understand the voice of the Holy One? The first part of his answer is that *Dor HaMidbar*, the generation of the wilderness, experienced Divine speech directly: the revelation at Sinai. At that moment, they were something like angels, endowed with a special kind of capacity for understanding. They could thus comprehend the limitless Divine as expressed through Moses, who at that point was himself more angel than human. The next generation, however, were not of that stature, and so did have that option. Thus, in order for the next generation—and, by extension, all future generations—to have access to the Divine as expressed through the Torah, Moses had to undergo a transformation in which he could be the vehicle by which the limitless, ineffable Divine voice could become intelligible to limited human beings. That transformation occurred, and the existence of Moses's book of words, *Devarim*, testifies to it.

## Renewing Words Through Practice

I find this teachicng, and the question at the heart of it, a powerful one in my own spiritual practice. While I have had a lifelong relationship with the words of Torah and Jewish prayer—or perhaps precisely *because* of that lifelong relationship—I find sometimes it can be a real challenge to experience these *devarim*, these words I know so well, as opening up something more. The words of the liturgy can become rote, my focus more on reciting them than on experiencing them as catalysts or aids to a deeper awareness. They become performances of my body, but do not help me go inward to the more expansive realms of spirit, which tend to be less linear, more associative, and infinitely open to meaning-making. Indeed, in taking the recitation of words as a requirement, they can even become a barrier to spiritual experience. From my observation, this isn't a problem unique to me.

At the same time, the lack of words can also be a problem, particularly when experiencing intense suffering. Traumatic experiences rob us of language, of the ability to express our pain and terror. When experiencing pain or loss, or even when dealing with less acute forms of suffering, I find it can be both challenging and debilitating to come up with words that help me establish order, structure, and meaning. Sitting in the grief of my father's death, I, like so many have before me, found tremendous comfort and spiritual sustenance in reciting Psalms and, later, in reciting Kaddish. I was far too broken at that point to come up with my own words, and my relationship with ritualized words was an anchor of stability.

Gradually, through both my own adult development and through being more intentional about my practice, that relationship with these familiar liturgical words and structures has deepened into something that is not hard and unchanging, but supple and useful. In the way that a craftsperson might hold her tools, or a musician might embrace his instrument, I've gradually grown into a relationship with the words of the tradition that is both familiar and challenging, by which they become less formulas that need to be recited than vehicles that help me commune with the Creator.

A key to that change has been embracing the practice of silent meditation, especially as preparation for and part of my *tefillah*, or prayer practice. "One should only enter prayer with a settled mind," teaches the Mishnah, which adds, "The Hasidim, or pious ones, of old would wait one hour before praying, in order to direct their hearts toward the Limitless One" (Brachot 5:1). I have found that taking this teaching to heart, and spending 10 to 15 minutes in silent meditation before uttering words of prayer, has been transformative in my relationship both with those words and with the Limitless One whose presence I aim to become ever more aware of through my practice.

While I might hope to spend hours working through the traditional liturgy at a slow and contemplative pace, I have commitments and responsibilities to others that lead me to put a limit on how much time I can devote to my prayer practice. (In making this choice I am enacting another teaching, that love of one's fellow is interwoven with love of the Divine.) When I sense I have sufficient time to recite them slowly and with intention, I focus my attention particularly on the morning blessings of *birkhot hashachar*, on the *Shema* and its surrounding blessings, and on the *Amidah*: *birkhot hashachar* because they help me ground my awareness of the Divine in my body; the Shema and its blessings because they bring me into a simple, elegant awareness of communion with the Creator and creation; and the *Amidah* because I find it a particularly personal, comprehensive, and expressive prayer. When I sense I have more limited time, I focus particularly on the *Shema* and *Amidah*. My practice generally follows that outlined in traditional Jewish law codes. Yet, taking more time to sit, and giving myself the compassionate gift to do less but better, rather than experiencing my prayer as a requirement to be checked off on my to-do list, has enabled me to experience my *tefillah*, and the traditional rules that inform it, as a wise discipline to be followed. It has renewed the words for me, and allowed me to renew them continually.

## Coda: From Tisha b'Av to Yom Kippur

By way of conclusion, I feel it important to note that, just as the book of Devarim opens at the time of greatest trauma on the Jewish calendar, when it is hardest to sense the presence of the Divine or to express meaning through words, we stay with this book through the seven weeks of consolation that follow, through Rosh Hashanah and on to Yom Kippur, a day that exists as a kind of photo-negative to Tisha b'Av. While the two days are both 25-hour fasts and, according to traditional practice, share the prohibitions of wearing shoes, bathing, anointing, and engaging in sexual relations, these shared observances have diametrically opposite valences. On Tisha b'Av they are meant to be expressions of our mourning, our awareness of our finiteness, and an attempt to separate our spirit from our physical being. They help us experience the chasm that exists between us and the Divine. But through the weeks that follow, we gradually shift our orientation such that, by Yom Kippur, these same observances become expressions of our status as "a little lower than angels" (Psalms 8:6). Our fasting and abstinence on Yom Kippur reflects not our distance from the Divine, but our intimate presence with and within It. Where Tisha b'Av harkens back to the breaking of the first tablets, and to the breaking of our language and our sense of intimacy with the Divine, Yom Kippur is the day when the second tablets were created, and with them, our language and our relationship were renewed. In that sense, the descent into which we enter with Tisha b'Av is, in the language of Hasidut, *yeridah l'tzorech aliyah*, a necessary descent in order to ascend. May our journey through Devarim be one of rediscovery and renewal.

## Questions for Reflection & Conversation

- Reflect on your own experience with the words of Torah and/or Jewish liturgy. Do you sense your relationship to be more one of rote performance, or of meaningful encounter—or something in between or otherwise? How, if at all, has your relationship with those words evolved and changed over time? What helped bring about that change? Was it a change in you, in someone else, or in someplace or something else? What in your relationship with those words might you want to change or develop further?

- *Shem MiShmuel* writes that, in order for the Divine to communicate with people, either the person needs to ascend to a level of prophecy, or an angel needs to be garbed in human trappings. How do you understand this? Does one or the other of these images resonate more with your own experience? When, how, why or why not?

- Have you ever felt that you were ascending to greater level of communion with the Divine, or that you were in the presence of an angel? What was that experience like? Is it one you sense you can cultivate regularly, or was there something special about the event—either in you or the environment—that you cannot replicate?

## Ideas for Practice

In his classic book on the season of *Teshuva* from Tisha b'Av through the fall holidays, Rabbi Alan Lew writes, "Our suffering, the unresolved element of our lives, is also from God. It is the instrument by which we are carried back to God, not something to be defended against, but rather to be embraced... We can enter the present moment of our lives and consciously alter that moment. We can end our exile."[93]

During Tisha b'Av and in the week that follows, consider this focus for your meditation practice, or perhaps for journaling. Make an intention to become aware of ways in which you are experiencing suffering—not only in more obvious registers, but, perhaps especially, in ways that are subtler or more obscured. Give yourself permission to be compassionate with your own suffering, to acknowledge that it, too, is real and part of the experience of living. Do not try to change anything. Rather, this week, simply make an intention to recognize, sit with, and hold those parts of your mind, heart, body, and spirit that are in pain. This recognition is the beginning of the process of *teshuva*, returning and renewing your relationship with yourself, others, and the Divine.

---

[93] Alan Lew, *This is Real and You Are Completely Unprepared: The Days of Awe as a Journey of Transformation*. Little, Brown, 2003, 63.

# Vaetchanan: Who Are You?

In her insightful, engaging, and often humorous book, *You Belong: A Call for Connection*, self-described "Nerdy Black Immigrant Tomboy Buddhist Weirdo" Sebene Selassie poses her reader a powerful set of questions:

> Imagine me sitting in front of you right now asking this: *Who are you?* Consider how you would answer. Maybe you would include your biographical history: where you were born, where you are from, your family growing up, the schools you attended, the friends you have, the work you do. You might connect with your physical and social realities: your gender, race, ethnicity, sexual orientation, religion, culture, nationality. Then there are aspects of our personality, patterns, proclivities, ways of being in the world. Perhaps a spiritual or existential sense of yourself would surface: your interconnection with the sacred, with all beings, with the whole of nature. And what if you met that question from an embodied place? A moment-to-moment exploration of who you are right now: sensations, thoughts, feelings—an ever-changing cascade of sensory data.

"There's no right answer here," Selassie concludes. "But the question is important… Without a deep understanding of who (and really what) we are, how can we build the bridges back to our fundamental interconnection? How do we know ourselves?"[94]

Selassie's project is to help us recognize that, while we need to work on structures and systems in which people can feel like they belong, as much or more of the work of belonging takes place within us. "Our moods, emotions, thoughts, our difficulties, fears, tendencies, our happiness, wellness, and joy—they are all experienced within this self, not externally," she writes.[95] Her book, and her larger teaching, is about how bringing awareness to the myriad and multi-layered dimensions of self can help us ultimately be present—that is, feel a sense of belonging—in the world.

## Knowing Ourselves, Knowing the Divine

Significantly, while Selassie discusses cultivating interconnection and belonging within a wide array of feelings, identities, conceptualizations, and

[94] Sebene Selassie, *You Belong: A Call for Connection*. HarperOne, 2020, 107-108.
[95] Ibid. 106.

things (all beings, the whole of nature), she doesn't quite go so far as to use the language of God or the Divine or the Holy One (she does say "the sacred"). Nor does she quite speak of "soul" or "spirit" to describe the essence within us. But that is because she is working from a Buddhist orientation. In Hasidic teaching, the sense of belonging and interconnection that Selassie describes is ultimately grounded in the reality of the Creator who continually infuses the universe, and our existence, with life force. Cultivating *da'at*, or awareness, is as much about coming to cleave to and know the Presence of the Holy One as it is about coming to know ourselves and the world.

Repeatedly in the Book of Deuteronomy, Moses exhorts the Israelites not to forget the miracles they have witnessed and the closeness with the Divine they have experienced. He warns them that, without active practice to remember and be conscious of the Holy One in their lives and in the life of the world, they are liable, ineluctably, to become deluded by their own egocentricity, particularly as they enter the promised land and assume a more overt role in their own self-sustenance. When they enter the land, they will assume a greater responsibility for their own survival and well-being. In doing so, he tells them, they will become susceptible to forgetting not only the Creator but, in the same breath, their true nature as beings ensouled by the Holy Blessed One.

This suggests a vital link between self-knowledge and knowledge of the Divine, a topic which forms the basis of the following gloss by Rabbi Elimelech of Lizhensk (1717-1787) on Deuteronomy 4:9:

נועם אלימלך ואתחנן ב'

השמר לך ושמור נפשך מאוד פן תשכח את הדברים אשר ראו עיניך. כי האדם צריך לילך תמיד בדביקות לחשוב ברוממות אל ית', לבחון בנפשו ובנפלאותיו אשר רואה תמיד ניסים ונפלאות ונוראים בברואיו, וההתחלה לבוא להמדריגה הזאת, צריך מתחילה לחשוב בחלק הניתן לו ממעל והוא הנפש שלו מה היא ואיך היא פועלת ניסים ונפלאות, כמ"ש בגמרא בחמשה דברים הנשמה שוה להבורא ב"ה וב"ש, אבל כשאין יודע את עצמו הוא מחוסר ידיעה ג"כ בבורא ב"ה, כיון שאפילו עצמו הוא אינו בוחן, וזהו "השמר לך ושמור נפשך", כי אם לא תעשה כך "פן תשכח את הדברים אשר ראו עיניך" הם רוממות הבורא ב"ה שאדם רואה תמיד בעיניו הפלאת הניסים והנפלאות, ע"כ צריך האדם להשגיח בעצמו תמיד. וק"ל.

Noam Elimelech, Vaetchanan 2

"But take utmost care and watch your essence scrupulously, so that you do not forget the things that you saw with your own

eyes and so that you do not turn your heart from them as long
as you live. And make them known to your children and to
your children's children." (Deut. 4:9)

For a person must always live in a state of cleaving to the
Divine, holding in awareness the exaltedness of the Blessed
One. One must discern within one's own self, and in the wonders one constantly encounters, the miracles, wonders, and
awesomeness of the Creator's world.

To begin to arrive at this level, one must focus on the portion that has been granted them from above, namely, their
essence: What it is, and how it performs miracles and wonders.
This is as we find in the Talmud, that in five ways the soul is
just like the Blessed Creator.[96]

But when one does not know oneself, one likewise does not
know the Blessed Creator, for then one does not even discern
oneself. This is the meaning of our verse, "Take utmost care
and watch your essence scrupulously," for if you fail to do so,
you will "forget the things that you saw with your own eyes"—
that is, the exaltedness of the Blessed Creator.

For a person constantly sees with their own eyes marvelous
miracles and wonders, and for this reason one must always be
mindful of oneself. This is simple to understand.

This teaching can be simultaneously simple and exceedingly challenging.
On the one hand, as both Moses and R. Elimelech instruct us, we have
to know ourselves. We should cultivate our awareness of our soul, of the

---

[96] Rav Shimi bar Ukva, said to Rabbi Shimon ben Pazi: The five instances of "Bless
the Lord, O my soul" [in Psalm 103] correspond to the five parallels between the soul
in a person's body and God's power in the world.

Just as the Holy Blessed One fills the entire world, so too the soul fills the entire body.

Just as the Holy Blessed One sees but is not seen, so too does the soul see, but is not
seen.

Just as the Holy Blessed One sustains the entire world, so too the soul sustains the
entire body.

Just as the Holy Blessed One is pure, so too is the soul pure.

Just as the Holy Blessed One resides in a chamber within a chamber, in the Divine
inner sanctum, so too the soul resides in a chamber within a chamber, in the innermost
recesses of the body.

Therefore, that which has these five characteristics, the soul, should come and praise
the One who has these five characteristics. (Brachot 10a)

wondrous, miraculous reality that we, along with the rest of the world of which we are a part and to which we bear witness, are continuously imbued with Divine life force from the Creator. On the other hand, that knowledge of ourselves is not intended to lead us to self-absorption, self-veneration, or solipsism. Instead, it should arouse a continual and deepening awareness of the Divine that forms us, imbues us with life, sustains and renews us from moment to moment, and does the same for the entire world.

That is, we should aim to recognize that our own existence—our bodies, minds, spirits, and the world we inhabit—are amazing and miraculous, and at the same time we have to be careful of the all-too-easy tendency for that awareness to lead us to think too much of ourselves and to see ourselves as separate, cut off from, and even over and against our own nature as part of the world. Our "somethingness," the fact that we are indeed something and not nothing, arises from our embeddedness in the vitality of the world as it is enlivened and brought into existence by the Creator.

## Re-membering: Toward Rosh Hashanah

The *Noam Elimelech* suggests that a key part of the practice lies in the act of remembering—that is, actively *not forgetting* that it is the Divine that animates our lives and the universe. To remember in this manner, we cultivate greater self-awareness, self-understanding, and self-knowledge. We do it not only on a cognitive or intellectual level, but with every aspect of our life and experience. We practice so that we can, as the text suggests, encounter every moment with a sense of wonder, awe, gratitude, and connection—to ourselves, one another, the natural world, and the Creator. This applies not only when it's easy, as when we encounter pleasant sensations and experiences, but even in those moments when we encounter unpleasant feelings. Our practice enables us to be present with ourselves, which in turn enables us to remember, to be present with the Holy One. In that remembering, we re-member ourselves—as part of the infinite interconnectedness that is creation.

Along these lines, Selassie quotes the 13th-century Japanese Buddhist teacher Dōgen Zenji: "To study the Buddha Way is to study the self. To study the self is to forget the self." What does it mean, she asks, "to 'forget the self' in a selfie society, in an economic climate where everyone is a brand?" Selassie continues:

> It's a package deal, studying and forgetting the self. We know ourselves through our ancestors, our experiences, and through our connection to everything around us. The less wrapped

up we are in our patterns—reactively avoiding pain or acting out unconscious conditioning—the more available we are for whatever life presents. As we forget the self, we remember that we are part of the whole. We can't have a connection to everything if we're trying to get rid of the self that is the very vehicle to experience connection.[97]

Forgetting the self, then, is not about erasing the self but, instead, remembering our membership in the larger cosmos—remembering what our eyes have seen and our hearts have felt, in Moses's words.

As we begin the 50-day journey from Tisha b'Av to Rosh Hashanah, I invite you to consider two themes in this teaching. The first is the question with which Sebene Selassie opened our study: "Who are you?" Rosh Hashanah is traditionally understood as the anniversary of the sixth day of Creation, the day on which the Divine created Adam and asked, *Ayeka,* where are you? It is the time when our tradition invites and expects us to take up these questions with particular awareness and focus: Where, who, what are you? At the same time, Rosh Hashanah is also called Yom HaZikaron, the day of remembrance, when, in a dance of mutual recognition, we remember the Divine and the Ineffable remembers us. It is, then, also a time when, even as we hear the Divine asking us, *Who are you?* we ask the same question of the Holy One: Who are *You?*

Through the practice of remembering and re-membering, Rosh Hashanah enables us to renew our understanding of self in and through our relationship with the Creator, to ask, How are you (and You) situated in this world? How are Y/you connected to everything? How are Y/you implicated in the unfolding of creation, and how does its unfolding affect Y/you? As we move toward Elul and Rosh Hashanah, these are questions we may discern in the call of the shofar.

### Questions for Reflection & Conversation

- Consider the Talmudic teaching referred to in the teaching of the *Noam Elimelech.* Review the five ways in which the Talmud compares the soul to the Holy One. Is there anything on this list that surprises you? What? Why or why not? Are there things you would add to or remove from it? If so, what are they and why would you add or remove them? That is, how do you sense the identity of the soul with Divinity?

---

[97] Selassie, 138.

- How do you respond to the *Noam Elimelech's* teaching that, in coming to know ourselves, we should actively cultivate a consciousness that it is the Creator who brings about the marvels and wonders of our lives from moment to moment? Do you find this teaching helpful or unhelpful, inviting or uninviting, or something else? Why?

- How do you understand Dōgen's teaching, brought by Selassie, that "to study the self is to forget the self?" Do you think Dōgen is talking about self-abnegation or, as we've interpreted here, rediscovering membership in a larger cosmos? Or is it something other than that? This is a difficult, paradoxical concept. How do you explain it in your own words? How do you understand the teaching in light of the *Noam Elimelech?* Are they saying the same thing or something different? If something different, how do you describe the difference?

### Ideas for Practice

Sebene Selassie offers the following journal prompts in connection with her chapter entitled "Know Yourself." Consider trying them this week.

- Where are your people from? What do you know about your ancestors? If there are gaps in your knowledge, is there anyone you can ask? If not, can you do a little research about the general information you have (e.g., if you are adopted, research your country or culture of origin and learn about the beliefs and practices of the place)?

- How would you describe yourself to a new friend? To a new colleague? To a stranger?

- What parts of yourself do you see? What parts of yourself do you not want to see?[98]

---

[98] Ibid. 236

# Ekev:
# How do we become—and remain—free?

Early in his majestic biography of Frederick Douglass, historian David Blight reflects on one of Douglass's great observations. "In his first two autobiographies," Blight writes, "Douglass seemed intuitively aware of Georg Hegel's famous insight about the mutual dependance of the master and the slave, of their inherent need for recognition from each other for the system to work." He continues:

> From experience, Douglass had his own ways of showing how the more perfect the slave, the more enslaved the master. And he showed how slavery, no matter how brutal its forms and conditions, was the meeting of two kinds of consciousness in a test of wills, and that total domination or absolute authority by the master was only rarely possible. He understood just how much the master's own identity as an independent, powerful person depended on the slave's recognition through his willing labor of that master's authority. But as Hegel put it, and Douglass lived it, in that labor, and the master's necessity of recognizing his humanity in performing it, 'the bondsman becomes aware, through this rediscovery of himself by himself, of having and being a *mind* of his own'. [Emphasis in original][99]

One has to be immediately careful not to blame an oppressed person for their own oppression. That is not what I understand Douglass to mean, nor for that matter Hegel or Blight. Rather, I understand him to be saying that a first and vital step in both individual freedom from servitude and, ultimately, collective abolition of forms of oppression, comes about through acts of awareness: The slave becomes aware that it is partially, and essentially, through their own authorization of the master over them, that the master has power in the first place. On a deep level, the master knows this, too, and thus the master acts to keep the slave subdued, unaware, and unconfident in their own agency to change their circumstances.

Douglass, of course, was the exception. The vast majority of slaves did not escape, nor even attempt to do so. Like oppressed people everywhere, most enslaved Africans in the United States, while living on some level with the awareness Douglass describes, ultimately could not overcome the various

---

[99] David W. Blight, *Frederick Douglass: Prophet of Freedom*, Simon and Schuster (2018), 40-41

forces—physical, psychological, spiritual—that their white oppressors used to keep them in fetters.

## Freedom From Egypt

If you are reading this, you are, I trust and hope, not a slave in the way Douglass or the ancient Israelites were. Yet the language of liberation from slavery is, of course, central to the Torah and to Jewish spiritual practice. Countless mitzvot have as their aim that we remember the Exodus from Egypt. Our recitation of the Shema is intended, among other things, to help us bring the Exodus to consciousness twice a day. And as the Hasidic masters taught, that was not an historical event long ago. Rather, we are constantly leaving psychological and spiritual forms of oppression—*Mitzrayim*, Egypt—in every moment.

With Douglass's observation in mind, we can ask, How is it that we become free? And, related, how do we become subservient, oppressed, enslaved in the first place? What is the spiritual work involved in both processes? And how can our spiritual practice help us to be free and to free others?

These questions form the basis for an exploration Deuteronomy 8:14 by Rabbi Chaim Tyrer of Tchernovitz (1740-1817) in his *Be'er Mayim Chayim*.

באר מים חיים דברים ח:יד

וְעוֹד יכוון בזה ורם לבבך ושכחת וגו'. כי הנה נודע אשר ישראל לא היו ראוין אז לגאולת מצרים. כי הלא היו ביניהם עובדי עבודה זרה כמאמר חז"ל (שמות רבה כ"א, ז') בטענת שר של ים הללו עובדי עבודה זרה וכו'. וידוע שאין גלות ישראל כי אם גלות עצמן. כפי שהם נשקעים בעבירות ובתאוות אשר תחת ממשלת הקליפה כן הקליפה ועמה שולטין עליהם. ועל כן הגאולה אינה גם כן כי אם גאולת עצמן כאשר נגאלין מהם ומכניעין את תאות לבבם הרע ויוצאים מרשות הקליפות. ממילא נשבר ונכנע כח המושלים ההם, וישראל יוצאים מהם. אבל ישראל במצרים שלא היו בבחינה זו לגאול את עצמן לא היו יכולין לצאת מן הגלות.

על כן נאמר בזה בשם אדומו"ר הרב המפורסם איש אלקים קדוש שמו מוהר"ר יחיאל מיכל זצלה"ה במה שהשיב הקב"ה למשה (שמות ו', א') עתה תראה אשר אעשה לפרעה כי ביד חזקה ישלחם וביד חזקה יגרשם מארצו. ולכאורה העבד אשר משועבד תחת רבו בכל מיני עבודת פרך. אחר כך כשיתגלגל הדבר שיוכל לצאת מאתו. האם צריך רבו לגרשו ממנו. הלא יברח בכל כוחו על ידיו ועל רגליו כצפור הנמלט מפח יוקשו. ולמה זה סיבב שמו יתברך שפרעה יגרשם דוקא ולא לצאת מעצמן.

ואמנם כי משה רבינו הבין שישראל הם בגלות עצמן ואינם רוצים
כלל לצאת מן גלותן להכניע כח ממשלת הקליפות אשר סביבם.
ועל כן אמר למה הרעות וגו' והצל לא הצלת את עמך ואמרו
חז"ל (שמות רבה ה', כ"ח) והצל לא הצלת ודאי. ועמדו המפרשים בזה.
ואולם כי בראותו שישראל אינן יכולין לצאת מן גלותן להיות תחת
ממשלתן ועל כן והצל לא הצלת ודאי.

ואמנם אלהינו ברוך הוא וברוך שמו המושל בכל ובידו כח וגבורה
ועצה ותושיה לכל דבר. ולמען הקים את בריתו אשר נשבע
לאבותינו. האיר אורו הגדול מול קליפת מצרים בפתע פתאום.
והחשיך וסימא את עיניהם. עד שלא יכלו כלל לסבול ניצוצי
הקדושה אשר בתוכם. כי מצא מין את מינו. וניצוצי הקדושה
בראותם אור אלהינו נבערו וניערו ברשפי אש שלהבת י"ה. עד
אשר לא יכלה הקליפות לסובלם. וגרשו אותם בכח גדול וחזק
מהם. וכן נעשה למטה בפרעה ועמו. שהאור התחיל לבעור בו מעט
מעט. והכהו במכות גדולות עד לבסוף שהיתה ההבערה קשה ולא
היה יכול לסבול. ושלחם וגרשם מארצו בכח גדול וביד חזקה. ולזה
אמר עתה תראה אשר אעשה לפרעה. לא כמו שאתה סובר שכיון
שישראל אינם יוצאים בעצמם יקשה להוציאם. אני אדריכו בדרך
אחר אשר ביד חזקה ישלחם וביד חזקה יגרשם מאתו.

ונמצא היציאה ממצרים היה רק בכח בכח ובטובת אלהינו יתברך שמו.
ולזה אמר הכתוב כאן ורם לבבך ושכחת את ה' אלהיך המוציאך
כלומר כי על ידי גבהות ורום לבבך תשכח שה' אלהיך הוא הוציאך
מארץ מצרים בכוחו הגדול בטובו. ורצה לומר שאתה תסבור שאתה
בעצמך יצאת משם. ועל כן אין אתה ירא ליכנס ביניהם להתאות
לתאותם ולחמוד חמדתם להכנע תחת ממשלתם ח"ו. כי תסבור
שתהא יציאה כביאה שתצא משם בנקל בעצמך אחרי שגם ממצרים
יצאת בעצמך שלא על ידי מעשים טובים (או אפשר יכחש זאת
מכל וכל לומר שהתאוה גורם להיות לעבד וראיה ממצרים והבן).

**Be'er Mayim Chayim, Deuteronomy 8:14**
"Beware lest your heart grow haughty and you forget the
LORD your God—who freed you from the land of Egypt,
the house of bondage." (Deut. 8:14).

There is a position which holds that Israel were not fit to be
redeemed from Egypt, for they were idol-worshippers among
Egyptians there, as our Sages taught… We also know that the
exile of the Israelites was, fundamentally, an exile of their own
doing, from themselves: They were sunken within the transgressions and desires of the dominion of the *klipah*, the shell
of superficial appearance separating them from their Divine

essence, and thus also the people of the *klipah*, Egypt. Thus, redemption must also have been a self-redemption: they subdued the lusting of their hearts, and became liberated from the *klipot*. When they did so, the power of their oppressors was broken, and Israel went free. But the Israelites in Egypt were not in such a state to redeem themselves, and so were not able to exit the exile.

In relation to this, Reb Yechiel Michel (the Zlotchover Rebbe) offered a teaching regarding the Holy Blessed One's words to Moses, "Now see what I will do to Pharaoh: With a mighty hand he will send you away, and with a mighty hand he will expel you from his land" (Exodus 6:1). At first glance, one would think that a slave, who is oppressed by his master with all manner of cruelty, would not need to be expelled by his master—as soon as the opportunity presents itself for him to escape, he will do so with all his power, on his hands and knees, like a bird escaping from a fowler's trap. Why, then, does the Blessed Name bring it about that Pharaoh must expel them, and not that they would leave on their own?

Moses our Teacher understood that Israel were in a state of their own exile, and they had no desire to leave their exile, to subdue the power of the *klipot* in which they were immersed. Thus, he said to God, "O Lord, why did You bring harm upon this people? Why did You send me? Ever since I came to Pharaoh to speak in Your name, he has dealt worse with this people. And deliver? You have not delivered Your people!" (Ex. 5:22-23). The Sages (Shemot Rabbah 5:28) teach that "you have not delivered your people" means, "You have not fully delivered them." There is much commentary on this. However, it was because he saw that Israel were unable to give up their exile to then rule themselves—thus, God's deliverance was not yet complete.

The Blessed Ineffable One governs all. In the hand of the Divine rests power, strength, wise counsel, and insight for every matter. "In order to fulfill the covenant the Divine made on oath with our ancestors" (Deut. 8:14): [The verse demonstrates that Israel were not yet in a state to leave the exile, and thus God had to act. Therefore,] the Redeemer, in an instant, shone Its great light toward the *klipah* of Egypt, darkening and blinding their eyes until they were unable to withstand the holy sparks that were among them [i.e., in the Israelites]. For like found like, and when the holy sparks [in the Israelites] saw the light of our Redeemer, they became enflamed, igniting with the flames of the Divine, to the point that the *klipot* were unable to contain them and the sparks cast them away with great force. The same was done in the lower realms, with Pharaoh and his people. The light began to flicker bit by bit. As the ten plagues struck the Egyptians, eventually the conflagration was strong, and they were unable to bear it—they then sent them away and expelled them from the land with great power and a mighty hand. For this reason the Divine said, "Now you will see what I will do to Pharaoh." It is not as you think, that because they will not leave of their own accord it is difficult for Me to liberate the Israelites. Rather, I have a different plan—that Pharaoh will send them out and expel them with a mighty hand.

It turns out, then, that the Exodus from Egypt was solely on account of the power and goodness of our Ineffable Blessed God. And this is why our verse here says, "Beware lest your heart grow haughty and you forget YHVH your God—who freed you." That is, 'through your pride and haughtiness, you will come to forget that it is YHVH your God who, in Divine goodness, brought you out from Egypt with great power.' You may think that you, on your own, came out of Egypt and therefore you will not be cautious when entering [the Land of Canaan, to live among the inhabitants], [ultimately] sharing in their lusts, and desiring what they find desirable, coming under their sway. You may reason that the exodus is like the entry into the Land—that, since you left Egypt by means of your own power, and not through God's good works, you will likewise be able to depart from the domain of lust and desire on your own. (Or, possibly, one could deny this dynamic and simply claim that it was the lustful desire which caused you to become a slave, and the proof is from what happened in Egypt. Understand.)

From the starting point of our verse in Deuteronomy, the *Be'er* asks, What is the relationship between being mindful of our hearts—our desires, drives, yearnings, lusts—and the state of freedom? In the first paragraph, he offers an initial answer, which is a strawman: Maintaining awareness and attention of our desires is sufficient to bring about, and therefore sufficient to sustain, the state of redemption. After all, this false argument goes, the Israelites had enabled themselves to sink to a state of degradation—not only physical and political enslavement, but spiritual poverty. They were enslaved not only to their Egyptian taskmasters, but to their base drives and desires. But because they brought their condition upon themselves, their redemption came about when they awakened within themselves the capacity to overcome their impulses and thereby leave that spiritual state. As soon as they did so, the Divine was awakened and they could go free.

But then the Tchernovitcher offers another, contradictory reading, courtesy of another teacher, the Zlotchover Rebbe. According to this view, slipping into a state of spiritual poverty is one thing, but liberating oneself from it is another. For when one gets to that place of degradation, one has no will or desire to leave it. Thus, they could not have brought about their own freedom—making it necessary for the Holy One to act. It was the Divine who activated the holy sparks within the people, which then enabled the liberation to occur—as evidenced by the fact that Pharaoh expelled them. They didn't just leave on their own, rather Pharaoh had to throw them out.

In the final paragraph he brings the focus back to our verse in Deuteronomy, and the implications of this exploration for not only entry into the land of Canaan, but ultimately the work of self-regulation and self-government that comes with crossing the River Jordan. Why does Moses need to remind the people to be mindful of their hearts, to not forget the Divine? For two reasons: First, because, without paying sufficient attention to their desires, they may—or, more likely, certainly will—fall victim to them; and second, because once that happens, it's not possible to leave that state without help from the Divine. Once we're in that state of diminished spiritual awareness, it will require yet another miracle to be liberated again. And as the Rabbis taught, we don't rely on miracles.

## The Divine Frees Us

The Tchernovitcher's point, then, is that our spiritual practice needs to transcend our selves. We can't do this on our own. Rather, we must actively remember that it was the Divine who took us out from Egypt—and it is that same Redeemer who, as we cultivate our awareness and conscious practice, enables us to liberate ourselves from our baser impulses again and again, in every moment of every day.

In my view, this is one of the most significant distinguishing features of Jewish spiritual practice, and also one of the hardest. So much of contemporary mindfulness focuses on the important work of self-awareness. Many meditation practices, for instance, help us cultivate awareness of our emotions, our drives, our desires. They help us notice what's going on in our bodies, hearts, and minds, and, through that awareness, they are powerful aids in living more intentional, aligned, purposeful lives. Yet there's something more to it, according to the Torah and, I think, to our own experience. The *klipot* are powerful. They include lustful desires and bad impulses. But they also include many kinds of unintentional, unaware conformity to parts of our surrounding culture that contribute to our individual and collective spiritual impoverishment: Consumerism, environmental exploitation, the hidden human exploitation in so many of the goods and services we use, a culture that values superficiality over deep human encounter, to name a few. There are *klipot* that are obvious to us, and then there are ones that are less obvious. To free ourselves from them—individually and collectively—will not come about solely through our own mindfulness. It requires that and more. It requires a continual and expanding awakening of Divine sparks within all of us—and God's help.

## Questions for Reflection & Conversation

- At the end of his teaching, the Tchernovitcher writes: "You may reason that the exodus is like the entry into the Land—that, since you left Egypt by means of your own power, and not through God's good works, you will likewise be able to depart from the domain of lust and desire on your own. )Or, possibly, one could deny this dynamic and simply claim that it was the lustful desire which caused you to become a slave, and the proof is from what happened in Egypt.)" What is the difference between these two readings? What does he mean by saying, "one could deny this dynamic"? What dynamic might we be denying, and what is the substitute understanding he offers?

- In your own spiritual practice, do you sense that you are liberating yourself? Do you sense that the Divine is working within you? Would you describe your experience a different way? If you do experience some force from beyond yourself working within you, say more about it: How does it feel? How are you aware of it? If you don't, can you say more about that? What is it that you sense is happening within you in your own practice?
  A key aspect of this teaching is its emphasis on calling the Israel-

ites to heightened awareness as they enter the land. In particular, Moses is concerned about the people's susceptibility to the values of the surrounding culture. I have transposed that charge into our own time and place, naming some of the meta-values (consumerism, superficiality, environmental and human exploitation, etc.). What, if any, of these kinds of *klipot*/negative forces, do you want to be more mindful of? What, if anything, do you find challenging in liberating yourself (and possibly others) from them? What, if anything, helps you to do so?

## Ideas for Practice

This week, consider a meditation practice that focuses on the following line from the traditional liturgy:

פְּתַח לִבִּי בְּתוֹרָתָךְ וּבְמִצְוֹתָיךָ תִּרְדּוֹף נַפְשִׁי

*P'tach libbi b'toratecha uv'mitzvotecha tirdof nafshi*

Open my heart to Your Torah and let my
soul pursue Your commandments.

Allow yourself to find a dignified posture. Soften your gaze or, perhaps, close your eyes. Find an anchor in your breath, a point of contact between your body and the chair or floor, or in a sound. Sit for a few minutes and allow your mind to settle, however much it may. Then, when you're ready, say these words out loud slowly. Notice what arises for you with each word: Open, heart, Torah, soul, commandments (or you might choose to leave it untranslated, as mitzvot), pursue. Repeat the phrase several times, and notice what arises for you.

# Re'eh: What Do You See?

In their classic work on leadership, Ronald Heifetz and Marty Linsky distinguish between leaders with and without authority. The former are those who are authorized by others through formal processes with an implicit or explicit charge to preserve order. Leaders without authority are those who lead others in agitating for change in the existing order. In their discussion of leading with authority, Heifetz and Linsky note that, "In adaptive situations, fulfilling the social functions of authority requires walking a razor's edge. Challenge people too fast, and they will push the authority figure over for failing their expectations for stability. But challenge people too slowly, and they will throw him [sic] down when they discover that no progress has been made… To stay balanced on the edge, one needs a strategic understanding of the specific tools and constraints that come with one's authority."[100]

Further on, Heifetz and Linsky note that, in exercising leadership, "one has to alternate between participating and observing." They invoke the metaphor of dancing on a dance floor. When participating in the dance, it is harder to see what is actually going on. "To discern the larger patterns on the dance floor—to see who is dancing with whom, in what groups, in what location, and who is sitting out which kind of dance—we have to stop moving and get to the balcony."[101]

While Heifetz and Linsky's observations may apply to people exercising formal leadership positions, Parker Palmer helpfully reminds us that, when it comes right down to it, all of us are doing this work all the time. "Everyone who draws breath 'takes the lead' many times a day. We lead with actions that range from a smile to a frown; with words that range from blessing to curse; with decisions that range from faithful to fearful. Friends lead friends, parents their children, teachers their students, bosses their employees, doctors their patients, politicians their constituents… As long as I am here, doing whatever I am doing, I am leading, for better or for worse. And, if I may say so, so are you."[102]

## Seeing and Choosing

These observations of Heifetz, Linsky, and Palmer frame our exploration

---

[100] Ronald A. Heifetz, *Leadership Without Easy Answers*. Cambridge: The Belknap Press of Harvard University Press, 1994, 126-127.

[101] Ibid. 252-253

[102] Parker J. Palmer, "Introduction" inn Intrator, Sam M. and Megan Scribner. *Leading From Within: Poetry That Sustains the Courage to Lead*. San Francisco: Jossey-Bass, 2007, xxiii-xxx.

of Parashat Re'eh, and in particular of the question, What do you see? When you see yourself, do you see someone exercising leadership, or something else? When you view a situation, do you sense a choice to be made, or are you compelled without a choice? What pressures do you sense to make a decision in one direction or another? What razor's edge do you find yourself walking? These are not only questions of presidents and CEOs: they are questions for you and me, for all of us, in every moment of every day.

The opening words of Parashat Re'eh articulate this theme, which, like others in the Book of Deuteronomy, Moses will repeat again and again: "See, I set before you today blessing and curse." The 16th-century Italian commentator Ovadiah Sforno notes, "Both of these options are before you. The choice is yours." What we see influences the choice we can make. How we choose to see is part of our choice-making, since having chosen to see or not see will affect what is available for us to choose later in the process. All of this is part of our own personal work of leadership.

Rabbi Yehuda Leib Alter of Ger (1847-1905) explores these themes of seeing and choosing with reference to the notion of the *yetzer hara*, often translated as our evil inclination:

**שפת אמת ראה תרל"ז**

במדרש ואל תדברו גבוהות כו'. דכתיב נותן לפניכם היום בו"ק. פי' שבכל עת וזמן יש ב' הדרכים לפני האדם. כמ"ש בספרי משל לזקן שעומד על פרשת דרכים ומזהיר זה הדרך תחילתו קוצים וסופו מישור כו'. נמצא הצדיק ג"כ עומד תמיד באמצעיות ב' הדרכים ימין ושמאל. וז"ש הגדול מחבירו יצרו גדול כו'. ואמרו חכמים לעתיד לבא הקב"ה מביא יצה"ר ושוחטו צדיקים נדמה להם כהר ובוכין איך יכלנו להלחם בו. ורשעים נדמה להם כחוט השערה ובוכין איך לא יכלנו לכבוש חוט שערה כזה. והענין כי לעולם יש רק חוט השערה. והצדיקים שגוברים עליו פוגעין אח"כ בחוט השערה אחרת וכן לעולם עד שמתרבה ונעשה כהר. אבל זה הרשע הנשאר עומד. הרי הוא עומד בחוט השערה אחת. וזה ענין הצדיקים אין להם מנוחה כו'. וז"ש שלא יתגאה האדם בהיותו נתעלה באיזה מדרגה. כי גם שם יש לפניו שני הדרכים כנ"ל. אמנם עי"ז מרויחין הצדיקים הברכה בהיותם מניחין דרך הרע ובוחרים בדרך הטוב. והוא השכר שלעתיד. וכן בש"ק מעין עוה"ב שנק' יום מנוחה. ומנוחה הוא רק אחר היגיעה. וכפי היגיעה בימי המעשה ובעוה"ז. כן המנוחה בש"ק ובעוה"ב. והאמת כי מנוחת הצדיק בשבת היא אות ועדות למנוחתו בעוה"ב.

Sefat Emet, Re'eh 5637 (1877)103

In the Midrash: "Listen and give ear; do not be haughty, for the Lord has spoken" (Jer. 13:15). Said Rabbi Tanhuma: The Holy Blessed One said, "Listen to the words of Torah and do not speak haughtily, for the Lord has spoken." Therefore, Scripture says [in the present tense]: "See, I place before you today blessing and curse"[104] (Deut. 11:26).

Indeed, these two paths stand before a person at all times. The *Sifre* offers a parable of an elder standing at the crossroads and warning those who pass, saying: "This path that begins in brambles ends up being straight [whereas the path that looks straight will end up in brambles]."

The *tzaddik* also stands always between two paths that branch off right and left. That is why they said: "Whoever is greater than his companion, his [evil] urge is also greater." The sages further said: "In the future, the blessed Holy One will bring forth the evil urge and slaughter it. To the righteous it will appear as a great mountain, and they will weep, saying: 'How were we ever able to battle it!' But to the wicked it will appear as a hairbreadth, and they will weep: 'How were we never able to conquer it!'"

The fact is that there is always only a hairbreadth. But the righteous, as they overcome each hairbreadth, go on to encounter another. They keep doing so forever, until they accumulate so many as to seem like a mountain. But the wicked is one who stands still, always facing that same hairbreadth. This is why "the righteous have no rest in this world."[105]

This is also the reason no one should become too proud for having ascended some rung. For in that place, too, there will be two paths. But this is how the righteous can earn their blessing, by ever leaving the wicked path and choosing the good. This is their reward for the future.

The *Sefat Emet* offers us a reflection on the opening word of the parasha, *Re'eh* "see" or "behold." What is it that we see? He gives us a few ways to

---

[103] Translation from *The Language of Truth: The Torah Commentary of the Sefat Emet*. Philadelphia: Jewish Publication Society, 2012.

[104] That is, the words of Torah are God speaking, placing blessing and curse before us always.

[105] Brachot 64a

consider the question. First, he mentions a midrash of a wise elder who stands at a fork in the road. One way appears to be a difficult, encumbered path, full of thorns and brambles, while the other looks to be open and clear. Yet the elder cautions the traveler that, though the first path appears to be difficult, it is only its initial appearance, as it ultimately ends in openness. The other, of course, also belies its true nature—though it appears open and clear now it winds up in thorns and brambles. This could be (and likely is, in its original context) an exhortation to choose the more difficult life—of Torah and *mitzvot*. Doing so in this world, the midrash suggests, will ultimately yield a peaceful life in the world-to-come; choosing what seems to be an easy, carefree life in this world will yield a painful life in the next. Yet, based on the *Sefat Emet's* next comments, he seems to be suggesting something subtler with this midrash. We'll return to it.

In the next two paragraphs, the *Sefat Emet* more directly takes up the question, When we confront our *yetzer hara*, the part of us which tempts us with a narrower vision of immediate gratification, what to do we see? In particular, he poses this question from a perspective of maturity. Looking back on our lives, how does the *yetzer hara* appear? Did we see the daily seductions of instant gratification, the impulse to take the easy way? Did we behold the inclination to satisfy ourselves rather than serve the greater need? For the righteous, he says, it will appear as a mountain, something overwhelmingly difficult to overcome that, with dedication and commitment, they were able to traverse. For the wicked—and here I would invite us to consider a more capacious conception than simply willful malice, instead acknowledging the all-too-human disinclination to deal mindfully with the *yetzer hara*—it appears as a tiny hairbreadth. How is it possible, they wonder in hindsight, that I couldn't get past that tiny little thing?!

This brings the *Sefat Emet* to the essential teaching, namely that "there is always only a hairbreadth." That is, in every moment we have before us a choice: "See, I have placed before you today blessing and curse." The two are separated by something infinitesimal, a hairbreadth. This brings us back to the midrash of the brambles and opens up another reading: That which appears as blessing (comfortable, comforting, pleasant, desirable) may, in fact, not be so; and that which appears as a curse (difficult, uncomfortable, disconsoling, undesirable) to us now, might turn out to be a blessing. To the unrighteous—not only the actively wicked but, we might say, even to the simply average person, that is, "us"—the *yetzer hara's* temptations will lead us to making unmindful choices. We are likely to follow our desires along what appears to be an easy path, only to find that it ends up somewhere much less blessed or beneficial than we anticipated. The more mindful practitioner—the righteous person, perhaps, the person we aspire to be—takes time to discern the choice before them. They create more time and space between sensing—seeing, beholding—the reality that presents itself, and their evaluation of it and ultimate response to it. They enable themselves to acknowledge the sensations of the *yetzer hara* operating within them, to feel its sensations and hear its seductive stories and then, mindfully, intentionally, choose their path.

## Perspective: How We See

Perspective is key in all of this. From our immediate vantage point, especially under the influence of our powerful, less-mindful drives (the *yetzer hara*), we might see the choice before us one way. Yet by pressing pause, as it were, and going up to the balcony of the dance floor, we might come to see other consequences—and other possibilities. Having seen those other options, we then have a greater capacity to make a more mindful choice, a choice of blessing, one beyond that which the *yetzer hara* is pulling us, a choice of curse.

The 19th-century Indian poet Mirza Asadullah Baig Khan, known as Ghalib, offers his own beautiful reflection on this dynamic of perspective:

> For the raindrop, joy is in entering the river—
> Unbearable pain becomes its own cure.
> Travel far enough into sorrow, tears turn to sighing;
> In this way we learn how water can die into air.
> When, after heavy rain, the stormclouds disperse,
> Is it not that they've wept themselves clear to the end?
> If you want to know the miracle, how wind can polish a mirror,
> Look: the shining glass grows green in spring.
> It's the rose's unfolding, Ghalib, that creates the desire to see—
> In every color and circumstance, may the eyes be open for what comes.[106]

As the verse from our parasha states, the Divine continually presents us with a choice in seeing. Taking the time to see more clearly, to open our mind's eye to what is but may yet be hidden from our view, whether in space or time or another dimension, is essential to discerning that hairbreadth's choice before us. It is not easy, nor is it a one-time affair: Just as the Divine continually imbues the world with life-force, so too the Holy One continually

---

[106] Ghalib and Jane Hirshfield (trans.). *For the raindrop, joy is entering the river.* n.d. 27 February 2022. https://thevalueofsparrows.wordpress.com/2015/07/22/poetry-for-the-raindrop-by-ghalib.

renews both the choices before us and our capacity to choose. It is an unending thing. In this very moment, you have the choice whether to continue reading or not, to sit with this text or do something else, to understand it on the level you currently understand it or try to find some new understanding within it, and so forth.

Even when it may not be apparent to us, we always have a choice—of action, feeling, thought, awareness. We practice so that we can see the hairbreadth and, in so doing, recognize the necessity for choosing, and our obligation and our ability to do so. May our practice nourish that capacity within us, and may we, like the righteous, choose life and blessing.

## Questions for Reflection & Conversation

- The *Sefat Emet* writes that, to the righteous, the evil urge appears as a mountain, while to the wicked it appears as a hairbreadth. He then observes that, in fact, "there is always only a hairbreadth," yet the righteous continuously confront and overcome the hairbreadth, while the wicked remain stuck in place. As you contemplate this image and this description, what arises for you? As you consider your own life, when do you sense that you have been more like the righteous or the wicked here? What contributed to the choices you made in those different situations?

- Do you agree with the characterization of righteous and wicked that the *Sefat Emet* employs here (the former constantly moving, making active, mindful choices, the latter standing still, not choosing actively)? Why or why not?

- I introduced the *yetzer hara* by noting that the term is traditionally translated as "evil inclination." Later I rendered it as "that part of us that tempts us with a narrower vision of immediate gratification." Does one or the other of these translations ring truer for you in your own experience? When, how, why or why not? In your own words (and, perhaps, your own experience), what do you understand the *yetzer hara* to be?

- How do you know that any choice is a "good" choice in the moment? In some sense the opening midrash suggests that we really only learn that in the end. Is it always that the "harder" choice is the good choice? Is it always a matter of self-denial/self-gratification? What have you learned from your own experience in this regard?

## Ideas for Practice

- This week, consider making an intention to "step onto the balcony" when you have a choice to make—at least once a day.

- Try to notice when you sense you are called to make a choice.

- Then, practice *hitlamdut*, bringing your awareness to what is working within you at the moment. What different forces, sensations, or voices are present for you? What intentions, commitments, relationships, or other aspects of your life are present? These might include the potential effects of your possible choices on yourself, on people close to you, people who depend on you, others whom you don't know but with whom you are no less in relationship by virtue of sharing the planet. They might include principles, causes, or institutions.

- Try to be aware of whether and how the *yetzer hara* is present for you. How might your desires—emotional, bodily, social, or otherwise—be calling to you? Do you want to listen to them? Can you sense how you might you be prone to rationalizing your choice in service of the *yetzer hara?*

- Then, consider the options you have before you (which could include the choice simply to honor whatever seems unavoidable in the moment). It is possible, even likely, that no single choice will honor all the aspects you've considered. Yet here you are, with the choice before you. How might each choice become a source of blessing, lifting up the factors most important to you? How might it become a source of curse, letting down those people or commitments? Will your choice be a life-giving one? Will it accommodate or accede to the call of the *yetzer hara?* Which choices seem like clear paths now but are likely to result in thickets and brambles later? Which seem more difficult now but are more likely to result in ease down the road?

- Give yourself time—you don't need to rush. Check out how your various options feel within you. Perhaps most particularly, aim to be honest with yourself about the implications of your choices. See if you can accept the likely reality that no choice is going to be perfect. Try to discern which is most aligned with the intention(s) you most wish to honor, which is most likely to be a source of blessing.

- Then, when you have discerned the choice that is most aligned with your intention, accept and internalize your decision. Try to hold in your awareness a whole sense of the matter—its fullness and its brokenness, its dimensions of blessing and of curse. Be kind to yourself: you've made a whole-hearted, difficult choice. If appropriate, consider the most mindful way to communicate your decision to others—especially to those you may be letting down.

# Shoftim: How Do We Judge?

After the five books of the Torah, *Pirkei Avot* is one of the most comment-ed-upon texts in the Jewish tradition. Often rendered in English as "Sayings" or "Ethics" of the ancient Rabbinic Sages, the six-chapter tractate of the Mishnah has been studied for centuries for its aphorisms and wisdom. "Say little and do much." "Make for yourself a teacher and acquire for yourself a friend." "If I am not for myself, who will be for me? When I am only for myself, what am I? If not now, when?" These and many more are among the teachings of the Rabbis that appear in *Pirkei Avot*.

Yet *Pirkei Avot* comes toward the end of a larger section of the Mishnah—the Order of Nezikin—that deals with civil law and jurisprudence. While we tend to read it as a source of folk wisdom, a plausible theory holds that it is, in fact, a guidebook for judges. After all, one of the key roles taken on by the Rabbis of the Mishnah and the Talmud was to develop and apply Jewish law. Thus, for instance, the very first teaching in *Avot* reads much better as words of counsel to judges and leaders than it does to average citizens:

> Moses received the Torah at Sinai and transmitted it to Joshua, Joshua to the elders, and the elders to the prophets, and the prophets to the Men of the Great Assembly. They said three things: Be patient in [the administration of] justice, raise many disciples and make a fence round the Torah.

Or consider Yehuda ben Tabbai's statement just a little later on (Avot 1:8): "Do not play the part of an advocate [when you serve as a judge]; and when the litigants are standing before you, look upon them as if they were [both] guilty; and when they leave your presence, look upon them as if they were [both] innocent, when they have accepted the judgment." These are clearly words for professional judges.

Yet the tradition of reading *Pirkei Avot* as folk wisdom, to inform the lives of every person, has its own logic. While judging is clearly a highly skilled profession, all of us, as human beings, make judgments all the time. Evolution has conditioned us to judge sights, sounds, smells, and sensations as friend or foe—most often subconsciously. But also on a conscious level, we live our lives through judging: What is the right decision in this case? What should I do? How shall I behave? This ranges from the mundane (should I eat this piece of cake?) to the sublime (should I say yes to this marriage proposal?). Our minds are constantly making judgments.

## Judging and Being Judged

This can get particularly tricky in our judgments about other people. Our evolutionary conditioning leads us to categorize and make judgments about people before we're even aware that we've done it. This is bias, and mindfulness practice can help us to become aware of those micro-judgments and potentially interrupt or counteract them.

Relatedly, while we may need to judge others to conduct our daily affairs and even for our health and wellbeing, we also have to be very careful not to become judgmental. This is a fine line, as reflected in the teaching of Yehoshua ben Prachya that I quoted above. Now, note the final phrase, which gives what precedes a finer point: "Make for yourself a teacher, acquire for yourself a friend, and judge every person with the benefit of the doubt" (*Avot* 1:5). Our judging can lead to judgmentalism, finding fault and flaw in everything and everyone. This can start us in a vicious cycle by which we start to judge ourselves negatively, too. Certainly in my own life, and also, I imagine, in yours, I've found that giving others the benefit of the doubt is intimately bound up with being compassionate toward myself. Thus, focused, intentional practice is key (otherwise Yehoshua ben Prachya likely would not have felt a need to say it!).

As its name indicates, Parashat Shoftim (a *shofet* is a judge) invites us to reflect on the question, How do we judge? "You shall appoint judges and officials for your tribes," opens the parasha, "in all the gates [of your cities, where courts of judgment were held] that the LORD your God is giving you. Judge the people with righteous justice" (Deut. 16:18). Elaborating on the theme of judging, and with the approaching Day of Judgment (Rosh Hashanah) in the background, Rabbi Levi Yitzchak of Berditchev (1740-1809) offers the following teaching:

קדושת לוי שופטים א

שופטים ושוטרים תתן לך בכל שעריך כו' ושפטו את העם משפט צדק (דברים טז, יח). דהנה הקדוש ברוך הוא שופט את הכנסת ישראל בבוא יום המשפט בגודל רחמיו וחסדיו. אך צריכין אתערותא דלתתא לעורר את המדה של רחמנות למעלה. ועל ידי מה נתעורר אותו המדה של חסד, כשאנו למטה מתנהגים בחסד ולמדים זכות על כל איש מישראל לדונן לכף זכות ואז על ידי זה גם מלמעלה נתעורר אותו המדה ולמדין גם עליו וגם על כל זרע ישראל חסדים. ואם כן האדם מעורר בעובדא שלמטה השער העליון לפתוח שערי חסד להריק ברכה על כל זרע ישראל. וזה שכתוב שופטים ושוטרים תתן לך בכל שעריך, רוצה לומר שאתה בעצמך תתקן ותכין המשפט

של מעלה על ידי שעריך, והוא השערים שלך שאתה עושה ומעורר
במעשיך. וזהו ושפטו את העם משפט צדק, רוצה לומר כל איש
ילמוד את עצמו להתנהג לשפוט את העם משפט צדק ללמד צדקה
וזכות על כל זרע ישראל ואז האדם מעורר השער של מעלה ועל
ידי זה יוצא בדין זכאי במשפט של מעלה, כי במדה שאדם מודד
מודדין לו:

### Kedushat Levi, Shoftim 1

The Holy Blessed One judges the Congregation of Israel on the coming Day of Judgment [i.e., Rosh Hashanah] in the fullness of Divine mercy and compassion. Yet that Divine mercy on high must be aroused through our actions in the lower realms.

What activates that quality of Divine love? To the degree that we below conduct ourselves with compassion and generosity of spirit, giving every member of Israel the benefit of the doubt, so too will these qualities be aroused on high. Each of us, individually and collectively, will then be treated with compassion [by the Divine]. This being so, then we, through our actions in the lower realms, arouse the opening of the highest gate, by which the gates of compassion are thrown wide to pour out blessing upon all of Israel.

This, then, is what is meant by "You shall appoint judges and officials for your tribes, in all your gates (sh'arekha)": that is, you, yourself, influence and establish the quality of heavenly judgment by means of your "favorable assessment (she'arim; a play on words with she'arekha, gates)." Your actions arouse the opening of heavenly "gates" (which parallel our favorable assessments).

And further, this is what is meant by "judge the people fairly and righteously." That is, each of us should train ourself to behave in such a way that we judge the people fairly and righteously—to seek the merit and righteousness of all members of Israel. Through this, we will arouse the gates [of compassion]/ [favorable] assessments in the upper realms and, as a result, reciprocally, emerge meritorious from Divine judgment [on the Day of Judgment]. For, as the Sages teach: in the manner that we measure others, we will be measured, in turn. (Megillah 12b)

The *Kedushat Levi* here makes a bold and, in my view, extremely helpful theological move. One view of Divine judgment in general, and Rosh Hashanah in particular, holds that God's judgments are inscrutable and that we must therefore beseech the Ominponent for mercy. Yet here, R. Levi Yitzchak offers us an understanding that is subtler, more intimate, and, as far as I'm concerned, more believable. Our individual and collective actions, *itrauta d'letata* in Aramaic, arouse the Divine to behave toward us in a similar manner. Our behavior and non-judgmental orientation toward others align more fully with the Divine will, so that the Beloved's true desire for us (life, health, wellbeing) can flow fully and effectively. If we are merciful, compassionate, and loving toward others, then the Holy One, reciprocally, behaves compassionately and lovingly toward us.

Thus, the question of how Divine judgment of us manifests in the world is really a question of how we judge others and ourselves. If we can be honest and righteous; if we can temper our strict judgment with compassion; if we can be mindful of our biases and tendencies toward judgmentalism and enable our faculties of judgment to remain clear, fair, and rooted fundamentally in *hesed* (loving connection), then the Holy One will mirror all of this. It is, in essence, an inversion of the Talmudic teaching, "Just as the Holy One is compassionate and slow to anger, so too should you be compassionate and slow to anger."[107] Instead, the *Kedushat Levi* suggests: Just as we are compassionate and slow to anger, so will the Holy One be as well.

To my mind, this is an empowering orientation for living, grounded in mindfulness practice. Not only might I help to bring about fairness and equity by being mindful of my biases as I judge; not only might I help others to experience love and compassion through my judgments, words, and actions; not only may I be able to be less judgmental toward myself and practice compassionate self-judgment: all these potential positive outcomes are manifestations of the Divine presence, of compassionate and loving Divine judgment in the world, facilitated and manifested through my practice. This is a theology that says that God wants to be visible and present in the world, that the Holy One wants to show up in our acts of love and compassion, and that we have the capacity to help ourselves and others be aware of the Divine presence in the world by behaving accordingly.

## Judging for Judges—and the All of Us

In an article entitled "Mindfulness and Judging," former Federal judge Jeremy Fogel reflects on how mindfulness practice can be beneficial for official judges:

---

[107] Shabbat 133b

As professional decision makers, judges typically become skilled at thinking reflectively and articulating reasons for their decisions. Most judges try to recognize and account for their reactions to the cases they hear and to avoid ruling impulsively. Judges also strive to treat people fairly. Yet despite these efforts, almost every experienced judge can think of cases in which a judgment missed the mark, in which the emotional impact of the situation made thoughtful reflection difficult or impossible, or in which there was lingering doubt about whether justice truly was done.[108]

Fogel also observes that "most cases involve real people with important, often very personal interests at stake. A judge's decisions frequently are made in and affect an atmosphere infused with passions that can confound the detached rationality with which decisions—at least in theory—are supposed to be made." For these reasons and more, he suggests, mindfulness practice can be extraordinarily helpful to judges. Developing mindful awareness of one's own biases, the emotions and bodily realities that influence how we may perceive the world in a moment, and the many other factors that naturally influence our judgments as humans, is vital in order to "be patient in the administration of justice," as *Pirkei Avot* exhorts.

This is not just good practice for professional decision-makers. All of us are judges all the time. As we enter Elul and prepare for Yom HaDin, the Day of Judgment, now is a time to bring greater attention to how our judgments come to be, how we can be more honest and truthful in our judgments, diminishing judgmentalism of self or others, and how we can renew the soil of compassion and loving connection in which our judgments take root.

### Questions for Reflection & Conversation

- The *Kedushat Levi* writes, "To the degree that we below conduct ourselves with compassion and generosity of spirit, giving every member of Israel the benefit of the doubt, so too will these qualities be aroused on high. Each of us, individually and collectively, will then be treated with compassion [by the Divine]." One might argue that this teaching is a variation on the statement, "Human beings create God in their image." Do you agree or disagree with this paraphrase? If you agree, how do you feel about that? If you

---

[108] Jeremy D. Fogel, "Mindfulness and Judging," 2016, *Federal Judicial Center.*

disagree, how would you state it differently? How, if at all, does your understanding affect your experience?

- Yehoshua ben Prachya teaches that we should give every person the benefit of the doubt. Likewise, the *Kedushat Levi* teaches that we should seek the merit and righteousness of others. In your own experience, do you find this kind of non-judgmental generosity difficult, easy, or something else? What, if anything, helps you to cultivate this disposition? When, if ever, do you find that greater circumspection, or even suspicion toward others might be warranted? If so, can you hold that suspicious orientation without judgment of yourself or the other, i.e., allow for something new to surface, some potential for reconciliation or positive outcome to arise?

- Is there someone in your own life or experience whom you view as exemplary in their capacity for judging with righteousness, fairness, and compassion? What, if anything, can you identify in their words, behavior, or practice that helped nurture that capacity? What, if anything, have you learned from them that you try to emulate in your own life?

## Ideas for Practice

There is actually quite a bit of material online related to mindfulness, judging, and the practice of law. In this video meditation, Scott Rogers, founder of the Institute for Mindfulness Studies and Director of the Mindfulness in Law Program at the University of Miami School of Law, teaches a short practice called "Just Us Holmes" which draws on Justice Oliver Wendell Holmes's instruction to "Stop, Look & Listen" from the Supreme Court decision in "Baltimore & Ohio Railroad v. Goodman:" https://youtu.be/8-8btX_PdhA.

As you engage in this practice, consider framing it for yourself in the words of the parasha: *tzedek tzedek tirdof,* "Justice, Justice shall you pursue" and, at the conclusion of your practice, journaling to yourself in response to the question: How might my practice bring greater clarity, compassion, and wisdom to a judgment I'm asked to make?

# Ki Teitzei: How Do We Recover?

The Los Angeles organization Beit T'Shuvah is a special place: a congregation and residential addiction treatment center. On its website, Beit T'Shuvah describes its philosophy this way:

> Addiction is a symptom of a divided self; an unhealthy dependence on substances or compulsive activities to provide a temporary sense of wholeness and well-being. Through a community rooted in the spiritual principles of Judaism, authenticity, and transparency, Beit T'Shuvah members are taught to live in concert with their own inner value, dignity, and *Kedusha*: holiness. We believe everyone has the right to redemption, which is why we never turn a single soul away due to their inability to pay... allowing all who wish to make *T'Shuvah*.[109]

Following general approaches to addiction treatment and recovery, Beit T'Shuvah understands addictions and compulsive behaviors as fundamentally spiritual challenges.

Alcoholics Anonymous founder Bill Wilson writes, "More than most people I think alcoholics want to know who they are, what life is all about, whether they have a divine origin and an appointed destiny, live in a system of cosmic justice and love."[110] In my own experience with people suffering from addiction, I've heard the phrase "there's a hole in my heart" or a "hole in my spirit." There's a sense that something is deeply, profoundly incomplete. And in their search for wholeness, the addict looks, is compelled by their own brain physiology to look, in dangerous and self-destructive places before—God-willing—they are able to find the help and spiritual sustenance they were looking for all along.

## Seeking Wholeness

Like many things, the reality of someone struggling with addiction or compulsive behavior is an intensified version of a reality many, even most of us, recognize in our own lives. Whether or not we have personally had experience with or been adjacent to addiction or compulsive behavior, we

---

[109] https://beittshuvah.org/about-us/.
[110] Bill Wilson., *The AA Way of Life: A Reader by Bill*. New York: Alcoholics Anonymous World Services, 1967, 323, quoted in Paul Steinberg, *Recovery, the 12 Steps, and Jewish Spirituality*, Jewish Lights, 2014.

can likely identify on some level with the feelings of incompleteness, isolation, and existential or spiritual loneliness. We likely harbor a deep desire to experience connection, completion, and wholeness.

In a creative reading of Parashat Ki Teitzei, Rabbi Nachman of Breslov, who struggled with his own profound psycho-spiritual challenges, offers us a powerful spiritual reflection on this search for wholeness. The Torah in Ki Teitzei instructs us in the *mitzvah* of *hashavat aveda*, returning a lost object:

> If you see your fellow Israelite's ox or sheep straying, do not ignore it but be sure to take it back to its owner. If they do not live near you or if you do not know who owns it, take it home with you and keep it until they come looking for it. Then give it back. Do the same if you find their donkey or cloak or anything else they have lost. Do not ignore it. (Deut. 22:1-3)

On its surface, this commandment deals simply with a basic ethical precept. We are responsible for others' lost items, and that we therefore have a duty to return to them the things they have lost. Rebbe Nachman, however, reads the passage as a reflection on the nature of our own spiritual quest and the process of becoming whole.

ליקוטי מוהר"ן א:קפח

דַּע, שֶׁצָּרִיךְ לִנְסֹעַ לְהַצַּדִּיק לַחֲזֹר עַל אֲבֵדָתוֹ. כִּי קֹדֶם שֶׁיּוֹצֵא הָאָדָם לַאֲוִיר הָעוֹלָם, מְלַמְּדִין וּמַרְאִין לוֹ כָּל מַה שֶּׁצָּרִיךְ לַעֲשׂוֹת וְלַעֲבֹד וּלְהַשִּׂיג בְּזֶה הָעוֹלָם, וְכֵיוָן שֶׁיָּצָא לַאֲוִיר הָעוֹלָם מִיָּד נִשְׁכַּח מֵאִתּוֹ, כְּמוֹ שֶׁאָמְרוּ רַבּוֹתֵינוּ זִכְרוֹנָם לִבְרָכָה (נדה ל:) וְהַשִּׁכְחָה הִיא בְּחִינַת אֲבֵדָה, כְּמוֹ שֶׁקָּרְאוּ רַבּוֹתֵינוּ זִכְרוֹנָם לִבְרָכָה אֶת הַשּׁוֹכֵחַ אוֹבֵד, כְּמַאֲמָרָם זַ"ל (אבות פ"ה): מָהִיר לִשְׁמֹעַ וּמָהִיר לְאַבֵּד וְכוּ'.

וְצָרִיךְ לַחֲזֹר וּלְבַקֵּשׁ אֲבֵדָתוֹ. וְהָאֲבֵדָה שֶׁלּוֹ הִיא אֵצֶל הַצַּדִּיק, כִּי הַצַּדִּיק חוֹזֵר עַל אֲבֵדָתוֹ עַד שֶׁמּוֹצְאָהּ, וְאַחַר שֶׁמּוֹצְאָהּ, חוֹזֵר וּמְבַקֵּשׁ אַחַר אֲבֵדוֹת אֲחֵרִים עַד שֶׁמּוֹצֵא גַּם אֲבֵדָתָם, עַד שֶׁמּוֹצֵא הָאֲבֵדוֹת שֶׁל כָּל הָעוֹלָם,

עַל כֵּן צָרִיךְ לָבוֹא לְהֶחָכָם לְבַקֵּשׁ וּלְהַכִּיר אֲבֵדָתוֹ, וְלָשׁוּב לְקַבְּלָהּ אֶצְלוֹ, אַךְ הַצַּדִּיק אֵינוֹ מֵשִׁיב לוֹ הָאֲבֵדָה עַד שֶׁיִּדְרְשֶׁנּוּ אִם אֵינוֹ רַמַּאי וְשַׁקְרָן, כְּמוֹ שֶׁכָּתוּב: עַד דְּרֹשׁ אָחִיךָ וַהֲשֵׁבֹתוֹ לוֹ—עַד שֶׁתִּדְרֹשׁ אֶת אָחִיךָ אִם אֵינוֹ רַמַּאי (ב"מ כז:):

Likutei Moharan I:188
Know that we must travel to the tzaddik to retrace our steps to retrieve that which we have lost.

For before we come into the world, we are taught and shown everything that we need to do, to labor at, to achieve in this world [—the shape and content of our service of the Divine.] And once we are out in the world, we are made to forget it, as our Rabbis teach.[111]

This forgetting is a kind of lost object. Thus, our Rabbis called the person who forgets "someone who has lost [something]," as they say, "Quick to hear—quick to lose."[112]

We must retrace our steps, returning to seek our lost object. But the lost object is with the tzaddik. This is because the tzaddik searches after their own lost object until they find it, and once they find it, they return and search for others' lost objects until they find those lost objects. [They do not stop] until they find the lost objects of the entire world.

Therefore, we must come to the wise person to request, and to [initially] recognize, our lost object, to return, and to receive it from them. But the tzaddik does not return the lost object to its owner until they examine (*yidrisehenu*) whether or not the seeker is a liar or deceiver. This is what the Talmud means when it interprets the verse "until they come looking for it (*ad d'rosh*), then give it back"—"until you examine (*tidrosh*) your fellow to know that they are not deceitful."[113]

There are two parts to this teaching. According to the Talmudic midrash, we experienced a primordial communion in the womb (to God, to Torah, to our mother, to oneness), but on our way into the world we were made to forget it. Rebbe Nachman takes this story and interprets it to mean that,

---

[111] Babylonian Talmud Niddah 30b: "A fetus is taught the entire Torah while in the womb, as it is stated: "And He taught me and said to me: Let your heart hold fast My words; keep My commandments, and live" (Proverbs 4:4)

... Once the fetus emerges into the airspace of the world, an angel comes and slaps it on its mouth, causing it to forget the entire Torah." (Steinsaltz translation via Sefaria.org)

[112] *Pirkei Avot* 5:12: While we have rendered text above literally, as "hear" and "lose," a more idiomatic translation might read "Quick to comprehend, and quick to forget," thus: "There are four types of disciples: Quick to comprehend, and quick to forget: their gain disappears in their loss; Slow to comprehend, and slow to forget: their loss disappears in their gain; Quick to comprehend, and slow to forget: a wise person; Slow to comprehend, and quick to forget: this is an evil portion." Rebbe Nachman's point is to draw an equivalence between losing and forgetting.

[113] Babylonian Talmud Bava Metziah 27b

from the very moment of our birth, we have lost that which makes us whole, complete, and united with the Divine. As we physically come into the world through birth, it would seem, we experience a sensation of separation—from our mother's womb, from the umbilical cord that connects us to her, from dependent interconnectedness to physical separation and (at least formal) independence. That separation shapes our feeling—ultimately incorrect, but no less real—that we are separate beings from other beings and from the Divine. Thus, from the very outset, we have a sensation that there is something more, a palimpsest to our lives that prompts within us, in conscious and subconscious ways, a yearning to find that lost aspect of ourselves, to connect and reconnect, to return.

This leads us to the second part of the teaching: the search. We must go looking for this lost aspect of ourselves. In our teaching, it turns out our "lost object" is with the *tzaddik*. It may be useful here to spend a moment unpacking the relationship between the *tzaddik* and the individual disciple/ Hasid who comes to them. In a study that originally served as his doctoral dissertation, Rabbi Zalman Schachter-Shalomi explored the dynamics of the rebbe/*tzaddik*-Hasid dyad:

> As early as R. Shlomoh of Karlin [1738-1792—ed.], the tzaddik, who could generally manage his spiritual economy better than the simple Hasid, took it upon himself to act and to lift his Hasidim with him. The Hasid was counseled to abstain from doing the great work himself. This attitude gave rise to Tzaddikism. Tzaddikism operated on the belief that "the tzaddik by his faith shall invigorate [the follower]."[114] In Tzaddikism, the gulf between rebbe and Hasid is well nigh unbridgeable... The Hasid might as well concede that the tzaddik is qualitatively different, and avail himself (for a consideration) of the tzaddik's saving work.[115]

Rebbe Nachman assumes this relationship when he describes the *tzaddik* as having first found the lost aspect of their own self. Having done so, and having developed themselves into a refined spiritual practitioner, they are then in a position to help others find the lost parts of themselves. There is much more to say about this relationship, about how it compares and con-

---

[114] This is a paraphrase of Habakuk 2:4, "The righteous lives by his faith." Here the verb "lives by" is read "revives, inspires, invigorates," ed.

[115] Zalman Meshullam Schachter-Shalomi, *Spiritual Intimacy: A Study of Counseling in Hasidism.* Jason Aronson, 1991, 23.

trasts with other therapeutic and master-disciple relationships, about how transference and countertransference show up as dimensions in the relationship—and R. Zalman's book is an excellent exploration of all of those questions. For our purposes here, the essential point is simply that this search is not something we can undertake fruitfully alone. We need help from guides, skilled in spiritual searches.

In the final paragraph, Rebbe Nachman gestures at the reality that, when we come to the *tzaddik*, we likely do not even know what the lost part of us looks like—its shape, its size, its quality. So the first step in the process with the *tzaddik* is to figure out, What is this lost part? What am I actually looking for? The tzaddik helps us discern its dimensions. Then, when we can recognize it, they return it to us—but first, they have to ascertain that we're being truthful.

Here, following the Talmud, Rebbe Nachman plays on a linguistic matter in the verse in the Torah itself. "If you see your fellow Israelite's ox or sheep straying," the Torah says, "do not ignore it—be sure to take it back to its owner. If they do not live near you or if you do not know who owns it, take it home with you and keep it *ad drosh akhikha v'hashevoto lo*, until your kinsperson demands it, and then return it to them" (Deut. 22:1-2). "Would it enter your mind," asks the Talmud, "that you should give back the lost item before the owner of the item claims it?"[116] Given that we already have a commandment to return lost items, the only reason we're holding onto this item is because we've been unable to return it! So why would the Torah say we have to wait for the owner to come and demand it? Instead, the Talmud rewrites the situation completely: *drosh* here does not refer to the owner claiming the object, but rather to the person watching the object: "*Darshehu*, scrutinize the claimant, to determine whether or not they are being deceitful." Only when you've determined that the claimant is being truthful should you return the item.

## Being Honest with Ourselves

This last part of Rebbe Nachman's teaching articulates the final stage—and, in another sense, the first stage of the rest of the process—of recovering what we've lost: We have to be honest. The *tzaddik* will know, and will be able to help us to know, whether we're really being truthful. Many things might prevent us from being fully honest with ourselves and/or the *tzaddik*. Ultimately, we cannot recover the lost part, we cannot become whole, until we

---

[116] Bava Metziah 28a

are willing and able to see clearly and speak truthfully. Then, and only then, is the *tzaddik* able to return to us that aspect of ourselves we lost so long ago.

If you have personally been in a 12-step program, or if you have been a caregiver or loved one supporting a family member through such a program, this last point may sound familiar. Twelve-step recovery programs begin with a person's honest recognition that a compulsive behavior—drinking alcohol, doing drugs, gambling, sex—has taken power over them and that they are powerless to stop it. Reaching that point of recognition can often take a long time—with a lot of damage and pain for self and others along the way. That is why, as support groups for loved ones of recovering addicts teach, until a person reaches that point of honesty, they can't begin to do the work they need to do. We can't fix someone else, and we can't even help them make meaningful change until they are truly honest with themselves.

Further, these programs hold that compulsive or addictive behavior is often rooted in what many describe as kind of spiritual hole, or missing piece, in their lives. The search for the missing piece might begin subconsciously, mindlessly, in an unhealthy way, and it may persist for a long time. But at some point, perhaps when their suffering has become too much to bear, the afflicted person arrives at a moment of honesty in which they recognize the shape of their missing piece—the reality of that missing piece which they need help to find. From that touchstone, they can begin a journey of finding wholeness—*shleimut*, from the same root as *shalom*. The journey requires the help of others; it requires continual honesty and accountability; it eventually grows to include helping others find their own missing pieces.

For all of us, there's much to learn from this process, particularly in this season of introspection and personal accounting before Rosh Hashanah and Yom Kippur. The combination of genuine honesty, inventorying our lives, out-loud articulation to others, cultivating a relationship with the Divine, and continuing accountability for our behavior is fundamentally a process of *teshuva*. And *teshuva*, as Rebbe Nachman teaches here, is, at its heart, a process of *hashavat aveda:* In recovering our lost objects, we return to our deepest selves, conscious of our interconnection with one another and Creation, aware of the Divinity of which we are a part.

## Questions for Reflection & Conversation

- Consider the Talmud's story that we are taught the entire Torah while in the womb and then, just as we enter the world, an angel taps us above the upper lip and causes us to forget it. How do you understand the message of this midrash? Do you now, or have you ever, felt this to be true? If you view it as simply a myth, how might taking it seriously affect how you live?

- In your own life, have you had a relationship with someone who functioned the way that the *tzaddik* functions in Rebbe Nachman's teaching? If so, what, if anything, was it about you that enabled that relationship to be useful, powerful, effective? What, if anything, was it about the other person? If not, what, if anything, do you sense might prevent such a relationship from coming about? Would you seek such a relationship? When, how, why or why not?

- The final section of Rebbe Nachman's teaching emphasizes the necessity for honesty: "But the *tzaddik* does not return the lost object to its owner until they examine whether or not the seeker is a liar or deceiver." As you consider your most intimate relationships—with a partner or spouse, best friend, therapist, clergyperson—do you feel you are able to be fully honest? If so, what, if anything, contributes to your ability to do so? If not, what, if anything, prevents it? What, if anything, might further enable you to be fully honest—with them and with yourself?

## Ideas for Practice

With Rebbe Nachman's teaching in mind, this week you might consider practicing deep listening with a spiritual *havruta*, or study partner. This practice draws on the broader area of spiritual direction. The instructions below are adapted from materials developed by my colleague, Rabbi Myriam Klotz.

Practice extending the quality of warmly welcoming guests as you engage with your partner. Notice what makes for safety, trust, and ease between you. When you are the sacred listener, pay attention to your body language, the tone of your voice, and pay deep attention to your *havruta* partner as they are speaking or holding space silently.

After your brief check-in and mindfulness time of invocation and silent grounding (see below for a suggested timetable), you might begin your sharing when you are the speaker with reflections based on the following or similar questions. Remember to take plenty of time in silence as you need it, to be deeply connected with what is showing up in your awareness in that moment.

- (How, when, where) do I experience spiritual completeness/ *shleimut* or incompleteness/*aveda*? (How, when, where) do I experience myself as missing, or having lost, a piece of me?

- Do I sense myself as on a search or quest? Do I sense that, perhaps, the Divine is searching for me?

- Do I have a sense of the shape of my "missing piece?" What might I know about it?

Suggested structure for your Spiritual Direction *havruta* time:

1. Brief check-in—10 minutes (5 minutes each)
2. Sit in Mindful silence; Offer a blessing, chant, or intention—10 minutes
3. First person shares about their spiritual life in relation to the process of discernment. *Havruta* partner practices sacred listening and holding space—10 minutes
4. Sacred listener reflects back the *Torat Hayim*, the living Torah, they hear, and offers a blessing (or invites speaker to state an intention or prayer)—5 minutes
5. Second person shares about their spiritual life in relation to the process of discernment. *Havruta* partner practices sacred listening and holding space—10 minutes
6. Sacred listener reflects back the *Torat Hayim* they hear, and offers a blessing (or invites speaker to state an intention or prayer)—5 minutes
7. Reflect together on the practice of your spiritual direction *havruta*—10 minutes

- How did you do together as spiritual direction companions?

- What opened up? What were the challenges, if you noticed any?

- What did you notice as the speaker?

- What did you notice or experience as a listening partner?

- What did you notice together about God's Presence with you in this practice, if you did?

# Ki Tavo: When Are We Enough?

In her book on self-compassion, University of Texas researcher Kristin Neff describes a practice she has used for years. "Whenever I notice something about my life I don't like," Neff writes, "or whenever something goes wrong in my life, I silently repeat the following phrases: *This is a moment of suffering. Suffering is part of life. May I be kind to myself in this moment. May I give myself the compassion I need.*"

Neff notes that this mantra touches the three key components of self-compassion she has identified in her research: self-kindness, common humanity, and mindfulness. In particular, she notes that the final phrase "firmly sets your intention to be self-compassionate and reminds you that you are worthy of receiving compassionate care."[117]

There is another aspect of this mantra Neff doesn't touch on but which I think bears mention: The last two phrases gently remind us that we have the capacity to be kind and compassionate to ourselves, even—or perhaps particularly—at moments when that capacity may feel most constricted. With these phrases we remind ourselves: Our hearts can break and heal, shatter and be reconstituted.

This is a lesson we particularly learn over time. For some, and hopefully for many, the more life we live and the more practice we have, we find that we can, indeed, suffer through hardship and come out on the other side of shipwreck. It isn't easy, and it isn't painless. But somehow our hearts can grow to respond to the moment. Praying, "May I be kind to myself in this moment. May I give myself the compassion I need," is a practice of activating our heart's ability to break, without being destroyed, and thus its ability to remake itself. We have everything we need within. We just need to bring our awareness and attention to the reality of our experience and remind ourselves that we are sufficient, we are enough, and we have enough.

## We're Never Really Lacking

Yet it isn't simply that we have that capacity within us, or that we can nurture it. Through Jewish spiritual practice, we cultivate awareness that that capacity comes from and is an expression of a Divinity of which we are a part. Thus, if and when we can recognize it, that truth is available to us as a constant source of renewal. Yes, we are enough: because the Infinite—that which has no end, for whom sufficiency is not even a question—works through us.

---

[117] Kristin Neff, *Self-Compassion: The Proven Power of Being Kind to Yourself.* William Morrow, 2011, 119-120.

This insight is beautifully explored in the following teaching from the *Degel Machane Ephraim* of Rabbi Moshe Chayim Ephraim of Sudlikov (d. 1800), a grandson of the Baal Shem Tov. The teaching is a commentary on Deuteronomy 26:11, which concludes the opening passage of Parashat Ki Tavo describing the ritual of bringing *bikkurim*, or first fruits, to the ancient Temple in Jerusalem.

**דגל מחנה אפרים כי תבוא ג'**

וְשָׂמַחְתָּ בְכָל־הַטּוֹב אֲשֶׁר נָתַן־לְךָ יְהֹוָה אֱלֹהֶיךָ וּלְבֵיתֶךָ אַתָּה וְהַלֵּוִי וְהַגֵּר אֲשֶׁר בְּקִרְבֶּךָ:

עוד י"ל ע"ד שאמרתי ע"פ ואברהם זקן בא בימים וה' בירך את אברהם בכל היינו שביר' אותו במדת כל: ואיתא בזו"הק כל היא רזא דמהימנותא וזהו ג"כ ויתן את כל אשר לו ליצחק היינו שמסר מדת כל רזא דמהימנותא אשר לו ליצחק וזהו ארץ אשר לא תחסר כל בה כנ"ל וכן אמר יעקב ג"כ וכי יש לי כל היינו שחנני ה' במדת כל ולכך לא יהיה לי שום חסרון במה שתקח המתנה מידי וזהו גם כאן הבטחה שלימה ושמחת בכל הטוב היינו שתזכה להשיג מדת כל שהיא שלימות וכללות הטוב כי דורשי ה' לא יחסרו כל טוב והבן:

### Degel Machane Ephraim, Ki Tavo 3

"And you shall rejoice in all the goodness that the Ineffable, your God, will give you and your household—you and the Levite and the stranger in your midst." (Deut. 26:11)

This can be understood in light of my teaching on the verse, "Abraham was now old, advanced in years, and the Holy One had blessed Abraham *bakol*—in all things" (Gen. 24:1). That is, the Divine blessed Abraham with the capacity for *kol*, for [holding or accepting] everything.

The holy Zohar states that *kol* is the mystery of faith. This is likewise implied in the verse, "And [Abraham] gave all that he had to Isaac"[118] (Gen. 25:5)—that is, he transmitted *kol*, the mystery of faith which was his, to Isaac. Likewise, [we find this in the description of the Land of Canaan]: "A land where you may eat food without stint, where *kol* will not be lacking" (Deut. 8:9).

[This applies as well] when Jacob said [to Esau], "Please accept my present which has been brought to you, for the Divine has favored me and I have *kol* [the capacity to hold or accept

---

[118] Which could be literally, and non-idiomatically, rendered as, "And Abraham gave to Isaac *kol*, which was his."

all]" (Gen. 33:11). That is, the Ineffable has graced me with the aspect of *kol,* and thus I will experience no lack when you take this gift from me.

So too here, it is a complete promise: "And you will rejoice in *kol hatov,* all the goodness"—that is, you will merit to internalize the aspect of *kol,* which is wholeness and the totality of goodness. "For those who turn to the Holy One shall not lack any (*kol*) goodness" (Ps. 34:11). Understand.

In this teaching, the *Degel* plays on the word *kol,* drawing connections between passages from around the Bible where the word appears. *Kol* means "all" or "every." Its use in the various passages he cites leads him to a simple and elegant point: *kol* is a consciousness of sufficiency. It is not so much about "having enough" as about living with the awareness that we lack nothing. When we realize we lack nothing, then the very concept of lack fades away—and with it, the mindset of scarcity.

In the verse from our parasha, *kol* is also coupled with *tov,* good or goodness. Not only are we able to cultivate a mindset of abundance and sufficiency; when we really internalize that the Holy One graces us with hearts that can dwell in that orientation, we are filled with goodness. We may then, with God's goodness, become able to share that goodness with others. It's a virtuous circle: the more we cultivate this awareness, the more we may soften our hearts and quiet our anxious minds which lead us to experience lack and scarcity, the more our hearts might grow in their capacity to help us recognize abundance and goodness.

## It's About All of Us

The context of our verse is important. As I mentioned, it comes at the end of a passage detailing the ritual of *bikkurim,* in which an ancient Israelite farmer would bring their first fruits to the Temple on the holiday of Shavuot. The Torah instructs that they were to place their items in a basket and give it to the kohen (priest). Yet then, unusually for Temple rituals, they, themselves, were to recite a formula that included a short recapitulation of Israelite history. This recitation may be familiar to us from the Passover Haggadah, where the ancient rabbis included it as part of the Seder ritual since, presumably, many people knew it by heart from practicing the annual Temple ritual on Shavuot.

Yet the traditional Passover version does not include the last two lines of the formula:

"The Holy One brought us to this place and gave us this land, a land flowing with milk and honey. And now I now bring the first fruits of the soil which You, Ineffable, have given me." (Deut. 26:9-10)

The passage then concludes with instructions, including the verse on which the *Degel* comments:

You shall leave it before YHVH your God and bow low before the YHVH your God. And you shall rejoice in all the goodness that the Ineffable, your God, will give you and your household—you and the Levite and the stranger in your midst. (Deut. 26:10-11)

With this context in mind, we can see more fully that the *Degel's* teaching is not only about cultivating a sense of personal sufficiency. As the very last part of the passage indicates, it is also about bringing about a broader social sense of abundance. When we are able to inhabit a mind-heartspace of sufficiency, of lacking nothing and dwelling within goodness, then we are able to share that mind-heartspace with others, in a potentially ever-expanding network of abundance and goodness. We are able to share it with others in our household and, crucially, with those who are more vulnerable, who do not necessarily have households of their own: the Levite (who in the times of the Torah was prohibited from owning property and was therefore usually materially poor), and the *ger*, the resident-alien without family, always a stranger, always at risk.

Cultivating our own inner awareness of abundance enables and leads us to recognize the people who, through the realities of the material world, are more vulnerable to the vicissitudes of material deprivation. Our practice helps us not only to share whatever abundance we have with them, but to counteract and even transform the societal structures that serve to separate us based on material wealth and possessions, or social status. Our spiritual practice of cultivating sufficiency within our mind-hearts is thus not merely about helping ourselves feel good, or even about managing the subconscious feelings of guilt we may experience over the fact that we have things that others don't. Ultimately it is about transforming our collective consciousness in a way that truly recognizes our interconnection and interdependence and that creates and maintains a world in which none of us experiences lack or want.

## Questions for Reflection & Conversation

- The *Degel's* teaching draws on a number of biblical sources including the stories of Abraham and Isaac, Jacob and Esau, and an earlier verse from Deuteronomy about the land of Canaan. Consider the passages he cites, even look them up and explore them in context. What, if anything, do you notice about the meaning of *kol* in each case? Is the *Degel* just mentioning these as exemplars, or is there something driving his choice of these examples in particular? In your reading, what might that be?

- One source the *Degel* does not bring in this context, but which nonetheless could prove fruitful as another passage for comparison, is Genesis 1-2:3. Take a look at that section, which describes the creation of the world and the first Shabbat. Note where the word *kol*, all, is used. Note where *tov*, good or goodness, is used as well. What, if anything, do you notice about *kol* and *tov* that could inform your understanding of the *Degel's* teaching on our verse here in Ki Tavo? In particular, what, if anything, do you think the practice of Shabbat might contribute to cultivating a sense of sufficiency and abundance in your life?

- In your own life and experience, is there someone who comes to mind as an exemplar of the kind of abundance-sufficiency that the *Degel* describes? What, if anything, do you know about that person's spiritual practice that helped them be that way? What, if any, spiritual practices do you imagine they might have engaged in? How, if at all, as their example affected you in your life?

## Ideas for Practice

Kristin Neff offers an exercise for developing your own self-compassion mantra:

> A self-compassion mantra is a set of memorized phrases that are repeated silently whenever you want to give yourself compassion. They are most useful in the heat of the moment, whenever strong feelings of distress arise.

You might find that the phrases I created work for you, but it's worth playing with them to see if you can find phrases that fit you better. What's important is that all three aspects of self-compassion are evoked, not the particular words used.

Other possible wordings for the first phrase, "This is a moment of suffering," are "I'm having a really hard time right now," "It's painful for me to feel this now," and so on.

Other possible wordings for the second phrase, "Suffering is a part of life," are "Everyone feels this way sometimes," "This is part of being human," and so on.

Other possible wordings for the third phrase, "May I be kind to myself in this moment," are "May I hold my pain with tenderness," "May I be gentle and understanding with myself," and so on.

Other possible wordings for the final phrase, "May I give myself the compassion I need," are "I am worthy of receiving self-compassion," "I will try to be as compassionate as possible," and so on.

Find the four phrases that seem most comfortable for you and repeat them until you have them memorized. Then, the next time you judge yourself or have a difficult experience, you can use your mantra to help remind yourself to be more calm and self-compassionate. It's a handy tool to help soothe and calm troubled states of mind.[119]

As you develop your own mantra grounded in Jewish spiritual practice, you might consider reviewing the *vidduy bikkurim*, the recitation uttered by the ancient Israelites on bringing their first fruits, in Deut. 26:5-9, which you could consider as its own form of mantra. In particular, you might consider modifying Neff's language to include not only giving yourself compassion but also becoming aware of or recognizing the compassion the Divine makes available to you. Try, as Neff suggests, composing your own language and see what is most helpful for you.

---

[119] Neff, 121-122.

# Nitzavim: What Does Your Heart Say?

The concluding chapter of Isabel Wilkerson's *Caste* is entitled, "The Heart is the Last Frontier." In it, Wilkerson tells the story of a plumber who comes to her house after she found water in her basement. The plumber is a white man, Wilkerson is a Black woman. At first, the plumber is visibly reluctant to engage her, or even to recognize the fact that she indeed owns her house. He is not helpful, forcing Wilkerson to move boxes around on her own. He is dismissive, not listening to her suggestions about where the problem might be coming from. Finally, the plumber says he can't fix the problem and that Wilkerson should simply buy a new sump pump. His heart, it seems, is hard. Wilkerson describes herself as "steaming."

"Since he wasn't helping," she writes, "I felt I had nothing to lose. Something came over me, and I threw a Hail Mary at his humanity." Wilkerson mentions that her mother had died the week before and asks, "Is your mother still alive?" This breaks the ice and, it seems, pierces the armor of his heart. The plumber and Wilkerson connect over their shared grief. They begin to tell stories to one another about loved ones they've lost. The plumber becomes engaged and energetic and solves the problem quickly (it was the water heater). He even winds up coming back after he leaves, realizing he should turn off the water heater, which was empty.

"How different things had been just minutes before," writes Wilkerson. "'My mother must've been talking to your mother,' I said, 'and telling her to get her boy to help her girl down there. 'My daughter needs your son's help.'"[120]

The story is a poignant conclusion to Wilkerson's historical reflection on systems of caste in India, Nazi Germany, and the United States. With it, Wilkerson reminds us that such systems rely upon and reinforce the idea that we do not share a common humanity, that some people are less human, less images of the Divine, less worthy of love and respect than others. Through the title of the chapter, Wilkerson reminds us that systems of separation and oppression are fundamentally built, maintained, overcome, and dismantled through the work of the heart—the part of us that is ultimately unknowable by others and only available to us and to the Divine whose spark lives within it.

Our words—in day-to-day interactions with plumbers and in legal documents like the Nuremberg Laws—convey our hearts: their encasement in a shell of fear, their openness to connection and trust. With this closing story, Wilkerson challenges us: Can we practice a language, in both our interpersonal relations and in our laws and policies, that is grounded in and helps to amplify our capacity for loving, compassionate hearts?

---

[120] Isabel Wilkerson, *Caste: The Origins of Our Discontents*. New York: Random House, 2020, 374-375.

## Putting Our Hearts Into Our Words

This brings us to a beautiful teaching of the Maggid of Mezritch on a mysterious verse from Parashat Nitzavim: "Hidden things belong to YHVH our God; but with revealed things, it is for us and our children ever to apply all the provisions of this Teaching" (Deut. 29:28). Classical commentators generally understood this to refer to God's capacity to punish those who secretly—in their hearts—worship false gods. Here, for instance, is Rashi: "I do not threaten to punish you because of secret thoughts, for these belong to YHVH our God, who will exact punishment from that individual; but those things which are revealed belong to us and to our children that we may put away the evil from our midst; and if we do not execute judgment upon them, the whole community will be punished." In this reading, the verse is a reminder that, no matter what we may say or do externally, God knows what is in our hearts, so we should be careful what we allow to take root in them.

The Maggid offers us a very different reading. (The selection below has been edited slightly for ease of reading.)

תורת המגיד נצבים

ובוודאי אם אדם מתפלל או לומד תורה בדחילו ורחימו... וכל כוונתו לשם שמים להעלותם אל שורשם אל הקדושה העליונה, בוודאי הדיבורים שלו מתחברים לעילא. ומה גם כי ידוע שבכל דיבור ודיבור, ובכל אות ואות, נכללין כל ס' רבוא אתוון דאורייתא, שהם נגד ס' רבוא נשמותיהן של ישראל, וכוונתו רצויה לעילא לעשות יחודים וזיווגים, ובשם כל ישראל שהם שורש הששים רבוא... ונמצא האדם הלומד וכוונתו אל הנזכר, אף שאינו לומד כל התורה כאחת, אף על פי כן יכול הוא לעורר ולקשר כל העולמות. וממנו יכול לברוא עולמות כמבואר בזוהר כי כל ס' רבוא אותיות נכללין זה מזה, אם כן במה שהוא לומד אם מעט אם רב נכללה כל התורה וכל נשמות בני ישראל....

ונחזור לענין "הנסתרות לה אלהינו וגו'". פירוש: "הנסתרות" הם יראה ואהבה, שהם חכמה ובינה, שהם אותיות י"ה מהשם הנזכר. אם האדם לומד ומתפלל בדחילו ורחימו, שהם הם הנסתרות, הוא עושה דבר גדול עד מאוד, שהוא מחבר ומקשר דיבוריו שהם חלק אלו"ה ממעל, שבכל דיבור מלובש שם הוי"ה שהוא שורש כל הדברים והמהווה כל הוי"ת, יכול הוא לקשר וליחד כל העולמות העליונים כנזכר. משא"כ "הנגלות" שהם רק קול ודיבור, שהוא נגלה לכל כשהוא מדבר ומשמיע קולו. אבל האהבה והיראה הם בלב האדם, הם נקראים נסתרות שאינם נגלים לבני אדם....

Torat HaMaggid, Nitzavim

Certainly, when we pray or study Torah with purpose and intensity... and all our intention is directed to Heaven, that we may
lift up our prayers and our study to their primordial source, then
without a doubt our words become connected above. Moreover,
we know this is so since every word and every letter contains the
600,000 letters of the Torah, which correspond to the 600,000
souls of the people Israel. Therefore, when our intentions are
welcomed in the supernal realms, and our devotions are performed on behalf of all Israel, who are the root of the 600,000
letters, we can perform these unifications and pairings. ... Thus,
when we study with our intention directed in this manner, even
if we do not study the whole Torah as one totality, nevertheless
we can awaken and connect all of the worlds. And from there
we can also create worlds, as explained in the Zohar. For all
600,000 letters contain one another. Thus, however much we
study, a small or large amount, our study will encompass the
entire Torah and all the souls of Israel ...

Now we can return to our verse: "Hidden things belong to
YHVH our God; but with revealed things, it is for us and our
children ever to apply all the provisions of this Teaching." The
hidden things refer to awe and love, which correspond to the
sefirot *chochma* and *bina,* which likewise correspond to the letters
*yod-heh* of the Divine Name YHVH. When we study and pray
with purpose and intensity—which are, themselves, these hidden dimensions—we do something very great: We connect and
bind our words, which are a manifestation of the recognizable,
this-worldly aspect of the Divine (corresponding to the name
*Elohim),* [to the higher, more concealed aspects of the Divine,
which correspond to YHVH]. For in every word is garbed the
name YHVH, the source of all things and the ultimate ground
of all reality. Thus, we are able to connect and unify all the
upper worlds. This is not the case with that which is "revealed,"
which is the nature of voice and speech. These are manifest to
everyone when we speak and make our voices heard. But love
and awe dwell in our hearts—thus they are called hidden, for
they are not discernable to others.

There are two parts to the Maggid's teaching. In the first paragraph, he offers
us a beautiful image: No matter how much or how little we study or pray, if we

do it with genuine purpose and intensity—if our hearts are truly in it—then we may experience an expansive and profound sense of unification between body, mind, and spirit, and between ourselves and all of creation through space and time. Even a single letter of the Torah, a single word of Jewish prayer, when uttered with genuine focus and attention, contains everything: the entirety of Torah, the entirety of the Jewish people. It may happen that we may be distracted by feelings of inadequacy, self-judgment, pride, or fear that may arise in us when we are praying or studying. But, says the Maggid, if we can manage to not be governed by those feelings, and instead attune our hearts to the invitation from the Divine that beckons to us from within them—then that's everything. One word recited with genuine attention and intention, with genuine focus and purpose, with an awakened and directed heart, has the power of all the words of Torah and all the souls of the Jewish people combined.

In the second paragraph, the Maggid connects this spiritual insight to the verse from our parasha. In doing so, he offers a dramatic contrast to the classical depiction of God as omniscient watcher over our inner lives. Yes, our hearts are our most intimate zones, ultimately unknowable by others. Yes, we are capable of being less than genuine with our words—saying one thing externally while telling ourselves something very different. The classical commentators understand the verse to focus on Divine punishment for improper belief. But the Maggid invites us instead to consider, in a positive way, the power of aligning our words with our hearts—our external expressions with our internal meanings. It isn't only that we tap into that network of 600,000 letters and souls that he described earlier. His point is that, when we pray and study with genuinely directed hearts, we unify the upper and lower worlds, the inner and outer; we bring together YHVH and *Elohim*, forming a conduit for the Divine flow through the cosmos and through ourselves. If we can really put our hearts into our words—if we can direct our words so they really express our hearts—that is nothing short of an act of cosmic significance.

## Expressing the Stirrings of Our Hearts

I'm not a Hasidic master, and I cannot claim to have achieved the quality of experience the Maggid describes. Yet I draw inspiration from it, particularly concerning my own practice of prayer. To me, as for the Maggid, *tefillah* is not only an opportunity for expression; it is also a duty prescribed by *halakha*. I live my life with a felt sense of obligation to recite the prayers of the traditional liturgy at their prescribed times. Yet by experiencing *tefillah* as an obligation in this way, I run into the challenge that when I recite the prayers at the right time, my intention may well be more focused on discharging my sense of duty than on attuning my heart to the Divine voice within. This is not an uncommon problem—not only for people who share my *halakhic* orientation, but also for people who have been educated and acculturated to perform prayers by rote. In both cases, it's often hard to say our hearts are in it.

So how might the Maggid's teaching help us? In my own practice, I find that the most essential thing is simply slowing down and exercising a dose of self-compassion. As David Mastie, a favorite high school science teacher, used to tell us: "Do less, better." In this context, Mr. Mastie's dictum might mean, first, to give myself permission that I don't need to recite every word in the siddur or read every line of the Torah or the Talmud or the rest of the awe-inspiring—and potentially overwhelming—library of Jewish texts. As the Maggid says, even one word recited with genuine intention and purpose contains within it the entire Torah and the entire Jewish people. So I begin by reminding myself of that (or, in the words of Joseph Karo, author of the *Shulchan Arukh*, the authoritative code of *halakha*: "Better few supplications with intention than many without intention").[121]

I find that mindfulness meditation can be a very useful aid, helping me cultivate a space in my mind-heart that is quiet, where I can be attentive to what is stirring within. For me, 10 to 20 minutes of meditation is often a good amount of time to prepare myself for prayer. But even when I choose, for whatever reason, not to give myself that much time, even just a few minutes of focused, quiet attention can make a world of difference.

Once I sense that I've reached a more settled, calmer mind, I begin to recite a part of the liturgy or a passage of Torah or other sacred text. In the case of prayer, the part I choose to recite is determined by the prayers traditionally prescribed for the particular time of day and what the *halakha* has to say about which of those are most central; in the case of study, the text might be suggested by the weekly Torah reading cycle, but might also come to me another way, through a commitment to study as regular practice.

In some cases—particularly in prayer—these are familiar words with which I have a long and intimate relationship. Yet whether or not they are familiar, these texts are sacred: they are letters and words that have created and continue to create worlds. (It is here that I differ from Mary Oliver, who suggests "it could be weeds in a vacant lot, or a few small stones" to which we pay attention.[122] While attention is necessary, in the case of Jewish spiritual practice it is insufficient.) Thus, as I return my attention to my breath as an anchor, ultimately, I seek to bring my heart-mind to the words I'm reciting, and to the Divine presence that these words can aid me in perceiving. I try keep my heart

---

[121] *Orakh Hayim* 1:4
[122] Oliver, "Praying"

open to sense the meaning the prayer stirs within me. As I articulate a word or words, I try to attune my heart-mind to that meaning, and thereby experience the alignment of inner and outer, upper and lower, YHVH and *Elohim*, that the Maggid describes. The meaning is not fixed; it is unique to that prayer or study encounter, even if the shape of it is similar. That, I think, is as it should be, providing both a stable structure of discipline, practice, and language, and, not in spite of, but *through* that structure, facilitating freshness and renewal.

## Renewing Old Structures and Unblocking the Divine Flow

There is, then, a lesson here about structure—and that brings us back to Wilkerson and her examination of caste. A caste system is a structure of language and practice that aims to keep people separated, and particularly to keep people in their place. It tries to fly in the face of our innate awareness that we are, in fact, interconnected, equally imbued with the spark of the Divine simply by virtue of being human, capable of renewal and change. As Wilkerson shows, caste systems go to extraordinary lengths to try and change the way we think, perceive the world, comport our bodies, and experience the Divine. And it often does so through a reading of sacred texts that does not serve our inner life but, instead, seeks to stultify and oppress it.

It is not an accident that the final chapter of Wilkerson's book is called "The Heart is the Final Frontier," and I don't think it's an accident that Wilkerson's interlocutor in that chapter is a plumber. The interaction she has with him, at first, is characterized by blockage and resistance. Something is stopped up. Language doesn't flow between them, and their relationship falls into the traps of disconnection, fear, anger, and resentment—not unlike the relationship too many Jews have developed with the words of the siddur or the Torah.

But then the relationship gets unclogged when Wilkerson's words open up the plumber's heart. He had a desire for loving connection in there all along, but it was blocked. In Wilkerson's question, "Is your mother still alive?" the plumber experiences a genuine expression of care which opens a connection, leads to more language and more connection, and ultimately yields a small, yet perhaps still cosmically significant, act of redemption.

As in the time of the Maggid, for so many people today the words of Jewish prayer and study can feel like dead letters or stale language. Too many people, tragically, experience Jewish prayers and texts as, at best, something to put up with and, at worst, something stultifying and even oppressive. They—we— don't experience our encounter with the siddur and the Torah as opening up channels through which the Divine presence flows. Our purpose in this series of essays has been to try and change that: to help us experience these texts as aids in cultivating a deeper inner life that helps us open up to a far richer relationship with ourselves, the Divine, the cosmos. And to that I will add, in the spirit of both Wilkerson and the Maggid: Redemption will come only when our hearts are opened. So let's keep opening them up.

## Questions for Reflection and Conversation

- Consider the Maggid's teaching that, "every word and every letter contains the 600,000 letters of the Torah, which correspond to the 600,000 souls of the people Israel." Try to explain this idea in your own words. What does the Maggid mean? Once you've para-phrased it, consider how it makes you feel: Is this image pleasant, unpleasant, inspiring, overwhelming, or something else?

- Have you prayed or studied Torah with the kind of intensity and direction the Maggid describes? If yes, how do you describe the experience? What happened within you? What about you, in that moment, if anything, enabled the experience to occur? What, if anything, about the words helped effectuate the experience? If not, what do you imagine such an experience might be like?

- How do you feel about your own relationship with Jewish liturgy? Do you find prayers to be a help, a hindrance, both, or something else? Does Jewish liturgy make you feel inviting into something larger? Does it seem to erect a barrier to expressing yourself? How, if at all, have you tried to enable Jewish prayer to be a meaningful form of heart expression?

## Ideas for Practice

Rabbi David Jaffe is the founder of the Kirva Institute and leads the Inside Out Wisdom and Action Project. He is the author of *Changing the World from the Inside Out: A Jewish Approach to Personal and Social Change*, which won the National Jewish Book Award for Contemporary Jewish life. In this episode of IJS's Open My Heart podcast, David shares a practice called "Turning Torah into Tefillah," which combines mindfulness meditation, an encounter with a passage of Jewish teaching, and prayer in a way that facilitates the kind of structured and renewed engagement we've discussed in this essay. Consider trying this practice this week. You can access both the audio of David's teach-ing and a transcript of the episode here: https://www.jewishspirituality.org/turn-your-torah-into-tefillah/.

# Vayelekh: How Do We Stay True To Our Intentions?

My first job out of rabbinical school was serving as the Hillel rabbi at Northwestern University. One of the blessings and curses of being a Hillel rabbi is that there is almost always food around. College students are hungry and often short of cash, so free food is a reliable draw. That includes candy, and that always seemed to be around in abundance. M&Ms, Hershey Kisses, Reese's Pieces—there was an endless supply in the lobby. And while I am a rabbi, I was no saint: I ate plenty of that candy, even though I knew I really didn't want to be eating it. I just couldn't help myself.

I have kept kosher all my life and have a deeply ingrained practice of waiting six hours between eating meat and milk. I wouldn't even think twice about eating something dairy within the six hours after eating meat. (You may recall that in the essay on Matot-Masei, I talked about my vow not to eat meat during the week. This story takes place before I made that vow.) So what did I do? Obviously, I went to the kosher dining hall and had a meat lunch—that way I wouldn't eat the candy when I came back to Hillel!

Now of course there's something cockamamie about this story. If I could maintain the discipline not to eat dairy for six hours after eating meat, why couldn't I just take that same discipline and say, "Josh, don't eat the candy!?" And yet I couldn't. My *kashrut* discipline was far more powerful than my will to eat healthfully. So, thank goodness for that—but also, what gives? Why is it, in this case as in so many others, our willpower seems insufficient to stay true to our intention? And why does one frame of reference—in this case, *kashrut*—seem to stick while another—my intention to avoid candy—fail to stick?

As we know from mindfulness practice, part of the answer to the first question is that while intentions are admirable, it takes consistent practice to align our actions with them. Returning over and over again to the felt sense of our intention can disrupt the process whereby our impulses and urges bypass what we say we want and move us straight to reaching for the candy jar. Our intention is necessary but not sufficient. Without building the neural and spiritual pathway that helps us see the candy and then pause to consider what's arising for us and what choices we have available to us, the candy is going to win most of the time.

## What Are These Rules To You?

But practice is also part of the answer to the second question, about relative stickiness. In this case, it might help to consider that *kashrut* isn't simply a set of rules about what foods are kosher or not kosher. In my experience, having lived it all my life, it's an embodied practice. For as long as I can remember, whenever I've confronted a bowl of ice cream or a glass of chocolate milk, a part of my mind immediately asks, "Are you *fleishig?*" That is, are you still within the six-hour period after eating meat?[123] That practice is so deeply ingrained in me that it can overcome my bodily urge. (Having largely given up meat, I have had to develop new practices to help me in my confrontation with dairy sweets.)

This sense that *mitzvot* and *halakhah* are not simply a set of laws but a rich set of embodied spiritual mindfulness practices is one I find deeply resonant. The Hasidic tradition in particular can help us enter into understanding *halakhah* this way. For instance, in the following teaching from his *Mei Hashiloach*, Rabbi Mordechai Yosef Leiner of Izhbitz (1801-1854) offers a spiritual understanding of a *halakhic* technicality that illuminates this approach. The commentary is based on the following verses (Deut. 31:10-11): "And Moses instructed them as follows: At the end of every seventh year, the Shemitah year, at Sukkot, when all Israel comes to appear before YHVH your God in the place that God will choose, you shall read this Teaching aloud in the presence of all Israel." The Izhbitzer begins by quoting a passage of the Talmud about the verse and then offers his own understanding.

מי השילוח וילך

איתא בגמ' (ראש השנה י"ב:) שנת השמטה מאי עבידתיה בחג הסכות שמינית הוא אלא כל תבואה שלא הביאה שליש בשביעית אתה נוהג בה מנהג שביעית בשמינית, והוא ע"פ פסוק (תהלים קט"ו,ט"ז) השמים שמים לה' והארץ נתן לבני אדם. וזה הוא רק כפי הנראה. אבל דהע"ה אמר (תהלים קל"ה,ו') כל אשר חפץ ה' עשה בשמים ובארץ. שהיה יודע בטוב שכל מעשי בני אדם אף שניתן הבחירה ביד אדם הוא רק דבר מועט כקליפת השום. וזהו שאנו אומרים ביום הראשון לה' הארץ וכו', דענין שבת הוא שתדע שאין שום כח ביד האדם לכל הל"ט מלאכות שנבראו בעולם שע"י יוכל אדם לפעול כל מה שירצה כולם נאסרים בשבת, וע"כ כשהתחילו ימי

<hr>

[123] *Fleishig*, in Yiddish, means "meaty." In American kashrut parlance, it can refer to a meat dish ("This stew is *fleishig*," or "We're having *fleishigs* = a meat dish for dinner") or a state of being ("I ate meat two hours ago, so I'm still *fleishig*"). In the latter usage, the term reflects that, to observe the rules of kashrut, where meat and dairy may not be consumed at the same meal, even if they aren't cooked together, and even when the meals may be distant (in our case, fewer than six hours after eating meat). The duration of the *fleishig* period varied anywhere from one to six hours according to the custom of the community. The tradition in which I was raised was to wait six hours.

החול ומותר בעשיית מלאכה יוכל האדם ח"ו לומר כחי ועוצם
ידי. ע"כ תיקנו חז"ל לומר מיד לה' הארץ ומלואה, וכן העניו
ג"כ בשמטה שציותה התורה, היינו שתדע כי לה' הארץ ומלואה,
וכשבא שנת השמינית והתורה התירה לחרוש ולזרוע פן תשכח
ח"ו ותאמר כחי ועוצם ידי, ע"כ צוה להיות נוהג בה בשמינית ג"כ
מנהג שביעית בתבואה שלא הביאה שליש כדי שתזכור כי לה'
הארץ ומלואה.

**Mei Hashiloach, Vayelekh**

The Talmud asks, "Why is the Shemitah year mentioned in connection with the festival of Sukkot in the eighth year? It comes to teach that any produce that has reached one-third of its growth in the Sabbatical Year before Rosh HaShanah is treated with the sanctity of the Sabbatical Year."[124]

This is in the spirit of the verse from Psalms: "The heavens belong to YHVH, but the Divine gave the earth to human beings" (Ps. 115:16). But this is only how things appear. Rather, King David also said, "Whatever YHVH desires, the Holy One does in heaven and earth, in the seas and all the depths" (Ps. 135:6). For King David knew well the truth about human endeavors: even though we are given the ability to choose our actions, our will is as insignificant as the skin on a head of garlic.

This is why we say, during the daily psalm for Sunday, "Of David, a psalm: The earth and all that it holds belongs to YHVH, the world and its inhabitants" (Ps. 24:1). For Shabbat comes to help us cultivate our awareness that, in truth, we have

---

[124] Rosh Hashanah 12b: It was taught in the Mishnah: Grain and olives are obligated in tithes from the time when they have reached one-third of their growth. The Gemara asks: From where are these matters derived, that the years of produce follow the first third of their growth? Rav Asi said that Rabbi Yohanan said, and some determined that this statement was said in the name of Rabbi Yosei HaGelili: The verse states: "At the end of every seven years, in the time of the year of release, in the festival of Sukkot" (Deuteronomy 31:10). What is the purpose of the Sabbatical Year being mentioned with the festival of Sukkot? The festival of Sukkot is already the eighth year. Rather, it comes to tell you that the halakhot of the Sabbatical Year continue to apply on Sukkot of the following year, as you must treat all produce that reached one-third of its growth in the Sabbatical Year before Rosh Hashanah with the sanctity of the Sabbatical Year, even if it fully grows and is able to be used only in the eighth year. (Steinsaltz translation via Sefaria.org)

no real mastery over the 39 forms of labor that were created by which we can do whatever we wish, but are otherwise prohibited on Shabbat.[125] Therefore, when the workweek begins again and we are permitted to do labor, we might, God forbid, [forget this reality] and say that whatever we do is through "My power, and the work of my hands."[126] This is why the Sages established that we should immediately say [on Sunday], "The earth and all that it holds belongs to YHVH."

This is also what we are to experience during Shemitah, which the Torah commanded so that we might become aware that the earth and all that it holds belongs to YHVH. And when the eighth year comes, and the Torah allows us to once again plow and plant, we similarly might forget—God forbid—and say that whatever we do is through "my power and the work of my hands." Therefore, the Torah commands that we continue to conduct ourselves in the eighth year according to the practices of the seventh, at least with regard to that produce which had reached one-third of its growth, so that we should remember that the earth and all that it holds belongs to YHVH.

The Izhbitzer starts this teaching with a Talmudic discussion that fleshes out one of the many complexities of Shemitah. It's all well and good, the Talmud seems to say, for the Torah to command that produce may not be actively cultivated in the land of Israel during the Shemitah year. But plants don't obey the Jewish calendar! Thus, inevitably, it will occur that some grain may grow during the Shemitah year. Following the conclusion of the year (which happens at harvest time), that grain could then be harvested and sold. The day before Rosh Hashanah of the eighth year, the produce

---

[125] A reference to the 39 forms of labor prohibited on Shabbat. See Mishnah Shabbat 7:2.

[126] A reference to Deut. 8:12-17: "When you have eaten your fill, and have built fine houses to live in, and your herds and flocks have multiplied, and your silver and gold have increased, and everything you own has prospered, beware lest your heart grow haughty and you forget YHVH your God—who freed you from the land of Egypt, the house of bondage; Who led you through the great and terrible wilderness with its seraph serpents and scorpions, a parched land with no water in it, who brought forth water for you from the flinty rock; who fed you in the wilderness with manna, which your fathers had never known, in order to test you by hardships only to benefit you in the end—and you say to yourselves, 'My own power and the might of my own hand have won this wealth for me.'"

was to be treated as Shemitah grain, not subject to our control—harvesting and selling—but left to be gleaned by whoever needed it. But as soon as the calendar changes, the very same produce—and the earth which produced it—is ours to exploit again. Is that really in keeping with the spirit of the law? Obviously one has to draw the line somewhere, but the Talmud seems to recognize that nature doesn't follow an arbitrary calendar, and we have to use our intelligence for the Torah to be meaningful. Intuitively, it seems, the Rabbis creatively applied an interpretation of the Torah verse, demonstrating that the Torah intended for a kind of buffer or transition zone to exist.

## Halakhah as Practice

The Izhbitzer goes further, however, to identify a spiritual dimension of the Talmud's teaching. Despite all our best intentions, despite an entire year of a profound spiritual practice of humility and surrender, the moment the Shemitah year ends, our good intentions are up against our *yetzer hara*. Our desires for control, power, money—to seize our lands for private use—are profoundly powerful drives. No matter how much practice we put in, the Izhbitzer suggests, we need to establish customs, rules, policies, and other systems of accountability to help us stay true to our deepest spiritual intentions. Thus, the tradition codified a practice to engage in every Sunday, reciting Psalm 24, as a means of reminding ourselves of the humility we tried to cultivate and experience during the spiritual retreat of Shabbat. Similarly, the Izhbitzer argues, in the weeks after the Shemitah year, the *halakhah* creates practices to help us remember our intention, to remain mindful of—and thus sustain—what we experienced on retreat.

This brings us back to the candy in the Northwestern Hillel lobby. I had every intention not to succumb to my hankering and avoid eating something unhealthy for me—that is, to uphold the *mitzvah* of *shemirat haguf*, keeping my body healthy, and thereby serving the Holy One. Yet, the minute that intention encountered my body's urges, it crumpled (like the skin on a head of garlic, as the Izhbitzer colorfully describes). So instead, I turned to a form of spiritual discipline in which I was deeply practiced: *kashrut*. That *halakhic* practice helped me stay true to my intention. (Well, at least partially and indirectly: the *kashrut* practice simply kept me from eating dairy after meat; it didn't stop me from eating non-dairy candy, or from eating dairy candy *before* I ate meat; and of course, eating meat wasn't necessarily the healthiest choice either. But I digress.) The *halakhah* of *kashrut*, having been inscribed in me from youth and embraced for decades, provided a sticky frame to enable me to stay truer to my intention than I would have been able to do otherwise.

It helped me not only eat less candy but, in the process, better live out my intention to be close to the Divine.

In a recent essay, Stanford University professor Ariel Evan Mayse powerfully explores what it might mean for us to approach *halakhah* not simply as a set of rules, but as a powerful form of embodied Jewish spiritual practice. Mayse begins his essay with a reminiscence of the day when, as a teenager, he became a black belt in karate. He proposes that, like karate, *halakhah* should be understood as a spiritual discipline. "A neo-Hasidic conception of *halakhah* begins with the affirmation that religious rituals and obligations should lead us to a life of devotion," he writes. "The mandates of the Torah lead us to overcome our natural drive toward banal self-centeredness, for through attuned discipline of practice and a rich inner world we come to bestow blessing and grace upon others."[127]

For Mayse, as for the Izhbitzer, the practices developed by the rabbis through what may sometimes seem like picayune arguments in the Talmud and legal codes are not simply interesting—or perhaps uninteresting—rules about how to blow the shofar or when the fast ends on Yom Kippur or whether an elephant can be used as the wall of a sukkah (yes, this is a real debate: See Sukkah 23a). They may be, if we choose to look at them this way, practices that support us in living out our intention to be manifestations of and vessels for the Divine presence in the world. If we practice them and allow them to be central to our lives, they can serve as a means of living with presence and intention from moment to moment, aware of and in communion with the Creator.

### Questions for Reflection & Conversation

- What, if anything, resonates for you in my story about the candy bowl? In your own experience, have you encountered a similar situation in which you invoked a different frame of discipline to help you stay true to your intention? If so, what do you understand helped make that frame stick for you? If not, do you think there might be, or might have been, a different way to approach the challenge?

- The Izhbitzer's teaching is not only about establishing rules and customs to help us stay true to our intention. He particularly

[127] Ariel Evan Mayse, "Neo-Hasidism and Halakhah: The Duties of Initimacy and the Law of the Heart," in Green, Arthur and Ariel Evan Mayse. *A New Hasidism: Branches.* Jewish Publication Society, 2019, 166, 173.

focuses on Shabbat and Shemitah, which I later referred to as forms of retreat, as experiences of humility, even surrender, to the Divine. Do you find this understanding pleasant, unpleasant, or something else? What, if anything, do you find compelling in the idea of surrender? What, if anything, do you find challenging about it?

- How would you characterize your own relationship with *mitzvot* and *halakhah?* Do you find "Jewish law" to be inviting, uninviting, or something else? How would you *like to* describe your relationship with *halakhah?* What, if anything, is a challenge for you in cultivating that relationship? What, if anything, might you do to address that challenge?

## Ideas for Practice

In this week between Rosh Hashanah and Yom Kippur, consider making a *kabbalah*, a commitment, to observe one *mitzvah* with particular focus and awareness, as a means of helping you stay true to an intention you've set for the New Year. It could be a ritual *mitzvah* like lighting Shabbat candles or praying daily. It could be an ethical *mitzvah*, like returning lost objects or honoring elders. Pick a *mitzvah* to focus on and, before you perform it, take a moment to center yourself and bring your awareness to what you are doing and why you are doing it. Notice what arises for you before, during, and after the *mitzvah*.

# Haazinu-Sukkot:
# What have we learned?

Haazinu marks the final Torah portion read on Shabbat, as V'zot Habra-cha is read in full only on Simchat Torah which, outside of Israel, always falls on a weekday. (The Shabbat before Bereshit falls during Sukkot, on which we read a special Torah reading, taken from Parashat Ki Tissa.) Therefore, this essay marks the final installment in our yearlong study. Like Moses himself, who sums up his teaching in this parasha, we find ourselves at a moment to take stock, to reflect, and to ask, What have we learned?

As I explained in the introduction to this book, I chose to title each essay with what I've called a Big Question. I offered some explanation of the idea of Big Questions there, but it seems to me that now, in this final essay, it will be helpful to unpack the term a bit more in service of our larger reflection. I'll start with my story of stumbling upon Big Questions.

## Discovering Big Questions

On a walk through the campus of Northwestern University one morning in the summer of 2005, I passed through the arch at the corner of Sheridan Road and Chicago Avenue that marks the entrance to the main campus. My family and I had just moved to Evanston, and I was starting my new job as the rabbi at Northwestern Hillel. Even though it was summer, there were still a few painted sheets tied to trees, advertising theater performances and blood drives going on during the hazy summer months. Like many rabbis in the summer, I was already starting to think about the High Holidays when, seeing the sheets on the trees, the thought occurred to me: What if WE hung a painted sheet? Something like, "Yom Kippur—Wednesday night! Repent!"

Good idea, but it could be better. Intuitively, I thought about using the banner to ask a question, rather than make a statement. The question was obvious: "What will you do better this year?" The High Holidays are about *teshuva*, personal transformation to mend our mistakes. So our banner could bring that question onto the campus, and it could extend the impact of the High Holidays from the immediate confines of services into the lives of anyone and everyone who happened upon the banner—which would be a lot of people.

Using the design skills acquired during my days as my Boy Scout troop's newsletter editor, I eschewed a sheet and instead made an 8-by-3-foot banner at Kinko's, with the question in big letters. I added ideas of things people could do better in smaller letters: donate blood, drink fair-trade coffee, vote, smile more. With some rope and some knots (skills also acquired in the Boy

Scouts), I hung the banner a few days before Rosh Hashanah. I waited to see what would happen.

As it turned out, my hunch was right. Students came up to me after services and said, "Rabbi Josh, that banner you posted on campus was really great. My friend and I were walking along and got into a conversation about what we'd do better this year!"

"That's awesome!" I replied.

"You know, you should really think about making more of those kinds of banners," they said.

Good idea, I thought. So, with the help of some student volunteers, we made some more banners. At family weekend we made one that said, "What do you wish you could say to your parents?" At Thanksgiving we printed one that read, "What are you thankful for?" During fraternity and sorority rush we hung, "Who is in your community?"

As time went on, students got more and more excited about the banners. The project began to grow. We got a small grant from the Jewish Outreach Institute and made a website with person-on-the-street videos answering the questions. We made post-it notes with the questions on them and put them on the backs of the chairs in large lecture halls. We invited faculty to reflect on the questions during evening salons in the campus Starbucks. Eventually, our work got the attention of a major philanthropy, the Einhorn Family Charitable Trust (now called the Einhorn Collaborative), who supported us to launch a campaign to bring Big Questions conversations to dozens of campuses across the country.

With the help of many smart colleagues and students, we developed a simple definition for Big Questions. They have to meet two criteria: First, they are questions that matter to everyone. Second, they are questions that everyone can answer. By everyone I really mean *everyone*: anyone with a body who has been on the planet for more than a few years, regardless of age, ability, race, socioeconomic status, religion, gender, sexuality, or anything else. They also have a few other rules: they're directed at a subject (you or we); they're usually shorter than seven words; they use plain language.

## Torah That Responds to Human Questions

Thus when I use the term "Big Question" to refer to the titles of these essays, it is, among other things, a technical term. If you go back through the essays, you'll see that the title questions conform to these rules. This is more than just a style convention. It's part of what I see as a larger project with this book, and with this approach to Torah study in general: to help many more of us experience Torah as a deep reservoir from which to draw as we respond to questions all of us share as human beings.

Abraham Joshua Heschel wrote in several of his books and essays something along these lines: "Religion is an answer to man's ultimate questions. The moment we become oblivious to ultimate questions, religion becomes irrelevant, and its crisis sets in."[128] My sense is that this orientation to religion derives from Heschel coming from the Hasidic world. He was also one of the essential figures in developing the Neo-Hasidic approach to Torah in the mid-20th century, from which this series draws inspiration. While I was not a Neo-Hasid at Northwestern in 2005, I was already, by that time, drawn to Hasidic texts—and, it seems, to this Hasidic orientation to Torah: it asks Big Questions.

In my experience, both then and now, the best Torah is Torah that responds to human questions. By Torah I mean not only the Five Books of Moses, but the entire corpus of Jewish text, ritual, practice, and tradition which seeks to guide or teach (relating to the Hebrew root, *l'horot*, from which "Torah" derives). My aim in these essays has been to help you, and all of us who form a community of reading and practice, to experience Torah this way. The Big Question titles are a key part of that, as are the personal questions for reflection and conversation at the end of every essay and the ideas for practice. These questions and prompts invite us to engage our full humanity—not only intellect, but body, heart, spirit—in the study of Torah.

But it's not only about our own personal experience. The prompt both to reflect, and have a conversation, points us toward another vital element of this practice of studying and living Torah: Doing it in community. *O Havruta o mituta*, says the Talmudic sage Rava: "Friendship or death" (Taanit 23a). Because they are questions we all share by virtue of having bodies and living on the planet, Big Questions form a common horizon for conversation about our lives as humans, enabling us to share our lives with other images of God. When framed with a Big Question, Torah can thus become the ground of that conversation, the object around which to center what Parker Palmer defines as truth: "An eternal conversation about things that matter, conducted with passion and discipline."[129]

Those last words, passion and discipline, are not a throwaway line. Indeed, they are equally as important to this project as the notion of conversation and shared humanity. Yes, Torah is an inheritance available to all of us, *morashah kehillat Yaakov*, as Moses puts it in his final blessing to Israel (Deut. 33:4). And: as an inheritance, it is something to be cherished, to be approached with humility, awe and reverence, and to be lived. Generations upon generations

---

[128] Heschel, 3.

[129] Palmer, *The Courage to Teach: Exploring the Inner Landscape of a Teacher's Life*, 130.

of Jews have studied these words, lived them, contributed to them, shaped them, experienced their lives through them. That means that Torah is both an extraordinary gift and comes with an extraordinary responsibility of custodianship. Yes, we aim to make Torah meaningful for us, but we also have to do that responsibly, allowing the text to breathe and open to meaning while not forcing it to bend to our will. To engage with Torah responsibly is itself a practice. Our passion and discipline, our *anavah*—attuned and balanced humility—is thus essential for our pursuit of truth through Torah study.

## A Torah of Awareness

Like everything else in our lives, our study, experience, and living engagement with Torah can be something we undertake with awareness, intention, and purpose, or it can be something we do with less than a full engagement of our mind-heart. Too many people in recent decades have experienced Torah and the larger world of Jewish ritual, prayer, text study, and tradition as something to be engaged with, if at all, primarily out of a sense of guilt or duty, not love. There are good reasons for that, from the Holocaust to the loss of Hebrew knowledge to the over-intellectualization of much of Jewish life. Mindful, heartful, intentional Jewish practice is, sadly, not something a lot of Jews have grown up with.

My hope and intention, alongside many wonderful teachers and colleagues, is to change that. It is, in Heschel's words, to rediscover the questions to which Torah helps us respond. In uncovering those questions and entering into Torah-centered reflection, conversation, and practice about them, we breathe life into the Divine spark that resides within us. For some of us, including myself, part of that process is renewing a tradition we've inherited; for others, your encounter with Torah in this way might be a process of entering into a centuries-long conversation for the first time. I don't know whether you, dear reader, identify as Jewish—and, truth be told, it really doesn't matter to me. You have found your way here, and Torah, when approached with a full, directed, and properly humble heart, can speak to us all. Whether or not you call yourself Jewish, I hope your encounter with Torah has been and will continue to be soul-nourishing. I hope you will continue to deepen your learning, your appreciation of this tradition, your love of Torah and your service of the Holy One.

This brings me to one final, short Hasidic text. It comes from the Netivot Shalom of Rabbi Sholom Noach Berezovsky (1911-2000), the Slonimer Rebbe. The Slonimer writes about the ceremony on Simchat Torah, the very last night of the fall holidays, when the custom is to dance with the Torah. As part of the special liturgy for that evening, when the ark is opened a collection of verses is recited, beginning with Moses's words: "You have been shown the way to awareness that YHVH is the divine and there is nothing beside that divinity" (Deut. 4:35). He writes:

נתיבות שלום שמחת תורה מאמר ב'

כי ע"י ההתבטלות הגמורה להשי"ת נעשה תיקון מדת הדעת. ואמנם א"א להגיע להתבטלות עילאית מתוך אהבה רק לאחר כל עבודת יהי בין המצרים ואלול, עשרת ימי תשובה ויום הכיפורים, סוכה וד' מינים, שכולם הכנה למדרגה של אתה הראת וגו'...

Netivot Shalom, Simchat Torah 2

By means of the total surrender to the Blessed Ineffable One, we refine the capacity for awareness. It is only truly possible to practice total devotion to the Holy One out of love after all the practice we have engaged in—from the weeks before Tisha b'Av through Elul, the Ten Days of Repentance and Yom Kippur, the sukkah and the four species: all of these were preparations to reach the level of "You have been shown the way to awareness."

All of our practice of the last year—all of our study, our prayer, our holiday observances, our performance of mitzvot—it is all, ultimately, in service of awareness. Asking Big Questions is meant to help us reach this point, to simply and fully *be here*, with the Torah and one another in community, to witness and experience but also make manifest the presence of the Divine in our midst. As we conclude the year and immediately renew our study and practice, may we hold this as our intention and support each other in staying true to it.

## Questions for Reflection & Conversation

- Take a look at the Big Questions we've explored this year (look at the Table of Contents). Consider the definition of Big Questions: They matter to everyone, and everyone can answer them. How, if at all, does this kind of question differ from other kinds of questions you regularly encounter or ask? If they are different, do you want to bring more of these questions into your life? If not, why not?

- Do you sense that these kinds of questions could be helpful to you in your spiritual practice outside of this text study experience? If so, how? If not, why not?

- Consider Parker Palmer's definition of truth: "An eternal conversation about things that matter, conducted with passion and discipline." What, if anything, do you appreciate about this definition? What, if anything, do you find challenging about it? In your experience of Torah study, do you find passion or discipline to be easier or harder to cultivate and maintain? What, if anything, helps you to sustain them?

- As you reflect on the past year, how, if at all, have you grown in your awareness of the presence of the Divine in your own life? How, if at all, has your Torah study contributed to that growth? What, if anything, would you like to set as an intention for your study in the coming year?

## Ideas for Practice

With a new year of study upon us, consider writing a letter—to yourself a year from now, to someone else to be opened sometime in the future—reflecting on the Big Question with which we opened this essay: What have we learned? What do you want the recipient of the letter to be aware and mindful of? What do you want to say to them about your relationship with Torah? With the Holy One? How might you invite them into their own experience of the Divine?

# Bibliography

Allen, Danielle. *Talking to Strangers: Anxieties of Citizenship Since Brown v. Board of Education*. Chicago: University of Chicago Press, 2009.

*Beit Tshuvah*. February 2022. https://beittshuvah.org/about-us/.

Benjamin, Mara H. *The Obligated Self: Maternal Subjectivity and Jewish Thought*. Bloomington: Indiana University Press, 2018.

brown, adrienne marie. *Emergent Strategy: Shaping Change, Changing Worlds*. AK Press, 2017.

Bruner, Jerome. *Acts of Meaning*. Cambridge: Harvard University Press, 1993.

Buchdahl, Angela Warnick. "'We Jews are not a race': A rabbi of color speaks personally on Yom Kippur." *The Forward*. 28 September 2020. Accessed October 2020. https://forward.com/life/455275/for-this-korean-american-rabbi-jewish-peoplehood-is-powerful-and-real-and.

Clawson, Mary Ann. *Constructing Brotherhood: Class, Gender, and Fratnernalism*. Princeton: Princeton University Press, 1989.

Douglas, Mary. *Purity and Danger: An Analysis of the Concepts of Pollution and Taboo*. Routledge, 1966.

Erdrich, Louise. "Fooling God." *Poetry* (1989): 223.

Faust, Drew Gilpin. *This Republic of Suffering: Death and the American Civil War*. Vintage Books, 2008.

Fogel, Jeremy D. "Mindfulness and Judging." 2016. *Federal Judicial Center*. Accessed February 2022. https://www.fjc.gov/content/321600/mindfulness-and-judging.

Frankel, Estelle. "Sacred Narrative Therapy: Hasidism, Storytelling, and Healing." In Green, Arthur and Ariel Evan Mayse (eds). *A New Hasidism: Branches*. Jewish Publication Society, 2019.

Gadamer, H.-G. *Truth and Method (2nd Revised Edition)*. Translated by J. Weinsheimer and D. Marshall. New York: Continuum Publishing, 1995/1960.

Ghalib and Jane (trans.) Hirshfield. *For the raindrop, joy is entering the river*. n.d. Accessed 27 February 2022. https://thevalueofsparrows.wordpress.com/2015/07/22/poetry-for-the-raindrop-by-ghalib.

Green, Arthur. *The Language of Truth: The Torah Commentary of the Sefat Emet*. Philadelphia: Jewish Publication Society, 2012.

Heifetz, Ronald A. *Leadership Without Easy Answers*. Cambridge: The Belknap Press of Harvard University Press, 1994.

Held, Shai. *The Heart of Torah*. Jewish Publication Society, 2017.

Heschel, Abraham Joshua. *God in Search of Man: A Philosophy of Judaism*. New York: Farrar, Straus and Giroux, 1976 reprint.

Hicks, Donna. *Leading with Dignity: How to Create a Culture That Brings Out the Best in People*. New Haven: Yale University Press, 2018.

hooks, bell. *All About Love*. William Morrow, 2001.

Hughes, Langston. "I Look at the World." *Poetry* (2009).

Jankélévitch, Vladimir. *Music and the Ineffable.* Translated by Carolyn Abbate. Princeton: Princeton University Press, 2003.

Keissar, Adi (trans. Ayelet Tsabari). "Anatomy." in Chazan, Barry (ed.). *Israel: Voices From Within.* Third Place Publications, 2020.

King, Ruth. *Mindful of Race.* Sounds True Press, 2018.

Ladin, Joy. "Wrestling." *The Future is Trying to Tell Us Something: New & Selected Poems.* The Sheep Meadow Press, 2017.

Leibowitz, Nehama. *New Studies in Bereshit/Genesis.* World Zionist Organization, n.d.

—. *New Studies in Vayikra/Leviticus.* The World Zionist Organization, n.d.

"Letter from the elders of the Six Nations to representatives of Maryland and Virginia, 1774." In Palmer, Parker J. and Arthur Zajonc. *The Heart of Higher Education.* San Francisco: Jossey-Bass, 2010.

Lew, Alan. *This is Real and You Are Completely Unprepared: The Days of Awe as a Journey of Transformation.* Little, Brown, 2003.

Lorde, Audre. "Sisterhood and Survival." *The Black Scholar* 17.2 (1986).

Magee, Rhonda V. *The Inner Work of Racial Justice: Healing Ourselves and Transforming Our Communities Through Mindfulness.* TarcherPerigee, 2019.

Mahmood, Saba. *Politics of Piety: The Islamic Revival and the Feminist Subject.* Princeton: Princeton University Press, 2005.

Mayse, Ariel Evan. "Neo-Hasidism and Halakhah: The Duties of Initimacy and the Law of the Heart." In Green, Arthur and Ariel Evan Mayse (eds). *A New Hasidism: Branches.* Jewish Publication Society, 2019.

Neff, Kristin. *Self-Compassion: The Proven Power of Being Kind to Yourself.* William Morrow, 2011.

Niatum, Duane. "Consulting an Elder Poet on an Anti-War Poem." *Drawings of the Song Animals: New and Collected Poems.* 1991.

Oliver, Mary. "Praying." *Thirst.* Beacon Press, 2007.

—. "What is there Beyond Knowing." *New and Selected Poems.* Beacon Press, 1993.

Palmer, Parker J. *Healing the Heart of Democracy: The Courage to Create a Politics Worthy of the Human Heart.* San Francisco: Jossey-Bass, 2011.

—. "Introduction." Intrator, Sam M. and Megan Scribner. *Leading From Within: Poetry That Sustains the Courage to Lead.* San Francisco: Jossey-Bass, 2007.

—. *The Courage to Teach: Exploring the Inner Landscape of a Teacher's Life.* San Francisco: Jossey-Bass, 1998.

Parks, Sharon Daloz. *Big Questions, Worthy Dreams: Mentoring Young Adults in Their Search for Meaning, Purpose, and Faith.* San Francisco: Jossey-Bass, 2000.

Piercy, Marge. "The Art of Blessing the Day." *The Art of Blessing the Day.* New York: Alfred A. Knopf, 1989.

—. "The Seven of Pentacles." *Selected Poems of Marge Piercy.* Circle of Water, 1982.

Polen, Nehemia. "Touches of Intimacy: Leviticus, Sacred Presence, Torah's Center." In Green, Arthur and Ariel Evan Mayse (eds). *A New Hasidism: Branches*. Jewish Publication Society, 2019.

Rankine, Claudia. *Just Us: An American Conversation*. Graywolf Press, 2020.

Rich, Adrienne. "In Those Years." *The Yale Review* 80.1 (1992).

Rosenberg, Shimon Gershon. "Justice and Ethics in a Postmodern World." In Rosenberg, Shimon Gershon. *Faith Shattered and Restored: Judaism in the Postmodern Age*. Jerusalem: Magid Books, 2017.

Rothstein, Dan and Luz Santana. *Make Just One Change: Teach Students to Ask Their Own Questions*. Cambridge: Harvard Education Press, 2011.

Sacks, Jonathan. *Studies in Spirituality: A Weekly Reading of the Jewish Bible*. Maggid Books, 2021.

—. *The Dignity of Difference: How to Avoid the Clash of Civilizations*. Continuum, 2003.

—. *The Home We Build Together: Recreating Society*. New York: Continuum, 2009.

Sarton, May. "All Souls." *Harper's* November 1957.

Schachter-Shalomi, Zalman Meshullam. *Spiritual Intimacy: A Study of Counseling in Hasidism*. Jason Aronson, 1991.

Selassie, Sebene. *You Belong: A Call for Connection*. HarperOne, 2020.

Soloveitchik, Joseph B. (trans. Lawrence Kaplan). *Halakhic Man*. Philadelphia: Jewish Publication Society, 1983.

—. "The Lonely Man of Faith." *Tradition* 7.2 (1965).

Steinberg, Paul. *Recovery, the 12 Steps, and Jewish Spirituality*. Jewish Lights, 2014.

The Fetzer Institute. *What Does Spirituality Mean to Us? A Study of Spirituality in the United States*. Kalamazoo: The Fetzer Institute, 2020.

Twist, Lynne. *The Soul of Money: Transforming Your Relationship with Money and Life*. W. W. Norton, 2017.

Villaneueva, Edgar. *Decolonizing Wealth: Indigenous Wisdom to Heal Divides and Restore Balance*. Berrett-Kohler, 2018.

Whyte, David. *Consolations: The Solace, Nourishment and Underlying Meaning of Everyday Words*. Many Rivers Press, 2014.

Wilkerson, Isabel. *Caste: The Origins of Our Discontents*. New York: Random House, 2020.

williams, angel Kyodo, Rod Owens and Jasmine Syedullah. *Radical Dharma: Talking Race, Love, and Liberation*. North Atlantic Books, 2016.

Wilson, Bill. *The AA Way of Life: A Reader by Bill*. New York: Alcoholics Anonymous World Services, 1967.

Zornberg, Avivah Gottlieb. *Bewilderments: Reflections on the Book of Numbers*. Schocken, 2015.

—. *The Beginning of Desire: Reflections on Genesis*. Doubleday, 1995.

# About the Author

Rabbi Josh Feigelson is President & CEO of the Institute for Jewish Spirituality. He grew up in Ann Arbor, Michigan and earned a B.A. in music at Yale University. Josh received rabbinic ordination at YCT Rabbinical School and a doctorate in Religious Studies from Northwestern University, where he served as a Hillel rabbi. He was founder and Executive Director of Ask Big Questions, a project of Hillel International which won the inaugural Lippman-Kanfer Prize for Applied Jewish Wisdom. Josh has published numerous articles and chapters in both academic and popular publications. *Eternal Questions* is his first book. Josh lives in Skokie, Illinois with his wife, Natalie Blitt, and their three children.

# Reflections on the weekly Torah portion from *Ben Yehuda Press*

**An Angel Called Truth and Other Tales from the Torah** by Rabbi Jeremy Gordon and Emma Parlons. Funny, engaging micro-tales for each of the portions of the Torah and one for each of the Jewish festivals as well. These tales are told from the perspective of young people who feature in the Biblical narrative, young people who feature in classic Rabbinic commentary on our Biblical narratives and young people just made up for this book.

**Torah & Company: The weekly portion of Torah, accompanied by generous helpings of Mishnah and Gemara, served with discussion questions to spice up your Sabbath Table** by Rabbi Judith Z. Abrams. Serve up a rich feast of spiritual discussion from an age-old recipe: One part Torah. Two parts classic Jewish texts. Add conversation. Stir... and enjoy! "A valuable guide for the Shabbat table of every Jew."—Rabbi Burton L. Visotzky, author *Reading the Book*

**Torah Journeys: The Inner Path to the Promised Land** by Rabbi Shefa Gold shows us how to find blessing, challenge and the opportunity for spiritual transformation in each portion of Torah. An inspiring guide to exploring the landscape of Scripture... and recognizing that landscape as the story of your life. "Deep study and contemplation went into the writing of this work. Reading her Torah teachings one becomes attuned to the voice of the Shekhinah, the feminine aspect of God which brings needed healing to our wounded world." —Rabbib Zalman Schachter-Shalomi

**American Torah Toons 2: Fifty-Four Illustrated Commentaries** by Lawrence Bush. Deeply personal and provocative artworks responding to each weekly Torah portion. Each two-page spread includes a Torah passage, a paragraph of commentary from both traditional and modern Jewish sources, and a photo-collage that responds to the text with humor, ethical conscience, and both social and self awareness. "What a vexing, funny, offensive, insightful, infuriating, thought-provoking book." —Rabbi David Saperstein

**The Comic Torah: Reimagining the Very Good Book.** Stand-up comic Aaron Freeman and artist Sharon Rosenzweig reimagine the Torah with provocative humor and irreverent reverence in this hilarious, gorgeous, off-beat graphic version of the Bible's first five books! Each weekly portion gets a two-page spread. Like the original, the Comic Torah is not always suitable for children.

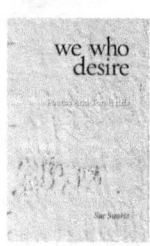

**we who desire: poems and Torah riffs** by Sue Swartz. From Genesis to Deuteronomy, from Bereshit to Zot Haberacha, from Eden to Gaza, from Eve to Emma Goldman, *we who desire* interweaves the mythic and the mundane as it follows the arc of the Torah with carefully chosen words, astute observations, and deep emotion. "Sue Swartz has used a brilliant, fortified, playful, serious, humanely furious moral imagination, and a poet's love of the music of language, to re-tell the saga of the Bible you thought you knew—and make its implications crystal clear for the life you are right now living." —Alicia Ostriker, author, *For the Love of God: The Bible as an Open Book*

**Words for a Dazzling Firmament: Poems/Readings on Bereishit Through Shemot** by Abe Mezrich "According to the mystics, the Torah was engraved with black fire on white fire. These poetic midrash too. Read them slowly." —Jay Michaelson, author of *The Gate of Tears: Sadness and the Spiritual Path*

**The Essential Writings of Abraham Isaac Kook.** Translated and edited by Rabbi Ben Zion Bokser. This volume of letters, aphorisms and excerpts from essays and other writings provide a wide-ranging perspective on the thought and writing of Rav Kook. With most selections running two or three pages, readers gain a gentle introduction to one of the great Jewish thinkers of the modern era.

**Ahron's Heart: Essential Prayers, Teachings and Letters of Ahrele Roth, a Hasidic Reformer.** Translated and edited by by Rabbi Zalman Schachter-Shalomi and Rabbi Yair Hillel Goelman. For the first time, the writings of one of the 20th century's most important Hasidic thinkers are made available to a non-Hasidic English audience. Rabbi Ahron "Ahrele" Roth (1894-1944) has a great deal to say to sincere spiritual seekers far beyond his own community.

**A Passionate Pacifist: Essential Writings of Aaron Samuel Tamares.** Translated and edited by Rabbi Everett Gendler. Rabbi Aaron Samuel Tamares (1869-1931) addresses the timeless issues of ethics, morality, communal morale, and Judaism in relation to the world at large in these essays and sermons, written in Hebrew between 1904 and 1931. "For those who seek a Torah of compassion and pacifism, a Judaism not tied to 19th century political nationalism, and a vision of Jewish spirituality outside of political thinking this book will be essential." –Rabbi Dr. Alan Brill, author, *Thinking God: The Mysticism of Rabbi Zadok of Lublin*

**Return to the Place: The Magic, Meditation, and Mystery of Sefer Yetzirah** by Rabbi Jill Hammer. A translation of and commentary to an ancient Jewish mystical text that transforms it into a contemporary guide for meditative practice. "A tour de force—at once scholarly, whimsical, deeply poetic, and eminently accessible." —Rabbi Tirzah Firestone, author of *The Receiving: Reclaiming Jewish Women's Wisdom*

**Enlightenment by Trial and Error: Ten Years on the Slippery Slopes of Jewish Mysticism, Postmodern Buddhist Meditation, and Heretical Flexidox Spirituality** by Rabbi Jay Michaelson. A unique record of the 21st century spiritual search, from the perspective of someone who made plenty of mistakes along the way.

**The Tao of Solomon: Finding Joy and Contentment in the Wisdom of Ecclesiastes** by Rabbi Rami Shapiro. Rabbi Rami Shapiro unravels the golden philosophical threads of wisdom in the book of Ecclesiastes, reweaving the vibrant book of the Bible into a 21st century tapestry. Shapiro honors the roots of the ancient writing, explores the timeless truth that we are merely a drop in the endless river of time, and reveals a path to finding personal and spiritual fulfillment even as we embrace our impermanent place in the universe.

**Embracing Auschwitz: Forging a Vibrant, Life-Affirming Judaism that Takes the Holocaust Seriously** by Rabbi Joshua Hammerman.The Judaism of Sinai and the Judaism of Auschwitz are merging, resulting in new visions of Judaism that are only beginning to take shape. "Should be read by every Jew who cares about Judaism." – Rabbi Dr. Irving "Yitz" Greenberg

CPSIA information can be obtained
at www.ICGtesting.com
Printed in the USA
JSHW011446190223
37771JS00004B/4